Speak Not

Speak Idle

Speak Not

Empire, identity and the politics of language

James Griffiths

BLOOMSBURY ACADEMIC

LONDON · NEW YORK · OXFORD · NEW DELHI · SYDNEY

BLOOMSBURY ACADEMIC
Bloomsbury Publishing Plc
50 Bedford Square, London, WC1B 3DP, UK
1385 Broadway, New York, NY 10018, USA
29 Earlsfort Terrace, Dublin 2, Ireland

BLOOMSBURY, BLOOMSBURY ACADEMIC and the Diana logo
are trademarks of Bloomsbury Publishing Plc

First published in Great Britain 2021
Paperback edition published 2023
Reprinted in 2023

Cover design by Adriana Brioso
Cover image © mikroman6/Getty Images

A catalogue record for this book is available from the British Library.

A catalog record for this book is available from the Library of Congress.

ISBN:	HB:	978-1-7869-9969-6
	PB:	978-1-7869-9970-2
	ePDF:	978-1-7869-9968-9
	eBook:	978-1-7869-9966-5

Printed and bound in Great Britain

To find out more about our authors and books visit www.bloomsbury.com
and sign up for our newsletters.

Contents

Introduction 1

Part One Welsh

1 Blue Books 13

2 Fire and fury 23

3 Nitroglycerine 35

4 Bilingual nation 49

Interlude: Afri-can't 57

Part Two Hawaiian

5 The princess who was promised 73

6 Sandwiched islands 83

7 I Mua Kamehameha 89

8 Ke Ea Hawai'i 101

9 Road closed due to desecration 107

Interlude: The old, new tongue 113

Part Three **Cantonese**

10 Dialectics 131

11 A Chinese alphabet 143

12 Common tongue 153

13 'Cantonese gives you nasal cancer' 159

14 Sounds of separatism 165

15 Language plateau 175

Epilogue 189

Author's Note 197
Notes 199
Bibliography 238
Index 242

It may be useful to notify the public that it is the wish of many leading men in America that all the children in the different States should learn the language in the same book, that all may speak alike.

— NOAH WEBSTER, IN A LETTER TO HIS PUBLISHERS, 1788

I lost my native language
For the one the Saxon spake
By going to school by order
For education's sake

— IDRIS DAVIES, 1927

Speak Putonghua. Write standardised characters. Use a civilised language. Be a civilised person.

— CHINESE GOVERNMENT CAMPAIGN, 2009

Introduction

A young girl stammers through an unfamiliar tongue in class, unable to express the thoughts in her head as her teacher frowns in frustration.

A man, an esteemed elder, speaks in a language his family no longer understands, telling stories of a people that barely now exist; he is the last to know them, they will die with him.

A mother, making decisions about her child's education, thinks back to her own school days, how she was punished and ostracised for speaking as she did at home; her child will not experience the same problem, she will speak the language of the future, of power.

Three men, abducted, sold and transported across the world, find solace in a shared tongue; but on their arrival, they are intentionally separated, for fear they will use it against their new masters.

Marching through a busy city centre, student protesters speak one language interspersed with words from another; their hybrid tongue informs their identity, and its loss is one reason they are taking to the streets.

An older man, his brow furrowed, listens with incomprehension and growing anger at the buzz of conversation around him on the bus; why can't these people speak the language of the country they're in?

A teenager types on their phone, thumbs moving across the screen with ease; a red squiggle appears under the text, the phone's spellcheck and autocorrect not recognizing the language being typed, attempting to turn the words into something different, alien.

In the muddy misery of a trench, the weather bitterly cold, two young men crouch together, ignoring official edicts as they murmur in their native tongue; a whistle blows further down the trench, ordering an attack, and one begins intoning the familiar words from his childhood, 'Ein tad … '

We are fascinated and frustrated by language. Humanity's 'greatest invention'[1] is what, more than anything else, separates us from the rest of the animal kingdom, and what likely put us on the path to dominating the entire globe, shaping its environment and even its geology, to the point that we now live in the Anthropocene: the age of man. While other species do communicate, some in impressively complex ways,[2] none demonstrate anything that approaches the intricacy and adaptability of human language,[3] the ability to express concepts both abstract and imaginary, to discuss the past, present and future. Uncertainty about the evolution of language, and the lack of comparable examples or proto-speech in either nature or the fossil record, has given language a touch of the divine, a 'god given' ability that can seem to defy explanation.[4] And while we are advancing towards a theory of language evolution,[5] it is unlikely that we will ever know the first word or the first tongue,[6] or whether it was *Homo sapiens*, or one of our older cousins, who was the original linguist.

So language fascinates, but it also frustrates. Throughout human history, language has separated us more than race, creed, or culture. Many ethnicities are, fundamentally, language groups, and linguistic diversity has led to division, confusion, hostility, war and genocide. This jars so much with the sense of language as a gift from the heavens that many myths have sprung up to explain the global confusion of tongues. In the Hebrew Bible, God responds to human arrogance at Babel by scattering a united people into thousands of different tribes all speaking different languages. In Greek myth, it was Hermes who confused humanity's tongues, making it hard for Zeus to communicate with his subjects and paving the way for the first king of men.[7] An ancient Bantu myth holds that during a severe famine, the first people went mad and wandered in every direction, jabbering incoherently, eventually giving rise to different languages.[8] The Kaska people of what is now northwestern Canada once held that a great flood scattered early humans across the world; by the time they met again after the waters subsided, their languages had changed and were now unintelligible.[9] Of the many myths, this is perhaps closest to the truth; while humanity was never split by a great deluge, we know now that languages drift and evolve in even a short period of time, so that soon after our ancestors spread out of and across Africa, as they separated and traveled to different corners of the world, if ever there was a unified tongue spoken it twisted and changed, a process that repeated endlessly and continues to this day.[10] Even the language you are reading this in is changing, and will not be the same in a hundred years, just as it was not a hundred years before.

This language drift not only creates new languages but also destroys, as tongues die out or merge with other languages. Sometimes the collision of two languages can create something new entirely. Beginning in the late first century, Britain was raided by Vikings from Denmark and Scandinavia. In 1066, the Normans (themselves of Viking origin) invaded. For a time, Old English was spoken alongside Old Norse and Norman French in parts of the country where all three cultures met, but increasingly the languages commingled and meshed together, eventually forming, along with other influences, something closer to the English we know today, with its mélange of Germanic, Norse, Latin and British elements.[11,12] While Old English is no longer spoken, it did not so much die out as evolved beyond recognition. We are able to read *Bēowulf* and other ancient texts not because Old English is the same language as the

English spoken today, it's not, but because we can trace its development backward, enabling it to be translated. Indeed, children in the English-speaking world often undertake this type of linguistic archaeology themselves, though they may not realize it, as they learn to read Shakespeare and Chaucer, adapting to less and less familiar versions of their own language.

When languages die, or, more often than not, are killed, this chain is broken. There was no last speaker of Old English, as the language gradually shifted into Middle and then modern English, but there was a last speaker of Kakan, a South American language which went extinct sometime in the seventeenth century.[13] While we know Kakan existed as a language from the writings of those who came across it, no word list, let alone a grammar or alphabet, was ever recorded, such that linguists today struggle to even categorize it. Alonsa de Barcena, a Jesuit missionary, was said to have written a grammar of the language, along with several other now-extinct South American tongues, but his manuscript has never been found, and no examples of the language – or living speakers – now exist.[14] Hundreds of languages died out in the centuries following the European invasion of the Americas,[15] many of which did not have a writing system, nor were recorded by outsiders, meaning they are lost to us forever, along with the myths, poetry, and history of their speakers. Even some scripts can be closed off to us: but for the Rosetta Stone, Egyptian hieroglyphs might never have been translated, severely limiting our knowledge of that culture.

On a hot, muggy day in July 2019, I made my way to a grand, seven-storey, white-fronted brick building on New York's West 18th Street. On the official map of the city, I was in the Flatiron District, just north of Union Square. According to a map of the city created by the Endangered Language Alliance (ELA), outside whose offices I stood, I was at the axis of Manhattan's Hindi-, Castellano-, Galego-, Marathi- and Tibetan-speaking areas. The ELA map catalogues all the languages and dialects spoken in New York, from Irish English down on the Rockaway Peninsula, to Mohegan, an indigenous language, north of the Bronx on the way to Connecticut, to the clusters of Eastern European, Chinese and South Asian languages that make up the mixing pot of Queens. New York is the most linguistically diverse urban centre in the world, with some eight hundred languages spoken within the city limit. This has enabled researchers to do important work that it was once thought only possible overseas.

I was visiting the ELA offices as part of the reporting for this book, a multi-year journey to try and answer the question of why some languages succeed while others are driven to minority status or even extinction. Many of the tongues the ELA supports are teetering on the edge of annihilation, but my interest in this topic was piqued by a language that, on the face of it, appears to be thriving. I live in Hong Kong, where the dominant language is Cantonese. More than six million people speak Cantonese as their native language in Hong Kong, part of a global community of around 73.5 million speakers, the majority of them in mainland China.[16] But the longer I spent in the city, talking to Cantonese speakers, learning the language myself, the more parallels I began to see between it and the language of my homeland, Wales.

I grew up speaking both English and Welsh, on Ynys Môn (the Isle of Anglesey) in North Wales. Mine was the first generation to have our schooling mainly in Welsh after a decades-long revival project had largely succeeded in creating a new political and educational base for the language, shoring it up after over a century of attrition had brought it to the verge of extinction.

Many other languages have not been so fortunate. Working as a journalist in China and Hong Kong, I have seen how the authorities in Beijing are pursuing exactly the same kind of policies which almost wiped out Welsh. Since the 1955 classification of Putonghua, or Mandarin, as the main official language of the People's Republic of China, there have been admirable advances in literacy and integration in that massive, and massively diverse, country. But this has come at the cost of many other languages and dialects, as policy makers in Beijing have pursued an aggressive monolingualism that would be familiar to officials of the British Empire. In recent decades, schools across China have increasingly switched to teaching only in Putonghua, and students are actively discouraged from speaking other languages or dialects, resulting in a generation that can sometimes struggle to communicate with grandparents or other relatives who were educated before the rise of Putonghua. This soft – and not so soft – imperialism is facing resistance in areas that were historically at the fringes of Chinese control, such as Tibet, Xinjiang and Hong Kong, and efforts to suppress local languages go hand in hand with a Han supremacist agenda that rejects the original promise of the People's Republic as a multiethnic, multicultural country, and seeks to unify and homogenize the population in order to stamp out any suggestion of separatism.

There is a pervasive idea, in popular discourse about language endangerment, that languages just slip away, becoming obsolete or falling out of use. In this view, languages are like fashions, that pass with time, or technology, that is replaced by the more advanced. Those clinging to the old languages are seen as quaint at best, and conservative, or even luddite, at worst. But this conception is wrong. It benefits the powerful at the expense of the powerless, reassuring the colonizer that they are not to blame. Languages are not lost, they are taken. They are uprooted by malice or neglect, their speakers assimilated into a new tongue, or left to struggle in the space between the fading old and the out of reach new.

Language endangerment has continually accelerated, as the rise of nation states and centralized, powerful governments, along with inventions such as the printing press and mass media, have created a handful of super tongues, which bulldoze all others in their path. While there are around seven thousand extant languages today, half the planet speaks one of just twenty-three tongues, with that proportion growing every year.[17] At the time of writing, according to UNESCO, some twenty-four-hundred languages are vulnerable or endangered, while almost six hundred are on the verge of going extinct.[18]

As a Welsh saying goes, 'cenedl heb iaith, cenedl heb galon', a nation without a language is a nation without a heart. Languages are deeply enmeshed with culture, they link people to their ancestors and help maintain traditions, oral histories and ways of thinking about the world. The loss of linguistic diversity is not merely an intellectual tragedy, but a continued consequence of colonialism and imperialism, as groups are forcibly assimilated and their diverse histories, cultures and tongues wiped out. This can literally be a matter of life and death: researchers in Australia and Canada have shown that indigenous communities that retain access to their languages are healthier and more cohesive, with less unemployment, alcoholism and suicide, and higher levels of education, than those unmoored from traditional culture and forced to use English alone.[19,20] Language diversity can also foster new ideas and thinking that can help us address many of the injustices and disasters wrought by colonialism and industrialization. The Mondragon worker's cooperative, a hugely successful exercise in attempting to find an alternative to capitalism, has its roots in the movement to revive Basque, a language spoken in the western Pyrenees along the France–Spain border.[21] Similar experiments were conducted in the kibbutzim by Hebrew revivalists in Palestine, while another, now-endangered, Jewish language, Yiddish, played an important role in the early-twentieth-century labour movement, through its radical press and literary scene.[22] Environmentally, economically, and culturally, language diversity holds the potential for new solutions for the problems often wrought by the world's linguistic monoliths. The United Nations, in declaring 2019 the International Year of Indigenous Languages, recognized that such tongues provide 'resources for good governance, peacebuilding, reconciliation, and sustainable development'.[23]

This book is built on hundreds of hours of interviews, archival research and reporting on three different languages and linguistic communities, in Wales, Hawai'i and Hong Kong, places that are simultaneously parts of the empires that consumed them, and separate and resentful of them; both proud of the greater nations and their achievements, and yearning for independence or autonomy. In each place, language is a key issue which sets the people apart from the metropole. Wales was the first colony of the English, later British, Empire, such that it is no longer thought of as such and much of its identity is enmeshed with its parent power, which has adopted or co-opted elements of Welsh identity, such as King Arthur, dragons and the name Britain (Prydain) itself. In Hawai'i, what was once an independent kingdom became first a colony, then a territory and eventually a state of the United States. Hong Kong, a former British colony, was subsumed by the People's Republic of China, which inherited and shored up the territorial reaches of the Qing Empire and has advanced an assimilatory language policy that previous Chinese rulers could only have dreamed of.

In examining these three diverse but analogous places – as well as two interludes to other parts of the world – we can see how language has shaped global politics and history more than is often acknowledged, with far-reaching effects. Each language in this book also provides lessons in how speakers of minoritised tongues can and are learning from each other as they attempt to exercise self-determination and defend their way of life and indigenous culture. This is not always a clean process, and a desire to preserve can often turn into an ugly obsession with the past, or a refusal to accept anything from outside. The stories recounted in this book are often violent and messy, including acts of terrorism, murder, bombings, arson, riots and protests, all carried out in the name of protecting a language. Efforts at preservation or revitalization are often met by government suppression or propaganda accusing language advocates of being separatists.

Welsh in particular, I believe, offers a clear path for revitalization. The revival of Welsh has coincided with political organizing towards greater autonomy and potentially even independence, and an explosion of Welsh culture, through Eisteddfodau – traditional literature and music festivals – Welsh-language TV, movies and literature. A child growing up in bilingual Wales today has a far greater connection to their country's past and its native culture than their parents did forty years ago, even as technology has meant Wales, like all nations, is increasingly globalized and affected by outside influences. Wales has also shown that the embrace of an endangered language need not be backward looking and xenophobic, but can embrace and integrate newcomers, as is currently done with Syrian refugees, many of whose children learn Welsh before they learn English. The revival of Welsh shows that language decline is not inevitable, and can be reversed. The recent history of the language provides a vital guide for doing so, one that has been followed around the world. But the story of Welsh is also a warning to other languages, of the need to fight against decline from a position of strength. Wales may not have lost its language, but the blueprint Welsh provides is one of a rearguard action, one that requires fighting tooth and nail to put off extinction. These are useful lessons, and relevant ones, given the woeful state of many of the world's languages, but they should not be taken alone. Within the British Empire, Wales was in a position to fight for and defend its language against English incursion. Instead, the Welsh elite helped accelerate the destruction of their culture, and bound the country ever closer to England. Even today, bilingualism in Wales is predominantly English-first bilingualism, with Welsh natives speaking both tongues but few English monoglots bothering to learn Welsh, confident that the law will protect their right to use either language, which inevitably means using only one. Bilingualism is an admirable goal, but only if it is achieved through the equality implicit in its name, not by relegating one language to an also-ran status. Wales has seen a commendable turnaround in the fortunes of Welsh, but the fight for the language's future has been anything but won, and terminal decline is still possible if it is not truly put on the same level as English.

Hawaiian is perhaps the most vulnerable language discussed in this book, due to the size of the native speaker population and a long history of marginalization, but its survival is no less impressive for that regard. The language was maintained over decades of colonial oppression and official neglect only through the diligent work of activists and teachers, many of whose stories I tell in this book. They set the stage for the current revival, pushing the language back into schools and enabling a new generation of Hawaiians to grow up in their native tongue. Many of these new speakers are active in advancing the cause of Hawaiian self-determination, empowering their community politically and protecting the islands' natural resources from exploitation. They are now poised to cement the revival of Hawaiian by making the language one for all peoples on the islands, the first officially bilingual state in America, guaranteeing its future prosperity and connecting both native and non-native populations to the history and culture of their home.

A language spoken by tens of millions worldwide, Cantonese might seem like an absurd inclusion in a book about endangered languages. But it is far more vulnerable than it appears on paper. In mainland China, Cantonese has already been marginalized, and while many in Hong Kong express a desire to protect it, they can sometimes also passively contribute to its denuding, encouraging their children to learn first English and now Putonghua at the expense of their native tongue. Unlike in other nations, where language and self-determination have gone hand in hand, the linking of Cantonese to the movement for Hong Kong independence may actually hasten its decline, as those promoting Cantonese are increasingly viewed with suspicion by the authorities in Beijing, who see them as crypto-separatists. Like Welsh, Cantonese speakers may be forced into a rearguard action. What remains to be seen is whether the language can survive the dark years to come, and thrive again in the future. During the reporting of this book, Hong Kong saw massive anti-government protests, which again showed how Cantonese maintains a divide between the city and its would-be rulers across the border. In 2020, these protests gave way to a sweeping new security law that radically changed the city's political and legal system, pulling it ever closer to China. That law likely portends a shift towards a more assimilatory policy overall that could rapidly accelerate the trends described in this book.

The fates of these three languages, as well as the stories of their speakers and those who fight to sustain them, are relevant to us all. Without a model for language revival, for revitalizing tongues that are under threat as well as sustaining those that could one day be, we risk losing more and more of our linguistic diversity, and the ideas, concepts, inventions, art, poetry and music that these tongues carry within them.

PART ONE

Welsh

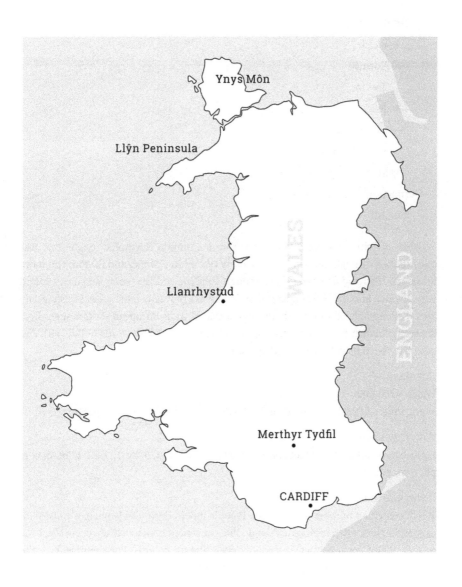

Cymraeg

(kəmˈraːɨg)

Language family
Indo-European

— Insular Celtic
    — Brythonic
        — Welsh
        — Cornish
        — Breton
    — Goidelic
        — Irish Gaelic
        — Scottish Gaelic
        — Manx
— Germanic
    — English

Welsh is a Celtic language, descended from a common Brythonic tongue that was once spoken throughout Britain. It is closely related to Cornish and Breton, and more loosely to Irish and Scottish Gaelic, though Goidelic and Brythonic languages sound very distinct, and the two language families are not mutually intelligible. Welsh is only very distantly related to English, through a shared Indo-European root, though there are many English-borrowed words in Welsh (and some Welsh words in English), and both have been heavily influenced by Latin.

Speakers
Wales: ~800,000
Worldwide: ~850,000 (primarily in Wales, England and Y Wladfa, Argentina)

Writing system
Latin-based alphabet of 29 letters: a, b, c, ch, d, dd, e, f, ff, g, ng, h, i, j, l, ll, m, n, o, p, ph, r, rh, s, t, th, u, w, y

Distinctive features
Welsh contains a number of phonemes that are rare in European languages and do not exist in English, often represented by double consonants, such as ll, ch, or ng (/ɬ/, / x /, or /ŋ/). Welsh consonants also mutate depending on context. For example, gan, the word for 'have', can become gen, ganddo and gennych chi depending on the context.

Cath, 'cat', shifts along with the possessive marker: fy nghath for 'my cat', ei gath, 'his cat', or ei chath, 'her cat'. Welsh follows the verb–subject–object order, in contrast to the SVO of English, and nouns have both feminine and masculine forms.

Examples

I'm a Welsh person, I speak Welsh.
Rwy'n Gymro, dwi'n siarad Cymraeg.

Where is the toilet?
Lle mae'r toiled?

Which road goes to Llanfairpwllgwyngyllgogerychwyrndrobwllllantysiliogogogoch?
Pa ffordd sy'n mynd i Llanfairpwllgwyngyllgogerychwyrndrobwllllantysiliogogogoch?

Chapter 1

Blue Books

Llandovery in October 1846 was cold and wet.[1] The tiny market town sits to the northwest of the Bannau Brycheiniog, the mountain range which separates it from the Welsh urban centres of Cardiff and Swansea. Near the centre was the Llandovery Union Workhouse, a low, grey limestone building topped with a slanted slate roof that made it even more squat in appearance. Unglazed windows in the shape of thin crosses did little to illuminate or ventilate the insides. The workhouse was a creation of the Poor Laws of 1834, which banned all other forms of relief for the destitute and made even the miserly Tudor-era welfare state they replaced seem generous.[2,3] Workhouses were designed to be miserable and punishing, a last resort for those unable to support themselves by any other means.[4] By 1839, almost half the population of the workhouses across England and Wales were children, both orphans and foundlings, and the offspring of adult inmates. In Wales, some three hundred years after the country was officially annexed by England, the workhouses also served an assimilatory function for a population that remained stubbornly independent-minded. At the workhouse schools, Welsh children were taught, in English, reading, writing and arithmetic for three hours a day, in addition to instruction in the Anglican faith.

At least, that was the theory. When Ralph Lingen visited Llandovery on 19 October 1846, he found a group of sixteen children of various ages sitting around a table in the bare, whitewashed stone room which served as the workhouse's school, writing on slates as they took turns reading monotonously from an English-language Bible. All the children looked 'stolid and lifeless' and one girl fell from her bench asleep as Lingen was talking to the schoolmaster, who then berated her harshly.[5] Few of the children were able to answer the master's questions, and he too had little grasp on the subjects he was supposed to be teaching. The textbooks he had to use were all in English, despite most of the children not understanding that language, and the master was unable to explain the principles of arithmetic beyond reading rote what was written in the book, leaving all none the wiser.[6]

The workhouse school was a paradise however, compared to another house of learning Lingen visited in Llandovery. The son of a rich Hertfordshire family and fellow of Oxford's Balliol College, who would go on to be elevated to the peerage, Lingen had never imagined, let alone experienced, such squalor.[7] The stench which emanated as he opened the door to the small building serving as a village school made him recoil. It was torrid, damp and nauseating, reminding Lingen of the engine room of a steamship on which several passengers have already succumbed to seasickness. The room inside was dark and low, packed to bursting with around fifty children who sat sprawled across benches and tables.[8]

Even that was not to be the worst Lingen found in his inspection of schools across Carmarthenshire, an impoverished farming county which covered much of southwest Wales. At least the Llandovery schools had a proper roof. Children in one village were taught inside a hut covered with thatch that did little to protect them from the frequent rain; pupils were instead given large quantities of straw to build makeshift shelters for themselves as they went about their lessons.[9] At another school, 'held in a ruinous hovel of the most squalid and miserable character', Lingen found the floor to be of bare earth and full of deep holes. Children were required to kneel as they wrote their lessons, and one table was constructed out of an old door. In the middle of the floor a heap of loose coal and rubbish gave off little heat and a lot of smoke which choked Lingen but didn't seem to bother the dozens of pupils packed inside, or their schoolmaster.[10]

Lingen had been despatched to Camarthenshire and its neighbouring counties to inquire into the state of the region's education, and he was not impressed. October was not a pleasant month to be traipsing around some of the poorest parts of south Wales, and in a report he filed later, Lingen's frustration and growing consternation at the conditions he found was palpable. He was particularly disgusted to find that, in his survey of almost seven hundred schools across the region, more than half were 'utterly unprovided with privies', children instead encouraged to use nearby fields or a hole in the ground dug for that purpose.[11] Read today, Lingen's report elucidates viscerally the crippling poverty of the regions he inspected and the resulting paucity of either good schools or capable teachers. It is surprising therefore that he and his two fellow commissioners – who inspected schools in North Wales and southeast Wales respectively – concluded the problem inherent in the country's education system was not poverty, or low standards, or a lack of teacher training, but the Welsh language.

'Education is in a greatly more neglected state in Wales than any other part of the United Kingdom,' William Williams intoned as he stood before the clerk's table in the centre of the House of Commons. 'The people of that country labour under a peculiar difficulty from the existence of an ancient language.'[12]

Williams was born in 1788 on a farm near the tiny village of Llanpumsaint, in Carmarthenshire.[13] After a brief education in the local parish school, he apprenticed as a shopkeeper in Carmarthen town before finding success as a cotton and linen wholesaler. He was first elected to parliament in 1835, and went on to become one of the House of Commons' leading radicals, advocating for extending the franchise and the separation of church and state. Williams was fifty-eight when he addressed fellow lawmakers in March 1846 on the topic of education in Wales, his round face framed by black mutton chops which stretched to his high upturned collar and bowtie.[14] Despite, or maybe because of, his coming from one of the most Welsh-speaking regions of Wales, Williams was clear in his belief that the country's native tongue was an inherent drawback to its future progress.

'The gentry and educated class universally speak English, as well as generally the inhabitants of towns; while the farmers, labourers and other inhabitants of the rural and mining districts speak the Welsh language,' he said. 'This being the language of the poorer classes, important works in literature have not for ages been produced in it; neither have scarcely been translated into it from other languages any works on literature, the arts, and sciences.'[15]

Because of this, 'although equally industrious with their English neighbours, the Welsh are much behind them in intelligence, in the enjoyment of the comforts of life, and the means of improving their condition'.

While he waxed lyrical about a desire to improve educational standards, Williams's concern, and that of other lawmakers, was largely motivated by growing unrest in parts of Wales. In the 1830s, worker-led uprisings had briefly seized the towns of Merthyr Tydfil and Newport, demanding better conditions and greater political representation, while throughout 1842, the so-called Rebecca Riots had targeted symbols of English wealth and economic oppression in agricultural regions of Wales, particularly workhouses and toll gates.

Williams demanded, successfully, that an inspection committee be formed for Welsh schools and despatched to all corners of the country. Thus it was that Ralph Lingen, along with two other commissioners, Jelinger Symons and Henry Vaughan Johnson, was sent walking from parish to parish in the winter of 1846. Lingen's fellow commissioners were, like him, wealthy sons of the English landed gentry. Symons was the son of a vicar and educated at Corpus Christi, Cambridge,[16] while Vaughan Johnson was a fellow of the same university's Trinity College and would go on to marry the daughter of a baron.[17,18] None of the three spoke any Welsh, nor had much familiarity with the country, though they were accompanied by assistants 'acquainted with the Welsh language'.[19]

The resultant *Reports of the Commissioners of Inquiry into the State of Education in Wales* was ponderously subtitled '[an inquiry] into the State of Education in the Principality of Wales, and especially into the means afforded to the labouring Classes of acquiring a Knowledge of the English language'. In it, the commissioners' findings were damning. Symons wrote in his most memorable passage that 'the Welsh language is a vast drawback to Wales, and a manifold barrier to the moral progress and commercial prosperity of the people'.[20]

It is not easy to over-estimate its evil effects. It is the language of the Cymri, and anterior to that of the ancient Britons. It dissevers the people from intercourse which would greatly advance their civilization, and bars the access of improving knowledge to their minds. As a proof of this, there is no Welsh literature worthy of the name.

While Lingen was less extravagant in his language, his assessment was no less critical.

Whether in the country, or among the furnaces, the Welsh element is never found at the top of the social scale, nor in its own body does it exhibit much variety of gradation. In the country, the farmers are very small holders, in intelligence and capital nowise distinguished from labourers. In the works, the Welsh workman never finds his way into the office. He never becomes either clerk or agent. He may become an overseer or sub-contractor, but this does not take him out of the labouring and put him into the administering class. Equally in his new as in his old home, his language keeps him under the hatches, being one in which he can neither acquire nor communicate the necessary information. It is a language of old-fashioned agriculture, of theology, and of simple rustic life, while all the world about him is English.[21]

The Welsh, the commissioners claimed, were filthy, uneducated, lazy, and prone to drunkenness and licentiousness. Despite the preponderance of churches, most did not properly observe the sabbath, and knowledge of the scriptures was poor, made worse by the fact the majority of religious institutions did not belong to the Church of England but were run by nonconformist sects such as the Methodists or Baptists. The commissioners were guided to these assessments by the testimony of local Anglican clergy, most of whom were English immigrants who also did not speak the local language, and were especially disdainful of their dissenting, Welsh-speaking neighbours.

'The poor seem ignorant on most subjects, except how to cheat and speak evil of each other,' Symons quoted the Reverend James Denning of St Mary's Church in Brecon.

They appear not to have an idea of what the comforts of life are. There are at least 2,000 persons living in this town in a state of the greatest filth, and to all appearance they enjoy their filth and idleness, for they make no effort to get rid of it. From my experience of Ireland, I think there is a very great similarity between the lower orders of Welsh and Irish – both are dirty, indolent, bigoted, and contented.[22]

All of these flaws, Symons and the other commissioners argued, could be traced back to the general lack of education in Wales, which was itself due to the evils of the Welsh language. Welsh hampered not only morals and learning, but even the effectiveness of the justice system, a point which harkened back to the original impetus for Williams's testament in Parliament and the commissioners' presence in Wales in the first place: worker unrest and the Rebecca Riots.

'The mockery of an English trial of a Welsh criminal by a Welsh jury, addressed by counsel and judge in English, is too gross and shocking to need comment,' Symons said. 'It is nevertheless a mockery which must continue until the people are taught the English language; and that will not be done until there are efficient schools for the purpose.'[23]

Efforts were underway to achieve this language replacement, and the commissioners found considerable support for advancing the teaching of English at the expense of Welsh even among Welsh-speaking people. In North Wales, Vaughan Johnson encountered 'a custom which has been invented in the hope of promoting a knowledge of English'.[24]

My attention was attracted to a piece of wood, suspended by a string round a boy's neck, and on the wood were the words, "Welsh stick." This, I was told, was a stigma for speaking Welsh. But, in fact, his only alternative was to speak Welsh or to say nothing. He did not understand English, and there is no systematic exercise in interpretation.

The Welsh stick, or Welsh [Not], as it is sometimes called, is given to any pupil who is overheard speaking Welsh, and may be transferred by him to any schoolfellow whom he hears committing a similar offence. It is thus passed from one to another until the close of the week, when the pupil in whose possession the Welsh is found is punished by flogging. Among other injurious effects, this custom has been found to lead children to visit stealthily the houses of their schoolfellows for the purpose of detecting those who speak Welsh to their parents, and transferring to them the punishment due to themselves.

Despite the use of harsh tactics like the Welsh Not, Lingen said that many parents supported the shift in languages, writing that 'you could not find in the most purely Welsh parts a single parent, in whatever class, who would not have his child taught English in school', while Symons quoted the Reverend Rees Price, who said that even though he was himself a Welshman, he rejoiced to see the ancient language in decline.

'When the English language shall supplant the Welsh, I doubt not that it will at the same time banish many prejudices that the people seem now to imbibe from their vernacular tongue, and improve their tastes and habits,' the clergyman said, though he noted that 'the really Welsh portion of the people are very tenacious of their native language, and would regard with displeasure any means of doing away with it'.[25]

Such displeasure exploded onto the commissioners when their report was put before Parliament in 1847 and later published in three volumes for public consumption. It became known as 'Brad y Llyfrau Gleision', the treachery of the Blue Books. The name, coined by Baptist bard Robert Jones, was a reference to the 'treachery of the long knives', an apocryphal event in which Saxon invaders were said to have murdered British chieftains at a peace conference in the fifth century.[26] The Blue Books were seen as no less insidious, in particular, complaints were raised against the commissioners' maligning of the chastity of Welsh women and the people's nonconformist faith. One thing that was not particularly remarked upon however, despite being the chief conclusion and recommendation of the report, was its attacks on the Welsh language and prescription for its extinction. While the report galvanized non-conformists and united rival sects against a common Anglican enemy,[27] the defence of the language was less full throated, and many who expressed outrage at sections of the Blue Books may have agreed with its linguistic prescriptions.[28]

Following the 1847 report, a great number of Anglican schools were built across Wales.[29] While many Welsh Anglican clergy were as critical of the Blue Books as their nonconformist brethren, with one memorably describing the commissioners as 'libellous and mendacious foreigners', the faith was emerging as the driving force of British Empire around the world, advancing both the state religion and language, and it would be no different in England's first colony. Anglicanism was not just English in origin, it was English in language, and by contrast non-conformism became characterized by Welshness, such that the former subsumed the latter, in a similar way to the centrality of Catholicism to Irish identity at the time.[30] While this may have helped retrench the language somewhat in parts of the country, with Welsh becoming more than ever the language of chapel and Sunday School, it would have deleterious effects later on, as a secular Welsh identity focused on protecting the language and unique culture of Wales was lost. When a new generation sought to throw off the confines of Baptist or Methodist faith decades later, it was natural for them to also split with Welsh, the language not of a glorious Celtic past of the Mabinogion and Arthurian legend, but stuffy Victorian Protestantism.

William Williams, the parliamentarian whose speech had inspired the creation of the Blue Books, was overjoyed by their findings, which confirmed many of his previous suspicions and prejudices. He wrote repeatedly to Lord John Russell, the prime minister, urging him to implement the report's recommendations.

The common people of Wales, from their want of an English Education, labour under difficulties and disadvantages, – and I may truly say privations, – far greater than any other portion of the British people, arising from their exclusive use of their ancient language.

... I trust, as your Lordship has the undoubted power, that you will be willingly instrumental in giving to the Welsh people that inestimable blessing, a good Education, as the only means by which they can be raised, from the woeful condition in which they are described by the Commissioners, and attested (as I have before observed,) by the concurring testimony of all classes. By doing this, your Lordship will have the proud gratification of placing another gem in the regal diadem, of more transcendent

lustre than any that now adorn our Sovereign's brow; while generations yet unborn, with heartfelt gratitude, will hail your Lordship as their greatest benefactor.[31]

Williams would have to wait almost twenty-two years to see his aims fully achieved, which would come with the passage of the Elementary Education Act 1870. In the intervening years, English was advanced at a local level throughout the country, enemies of Welsh language education having been emboldened by the report's findings and the government's support for them. As the industrial revolution reached its zenith mid-century, thousands more English-speaking workers poured into the coalfields and ironworks of South Wales, such that the language spoken at the pits began to shift in that direction and newer arrivals no longer felt the need to learn Welsh. The continued privations of poverty and a rising tide of Englishness led some Welsh to move overseas, setting up communities in Canada and the United States where Welsh 'could remain the language of home, chapel and immediate community'.[32] Some responded to English imperialism by becoming themselves colonizers. Led by Michael D. Jones, a community of Welsh settlers began travelling to Patagonia, where they leased land from the Argentinian government to establish Y Wladfa Gymreig, the Welsh colony. The existence of a Welsh-speaking community overseas, long after those in North America had been Anglicized, was a point of pride for many Welsh patriots, and Jones was described by some as 'the most important Welshman of the nineteenth century'.[33]

Inspired by Jones's linguistic nationalism, a strong Welsh literary and educational culture was established in Y Wladfa, such that the community remains Welsh-speaking to this day, though Spanish is now the primary language.[34] As the only Welsh-speaking place outside of Wales, Y Wladfa is ripe for over romanticization, with many earlier writers in particular blind to the hypocrisy of the community's interactions with the indigenous Tehuelche people, whose displacement and oppression by Spanish and Argentinian colonists was vital for the success of the venture. Even as he lobbied for more Welsh patriots to travel to Patagonia, Jones, splendidly bearded, with fierce eyes and a habit of wearing a traditional poncho like an Argentinian gaucho, remained in Wales, where the situation of the language was worsening just as he had predicted. By the 1850s, the number of Welsh speakers was approaching 50 per cent, down from nearly one hundred at the turn of the century; this as the population had exploded in size thanks to immigration and the Industrial Revolution.[35] Despite the evident decline of the language, many did not see a way to reverse this. In the era of Social Darwinism, it was considered natural that one language would triumph and if a people wanted to get ahead they should come to terms with that. Speaking at the 1865 Eisteddfod, the traditional celebration of Welsh literature, poetry and music, the industrialist and future Liberal MP David Davies told the crowd that 'I have seen enough of the world to know that the best medium to make money by is the English language'.[36]

'I want to advise every one of my countrymen to master it perfectly; if you are content with brown bread, you can, of course, remain where you are,' he continued. 'If you wish to enjoy the luxuries of life with white bread to boot, the only way to do so is by learning English well.'

Across the border, the sentiment was all the more damning, without even the slightest genuflections in the direction – as Davies had done – of respecting the heritage of the Welsh tongue. A report in *The Times* from 1867 warned that 'the Welsh language is the curse of Wales'.[37]

> *Its prevalence, and the ignorance of English have excluded, and even now exclude the Welsh people from the civilisation of their English neighbours. An Eisteddfod is one of the most mischievous and selfish pieces of sentimentalism which could possibly be perpetrated. It is simply a foolish interference with the natural progress of civilisation and prosperity. If it is desirable that the Welsh should talk English, it is monstrous folly to encourage them in a loving fondness for their old language. Not only the energy and power, but the intelligence and music of Europe have come mainly from Teutonic sources, and this glorification of everything Celtic, if it were not pedantry, would be sheer ignorance. The sooner all Welsh specialities disappear from the face of the earth the better.*

Even the literati would not stand up for Welsh. Speaking about the decline of Celtic languages throughout Britain, Matthew Arnold, distinguished professor of poetry at Oxford University, said that 'it may cause a moment's distress to one's imagination when one hears that the last Cornish peasant who spoke the old tongue of Cornwall is dead; but, no doubt, Cornwall is the better for adopting English, for becoming more thoroughly one with the rest of the country'.[38]

> *The fusion of all the inhabitants of these islands into one homogeneous, English-speaking whole, the breaking down of barriers between us, the swallowing up of separate provincial nationalities, is a consummation to which the natural course of things irresistibly tends; it is a necessity of what is called modern civilisation, and modern civilisation is a real, legitimate force; the change must come, and its accomplishment is a mere affair of time. The sooner the Welsh language disappears as an instrument of the practical, political, social life of Wales, the better; the better for England, the better for Wales itself. Traders and tourists do excellent service by pushing the English wedge further and further into the heart of the principality; Ministers of Education, by hammering it harder and harder into the elementary schools.*

And so the Welsh Nots advanced across the country. Signs went up in English for the benefit of tourists and new immigrants, and went down in Welsh for the benefit of future civilization. Modernity – English, Anglican, imperial progress – infiltrated almost every part of the country, with monoglot Welsh speakers pushed to the furthest impoverished reaches. By the 1911 census, Welsh was a minority language in Wales for the first time, spoken by just 43 per cent of the population, concentrated in the less developed regions in mid-Wales and the northwest.[39] The Blue Books hastened this decline, but they also precipitated a resistance, one that would take almost a century to be fully realized, when it exploded into the consciousness both of the Welsh public and the English, a final attempt to save the ancient language.

Chapter 2
Fire and fury

The Llŷn Peninsula juts out like an arm from the northern Welsh landmass into the chilly waters of the Irish Sea, the tip narrowing like an extended finger pointing at Ynys Enlli, an island made inaccessible at times by fierce winds and treacherous currents. Beyond Enlli, the path of the Llŷn's finger traces across the sea itself, to the southeastern tip of Ireland, bordering St George's Channel. Visiting in the 1770s, the celebrated naturalist and antiquarian Thomas Pennant found Llŷn 'in general flat, but interspersed with most characteristic hills or rocks, rising insulated in several parts'.[1] From the top of one of these prominences, 'South Wales may be seen plainly, and in clear weather Ireland; and in front the whole tract of Snowdonia exhibits a most magnificent and stupendous barrier'.[2]

This barrier was attractive to those who sought to use it against their enemies. After Einion ap Owain, 'the golden-handed prince of Lleyn',[3] invited the future Saint Cadfan to found a church on Enlli around the year 530,[4] 'saints came there from across the Isle of Britain', fleeing the advance of the 'pagan Saxons', according to one history, until there were as many as 'twenty thousand' on the isles.[5] The island would go on to become an important pilgrimage site, such that three trips there – over the rugged Welsh mountains and across the dangerous seas – were as good as a single visit to Rome.

Making the journey himself, Pennant found 'a very fertile plain, and well cultivated, and productive of every thing which the main land affords'.[6] But the onetime Insula Sanctorum was a shadow of its former glory, spiritual concerns 'at present under the care of a single rustic'.

'The British name of the island is Ynys Enlli, or the Island in the Current, from the fierce current which rages particularly between it and the main land,' Pennant wrote. 'The Saxons named it Bardseye, probably from the bards who retired here, preferring solitude to the company of invading foreigners.'

In the nineteenth century, Enlli, along with the whole of Llŷn, became another kind of haven from Saxon advance. Far from the ironworks and mines of the south, with their largely immigrant workforce, and detached even from the slate quarries of North

Wales, where English owners had to use interpreters when speaking to their workers,[7] Llŷn remained a bastion of the Welsh language and traditional culture through the First World War. In 1936 however, its distant English rulers looked at the rolling green expanse, and decided to blow parts of it up.

At the beginning of February 1932, members of the new League of Nations, along with the obstinate holdouts of the United States, met in Geneva. Though the league had already started down the slow slide of disunity and hostility that would lead inexorably to the Second World War, members came together in Switzerland to discuss disarmament, a final chance to avoid another global conflagration and millions more wasted lives. With Japanese forces occupying Manchuria, the Italians eyeing Ethiopia and the British hanging revolutionaries in India, the idea of a world without war might have seemed absurd, but absurdity was what the league did best.

The Treaty of Versailles had committed its various signatories to working towards disarmament, but few in Geneva expected this to take place. Indeed, Hitler's representatives were there to demand Germany be allowed to increase the size of its military, back to parity with those of France and the UK.[8] It was a surprise then when Herbert Hoover, the US President, suggested a reduction of one third in all land armies, based on Germany's own drastic disarming post-First World War, as well as the abolition of all bomber planes, tanks, chemical weapons and heavy mobile guns, and a massive drawdown in naval forces, particularly by the UK.[9] The Soviet Union, which had made a similar proposal ahead of the meeting, backed Hoover's plan, as did most of the countries who had suffered during the war. The British immediately set about quibbling. In particular, London wanted to protect its right to use aerial bombardments on its frontiers, where imperial power was being challenged. 'We were actually attaching more importance to preserving the amenities of being bombed for a few Pathan and Iraqi villages ... than to joining the rest of the civilised world in a practical attempt to remove the menace of the bombing aeroplane,' wrote Major General A. C. Temperley, the UK's military adviser at the conference, in a contemporary account. In the end, London's objection to banning aerial bombardment ensured that nothing would come of Hoover's proposal, foreshadowing the ultimate collapse of the conference entirely in the wake of Germany's withdrawal the following year.[10]

Now facing not a push for disarmament but an arms race, the British government began expanding its aerial forces and set about looking for a site for a new bombing school. Speaking before the House of Lords in May 1935, Charles Vane-Tempest-Stewart, the Minister for Air, proposed tripling the size of the Royal Air Force, adding hundreds of new planes and building dozens of bases around the country. In an embarrassing performance that would ultimately spell the end of his tenure as minister,[11] Vane-Tempest-Steward referenced his experience as one of Britain's representatives in Geneva, complaining he had 'the utmost difficulty at that time, amid the public outcry, in preserving the use of the bombing aeroplane even on the frontiers of the Middle East and India, where it is only owing to the presence of the Air Force that we have controlled these territories without the old and heavy cost in blood and treasure'.[12] When word got out that spots in northwest Wales were being considered for a future bombing school, local politicians and religious leaders began rallying opposition, initially on pacifist grounds.[13] At a conference of Plaid Cymru, the Welsh nationalist party, on 13 August 1935, representatives resolved 'that the Party opposes any attempt on the part of the English Government and of Local Authorities to establish vested interests in weapons of war in any part of Wales'. Plaid had been founded a decade earlier, focused on defending and promoting the Welsh language, though it remained more of a pressure group than an effective electoral force for years to come. In 1936, as the drumbeat of war increased, an editorial in the party's monthly magazine, *Y Ddraig Goch*, asked, 'are the Welsh communities of Llŷn to be turned into a practice ground for the fiendish bombs of the English? Shall Whitehall officials be allowed to smile in cold disdain when we insist on the wrong this will do to the Welsh way of life and Welsh traditions?'[14]

Objection quickly turned to not just the militaristic imposition of the bombing school, but the intrusion of England and Englishness into the most Welsh part of Wales that the plan would entail.[15] Llŷn was 'virgin ground almost completely unaffected by modern building and the effects of tourist and English influences', wrote one correspondent to the Council for the Preservation of Rural Wales, demanding it take action to protect the area.[16] Not only was Llŷn a beautiful unspoiled piece of countryside, the 'purity of the linguistic tradition' was stronger there, the local tongue 'unadulterated by any mass-borrowing from English'. The bombing school was, in the words of another critic, a threat to 'one of the few remaining homes of Welsh national culture'.[17,18]

Nationalist opposition to the bombing school only increased when it emerged during the campaign that a proposal to build on site near Lindisfarne – 'Holy Island', an important site of early Anglo-Saxon Christianity – had been defeated after local dignitaries objected to the idea.[19]

'To us, the unsullied beaches of Llŷn, Bardsey Island and the Pilgrims' Way are holy ground just as much as is Holy Island to the English of Northumbria,' Saunders Lewis, Plaid's founder and leader, said in a speech to party members in Caernarfon on 29 February 1936. 'Their peace and quiet are an inheritance. The beauty and peace of Llŷn are not something accidental. Llŷn has been holy ground through all the centuries of our nation's history.'

Let us also consider the role of Llŷn in Wales's literature. From it Welsh literature received its Mabinogi, and from the days of the Mabinogi to the time of Eben Fardd and Robert ap Gwilym Ddu the rural life of Llŷn and the pure Welsh nature of the neighbourhood and its rich literary tradition have been a part of the strength of Gwynedd and part of the strength of the Welsh language. It was there, at least so we were able to believe until very recently, that the purity of the Welsh language would be safeguarded despite every alien system of education. While Llŷn remained Welsh-speaking the Welsh nation would not perish.

And that is the worrying difference between [Llŷn's] Porth Neigwl and Holy Island. When the bishops and ministers of religion and scholars and men of letters of the English nation arose to call for Holy Island to be saved from the bombs of the Air Force, they foresaw no mortal danger to the culture of England. All they wished to preserve was a piece of beautiful and unsullied countryside with important and ancient religious associations. In Llŷn and at Porth Neigwl the Welsh nation has relics quite as dear to us as is Holy Island to the English. But to us Llŷn is inexpressibly more important. This threat from the Air Force is aimed directly and unerringly at the heart and very life of our language and our literature and our culture and our existence as a nation.

Since Cadwallon Lawhir won the land of Llŷn and Anglesey from the Irish, there has never until today been any danger that the Welsh language would ever be lost in Llŷn. If this bombing camp is now set up there, and if it grows as the military experts say it is sure to grow, then, there can hardly be any doubt, it will deal a death-blow to the Welsh language and to our nation.

Even as opposition to the plan continued to build, in early September 1936, some two hundred workmen arrived at Pen-y-berth on the southern coast of Llŷn. There they demolished an old farmhouse which had stood on the site for centuries, and began building a new road to the main thoroughfare so more supplies could be transported. Wooden sheds, offices and workshops were erected, and piles of timber and other materials stacked across the site. Despite the vocal opposition to the plan across Wales, the workers showed little concern, and security at the site was limited to one guard, a disabled First World War veteran.

There is a deep darkness unique to places far from urban centres and the light pollution they bring with them. This existed on the Llŷn Peninsula, where houses were scarce and people even scarcer. In the early hours of the morning of 8 September, this darkness was illuminated by a huge fire, the strong wind sending smoke billowing up into the hills, as the half-built bombing school burned. On the hill nearby, silhouetted by the flames, three figures began the forty-minute walk along the coast to the town of Pwllheli. 'It was a glorious fire,' one said later. 'We didn't need lights.'[20]

The men who burned the bombing school were an unlikely trio of arsonists. Saunders Lewis, the Plaid Cymru founder and a professor of Welsh at the University of Swansea, was one; he was joined in setting the fire by the Reverend Lewis Valentine of nearby Llandudno, and David John 'D.J.' Williams, a schoolmaster from Abergwaun on the southwest Welsh coast.

After the three men arrived in Pwllheli a little after half past two in the morning, they made their way to the local police station and asked to see the superintendent.[21] When the duty constable quite reasonably asked what was so important that he need wake his boss at that hour, Valentine replied that 'Pen-y-berth is on fire'.[22] They presented the officer a letter, addressed to the Chief Constable of Caernarfon, which read:

Sir, we who sign this letter acknowledge our responsibility for the damage which was done to the buildings of the bombing camp this evening. Ever since the intention to build a Lleyn bombing camp was first announced we and many of the leaders of the public life of Wales did everything we could to get the English Government to refrain from placing in Lleyn an institution which would endanger all the culture and traditions of one of the most Welsh regions in Wales.

Burning the bombing school, the letter continued, was 'the only method left to us by a Government which insults the Welsh nation'.

Meanwhile, members of the local fire brigade were struggling to get the fire under control. Most of the buildings on the site were wooden, as was much of the material stacked nearby, which the trio had doused with petrol before setting alight. The firemen were largely left to watch as the blaze burned itself out; Pen-y-berth's isolation, which had made it such an attractive site for the bombing school, ensured the fire could not spread very far.[23] Despite its relative containment, the government estimated the fire caused some two and a half thousand pounds of damage to buildings, timber and 'other articles of property of the King' (the equivalent of £175,000 or $230,000 today).[24,25]

The three men, the youngest of whom was forty-two, were held overnight in the cells at Pwllheli police station, where they passed the time discussing Welsh literature and reciting sonnets.[26] The following morning, they were charged with contravening Section 51 of the Malicious Damage Act of 1861, which, due to the timing of their offence – the act had a special provision for crimes 'between the Hours of Nine of the Clock in the Evening and Six of the Clock in the next Morning' – carried with it a maximum sentence of five years hard labour, or imprisonment for up to ten years.[27] They were each granted bail at £100 and released on their own recognizance.

By the time Lewis, Valentine and Williams came to trial on 13 October, another charge had been added to their docket – that of arson – and money had poured in from supporters around the country to a fund set up by Plaid Cymru. They were greeted by cheers outside the court in Caernarfon, where people had been queuing since the early hours of the morning to get a seat inside. Those who could not enter sang the Welsh national anthem and other patriotic songs as the trial proceeded and they waited for news.[28] Other supporters sent telegrams, which were delivered by hand to the defendants inside, including one from the men of a local quarry: 'May you be given strength for the sake of Wales and of civilisation.'[29]

The trial quickly dissolved into farce as the three insisted on their right to speak Welsh in a Welsh court, to the consternation of the English-speaking judge, Sir Wilfred Lewis. Asked for his plea, Saunders Lewis gave it in Welsh, 'not guilty'. Twice the judge asked him, 'Do you tell me you cannot understand or speak English?' Both times Lewis responded, first in Welsh and then translating for the benefit of the judge, 'I can understand and speak English, but Welsh is my mother tongue.'[30]

The judge continued to insist that he give his plea in English until finally, after he was threatened with contempt, Lewis did so 'under protest', as, eventually, did Valentine and Williams. Linguistic legal wrangling continued as lawyers for the defendants objected to juror after juror on the grounds that they could not speak Welsh, until Justice Lewis, his patience and temper already lost, snapped that an interpreter would be provided where needed.

Various witnesses were called, including the police constable who had taken the men's confession, and men of the fire brigade who had responded to the blaze. Also giving evidence was David William Davies, the Pen-y-berth night watchman. Here was the only place where the crown's account of the night differed from that of the defence. Davies, who had lost an arm in the Battle of Ypres, said he had been jumped from behind by two unidentified men and held down while the fire was set.

'I suggest you were not attacked by any man that night', the defence barrister said to Davies after a long back and forth over his story.

'Well I ought to know, oughtn't I?' the man responded.

'There was nothing on you afterwards to show that you were attacked?'

'No, sir.'

Giving testimony later, Saunders Lewis again refuted Davies's account:

Before we began to fire one part of the bombing camp I myself searched every part of the camp from one end to the other in order to discover if there was one living man on the field. There was not one living man about. The night watchman was not there. The main thing we had in view was to watch carefully that no one should come to any harm at all from our act of protest. That is the only evidence I believe it to be necessary for me to give here.

All three men addressed the jury, arguing throughout with the judge over the reasonable bounds of what might be said in their defence. As Valentine, a baptist minister, tried to reference a motion passed by churches against war, the judge intervened, 'You will certainly not draw the attention of the jury to the resolution of anybody'.

Stopped again moments later, Valentine said 'I plead with you in my difficulty'.

'I see no difficulty. You describe yourself as a minister of the Gospel and are presumably a man of intelligence', the judge responded. 'You will address the jury on matters relevant to the charge.'

'You may not know much about Welsh preachers, but it is necessary to have this preamble.'

'It is not necessary, and it is not permissible in this court.'

As Valentine again sought to settle into the soaring rhetoric with which he addressed his congregation, the judge interrupted once more: 'I shall ask you to sit down if you don't address the jury on what is relevant.'

The preacher did so, saying, 'I am sorry. I must obey your ruling.'

Saunders Lewis spoke to the jury in English, saying the fact 'that we set fire to the buildings and building material at the ... bombing-range is not in dispute'.

Yet we hold the conviction that our action was in no wise criminal and that it was an act forced upon us, that it was done in obedience to conscience and to the moral law, and that the responsibility for any loss due to our act is the responsibility of the English Government.

It was the terrible knowledge that the English Government's bombing-range, once it was established in Llŷn, would endanger and in all likelihood destroy and essential focus of Welsh culture, the most aristocratic spiritual heritage of Wales, that made me think my own career, the security even of my own family, things which must be sacrificed in order to prevent so appalling a calamity.

He got no further before he too was interrupted by the judge: 'I tell you in your own interests that that is no excuse in law, and the more your persist in telling the jury your ideas about Welsh nationalism and Welsh culture the less excuse is there for having committed this act. So far your argument has been totally irrelevant to the charge.'

'I thought I was speaking on it the whole time. I am sorry,' Lewis responded.

He turned back to the jury. 'If you find us guilty the world will understand that here in Wales an English Government may destroy the moral character of a nation – ' Lewis said.

'That is absolutely untrue,' the judge interjected.

'– you may shatter the spiritual basis of that nation's life–'

'That is untrue,' the judge repeated. 'Will you stop? I am not going to allow you to make statements that are untrue and almost blasphemous.'

'– if you find us guilty –'

'You must not repeat that statement,' the judge warned Lewis.

'I was not going to, my lord,' he responded, before continuing, 'If you find us guilty you proclaim that the law of the English state is superior to the moral law of Christian tradition, that the will of the government may not be challenged by any person whatsoever.'

In his summing up, the judge, by now thoroughly incensed, tried to undo Lewis's appeals to Welsh nationalism and the protection of Llŷn's unique cultural and linguistic heritage. In doing so, he used the words England or English more than a dozen times, inadvertently emphasizing the point being made by the defence that this was a foreign power imposing its will without thought to the feelings or desires of the people of Wales.

'I am here to do to the best of my ability the duty which I have sworn to do, namely to administer the law of England,' the judge said. 'You when you went into the jury-box took an oath to administer the law of England, and it is your duty to accept from me what the law of England is.'[31]

He added that it would be a sorry day were it to be said that because a man had strong and sincere views and thought his neighbour had done him an injury, that he would be entitled to go and burn his house down.

'You have heard from the lips of two of the accused, the suggestion that the whole of Wales approved of this act,' the judge said. 'There are many patriotic Welshmen who would shudder at such an act of violence as this. But whether that act has or has not received the approbation of Wales is nothing to do with this court, and if you are satisfied that this was done then your duty is to find a verdict of guilty.'

They did not. After forty-five minutes of deliberating, the jury returned to the court and the foreman informed the judge that there was 'no chance' of them reaching an agreement on the verdict. As the news of the decision filtered to the crowd outside, to an eruption of cheers and singing of the national anthem, the judge said the case would be transferred to another jurisdiction, in the hopes that a jury there would face less difficulty reaching an accord. Emerging outside, Lewis, Valentine and Williams were greeted by more cheers, and carried through the streets in triumph, before they departed for the local Plaid headquarters in Bangor, where celebrations continued well into the night.

The trio's victory at Caernarfon was not absolute, the jury had deadlocked but it had not found them innocent. Nor was the next court likely to do either, a fact that was made all the more clear when the case was transferred to the Old Bailey, the central criminal court, in London. The move outraged many in Wales, nationalist or not, smacking of a distrust of any Welsh jury to decide the case in the government's favour. David Lloyd George, the Welsh-speaking, former Liberal Prime Minister and one-time great hope of nationalists across the country, wrote in a letter to his daughter Megan, member of parliament for Ynys Môn, that the government of the day cringed before Mussolini in Ethiopia, but did not hesitate to bully gallant little Wales.

'This is the first Government that has tried Wales at the Old Bailey … they might at any rate have had a second trial, or removed it to some other part of Wales, but to take it out of Wales altogether and, above all, to the Old Bailey, is an outrage that makes my blood boil,' he wrote, though the great statesman kept his objections private.[32]

Nationalist sentiment was further enflamed when the trio refused outright to speak English at the trial. In first comments before the court, Lewis said in Welsh that he protested 'against the removal of the trial' to another country.[33]

The judge asked him if he could speak English.

'I intend to speak in Welsh,' Lewis responded in that language.

'You must speak in English.'

'I will not. I am not as fluent in English as I am in Welsh.'

'Do you speak English?'

'Yes, sir,' Lewis said, still in Welsh.

Though witnesses were found to attest to Lewis and Valentine's ability to understand English, there were none for Williams, and so an interpreter was eventually sworn in.

However, after the judge told the trio that if they wanted to say anything they would have to do so in English, all three declined to testify.

'I am not going to plead my case, as I consider, with every respect to the English jurymen, that they cannot do justice to our cause,' Williams said. 'No one can do justice to our cause except jurors chosen from among our own countrymen.'

The jury did not have to leave their seats to agree on a verdict; after a brief whispered discussion in the box, they found the defendants guilty of arson and malicious damage.

'You three men – educated men – have resorted to a most dangerous and wicked method of calling attention to what you believe to be the propriety of your views,' the judge said.

> I must sentence all of you, for it would be in ill-accord with the legal history of this country if it were to be understood for one moment that justice would not be administered properly because of some reason put up by the accused which is not a reason for doing that which he did, but merely an opinion which he says is the basis of his offence.[34]

He sentenced them to nine months in prison, after which both Valentine and Lewis left the dock. Williams however remained seated, until the judge realized that his verdict had not been translated, and called on the interpreter to do so.

'I thank you, my lord,' Williams said in Welsh, after the translation was complete, and then followed his companions to the cells below.

Saunders Lewis, Lewis Valentine and D.J. Williams were released from Wormwood Scrubs prison on 26 August 1937, as heroes. They were greeted in Caernarfon a fortnight later by a crowd of fifteen thousand, and though Lewis lost his job at Swansea University, his profile and that of Plaid Cymru were boosted tenfold, and he quickly became one of the leading Welsh nationalist intellectuals, as well as a celebrated playwright and novelist.

While it galvanized Welsh nationalist opinion, the arson did not permanently halt construction at Pen-y-berth. RAF Penhros opened on 1 February 1937, and operated as a gunning and bombing school until October 1946, when it became a resettlement site for Polish soldiers who did not want to return to a country now under Soviet control.[35] Despite this apparent failure however, the case did have repercussions for the law itself. Outrage over the original trial judge's refusal to allow testimony in Welsh sparked lawmakers to push for the legalization of the use of the language in the country's courts.[36] In a debate on a bill introduced in February 1937 – while the three were still serving their sentence – Megan Lloyd George asked the Attorney General:

> Supposing a Welshman understands English and can speak it, but he prefers to give his evidence in his own language. Would the judge be entitled in that case

to say: 'You understand English and speak it well; therefore I cannot allow you to speak in Welsh?'[37]

While that effort failed, five years later, the Welsh Courts Act of 1942 secured 'the right of Welsh speaking persons to testify in the Welsh language in courts of justice in Wales'.[38] Though it was criticized by nationalists for not going far enough, the law was 'the first legislative step since the [1536] Act of Union towards the restoration of the legitimacy of the Welsh language in the courts of Wales'.[39] It also set the stage for more sweeping laws to come, pushed forward by a newly invigorated Welsh nationalist community.

Two decades after that act was passed, Lewis made his second major contribution to the fate of the Welsh language. By now he had largely retreated from politics, sticking to writing and broadcasting. A difficult man at the best of times, Lewis had always been an uneasy fit with the party he helped found. While he was never as right wing as some of his critics claimed, he was undoubtedly incompatible with the socialist beliefs of Plaid Cymru's base and most of its other leaders.[40] A Roman Catholic who dreamed of a Welsh aristocracy and wanted to roll back industrialization, Lewis was out of step not only with nationalists and others on the left, but most Conservatives and Liberals too. In February 1962, some months shy of his seventieth birthday, he sat in a small radio studio in Cardiff. Dressed in his customary suit and tie, his thick black hair was finally showing signs of grey, having retreated so far up his head that he appeared to be being lifted up by it. Lewis's face was deeply lined, but his high voice was clear and confident as he began reading from an essay titled 'Tynged yr Iaith', the fate of the language. He began by discussing the impending publication of a census of Welsh speakers that was expected to 'shock and disappoint' proponents of the language, adding that 'Welsh will end as a living language, should the present trend continue, about the beginning of the twenty-first century, assuming that there will be people left in the island of Britain at that time'.

> *Thus the policy laid down as the aim of the English Government in Wales in the measure called the Act of Union of England and Wales in 1536 will at last have succeeded. To give the Government its due, throughout some four centuries of governing Wales, despite every change of circumstance, despite every change in parliamentary method and in the means of government, despite every social revolution, it has never wavered in applying this policy of excluding the Welsh language as a language of administration from office, court and legal writing.[41]*

Referencing the Blue Books and the suppression of the language which followed their publication, Lewis acknowledged that some progress had been made in education, 'but outside the world of the child and school it is English only which is essential for every post or administrative office in Wales'.

If England and Wales are one totally united kingdom ... then the existence of an historical Welsh language is a political stumbling-block, a reminder of a different state of affairs, a danger to the union. That was precisely what was said in the Act of Union, in the Blue Books, and many other times.

'It was the reaction against the Blue Books which initiated Welsh nationalism in the second half of the century,' Lewis noted. 'It must be confessed, too, that it was the Blue Books which triumphed.'

He bemoaned the failure of Welsh lawmakers in Westminster to defend the language, even though Wales had long been a steady supply of first Liberal and later Labour votes, without which both parties would have struggled to gain power. 'Several of the leaders of the political parties and local authorities in Wales are full of poison towards the Welsh language,' Lewis said. 'And many thousands of steel, coal and nylon workers and workers in the various new industries do not even know of the language's existence any more.'

Is the position hopeless? It is, of course, if we are content to give up hope. There is nothing in the world more comfortable than to give up hope. For then one can go on to enjoy life.

He ended with a call to action: 'Let us set about it in seriousness and without hesitation to make it impossible for the business of local and central government to continue without using Welsh.'

Let it be insisted upon that the rate demand should be in Welsh or in Welsh and English. Let the Postmaster-General be warned that annual licences will not be paid unless they are obtainable in Welsh. Let it be insisted upon that every summons to a court should be in Welsh. This is not a chance policy for individuals here and there. It would demand organising and moving step by step, giving due warning and allowing time for changes. It is a policy for a movement, and that a movement in the areas where Welsh is the spoken language in daily use. Let it be demanded that every election communication and every official form relating to local or parliamentary elections should be in Welsh. Let Welsh be raised as the chief administrative issue in district and county.

Beyond this, Lewis prophetically predicted the reaction to the campaign of civil disobedience he was urging on the people of Wales:

There would be storms from every direction. It would be argued that such a campaign was killing our chances of attracting English factories to the Welsh-speaking rural areas, and that would doubtless be the case. It is easy to predict that the scorn and sneers of the English gutter journalist would be a daily burden ... Fines in courts would be heavy, and a refusal to pay them would bring expensive consequences, though no more expensive than fighting purposeless parliamentary elections.

'I do not deny that there would be a period of hatred, persecution and controversy in place of the brotherly love which is so manifest in Welsh political life today,' he said. 'Success is only possible through revolutionary methods.'

The impact of Lewis's lecture cannot be overstated. More than he had done so on that night in 1936, he lit a fire which blazed across Wales, inspiring a new generation of activists whose achievements would outpace even his wildest hopes. The revival of the Welsh language might have happened without the fire on the Llŷn, but it would not have happened when it did, or how it did, without Lewis's 'Tynged yr Iaith'. By the time Lewis died in 1985, at the grand age of ninety two, there was a secretary of state for Wales, Plaid had sent nine members of parliament to Westminster, the Welsh language was properly recognized in court, and there was a flowering of activism and cultural activity across the country, supported in part by new publicly funded television and radio channels in Welsh. This success would not come easy however, and Lewis, Valentine and Williams would not be the last to go to prison on behalf of their language.

Chapter 3
Nitroglycerine

On the northern edge of Cathays Park, a short walk from the grounds of Cardiff Castle, stands the Welsh National Temple of Peace and Health, an ostentatiously large, three-storey art deco building constructed of grey limestone. Built in the 1930s, aspirations for the temple were as outsized as its appearance, chief among them that international cooperation and understanding could prevent another devastating war. The temple's opening ceremony included speeches by the mothers of those who died in the trenches of France and Belgium, and a wing of the building was dedicated to the work of the League of Nations. Another goal was a more local one, shared by the other occupants of Cathays Park, from the baroque, domed City Hall, to the National Museum and war memorial. All were situated on King Edward VII Avenue, named for the ruler who first declared Cardiff a city in 1905, and spoke to a dream of future glory, of transforming the one-time coal port, eclipsed both in culture and pedigree by the ancient northern towns of Caernarfon and Aberystwyth, into the first city of Wales, and future national capital.[1] For decades after the temple was opened in 1938, both dreams would remain out of reach. Cardiff did not gain capital city status until 1955,[2] and it was not until the turn of the millennium that Wales would achieve any real measure of self government, making this anything more than ceremonial. And less than a year after the temple opened to the public, the League of Nations disintegrated, as the world was plunged once again into war.

Twenty-nine years after that opening, almost to the day, conflict came to the steps of the temple itself. In the early hours of 17 November 1967, as a bitter gale blew through the city and frost covered the ground,[3] residents were awoken by the sound of an explosion.[4,5] The blast ripped a hole in the front of the temple, throwing chunks of masonry into the air and blowing apart the two-and-a-half-metre tall metal doors. Bronze window frames were torn asunder, glass disintegrating, as much of the furniture inside the greeting hall was splintered beyond recognition. Across the street, all the plate glass windows of the Welsh Board of Health were blown out, as were those of the National Museum, over half a kilometre away. The sound of the blast was heard throughout the city, rousing people from their beds and sending dogs barking, soon to be followed by the wail of sirens.

It was still dark when Major Clinton Jefferies arrived at the scene. A ten-year veteran of the Royal Army Ordnance Corps, the thirty-six-year-old was one of the country's chief bomb disposal experts. The following year, he would be made a member of the Most Excellent Order of the British Empire, after spending five hours in a water-filled trench, defusing by hand a six-pound explosive that threatened a power station.[6] Walking through what was left of the entranceway, Jefferies surveyed the destruction. The steps and pavement outside were carpeted with shards of glass and bits of metal. Dust poured from the engraved plaster ceiling, chunks of which had been torn off by the explosion. Tiles hung off the wall and debris covered the floor, the remnants of furniture and fittings that had been flung backward by the blast or smashed apart by flying chunks of bronze and stone. As police set up road blocks around the city in a futile attempt to catch the bombers,[7] Jefferies began piecing together how the explosion had occurred. From the fragments recovered, he was eventually able to deduce that a roughly nine-kilogram charge of nitroglycerine, an explosive often used in mining, had been placed in a canvas bag above the temple's main door. It had been fitted with a battery-powered electric detonator, along with a timer of the type used in street lights, set for 4 am.[8] It wasn't a particularly complicated bomb, as explosives go, but it was a set-up Jefferies would become deeply familiar with.

The 1960s were a decade of growing nationalism and economic uncertainty in Wales. Unemployment was on the rise, as coal pit closures left thousands out of work, and by 1970, for the first time in over a century, there would be more people working on the land than under it.[9] Farmers were little better off however, as increasing mechanization led to a shrinking workforce there too, while flocks were devastated by a foot-and-mouth pandemic in the middle of the decade.[10] Britain was teetering on the edge of recession for much of the 1960s, and Harold Wilson's Labour government was forced to devalue the pound to deal with a trade deficit inherited from the Conservatives,[11] caused in part by numerous overseas misadventures. While support for Labour was strong in Wales, particularly in the socialist mining towns of the south, discontent with the ruling class in general was growing.

The modern Welsh nationalist movement had been kickstarted in 1957, when the British Parliament voted to approve a plan to drown the Welsh valley of Tryweryn, including the ancient village of Capel Celyn, to create a reservoir that would supply water to the English city of Liverpool.[12] The destruction of a Welsh-speaking village and displacement of its people in order to benefit the residents of a city in another country was too much for even conservative Welsh opinion, and newspapers, politicians and clergyman railed against the proposal, but to no end. Despite not gaining the vote of a single Welsh member of parliament, the bill passed, and increasingly desperate attempts to block it – including a march through Liverpool by Capel Celyn residents and an appeal to the Queen – all failed.[13,14] Four attempts at sabotage, including the bombing of a transformer on the work site, only delayed the reservoir, which finally opened on 21 October 1965. On that day, speeches by grandees from Liverpool, including the Lord Mayor, were drowned out by the chants of protesters, who threw stones and scuffled with police.[15] Leading the violence were a number of men wearing green uniforms and caps bearing a white eagle insignia, representatives, they said, of the Free Wales Army.[16] Some protesters held a banner reading, 'FWA, for action, not words'.

Words, however, were what the FWA was best at. Founded by Julian Cayo Evans, a Lampeter horse-breeder, the 'army' never consisted of more than a handful of members, and spent far more time courting press attention than challenging the British state. Evans was a master publicist, staging elaborate training exercises for journalists in the hills around his farm, boasting of plans for guerrilla warfare and traveling to Dublin to join a march on the fiftieth anniversary of the Easter Rising.[17] For all his growing fame, the authorities did not take him seriously, and Evans and his men were permitted to operate relatively unmolested, an army without an enemy.

That ambivalence began to shift however after the government announced plans to hold a grand ceremony at Caernarfon Castle for the investiture of the Queen's eldest son, Charles, as prince of Wales on 1 July 1969. For Wilson's government, the ceremony – which would be broadcast live on television – was a chance to focus the world's attention on the newly modernizing, post-industrial Britain that they were creating.[18] It was to be preceded by a year-long campaign designed to increase Welsh support for the monarchy and stamp down growing nationalism. As part of the preparations, Charles was to be sent to the University of Wales in Aberystwyth, where he would study Welsh language and history.

Many nationalists were outraged. The last native ruler of Wales – Llywelyn Ein Llyw Olaf, 'Llywelyn the last' – had died in 1282, during the country's conquest by Edward I, who appointed his son as prince of Wales soon after. For many Welsh patriots, the position was a symbol of English subjugation, and holding a grand ceremony to reinforce Charles's title showed indifference to Welsh opinion and history, something the young prince did not help by asking a protester, on arrival in Aberystwyth, who the 'Llywelyn' on his sign referred to. Protests dogged plans for the investiture from the beginning, led in part by Cymdeithas yr Iaith Gymraeg, the Welsh Language Society, which had vowed to block the ceremony, along with Plaid Cymru, the Welsh nationalist party.

In November 1967, the Temple of Peace was due to host the first meeting of the committee organizing the ceremony, led by Anthony Armstrong-Jones, husband of Princess Margaret, who had been made the earl of Snowdon following their marriage. When Snowdon arrived at the temple shortly after the bombing, he was greeted by Cymdeithas protesters, who held up banners proclaiming 'No Prince', and 'Republic, Not Royalty'. Fourteen people were arrested in scuffles with police, which failed to prevent Snowdon and other dignitaries entering the building.[19] Following the meeting, held far away from the debris still being poured over by Jefferies and police crime scene investigators, the lord mayor of Cardiff, Eric Dolman, condemned the bombing as a 'puerile gesture' by a 'lunatic fringe'.[20]

Attention soon turned to Cayo Evans and the Free Wales Army, which denied all responsibility for the blast. Indeed, the FWA only carried out one bombing during this period, a failed attempt to destroy a water pipeline near Llandrindod Wells.[21] The explosives for that operation were provided, though without the knowledge of the eventual recipients, by the true culprits behind the Temple of Peace attack: a shadowy group known to the few who were aware of its existence by the initials MAC, for Mudiad Amddiffyn Cymru, the 'Movement for the Defence of Wales'.

Like the FWA, MAC had its roots in the anger over Tryweryn. The attack on the reservoir work site in 1963 that resulted in the destruction of a transformer was the work of MAC founders Emyr Llywelyn Jones, Owen Williams and John Albert Jones. These were not sophisticated terrorists however, and all three men were soon arrested, after Emyr Llywelyn Jones left a handkerchief with an incriminating letter 'E' embroidered on it at the scene.[22] Many observers suspected that Jones, who idolized Saunders Lewis and the other bombing school arsonists, intended to get arrested and stage his own public court protest in defence of nationalism.[23] If this was his goal, it failed at stopping the reservoir being opened, as did all other protests at the time.

With its founders in prison, command of MAC passed to John Barnard Jenkins, a sergeant in the Royal Army Medical Corps. A non-descript man of medium height, medium build and a bland, long face, the only thing that stood out about Jenkins were his slightly larger than average ears. He did not attract attention, and this was perfect for MAC's purposes. Unlike the FWA, whose flashy antics he found embarrassing, Jenkins stayed in the background, reconfiguring MAC into a true militant organization, with small cells around the country and a commitment to absolute secrecy.[24]

It was clear to the security services by the time of the Temple of Peace bombing that a more serious organization had stepped onto the scene.[25] In a classified note to members of Wilson's Cabinet, Goronwy Daniel, the top civil servant in Wales, said if 'the timing mechanism of that bomb had functioned a few hours in arrears there would have been very serious loss of life'.[26]

'Moreover, the fact that a bomb was used to protest against a meeting arranged to prepare for the investiture of the Prince of Wales carries with it the threat that the same means of protest will be used again as arrangements for the Investiture proceed and there is the danger that the consequences of this could be very serious indeed', Daniel wrote, adding the culprits 'would appear to be a small group with expert (perhaps ex Army) knowledge of bombs and access to explosives. They are also likely to be Welsh speaking and to have links with extreme nationalist and Welsh language movements'.

In fact, Jenkins's Welsh was middling at best. He grew up in the Anglicized south, and spent much of his early adulthood out of the country, stationed in Cyprus and England, where there was little chance to practise. But he was a passionate advocate for the language, and its decline was one of his main motivations in taking up arms against the British state.

In the run up to Charles's investiture, both the police and MAC stepped up their activities. Using explosives stolen from a colliery in Wrexham, MAC bombed targets across Wales, including several water pipelines, an Inland Revenue building and the Welsh Office, a few doors down from the Temple of Peace on Cathays Park.[27] For their part, the security services increased surveillance of Cymdeithas and Plaid Cymru, and moved to prosecute Evans and the rest of the FWA, though the most they could charge them with were public order offences related to the wearing of paramilitary uniforms, more often used against IRA supporters. It would be several more years, however, before the authorities came close to their true target.

'They were wasting their time,' Jenkins said later.

> *The authorities wanted to prove that [militant protest] was all about the Free Wales Army and Cymdeithas yr Iaith: organisations that they could quite easily deal with. What they couldn't deal with was the secrecy with which we were surrounded, and the fact that they simply didn't know who we were, where we were, or what we were going to target next.*[28]

Despite the success of his clandestine organization in avoiding arrest, privately Jenkins was frustrated by the reaction to the bombings. The authorities seemed to be acting more due to media pressure than any real concern over the investiture, plans for which were still steaming ahead. MAC had always ensured to avoid casualties in all its bombings, but Jenkins was facing calls from within the organization to carry out more radical action, including attempting to assassinate Charles while he was in Aberystwyth or during his tour around the country ahead of the investiture. The public was getting used to the explosions, and the police did not seem to be taking the campaign seriously, even as the investiture date got closer and closer. To get his message across, Jenkins and MAC would, for the first time, have to break cover.[29]

The gravel driveway crunched underneath the tires as Ian Skidmore turned his car off a narrow country lane on the outskirts of Chester, an English town near the Welsh border, on 2 May 1968.[30] A freelance journalist, Skidmore had been promised a meeting with the men responsible for the anti-investiture bombing campaign. He'd brought with him Harold Pendlebury, a Manchester-based reporter for the *Daily Mail*, to whom he often sold tips and stories. As the car made its way up the driveway towards the large white house, Skidmore heard running feet and suddenly two men appeared on either side of the vehicle. It was nearing 10 pm and dark outside, but he could see that both men were young, in their early twenties, wearing green combat jackets. One opened the driver's side door and ordered the two journalists to get out, before taking Skidmore's keys.

The house was pitch black as Pendlebury and Skidmore were led inside. One of the men told the other to go get a lamp and set it up in the drawing room, before turning to the two journalists: 'I'm sorry, there will be no other lights allowed.'[31]

The drawing room was so dark that one of the men stumbled into a low table and knocked it over, before the lamp was located and set up, offering some illumination.

The journalists were ordered to empty their pockets before being patted down, as other men could be heard searching the house from top to bottom. Finally, one of the men went to a large desk in the dining room and picked up a telephone, saying into the receiver 'right Mac, move in'.

After a few minutes, a car could be heard arriving and a dark figure walked into the drawing room. 'No lights,' he said sharply, and the desk lamp was switched off. The man introduced himself as director of operations of MAC and said he was willing to give an interview about the organization and its aims.

Pendlebury pointed out that he couldn't take notes if he couldn't see, and one of the men dug out a small torch and shone it on his notepad, leaving the rest of the room, including the interviewee, shrouded in darkness. Pendlebury asked the man about MAC, and was told it had a supreme council of five and an executive committee of three. This was nonsense, of course. The man who had introduced himself as director of operations, implying a subordinate role, was John Jenkins, absolute leader of MAC and mastermind of the bombing campaign.[32]

'Our aim is to reawaken the national consciousness of the Welsh people, by propaganda and action with explosives,' Jenkins said, gesturing with a cigarette in his hand, the only point of light in the room other than the torch. 'We are prepared to kill, we don't make the rules, we are dealing with a government which apparently puts aside logic and reason, we aim to make them sit up and take action. The only way to make them see that we mean business is to carry out acts of extreme violence.'

Jenkins told the reporters that MAC had a 'battle plan' and considered itself 'the soul of nationalism and the conscience of Wales'.

He listed off a number of bombings that he said MAC was responsible for, providing bits of information that had never been made public by the police as proof, such as the fact an unusual timing device – the street light switch – was used in the Temple of Peace bomb.

'A lot of rubbish was written about the dangers of the effort to the counsellors and Lord Snowdon. Had we had wanted to hurt them we could have blown up the whole place at the time of the meeting, including Lord Snowdon,' Jenkins said. 'We were not throwing the gauntlet down we were picking it up. These people were using this building as a political forum to preserve English rule in Wales, they threw the gauntlet down.'

Jenkins boasted about having raided the Hafod Colliery near Wrexham and stealing almost a hundred kilograms of explosives.

'Our armoury is well stocked,' he said. 'Our organisation is composed of trained saboteurs, and others [who] could be described as an assassination squad. We do not propose wholesale armed insurrection, we simply want to draw attention to the plight of Wales and awaken the spirits of the people. They will take it from there. The people will back up the demands.'

He dismissed the FWA as 'top of the shit parade' and Plaid Cymru as 'far too saintly to recognise the facts of life'.

When Pendlebury asked about the investiture, Jenkins's tone became threatening. He warned that the organization was determined to stop the ceremony, and while MAC was not targeting Charles directly, 'we have a lunatic fringe'.

'There may come a time where some person fired only by patriotic ideals may perform a "Lee Oswald." Who knows. If I was the Queen I would start thinking about being a mother. We have nothing against Charlie, but we hate and detest the Prince of Wales. He isn't coming as a friend, he's coming as a political overlord into his inheritance by right of conquest,' Jenkins said.

As Pendlebury scribbled furiously, Jenkins went on: 'We've reached a conclusion in that unless something is done in the next five to seven years, Wales will have reached the point of no return. In terms of language, in terms of economy, after ten years there will be nothing left.'

He rattled off a list of statistics about declining Welsh language use across the country. 'This is due to two factors, a lack of employment for local people, and the influx of English people to live there and destroy the Welsh language,' Jenkins said.

'We have nothing against the English, but the fact remains an Englishman will spend fifty weeks of the year learning French, Italian, or Spanish to spend a holiday there. He won't spend a second trying to pronounce a Welsh place name. We feel Wales should get independence from normal political channels but by the time she does the only people left to celebrate will be Liverpudlians'.

As the interview wrapped up, Skidmore asked what would happen if the two men went to the police.

'The consequences will be serious,' Jenkins said, in his soft Welsh accent, his face still shrouded in darkness.

The two journalists asked him to explain.

'If you [squeal] and we find out, you will be killed.'

No matter the desires of some of the more radical MAC members, Jenkins had no intention to kill Charles, or indeed anyone else. Wales was not Northern Ireland, where the level of oppression suffered by Catholics, and their political marginalization, made people willing to support the IRA's violent campaigns. While Plaid Cymru saw electoral success in this period, nationalist politics remained a minority preoccupation, and most Welsh voters were loyal to the unionist Labour party. To kill a member of the British royal family would have been a public relations disaster for MAC. But Jenkins wanted to send shockwaves through the British establishment, and he felt this had been successful when no story resulted from the meeting with the journalists. Jenkins was confident that tabloid reporters like Pendlebury and Skidmore would never turn down a scoop on the level of a threat to assassinate the heir to the throne, especially after the press had engaged in a feeding frenzy over the FWA, and so the story must have been suppressed by the authorities.[33]

In London, panic was starting to set in over the investiture. Officials were suddenly having visions of the royal party being blown apart in front of the international media.

The home secretary, James Callaghan, a hard-nosed trade unionist and former Naval officer, ordered the establishment of a dedicated task force, to be based in Shrewsbury, just over the border in England, and led by counter terrorism officers from the Metropolitan Police.[34]

MAC bombings continued throughout 1968, and concern grew in London as Charles prepared to begin his studies in Aberystwyth the following year. In a private letter to Wilson following the bombing of a tax office in Chester in early April 1969, Callaghan admitted to finding the increased violence 'disturbing'.[35]

'The plans I described [previously] for protecting the Prince while he is at Aberystwyth are being put into effect,' Callaghan said. 'The Security Service and the Special Branch Unit at Shrewsbury both conclude that the risk he runs is more a matter of personal embarrassment than of physical harm, although it is never possible to rule out the activities of a determined fanatic.'

He told the prime minister the security services were aware of plans to bomb railway tracks and derail trains on the day of the investiture itself, when it was planned Charles would travel up by rail from Aberystwyth to Cardiff. Other extremists were believed to be targeting pipelines, bridges and even planning to kidnap prominent dignitaries associated with the event.

A month after Callaghan's letter, police in Caergybi, a port on the northwest tip of Môn and the main link to Ireland, were alerted to a suspicious-looking bag on McKenzie Pier.[36] Inside were sixteen sticks of nitroglycerine wrapped in brown paper, connected to a battery and a white plastic alarm clock, which was ticking. The bomb had been placed next to a plinth upon which sat a plaque commemorating the day in August 1958 when Charles, aboard the royal yacht Britannia, had come ashore, the first time he set foot in the country after the Queen designated him the future prince of Wales.

Jefferies, the bomb disposal expert, was once again called to the scene. As police cordoned off the area, he delicately opened the bag and peered inside. The minute hand of the clock had been removed and a small hole drilled in its face. Out of this hole poked a yellow wire. When the hour hand reached six, the metal would have touched the exposed wire, completing the circuit and detonating the bomb.

The Caergybi bomb was perhaps the closest MAC came to killing innocent people. The original man tasked with planting the explosives, Gordon Jones, had got cold feet after seeing how busy the area was, and the risk to public safety.[37] Jones later told police that he'd hidden the bomb materials given to him in an old disused farm, before blowing them up during a fireworks display to conceal the noise. To this day, no one has claimed responsibility or been prosecuted for planting the bomb in Caergybi.

Despite the defusal of that device, the MAC campaign was not without casualties. On the eve of the investiture, Alwyn Jones and George Taylor were planting a bomb outside the Social Security office in Abergele, a small town on the North Wales coast, when the device was triggered accidentally, killing them both. The bomb was one of three intended to go off during the ceremony, while another was timed to explode at a pier in Llandudno the day after, preventing the royal yacht intended to carry Charles on a tour of Wales from docking. Only one of the devices worked as planned, during the twenty-one gun salute which greeted the royals on their arrival in Caernarfon. Another had been hidden near the castle, intended to go off during the ceremony itself, not to hurt anyone but to disrupt the investiture and embarrass the prince. But the timer didn't work, and the bomb lay dormant, until four days later a ten-year-old boy visiting from England, Ian Cox, saw what looked like a football and kicked it, blowing off part of his right leg.[38] Jenkins said later that he had called in both failed bombs to police after they didn't detonate, but the force had received some sixteen thousand hoax calls that week, and did not act on his tip until it was too late.[39]

The investiture went ahead as planned. Charles was crowned prince of Wales, and in his speech, delivered partly in heavily accented and rather halting Welsh, he said:

It is with a certain sense of pride and emotion that I have received these symbols of office, here in this magnificent fortress, where no-one could fail to be stirred by its atmosphere of time-worn grandeur, nor where I myself could be unaware of the long history of Wales in its determination to remain individual and to guard its own particular heritage.[40]

MAC had failed to stop the ceremony. Its actions had crippled a young boy and led to the deaths of two of its own members. And the police were closing in. On the morning of 2 November 1969, Jenkins's home was raided, along with that of another leading MAC member, Ernie Alders. The two men were charged with nineteen counts, ranging from possession of explosives, larceny, and conspiracy, as well as being accessories to the bombing of the Temple of Peace.[41]

Alders, who had met Jenkins through the Territorial Army drumming corps, and was involved in most of the bomb plots, soon turned Queen's evidence. He pleaded guilty to eight offences, and fingered Jenkins as the MAC ringleader.[42] Multiple other MAC associates, including Alders's former fiancé Ann Woodgate, and Gordon Jones, the aborted Caergybi bomber, also testified against Jenkins. Realizing that the odds were stacked against him, and keen to avoid a drawn out trial that could have exposed more MAC members, Jenkins changed his plea to guilty. At trial, the prosecution denounced the 'sinister organisation known as Mudiad Amddiffyn Cymru' which it said was 'wedded to the use of violence' and comprised of members who 'scorn the ordinary peaceful methods of achieving political objectives'. Jenkins was eventually sentenced to ten years in prison. Alders received six.[43]

Throughout the MAC offensive, Cymdeithas yr Iaith Gymraeg, the Welsh Language Society, had been conducting its own civil disobedience campaigns against both the investiture and the failure of the government to protect the Welsh language.[44] Inspired by Saunders Lewis, who in 1962 had called for direct action in protection of the language, Cymdeithas members staged sit-ins, refused to pay taxes or other government fees unless they were in Welsh, ignored English-language court summons, and vandalized English-only road signs. Though members of the society, along with Plaid Cymru, which sent its first MP to Westminster in 1966, were careful to distance themselves from MAC, some did express support or at least sympathy in private. In a way, the two sides, the non-violent civil rights protesters and the militants, worked in tandem to pressure the government to make concessions to Welsh nationalism.[45] Even as police failed to track down Jenkins, court cases involving members of Cymdeithas became increasingly common, and many prominent members were jailed, increasing public sympathy for the cause.[46] Plaid Cymru also saw its electoral fortunes improve during this period, not just in Welsh-speaking areas in the northwest but also in Labour strongholds of the south where English was the norm. This was thanks to a growing tide of nationalism of which the bombings were key part.

With the investiture having created more division rather than healed it, the British government was facing immense pressure to make some kind of concession to Welsh nationalist causes. This came in the form of the Welsh Language Act of 1967, which decreed that 'it is proper that the Welsh language should be freely used by those who so desire in the hearing of legal proceedings in Wales', and also cleared the way for some Welsh-language statutory documents.[47] The law stopped short however of making Welsh an official language, and was met with little enthusiasm in Wales, and outright hostility from Cymdeithas.[48] While some local authorities took full advantage of their new ability to use Welsh in official documents and proceedings, much of the country remained as English as before. The Labour Party, which included many Anglo-Welsh MPs who were not altogether sympathetic to the cause of the language, was split on the issue, and sensing an opportunity to break its electoral stranglehold on the country, both the Conservatives and Liberals began to promise to do more to protect 'Welsh culture'.[49] Amid this growing pressure, as well as the ongoing threat of Plaid siphoning off Welsh votes, James Callaghan, by now prime minister, made two major concessions: first, he agreed to support a new, publicly funded Welsh television channel, a key goal of language campaigners; and secondly, he agreed to a referendum on a Welsh Assembly, a devolved parliament that would have responsibility for legislation in Wales.[50] The date of the vote was 1 March 1979, St. David's Day, and it ended in bitter disappointment for Welsh nationalists, with the 'no' vote winning four-to-one. Every single county, including in the Welsh-speaking northwest, voted against devolution.[51] This result was achieved in large part by scaremongering over the potential fate for Anglo-Welsh and English immigrants in an autonomous Wales, fuelled by anti-devolution Labour MPs like Neil Kinnock, who argued that 'we do not need an Assembly to prove our nationality or our pride. This is a matter of hearts and minds, not bricks, committees and bureaucrats'.[52] His fellow anti-devolutionist, Leo Abse, argued that an Assembly would represent 'xenophobia and nineteenth century nationalism'. He spoke of 'a packed gravy train' headed for Cardiff, where the new body was to be based, with the 'first-class coaches marked "For Welsh speakers only"'.[53]

By now, Jenkins had been released, leaving prison on 15 July 1976. Boarding a train for Wales, wearing square sunglasses and carrying a green, prison-issue holdall, he was asked by a reporter if he harboured any regret for his actions, retorting, 'does a man have to apologise for fighting for his country?'[54]

His imprisonment had stopped the MAC campaign, but it did not end political violence in Wales. The year 1979 saw not only the failed devolution vote, but also the election of a Conservative government in London, led by arch-unionist Margaret Thatcher. Around this time, a new militant organization emerged on the scene. Calling themselves Meibion Glyndŵr, after the Welsh prince Owain Glyndŵr who led a revolt against English rule in 1400,[55] this shadowy group, whose commitment to secrecy put even MAC to shame, began fire-bombing English-owned holiday homes across the country.[56] Eventually some two hundred cottages were burned, the majority in the north, where English migration was increasingly undermining the last redoubt of Welsh-speaking Wales.[57] A massive police operation, including the detention, search and surveillance of leading Welsh politicians and activists, completely failed to track down the masterminds, who attracted widespread sympathy from local populations, particularly in the north, where police complained of a conspiracy of silence against them. Speaking to the BBC about the arson attacks, Jenkins denied any involvement, but said the campaign was a 'last-ditch stand by people who are determined to resist, in any way possible, the infiltration, and basically cultural genocide of all they believe in'.[58] He dismissed a suggestion that the campaign was unjustified given that Wales had overwhelmingly rejected devolution in the recent referendum. 'The people of Wales have been brainwashed for close on eight hundred years,' he said. 'You can hardly expect someone who hasn't had full control of his environment or control of any decisions concerning his environment, suddenly to get up and take a great step forward as this [referendum] would have been.'

By March 1980, more than two-dozen properties had been torched, most on the Llŷn Peninsula, the site of the original Welsh nationalist arson attack on the bombing school. Thatcher's government was also facing pressure from non-violent Welsh-language activists, with Plaid Cymru president Gwynfor Evans planning a hunger strike in protest at Westminster's backtracking on plans for a Welsh-language television channel. While Thatcher would go on to let ten Irish republicans die during a hunger strike at Long Kesh prison in 1981, she was convinced that to do so in this case would have been a disaster. Dafydd Wigley, Plaid's MP for Arfon, in the northwest, wrote to Thatcher to 'stress the gravity of the situation that would develop in Wales if Mr. Evans were to sacrifice his life on this issue'.[59] Inside Cabinet, Thatcher was warned that were Evans to go through with the strike, 'there could be much tension and unpleasantness in Wales later in the year … and there would be a danger that Plaid Cymru would fall into the hands of extreme left wing leaders'.[60]

'The last thing the government needs is to inflame nationalism again,' Thatcher said in one meeting.[61] She eventually agreed to support a Welsh-language channel, an early reversal for the lady who would later claim she was not for turning, though the Tories had initially supported such a channel during the 1979 general election. Sianel Pedwar Cymru, S4C, began broadcasting on 1 November 1982, one day before a fourth channel was launched for the rest of the UK.[62] It was a major victory for Welsh-language campaigners, true to Saunders Lewis's demands that there must be a space to support and promote Welsh-language culture if the tongue was to survive.

Nor would this be the last major concession the Conservatives made to the cause.[63] In 1988, Thatcher's educational reforms made Welsh a compulsory subject for all students in Wales until age fourteen, ensuring children had at least a decade of learning Welsh, helping to shore up the language for the next generation. Five years later, under Thatcher's successor John Major, the language activists got their white whale, an act decreeing that Welsh and English 'should be treated on a basis of equality'.[64] The law also established the Welsh Language Board, which was given the power to require public bodies to promote the language and aid in its use.[65] These victories, while they came in quick succession, were the result of decades of work by language campaigners, who lobbied consecutive governments, both in parliament and the press, as well as through direct action, to do more to protect and promote Welsh. On the Conservatives part, Evans's threat to starve himself to death appears to have genuinely shaken London, and there may have also been a sense that here, finally, was a way to win votes in Wales, long a Labour stronghold. In one Cabinet meeting with her Welsh Office minister Wyn Roberts, Thatcher complained that the 'only Conservatives in Wales are the English who moved in'.[66]

While the Welsh nationalist establishment, exemplified by Plaid Cymru and Cymdeithas, always distanced itself from the militants, it cannot be denied that the achievements of the civil rights movement happened in the context of a bombing and arson campaign carried out by multiple groups committed to violent direct action. Consecutive British governments were wary of Wales heading in the direction of Northern Ireland, where a bitter insurgency cost some 3,500 people their lives between the late 1960s and 1998.[67] At their most extreme, members of MAC occasionally fantasized about provoking a British army occupation of Wales, as in Northern Ireland, and staging atrocities to spark a mass uprising.[68] This, thankfully, never came to pass, and the bombing and arson campaigns ended in 1993, around the time of the Welsh Language Act.

Nor was the situation in Wales ever as heated or parties as intransigent as in Northern Ireland. Plaid supported home rule, but not necessarily full independence from the UK, and Welsh-language activism was for thoroughly reasonable demands, that, despite the scaremongering of Kinnock and others during the referendum campaign, did not threaten the English-speaking majority. Concessions were easy to make, and the existence of a peaceful civil rights movement made it possible to genuflect in that direction when doing so, without making it seem like the government was giving in to the threat of terrorism. Each legislative step begat the next, as exposure to the Welsh language, on the airwaves, on road signs and official forms, and in schools, increased support for its protection, even among English speakers.

Though the Welsh language was relatively successful under Thatcher, the country at large suffered greatly, with her war on the miners causing untold misery throughout south Wales in particular.[69] Whatever goodwill there might have been for the Tories was expunged by the mass unemployment and outward migration their economic policies wrought on the country.[70] A renewed campaign for a devolved government advocated for Welsh solutions to Welsh problems, and, with the language and cultural issues somewhat addressed, began to gather support. In 1992, John Smith, the Scottish MP who had spearheaded the 1979 push for devolution,[71] became Labour leader, and while he died suddenly of a heart attack two years later, the party remained committed to the cause. When Tony Blair became prime minister in 1997, his government legislated for a new referendum on a Welsh assembly, and threw its weight behind a 'yes' vote. This time there would be no dissenting MPs, at least in public,[72] and the party was joined by Plaid and the Liberal Democrats. Only the Conservatives, bereft of any MPs in Wales after the crushing 1997 election defeat, campaigned against the proposal. The result, on 12 September 1997, was far narrower than the 1979 referendum. It came down to Carmarthenshire, the last authority to declare. In halting, painful Welsh, which did little to promote the language as a living, vibrant tongue to the UK-wide audience watching the BBC, the local returning officer read out the final figures, 49,115 in favour of an assembly, 26,911 against. Added to the cumulative total, that gave the 'yes' campaign a majority of 6,721, and a victory.[73]

'Quite incredible. A night of absolute drama', the Welsh BBC presenter Huw Edwards said as he digested the results live on air, trying not to appear too happy. 'All evening, the "no" campaign was looking at a narrow victory for themselves, and they've been robbed of that at the last minute.'

It was a remarkable reversal of the 1979 result, and the Labour government swiftly acted to turn the decision into law. The Government of Wales Act was passed in 1998, and the National Assembly for Wales created the following year. As the country, and the language, greeted a new millennium, it would do so under a new Welsh government, one committed to upholding and preserving the Welsh tongue.

Chapter 4
Bilingual nation

My father has been learning Welsh again.

'Welsh speakers, what is wrong with "fasai i ddim hoffi'r noson carioci o gwbl"?' he asks on our family group chat. For several months now, he has been studying the language on Duolingo, a gamified flashcards app that occasionally throws up confusing results. To me, his translation of 'I wouldn't like a karaoke night one bit' seems fine.

'What was the correct sentence?' I type back.

'Liciwn i mo'r noson carioci o gwbl.' ('I wouldn't mind a karaoke night'.)

My brother-in-law, who grew up with Welsh as his first language, chimes in: 'That's very South Walian!'

Welsh is split into two broad dialects north and south, with the divide generally given as where the mountains of Snowdonia give way to the flat pastures of central Wales, around Aberystwyth.[1] In the north, the dialect of the south is known as 'hwntw', a term which derives from 'tu hwnt' or 'from yonder'; the language they speak beyond the mountains. South Walians refer to northerners as 'gogs', from the word for north, 'gogledd', and the dialect takes the same name. While mutually intelligible for the most part, hwntw and gog Welsh differ on some grammatical points as well as vocabulary, far more so than northern and southern English. Like other languages, there are also sub-dialects and regional peculiarities, further confusing the matter for Welsh learners. In the northwest, for example, the word for milk is 'llefrith', while the rest of the country all say 'llaeth'. Duolingo, in attempting to teach Welsh as a cohesive language, uses both dialects, and occasionally dedicates whole lessons to the differences between them. But for ears accustomed to gog Welsh, the southern dialect can be jarring at times, particularly for those learners, like my father, whose exposure to Welsh is almost entirely person-to-person, rather than through television or literature, and therefore limited to our local dialect.

Despite these occasional hiccups, he was thriving on Duolingo. I introduced him to the app in June 2019, and he soon texted me to say he was 'converted'.

'Busy whizzing through the Welsh', he messaged me a couple of days later, followed soon after by 'I am level 17 Welsh'.

In July, he told me he was aiming for half my score on the app (I use it for studying Chinese) and had just hit that goal. Within months, he had overtaken me. At the time of writing, he's clocked up a score of over 36,000 experience points, to my paltry 8,000, and has completed the Welsh course several times, returning to lessons for revision and to keep his vocabulary up.

My father is something of a connoisseur of Welsh-language learning techniques. On a bookshelf in my parents' house is an old record produced by the Linguaphone Institute, its sleeve decorated with illustrations of people carrying out the distinctly un-Welsh activities of playing the mandolin and wearing lederhosen. On the record label is written 'Listen and Learn Welsh', and, in smaller type, 'Made in England'.

'I suspect that the Welsh on these 78s was so far from that spoken on the streets, that their contribution to the resurgence of the language was negligible,' my father said. 'I do still remember, however, "cnoc, cnoc, yr postman wrth y drws"'.

He had more success with Wlpan, an immersive language programme based on the Hebrew Ulpan method, which aims to introduce learners to both language and culture. He sends me one of the lessons, so good is its encapsulation of life in post-industrial Wales, where many villages – including the one I grew up in, Dwyran – have seen all their businesses close, becoming just collections of private houses, with no shops, post offices, or any other community institutions.

'Does a bus go from here?', a man visiting some unnamed village asks a woman in the Wlpan lesson.

'There was a bus to Bangor half an hour ago, but there won't be another until tomorrow,' she replies.

'Is there a train?'
'A train? There's been no station here since 1996.'
'Is there a taxi company around here?'
'There's a company in the town.'
'Is there a kiosk here?'
'Yes, but there's no phone in it, there's been a problem with vandals.'
'Do you have a phone?'
'Yes, but it hasn't worked since the storm. There was a terrible storm last Saturday.'
'Is there a hotel here?'
'There was … but there wasn't enough business. It shut, yesterday.'
'What am I going to do?'
'Do you want to buy a bike? A bargain for £100.'
'Oh well, ok, is it possible to pay with Visa?'
'No.'
'A cheque?'
'No, just cash.'
'Is there a bank around here?'
'No.'

My father was born in Gillingham, in the south of England, near London. Our roots are in Wales however, and our family history tracks with the prevailing state of the Welsh language.

In the 1901 census, the Griffiths were living in Llanrhystud, a small farming village whose best days were long past, on the central Welsh coast. With Ceredigion Bay and the Irish Sea on one side, and the mountains that protected Wales from invasion for centuries on the other, this was once the heart of monoglot Welsh country, where English was rarely heard. But by the turn of the twentieth century, even Llanrhystud was changing, as subsistence agriculture gave way to mechanized farming and people looked outwards for work. At the time of the census, all members of the family were recorded as speaking both English and Welsh, apart from the youngest member, the splendidly named Redvers Octavius Price Griffiths,[2] who was still then a baby. My great grandfather, he would grow up speaking only English, after the family moved to the outskirts of London in 1904. While the household remained somewhat bilingual through Redvers's early childhood, and his parents may have spoken Welsh together in private, he never learned the language himself, and a stint in the ferociously-Anglo British Army during the First World War finished off any lingering Welshness. As my grandfather recalls of his father, 'Although he had an ear for Welsh, he had no cohesive recollection of that language by the time he was an adult.' That the family made no effort to retain its native language while living in England, despite deep roots stretching to the most Welsh parts of Wales, was common for poorer emigres at the time, who could not afford to do anything but assimilate. Some of this they shared with other immigrants from further afield, who were dealing with a community hostile to outsiders and multiculturalism – despite its diverse population, east London was also a stomping ground for the British Union of Fascists prior to the Second World War.

Redvers did not teach Welsh to his children, and both my grandfather and father grew up with little knowledge of the language, or much of an assumption that they should have any. The connection to Wales itself remained however. My grandparents bought a holiday cottage in Corris, south of Snowdonia, where my father spent most summers, picking up snatches of Welsh while playing with local children. My grandfather attempted to learn the language through the Linguaphone records that eventually ended up in my parents' house. The Welsh that resulted from this however was so archaic and South Walian that it was more often prone to spark laughter than understanding.

Aside from the occasional holidays in Corris, my father spent most of his life in England, attending university in Lancaster in the northwest, where he met my mother. Shortly before I was born, in 1988, my parents moved to Ynys Môn, about one hundred sixty kilometres north of the old family farm. I became the first of Redvers Griffiths's direct line to be born in Wales for almost a century. I was also the first in four generations to grow up speaking Welsh, attending a Welsh-language primary school, which were growing in number all over the country as the momentum in favour of the language snowballed in the last decade of the twentieth century.

Since the turn of the millennium, the fortunes of the Welsh language, in decline for so long, have rebounded. Between 2001 and 2018 the number of Welsh speakers rose from around half a million, to over 800,000, with the highest concentrations in Ynys Môn and Gwynedd in the northwest.[3,4] The Welsh government, which unlike the British administration has remained solidly Labour since 1997, is committed to a million speakers by 2050. 'We need to reach a position where the Welsh language is an integral element of all aspects of everyday life,' ministers wrote in announcing the plan. 'If we want to achieve this, the whole nation has to be part of the journey – fluent Welsh speakers, Welsh speakers who are reluctant to use the language, new speakers who have learned the language, and also those who do not consider themselves to be Welsh speakers.'[5]

The success of this transformation depends less on historically Welsh-speaking families, who have long stopped being embarrassed about their language or refusing to teach it to their children, but on Anglo-Welsh households and English-speaking migrants. Wales, having already provided a model for language revitalization, stands now on the precipice of restoring the country to being a truly Welsh-speaking nation. It is not there yet. While advances in Welsh representation have helped shore the language up, English remains the dominant tongue throughout most of the country, and many people do not have much contact with Welsh beyond seeing it on the occasional road sign. Though some migrants do learn the language, many more do not, and tired tropes about Welsh speakers being hostile to outsiders ('they stopped talking English when I entered the pub', etc.) are still common in the British press. Government support for bilingualism has often contributed to the marginalization of Welsh through what writer Simon Brooks terms 'one-directional bilingualism', which focuses on ensuring that everything not in English is bilingual, rather than advancing Welsh into Anglophone spheres.[6] Brooks, who is highly critical of the 'fetishization' of bilingualism, argues that the current approach will always result in Welsh being a supplementary language to English, given the latter's prestige and the facts of geography. He compares the situation in Wales unfavourably to that of the Basque Country and Quebec, where minority-language communities have been able, both historically and today, to promote their own language as the primary tongue. The result is still bilingualism in both places, but one that advances and sustains Basque and Quebecois rather than relegates them to supplementary languages.

There are reasons for optimism however.

'We've turned the tide in that people genuinely expected the Welsh language to have been destroyed by now,' said Toni Schiavone, a long-term member of Cymdeithas yr Iaith Cymraeg, the Welsh-language pressure group that helped drive so many of the changes in the twentieth century. Now sixty-nine, Schiavone is a veteran of the language wars, and has seen what were once fringe issues become mainstream opinion.

Born in Carmarthenshire not far from my ancestors' village, Schiavone grew up in an English-speaking household. His father was Italian and his mother Welsh, and since neither spoke the other's language, they settled on English. After graduating from university, Schiavone went to teach in 'a very deprived part of London'. There he felt a great deal of solidarity with Asian and Afro-Caribbean immigrants, whose situation awakened long-held feelings about his own culture and heritage.

'I could see the subtle ways in which they were being oppressed and being treated as second-class citizens,' he said. Eventually, Schiavone moved back to Wales, where he joined Cymdeithas and began taking part in civil disobedience actions, including the road sign protests. Today, he is the group's education spokesperson, working to pressure the Welsh government to actually live up to the lofty goals it has set. Cymdeithas has attacked Cardiff for not legislating to make all schools in the country Welsh medium,[7] after pushback from some English parents who objected to their kids being taught in the language. While the Welsh government is aiming to have 40 per cent of schools in the country be Welsh medium by 2050, this still leaves tens of thousands of children whose exposure to the language is sporadic at best.

'The education system as it stands means that the vast majority of our children and young people are denied the ability to speak Welsh,' Schiavone said. 'The government is running a system which is going to lead to a decline in the language. The system needs radical change so that every pupil leaves school fluent in Welsh. That's what will be needed if the Welsh government is going to meet its target of a million speakers.'

My own experience speaks to both the success and failure of the post-2000 education system. Though I was in a Welsh-medium primary school from ages four to eleven, I then transferred to Ysgol David Hughes for high school, where students were sorted into three streams: Welsh, English and bilingual. The first two had their classes wholly in those languages, while bilingual students were mixed in with both (e.g., I learned geography in Welsh, but history in English). The idea behind this was a noble one, allowing Anglo-Welsh students like myself (my parents, though both Welsh learners, do not speak it fluently, and the language of our home was English) to take as many Welsh-language courses as we felt able, while not leaving us adrift in the Welsh-only stream, or completely detached from the language in the English. Inevitably however, this created a degree of segregation between Welsh speakers and the rest of the school, which was overwhelmingly English speaking, including in the bilingual stream. Instead of improving my Welsh, my grasp of the language declined significantly, and the only class I took in it by the time I was nearing graduation was Welsh Language and Literature.

'There was definitely an idea that there was "everyone," and then there were the "Welshies",' said Ellis Vaughan, who attended David Hughes several years after me and now studies Welsh language at Bangor University. 'There were people from Welsh speaking homes who used Welsh at school, but a lot of people definitely distanced themselves from a Welsh identity.'

This was my own experience as well. I'm not sure if I was aware of it at the time, but looking back I can see how the distinction between the Welsh stream and everyone else alienated me from a Welsh identity, which I didn't really embrace until after I started university in England. Even within the bilingual stream, we were further divided into those taking 'first language' Welsh like myself, and those taking 'second language', which was structured more like foreign-language courses and assumed no prior knowledge before secondary school.

'I never liked the title of first language for Welsh because it cut off so many pupils,' said Alwen Derbyshire, who taught me Welsh Language and Literature. A slight, short-haired woman with an easy laugh and a heavy, musical Welsh accent, Derbyshire was one of my best teachers, in one of my worst subjects. In class, she would play music to fit the poetry we read, and was passionate about Welsh culture, writing several musicals that are still performed today at David Hughes. She retired from teaching a number of years ago, going instead to work at Trawsfynydd, the birthplace of the great Welsh poet of the First World War, Hedd Wyn.

When we spoke, Derbyshire was still animated about what she saw as the lost opportunity to gain many new speakers for the language, through misguided policies such as the first-/second-language divide, and the attitudes of many Welsh speakers that made them hostile to language learners, and unfriendly to those that tried to speak Welsh less than perfectly.

'Don't get me started!' she exclaimed, as I asked about the obsession with 'perfect Welsh' among some more conservative parts of society.

'This attitude that you have to speak perfect Welsh, that your mutations have to be bang on before you can use the language, it's totally wrong in my opinion,' she said. 'The language is going to survive only as long as people speak it. It's not just a matter of encouraging parents to pass on the language to children, it's also a matter of using the language socially. It's a living language, and the more you see of it and hear of it the better.'

This visibility (and audibility) has been the great success of the campaigns which began in the 1960s. Any visitor to the country is greeted, right at the border, by a sign saying 'Croeso i Gymru', welcome to Wales. Road signs throughout Wales are written in both languages, as are all official documents, forms, press releases and the like. In the days when people were still turning on devices and consuming whatever was put in front of them, they could easily come across a Welsh soap opera on S4C (one, *Rownd a Rownd*, is filmed just down the road from my old school) or listen to a Welsh-language broadcast on BBC Radio Cymru. Welsh speakers are, more than at any point in the last century, able to live in an entirely Welsh world should they choose, in their jobs, private lives, schools and through popular culture.

This, as well as the legislative successes and educational policy, has created a model for other minoritized languages. In Cornwall, people for centuries spoke a Brythonic language related to Welsh, but it experienced a rapid decline in the eighteenth century and largely died out.[8] Recent decades have seen a major push for revival however, modelled on the success of Welsh, with a Cornish Eisteddfod, the Esedhvos, and a national anthem, 'Bro Goth agan Tasow', which borrows the music from Wales' 'Hen

Wlad Fy Nhadau', as does that of another Brythonic language, Breton, 'Bro Gozh ma Zadoù'.[9] Proponents of Scottish Gaelic too have drawn on the example of Welsh.[10]

Through the European Union, Wales received a large amount of funding both for development and programmes supporting the Welsh language.[11] The vote in 2016 to leave the EU threatens this, and many pointed to the irony that parts of Wales that received among the greatest amounts of money from the bloc voted in favour of Brexit, with the country as a whole voting 52 to 48 per cent in favour of leave.[12] The vote split along linguistic lines, with majority Welsh-speaking areas more likely to opt to remain, while parts of the country where there were large numbers of English migrants voting to leave.[13] But not all Brexit voters were English, nor were all those who chose to remain Welsh speaking, and the results were a major blow to the country's biggest political parties, all of which had campaigned to remain (the pro-Brexit Conservative Party remains a marginal force in domestic Welsh politics).

Following the Brexit vote, in which all parts of mainland Britain opted to leave apart from Scotland, it was widely assumed there would be a big swing towards independence in that country. What was not expected was a similar shift in Welsh opinion, where a substantial and growing minority now supports independence from the UK.[14] The coronavirus pandemic helped drive this change. Wales sets its own health policy, and Cardiff was far more successful in containing the virus than Westminster, enforcing tougher restrictions than across the border in England, something which served to highlight the distinctions between the two countries. Plaid Cymru, along with the pro-independence pressure group, YesCymru, quickly moved to capitalize on this shift, using the coronavirus as an example of how an independent Wales could effectively manage its own affairs, without support or interference from Westminster. Writing in mid-2020, Adam Price, Plaid's popular young leader, said that '62 countries have gained their independence from the UK and not one has looked back. After gaining its independence from the United Kingdom, Ireland went from being one of the poorest parts of Europe to one of the most prosperous'.[15]

One of Price's successes has been in connecting the situation in Wales, and arguments about Welsh independence and protecting the Welsh language, to that in other countries. For a long time, one of the strongest criticisms of the Welsh-language movement, and the nationalist movement more generally, was its insularity, an instinct to look backwards and bemoan a lost past. Even as other minority-language communities looked to Wales for inspiration, Welsh speakers could be ignorant of those they should have been building solidarity with. As a teenager, I was only aware that Breton was related to Welsh because one of the teachers in our school happened to be from Brittany, and had no idea of the state of Cornish or Irish, or the historical context around those languages, how they were oppressed, or the efforts to revitalize them.

Vaughan, the former Ysgol David Hughes student, said that growing up, 'it was so often emphasised that we had something unique and different' in the Welsh language. While this was intended as a way of celebrating the ancient tongue, it cut young people off from a pro-indigenous rights and minority-language movement that spanned not only Europe, but the entire globe.

'When I started studying other Celtic languages, I almost got annoyed. You don't have to go far to find a whole slough of minority languages who have typically suffered very similarly in the past and have a similar fight ahead of them,' Vaughan said. 'I remember wishing that we would have been taught that we're not the only ones doing this. That we're not alone in this fight.'

Interlude: Afri-can't

Before they divided the country by race, white South Africans separated themselves by language. As late as 1910, almost three hundred years after the first Cape Colony had been established as a Dutch slave state, whites referred to the 'racial question' as the cleavage between English-speaking British settlers who had begun arriving in large numbers in 1820, and the descendants of the early Dutch colonizers.[1] These Afrikaners, as they came to refer to themselves, made up the majority of the white population but held little political power, the British rulers of South Africa having fought two bloody wars to subjugate them to the Crown's control. While the purpose of these wars was largely financial – both diamonds and gold had been discovered in Afrikaner-controlled territory – they were justified on racial grounds. As South African historian Leonard Thompson writes, Anglo-South Africans 'kept aloof from Afrikaners, despised their language and culture, and underestimated their achievements'. Afrikaners, who lived in closer proximity and interacted more with Black Africans than did many other whites, were seen by some in the colonial administration as indelibly tainted because of this. Such an attitude was exemplified by Sir Alfred Milner, who in 1897 was appointed high commissioner to South Africa. Milner believed that 'the "British race" had a moral right to rule other people – Asians, Africans, and Afrikaners'.[2]

After being fought to a draw in the First Boer War – 'boer' means farmer in Dutch, and most Afrikaners lived in agricultural and pastoral communities in the southern African interior – the British Empire drew on its full might to crush Afrikaner resistance when fighting broke out again in 1899. Almost half a million troops, from Britain, Canada, Australia and New Zealand, poured into the country, and the empire adopted scorched earth policies, burning farmsteads and moving Afrikaner civilians into concentration camps, where some twenty-eight thousand died of dysentery, measles and other diseases. More than a hundred thousand indigenous Africans were also moved to the camps, where at least fourteen thousand died,[3] without the condemnation and handwringing in the UK that accompanied the abuse of the Boer.[4]

Even in the face of such overwhelming force, through the Peace of Vereeniging that ended the war, Afrikaners negotiated key concessions that would set the stage for the resurgence of their own power. Chief among these was a guarantee that Dutch would continue to be taught in the former areas of the Boer Republics, and could be used in courts.[5] The treaty also stated that 'the question of granting the Franchise to Natives will not be decided until after the introduction of Self-Government'. The British had abolished slavery in South Africa and often justified seizing control of Boer territories in the name of protecting indigenous peoples' rights. But when the opportunity came to put Black citizens on an equal footing with whites, they put off the matter in a way that, given the demographics of what would become South Africa, guaranteed any decision on granting the franchise to indigenous people would be made by Afrikaners, not London, setting the stage for minority control well beyond the point that most other former colonies gained independence. The war also created a more unified Afrikaner identity, one with a strong foundational myth and legitimate complaints of colonial abuse and historical suffering that would propel their future nationalist project.

After the newly formed Union of South Africa gained self-governing dominion status in 1910, Afrikaner political groupings soon won back control of the former Boer Republics, with pro-British parties only securing a majority in the predominantly English-speaking Natal.[6] On 31 May 1910, Louis Botha, who had led Afrikaner forces in the Boer wars, became prime minister, under a constitution that made both Dutch and English (and only them) the official languages of the new country. In 1925, Dutch was replaced as an official language by Afrikaans, a reflection of just how far this one time creole had split from its mother tongue.

While it would become associated with white supremacy and a fetishizing of traditional Boer frontier identity, Afrikaans emerged from the racial and linguistic mixing pot of the early Cape Colony, where Europeans of various stripes, slaves from across Africa and Asia, and the indigenous Khoisan people (called Hottentots by the Dutch), interacted, traded and married.[7] During the Great Trek, when tens of thousands of Dutch-speaking colonists moved to the interior to get away from increasing British control of the colony, most spoke a version of the language that had been heavily influenced by the creole or pidgin tongues used by Khoisan and non-indigenous slaves. Though Dutch traders who remained in the British-controlled coastal cities, and retained their connection to Europe, continued to speak the traditional language, the isolated Trekboers, both white, Black and Asian, continued to develop their own tongue, and by the end of the eighteenth century this had evolved into what would be called Afrikaans.[8]

The new language – with its hints of race mixing and native influence – was despised by both the English and Dutch elites on the coast, who saw it as proof of the degenerate backwardness of the interior Boers. A Cape Town newspaper described it as a 'miserable, bastard jargon', not worthy of the name language at all, and called for the 'atrocious vernacular' to be stamped out.[9] Dutch writers were equally scathing, dismissing Afrikaans as a 'Hotnotstaal', or language of the Khoisan, unfit for whites.[10] Such concern had a long legacy among the Dutch elite. As early as 1685, Hendrik van Rheede, commissioner general of the Dutch East India Company, wrote in his diary:

> *There is a custom here among all our people that when these natives learn the Dutch language and speak it, in their manner very badly and hardly intelligibly, our people imitate them in this so that, as the children of our Dutchmen also fall into the habit, a broken language is founded which it will be impossible to overcome later on.*[11]

By the time they emerged from the crucible of the Great Trek and the Boer Wars, Afrikaners were as attached to their language as they were their strict Presbyterian faith, and the changing of the constitution in 1925 'fulfilled a major Afrikaner cultural goal', in the words of historian Thompson.[12] That goal was furthered by the rise, in the 1930s, of the Broederbond, a secret society which counted among its ranks much of the Afrikaner elite. That decade saw the cementing of Afrikaner primacy over English-speaking whites and all non-whites in South Africa.

Though functionally independent, South Africa was still part of the British Empire, and a further wedge was driven between many Afrikaans speakers and London when the country was pulled into the Second World War on Britain's side. Many Afrikaners felt more of a cultural affinity with the Germans, and shared the Nazis' concerns with racial mixing, feeling the state needed to do more to maintain white supremacy and blood 'purity'. The solution, proposed by prominent Broederbonders, was a system of complete economic and cultural segregation of the races. In 1945, as Nazism was being defeated in Europe and the Charter of the United Nations drafted, Afrikaner academic Geoff Cronjé published 'A Home for Posterity', a stridently racist tract that demanded a 'national home' for Afrikaners. Nothing less than full separation, he wrote, could stave off 'miscegenation and racial conflict', the 'core of South Africa's racial problems'.[13] Cronjé and his fellows went beyond just white supremacy, they wanted to carve out a wholly white homeland in southern Africa, with indigenous peoples transferred to their own self-governed territories. While the plan provided for a period of transition, whereby Black migrant labour would have to be depended upon, the hope was that the white state would eventually be wholly self sufficient.

In the election of 1948, the National Party adopted the ideas put forth by the Broederbond intellectuals, now widely referred to as apartheid, or 'apartness'.[14] A promise to enact apartheid and end the economic divide between English and Afrikaans-speaking whites carried the Nationals to power, and on 1 June 1948, D.F. Malan, arriving in Pretoria to take up the premiership, said that 'in the past, we felt like strangers in our country, but today South Africa belongs to us once more. For the first time since Union, South Africa is our own. May God grant that it always remains our own'.[15] Afrikaans was ascendant.

*

On 16 June 1976, Hastings Ndolvu was among the first to die. He was seventeen.[16,17] The bullet that killed him, fired from a police revolver, its retort rising above the din of the crowd, passed straight through his skull and out the other side, spraying blood and grey matter onto those nearby. The crowd, which had been screaming defiance moments earlier, now scattered and fled as the bullets screamed back. Many of the students were even younger than Hastings, and had come to the protest dressed in their school uniforms, looking like they were on a field trip. Now they ran for their lives, dropping their carefully painted placards and protest signs as they did. One read: 'To hell with Afrikaans'.[18]

Around ten thousand students marched that day in Soweto, the sprawling, impoverished township outside Johannesburg, South Africa's largest city, and, at the height of apartheid, one of its most divided. The children had come out to protest a new decree making Afrikaans the medium of instruction in all Black schools, alongside English. The move was the latest in a series of policies whose crafters saw the purpose of schools not to educate the next generation of Black leaders – the missionary schools that had produced the likes of Nelson Mandela, Oliver Tambo and Thabo Mbeki were now seen as a major mistake – but to train a new crop of labourers and servants. Never mind that most Black schools were poorly funded and struggling, and that many teachers lacked the skills to cope in English, let alone a third language; Afrikaans was the language of the white employer, and therefore it was deemed necessary that future workers be able to understand what the 'baas' said, without him having to resort to English or, even worse, an indigenous language.[19] Black South Africans, particularly those living in urban areas who had little need to speak Afrikaans normally, resented this. They saw Afrikaans as the language of colonialism, and were damned if their children's education was going to suffer in the name of promoting it.

Of course, English too was a language of colonialism, but this legacy had also made it a world language, a path not only to employment and success within South Africa, but potentially anywhere one might go. In any case, the British who had imposed the language on South Africa were long gone, and English-speaking whites were a minority, albeit a hugely wealthy, privileged one. By contrast, Afrikaans had become more than ever the tongue of the Afrikaner; the one-time creole, created by a mix of all South Africans, had become the language of white supremacy and the brutality of the Boer state.[20]

This development was recognized and regretted by many leftist Afrikaans speakers, but just as there was little progressive white South Africans could do to push back against apartheid, so too was the language out of their control. 'Towards the end of the nineteenth century the language was regrettably appropriated as a political tool by a small band of white men to challenge the domination of English and Dutch at the Cape,' wrote the late Afrikaans intellectual and dissident André Brink. 'When, after sickening humiliations and tribulations, they finally came to power, Afrikaans became, in its own turn, the language of oppression and power. The language of apartheid.'[21]

The architects of apartheid were cruel, but they were not stupid. They understood that demographics were against both white rule in South Africa and the continuation of the Afrikaans language, and that to preserve both would require the drastic exercise of state power. They had seen that, given a choice, black schools would always pick English over Afrikaans as the non-indigenous language of instruction, and that gradually, just as the creole Dutch spoken by slaves and servants in the original Cape Colony had become the language of the white masters, Afrikaans would slip out of use, buffeted on one side by growing international Anglo-supremacy, and on the other by the necessity of using English when talking to Black workers or servants. In any case, as one school inspector wrote in justifying the new language policy, 'in urban areas the education of a black child is being paid for by the White population, that is English and Afrikaans speaking groups'. Schools therefore had the 'responsibility of satisfying the English and Afrikaans-speaking people' in producing workers who could understand them.[22]

The mostly teenage demonstrators who took part in the initial Soweto protests could see that their futures were being stolen from them. In June, the older students were facing final exams, ones they felt sure they would fail were they forced to write in Afrikaans. Without the involvement of the traditional opposition – many of whom had been forced into exile – students began organizing against the new language policy. At 9 am on 16 June, eleven columns of students marched to Orlando Stadium from across Soweto, with the intention of holding a mass rally against the Afrikaans decree.

Initially joyous, as the columns neared Orlando, the mood turned tense, and one of the student leaders, Tietsi Mashinini, warned the crowd to be 'calm and cool' as a large police force approached them. 'Don't taunt them, don't do anything to them,' he shouted from atop a tractor. 'We are not fighting.'

Such restraint was not shown by the police, who fired tear gas at the crowd and ordered them to retreat over loudspeakers. When they did not, the first shots rang out, and pandemonium soon followed. At least 575 were killed in the violence that followed, and another twenty-three hundred wounded. Most of the victims were under twenty-five and many were school children.[23] Within hours of the initial shots being fired, much of Soweto was in chaos, as anger at the killings spilled onto government buildings and other symbols of the apartheid regime, such as state-owned bottle shops and beer halls, seen as a way to keep the Black population docile. Police launched a huge operation to pacify the township, but it was too late.

South Africa's leaders did not know it at the time, but their overstepping in defence of Afrikaans had created a ripple effect that would eventually lead to the end of minority rule altogether. The unrest which began in Soweto spread to more than two hundred towns and cities across South Africa, an explosion of fury and frustration that had been bottled up for too long.[24] These sympathy protests were met with aggression equal to that used in Soweto, as Prime Minister John Vorster said that 'the government will not be intimidated'. In the name of 'maintain[ing] order at all costs', all outdoor public meetings were banned and policing of Black communities, already stifling, was escalated even further. The arbitrariness of the original language decree, the bloody crackdown on a peaceful protest and the heavy oppression required to contain its aftermath helped radicalize a generation of young people. Before the Soweto uprising, Black opposition movements such as the African National Congress (ANC) had been marginalized and were struggling to attract new members. After the protests, thousands of young people joined the ANC, and many travelled across the border to camps in Angola and Tanzania where they received military training and began plotting the overthrow of the white state.[25] Soweto also magnified and focused international condemnation on the apartheid regime, spurred by the images of children, many wearing school uniforms, being shot dead by white police officers.

'The Soweto uprising was a turning point not only politically in South Africa, but also linguistically,' writes author Kwesi Kwaa Prah.

> It marked the beginnings of the end of Afrikaans hegemony, which had been on the rise from 1948. The road travelled from 1976 to 1994 was politically that of a slowly unravelling Afrikaner power grip over the state, and the beginnings of discussions regarding the foundations for a more emancipated and more democratic order in the country. The insurgent social groups were largely focused on the conquest of political power rather than cultural concerns. Where these concerns existed, they implicitly were directed towards the practical replacement of Afrikaans language supremacy with English.[26]

*

The bronze statue was weathered and worn, its metal turned a green-blue by years of sun and rain, the streaked patina further diminished by the occasional blob of bird droppings. Despite this, the seated figure still had a cold dignity; one elbow rested on a knee, its palm propping up a moustachioed face which gazed impassively into the distance, with an expression of calm superiority. On the morning of 9 March 2015, the sun already high in the clear blue sky, threatening an oppressive midday heat, the statue had been staring at the same spot for over eighty years. It continued to stare as shit, semi-liquid, brown and stinking, splashed across its concrete base and onto the statue itself.[27] It continued to stare as, for the next month, it became the most divisive issue in a country famous for, and built upon, division.[28]

On the front of the statue's base, the opposite side to that now stained with shit, which had been flung from a plastic bucket used to collect raw sewage in a neighbouring poor community,[29] the inscription read:

> I dream my dream, by rock and heath and pine,
> Of Empire to the northward. Ay, one land
> From Lion's Head to Line!

The words were those of Rudyard Kipling, and no man better exemplified the jingoism and unashamed imperialism that Kipling spent most of his career extolling than the statue's subject: Cecil John Rhodes, seventh prime minister of the Cape Colony, founder of the eponymous country of Rhodesia, and for a time one of the wealthiest men in the world.

'The native is to be treated as a child and denied the franchise,' Rhodes told his fellow white lawmakers in 1887. 'We must adopt a system of despotism in our relations with the barbarians of South Africa.'[30] He would have been appalled that one day the people he so despised would not only have the franchise, but would succeed in having his own statue removed from the grounds of the university he helped found, part of a wave of decolonization that has swept South Africa in the decades since the end of apartheid.

'Rhodes Must Fall,' as the campaign to remove the statue was called, was just one small part of this wave, which took aim at an educational system that many felt maintained the divisions put in place under white rule, and did not reflect the desires or needs of Black students. Rhodes in fact was something of an anomaly, in that he represented above all else British imperialism; whereas the primary focus of the decolonization campaign was in pulling down the language of the country's post-independence rulers: Afrikaans.

In the election campaign of 1948 which brought them to power, the National Party ran on the slogan, 'our own people, our own language, our own land.'[31] During the four and a half decades the Nationals were in power, Afrikaans was in the ascendancy, and the government worked to entrench it in all aspects of South African life, white and Black. This reached a head with the 1976 educational reforms, an overstep that sparked a backlash that would eventually bring down the apartheid regime altogether. But the failure of the Afrikaans-first policy went beyond the events of Soweto.

The uprising, along with sympathy protests that spread out across the country, forced the government to roll back its language policies, leaving Black schools free once again to choose either English or Afrikaans and an indigenous 'home language' as the medium of instruction. They overwhelmingly chose English. As Nkonko Kamwangamalu writes, for Black South Africans, 'English became the language of liberation, despite the fact that prior to the rise of Afrikaans both the Boers and the blacks viewed English as an instrument of domination.'[32] In so indelibly linking the language to apartheid and the white supremacist state, the Nationals traded away the future of Afrikaans, making a backlash against the language inevitable when finally, in 1994, minority rule ended and South Africa became a full democracy.

Following his election as the country's first Black president, Nelson Mandela went to great lengths to reassure the Afrikaner minority – which still possessed a great deal of the country's wealth, and a large number of its weapons – that they had a part to play in the rainbow nation.[33] During his inaugural address, Mandela, who had studied Afrikaans while imprisoned on Robben Island, read a poem by the dissident Afrikaner writer Ingrid Junker (though he did so in English). He embraced rugby, and praised Boer generals who had fought against British imperialism. In doing so, Mandela alienated some within the liberation movement who wanted to see those who benefitted from apartheid suffer for it, but he staved off any chance of armed white resistance or a cleavage of the country that some thought might come about after the end of apartheid. But while Afrikaners may have been pleasantly surprised to not find themselves oppressed within the new South Africa, their role was nonetheless greatly changed, and many privileges removed, not least of which the position given their language. 'It has been stated openly that Afrikaans is the price that Afrikaners will have to pay for apartheid,' Afrikaner author and journalist Antjie Krog wrote while covering the post-apartheid truth and reconciliation commission in the late 1990s. 'Was it not a debate for years on Robben Island: What do we do with the language of the Boer?'[34]

In the 1996 constitution, there are eleven 'official languages of the Republic'; Ndebele, Sepedi, Sesotho, Setswana, Swazi, Tshivenda, Xitsonga, Xhosa, Zulu, Afrikaans and English. The country's founding document also states that 'recognising the historically diminished use and status of the indigenous languages of our people, the state must take practical and positive measures to elevate the status and advance the use of these languages'.[35]

A year after the constitution's promulgation, a new education policy made schooling compulsory for all South African children and created a single, unified system to replace the nineteen departments of education the apartheid regime had set up to regulate the teaching of various races and subgroups. While parents were free for the first time to send their children to any school, and have them taught in their own language, many increasingly chose English-medium schools, both from a desire to set their children up for success in an increasingly Anglicized country and global economy, and from an ingrained prejudice against indigenous language schools, which had been severely underfunded during apartheid.[36] Afrikaans schools had been among the best in South Africa, particularly those that had been whites-only and provided with the most funding and best teachers. But Black parents had not fought in Soweto and elsewhere to have their kids taught in the language of the Boer, and so they overwhelmingly chose English-medium schools, leaving Afrikaans-medium institutions majority white or coloured. (Under apartheid, so-called coloured South Africans were a class apart, with more political power than Blacks but still officially discriminated against. While the designation originally referred to the children of white and Black or white and Asian parents, it developed into more of a social, rather than racial category, and many coloured people today continue to identify as such, rather than as Black or white, or mixed race.)

At least initially, this process could be seen as a natural realignment of the languages; where once Afrikaans had been prioritized and privileged, now it was one among many. Most schools that switched to English or another non-Afrikaans language were also, thanks to the segregationist policies of apartheid, in predominantly Black areas, while schools in Afrikaner parts of the country, even if they now had more Black and brown faces among the students, could continue teaching in Afrikaans with the approval of the majority of parents. For some in the ANC however, the continued prominence of Afrikaans – as well as the continued wealth and power of

Afrikaners – was a sign that the country was not truly moving beyond apartheid. Once Mandela, with his moderating presence and eye for compromise, stood down as president in 1999, this attitude began to come to the fore. In particular, Black politicians took aim at the country's universities, arguing that Afrikaans acted 'as a barrier to access' for Black students, and so perpetuated the type of separation made illegal under the post-apartheid constitution.[37]

The increasingly bitter tone of the debate shocked even those Afrikaners who supported the ANC. André Brink, who had the dubious honour of being the first Afrikaans author to have a book banned by the apartheid regime,[38] wrote in his memoir:

> After the interminable rule of the apartheid regime, when the Afrikaans language became the de facto language of the oppressor, it was good to see the language cut down to size as one of eleven official languages. But as the new rulers became more safely ensconced, and more arrogant, in their new-found positions of power, an alarming vindictiveness crept into their dealings with Afrikaans.[39]

If white leftists were alarmed, conservative Afrikaners were appalled. As a debate sprung up over the teaching of Afrikaans at Stellenbosch University in 2002, right-wing commentator Dan Roodt excoriated education minister Kader Asmal, writing that 'no one is more hated today by Afrikaners than Asmal, who has patiently set about undermining the ultimate repository of Afrikaner identity their education system'.[40] He warned that 'the current sense of crisis among Afrikaners, compounded by crime, farm murders, affirmative action and Asmal's Anglicisation policies, provides an ideal environment for recruitment to extremist groups'.

That a major transformation in the linguistic life of the country was underway could not be denied. At the beginning of the 1990s, there were around two thousand schools teaching in Afrikaans; less than a decade later, only three hundred remained. As these students graduated and applied for university, the pressure for historically Afrikaans institutions to provide classes in English became overwhelming. The government decreed that schools could no longer only teach in Afrikaans, nor were they permitted to impose language tests on South African students, as they did for applicants from overseas.[41]

Critics of Afrikaans did not stop there. While the Rhodes Must Fall campaign of 2015 and 2016 began in Cape Town with a British imperialist, students of the 'born free' generation, those who had never experienced apartheid, soon turned their sights on the country's historically Afrikaans universities. In its manifesto, the Open Stellenbosch Collective (OSC), which helped lead the protests, said it was challenging 'the hegemony of white Afrikaans culture and the exclusion of black students and staff'.[42] Twenty years after the end of apartheid, the students wrote, 'there are more professors named "Johan" than there are black professors at our institution.' OSC demanded that no student should be 'forced to learn or communicate in Afrikaans,' and all classes must be made available in English.

Named for the governor of the original Dutch Cape Colony and the intellectual home of apartheid, for many Afrikaners Stellenbosch was not just an Afrikaans university, it was *the* Afrikaans university. If the language could not survive at Stellenbosch, could it be preserved at all? Writing after Stellenbosch assented to the students and agreed that 'all learning … will be facilitated in English',[43] Hermann Giliomee, a prominent Afrikaner writer and intellectual, said the decision 'represents a cruel irony in the case of a university established in 1918 to escape from English cultural hegemony'.[44]

Conservative Afrikaners did not take the challenge lying down. If university administrators would not stand up for the language, they would take it on themselves to do so. They waged a legal war against each university in turn – from Pretoria, to the Free State, to Stellenbosch – as they all gradually switched from Afrikaans to English. The cases almost all ended up before the constitutional court, South Africa's highest seat of judgement, with the plaintiff in most cases a group that has increasingly dominated the conversation around the language and its future, AfriForum.

Founded in 2006 with the stated goal of re-engaging Afrikaners in the public sphere,[45] AfriForum is an offshoot of Solidarity, a predominantly white trade union that had long fought a losing battle against the retreat of Afrikaans as the language of official South African life. Solidarity remains controversial in South Africa, having its roots in the Mineworkers' Union, the openly racist apartheid-era organization that once notoriously marched under the banner, 'Workers of the world unite for a white South Africa'.[46] In the decades since 1994, Solidarity has adopted a far more slick presentation and the language of racial inclusivity, but according to its critics, much of the underlying motivations remain the same, with some critics describing it as an Afrikaner 'state within a state'.[47]

AfriForum is even more politically adept, lobbying on behalf of minority – almost always white – rights and taking institutions and individuals to court when the government will not. The group describes itself as South Africa's largest minority rights group, and purports to stand up for the 'continued existence of Afrikaners', and work to 'establish sustainable structures through which Afrikaners are able to ensure their own future independently'.[48] According to writer Max du Preez, 'No other interest group, NGO or political party even remotely has a similarly booming voice in the Afrikaans media. AfriForum is further sanctioned by soft editorials and columns by prominent members of the Afrikaans commentariat.'[49]

It has gained this position through its aggressive and highly public lobbying on two issues: Afrikaans and farm murders.

The crimes are horrific. Men burned with irons and drowned in bathtubs filled with boiling water. Children's throats cut. Women raped and mutilated. Animals dismembered, their blood used to paint racist slogans on the wall.[50] First-hand accounts of the aftermath of the killings, and of those who managed to get away or fight off their attackers, are shared on Facebook and in long, gruesome threads on

WhatsApp. They are compiled into seemingly endless litanies of horror that demand a police or government response.

For some rural white South Africans, farm murders are a near-constant terror, a sign of how far the country has slipped into lawlessness and barbarism since the beginning of Black rule. Those who lobby for greater recognition of the issue say the government is downplaying or ignoring an epidemic of murder and crime targeting white farmers. They point to openly racist, even genocidal rhetoric from some Black politicians as evidence of a coordinated campaign of killings, proof of which can be seen in the hundreds of deaths – some of them unspeakably horrific – recorded across rural South Africa in the last decade; and warn of worse to come if the issue is not tackled soon.[51]

The deaths are real, the pattern isn't. According to statistics compiled by AgriSA, an agricultural union, contrary to reports that there has been a 'surge of violence' against white farmers in recent years, farm murders actually peaked around 2002, and hit a twenty-year low of forty-seven in 2018.[52] Even if the higher figures put out by some Afrikaner groups are accurate, these must be taken in the context of South Africa's staggering murder rate. There were more than twenty-one thousand recorded murders in the country in 2018, according to official statistics,[53] and South Africa has one of the highest intentional homicide rates in the world, at thirty-six per 100,000 citizens, compared to 4.96 in the United States.[54] There is also no legal definition of what exactly constitutes a farm murder, and Afrikaner groups frequently lump in racially motivated crimes with those that have clear alternative motives.[55]

Scepticism hasn't stopped certain groups pushing the idea that farm murders are an epidemic, indeed it may have helped spur them on, fuelling claims the media is biased against white victims and engaged in a conspiracy with the authorities to underplay the issue. This narrative has received considerable support from right-wing tabloids in the United Kingdom and United States, which have revelled in gory pictures and accounts from farm attacks in South Africa, warning of a Zimbabwe-style campaign to confiscate white capital, and confirming their readers' worst prejudices about Black power. The issue has become something of a cause célèbre among right-wing circles in both countries, with President Donald Trump tweeting about the issue in August 2018, much to the delight of many white South Africans and those on the far-right worldwide who claim that a supposed 'white genocide' is imminent.[56]

It is in this context then that AfriForum has emerged as the leading defender of Afrikaans. In arguing that the language is no longer that of apartheid, and that it is another indigenous language deserving of the same protection as all others, the group is often hamstrung by its roots in white Afrikanerdom, either because it is perceived as representing a revanchist white supremacism, or that, despite its paeans to diversity, it fails to recognize how South Africa has changed since 1994. In a stinging rebuke to AfriForum in a 2017 case over the University of the Free State, Justice Johan Froneman, an Afrikaner and graduate of Stellenbosch, said the application lacked 'any recognition of the complexity of the language rights of others and the unequal treatment of oppressed people of other races in the past, let alone the continued existence of historic privilege'.[57]

> *No practical suggestions were apparently made to accommodate the needs of other race groups and facilitate language instruction during the University's extensive inquiry into the problem. There is no apparent insight into these realities, nor any realisation of the perception that this creates in others. These failures entrench the caricature of Afrikaners as intransigent and insensitive to the needs of others. The applicants need to ask themselves whether their manner of attempting to protect language rights advances the cause of Afrikaans or hinders it.*
>
> *The future of Afrikaans lies in the hands of a younger generation of Afrikaans speakers. Whether there will ever be a 'Derde Taalbeweging' [Third Language Movement], this time for an inclusive Afrikaans shorn of racial and other prejudices, only time will tell.*

In late 2019, I spoke to Alana Bailey, head of cultural affairs at AfriForum and the main driver of its language policy.

'I grew up in the really dark days of apartheid,' she told me. 'I think we took Afrikaans for granted, the fact that you had access to any service, whether it's a civil service, or your school, or the business you used, we really took it for granted because the language was so strong and it was supported by the state so strongly.'

Fifty-four, with short brown hair and a propensity for blue jackets, Bailey is an author and cultural historian, and well versed in the history of Afrikaans and its challenges. Pragmatic and reasonable, with the polished air of someone accustomed to media interviews, she nevertheless had a habit, common among some white South Africans, of speaking about apartheid as something that ended in the distant past, not just under three decades ago.

While Bailey was quick to emphasize that the majority of Afrikaans speakers were non-white, she disagreed that white organizations like AfriForum dominate the debate and shape non-Afrikaans-speaking peoples' views on the language. When I asked her about whether it hurt the debate to have Afrikaans adopted as an issue by the far-right, she agreed it did, but the example she gave was one of an Afrikaner being irate about not getting service in their own language.

'The way we try to get beyond that, is by not just looking at Afrikaans as a language in isolation, but looking at the whole argument of mother language education,' Bailey said. 'So that people realise that the promotion of a language is not just beneficial to one community but to the country as a whole.'

It's on this point that groups like AfriForum have the strongest argument, because if Afrikaans is suffering under the advance of English, it is nothing compared to the continued denuding of other indigenous languages. Forcing schools to teach in languages other than English could empower tongues other than Afrikaans, and wins for AfriForum could have wider applications to minority rights. According to the most recent survey of language use in South Africa, Afrikaans is actually the fourth most widely spoken tongue, behind Zulu, Xhosa and English.[58] Other minority languages, including Swazi, Tshivenda, Xitsonga, Ndebele and the Khoisan languages, are barely heard outside of the home, and rarely used in education, where English dominates above all else.[59]

I come out of my conversation with Bailey feeling somewhat sympathetic to her: we can't always choose our allies, and isn't it possible that, given their funding and experience, Afrikaner groups may be best positioned to push back against English hegemony in favour of all South African languages, even if they do so for self-serving purposes?

Peter Du Toit brings me back down to earth. A muckraking Afrikaner political journalist who has clashed with AfriForum in the past, he said that 'the fact that right-wing organisations have hijacked the debate around Afrikaans for their own political ends has been absolutely tragic and devastating for Afrikaans and the future of Afrikaans'.

Du Toit, like Bailey, pointed out that the majority of Afrikaans speakers are non-white, but unlike her he had deep misgivings about them being represented by a group with ties to the Afrikaner right and white nationalists abroad. He highlighted the 'strong drive to claim Afrikaans as a language of all its speakers, not only white Afrikaners'. This effort has seen some success in centring the role of non-white Afrikaans speakers, who make up the majority of speakers, and reclaiming the legacy of the language as a multi-ethnic one. Some of the earliest Afrikaans books were written by non-white authors, and throughout apartheid, non-white Afrikaans speakers used the language to organize against oppression, in solidarity with left-wing Afrikaners. As early as the 1980s, these Afrikaans speakers warned that the presentation or perception of the language as one only of whites could have a detrimental effect in future. 'Afrikaans has to be purified from racial judgements and ... prejudices, and from its white favouring,' a teachers' conference warned in 1988. 'Afrikaans belongs to all its speakers. It is not so that one subgroup can claim the language.'[60] Du Toit pointed to ongoing work by organizations like the Afrikaans Language and Culture Association, which does outreach, particularly among Black South Africans, who may be the most hostile towards Afrikaans. But he warned that this progress risked being undone by the work of white Afrikaner groups.

'Unfortunately, an organisation like AfriForum, an ethnonationalist right wing organisation, has, because of its financial clout and its tactical and strategic nous, been able to hijack the Afrikaans debate for its own ends and has been able to hijack the language for itself and its members, and cast itself as the only organisation capable of defending Afrikaans,' Du Toit said.

Ominous warnings about the death of Afrikaans also risk overstating the danger, and underplaying the language's many successes. There is reason to be, if not wholly optimistic, then not completely despondent about the future of Afrikaans, particularly in the cultural sphere.

'As a language of the arts, as a language of literature, as a language of culture, Afrikaans hasn't been in a better space in its existence as it is now,' Du Toit said. 'The proliferation of Afrikaans language arts festivals, cultural festivals, which have embraced non-white Afrikaans speakers, has had a major effect.'

In terms of books, TV shows, movies, music and journalism, Afrikaans is second only to English, and on a par in some cases, in spite of its considerably denuded role in the political and academic spheres.[61] The Third Language Movement hoped for by Justice Froneman is slowly getting off the ground, led by non-white Afrikaans-speaking authors, poets and musicians. For these speakers, it is not a matter of redefining Afrikaans so much as reclaiming it as a language of mixed foreign and indigenous roots, one that was developed in large part by non-white speakers, and only reclassified as a racialized tongue by the architects of apartheid.

'One of the undoubted successes of Afrikaner nationalist hegemony was the creation of the myth that they, and only they, spoke for those identified as "Afrikaners",' writes Black Afrikaans speaker and academic Hein Willemse. 'Also, that their worldview was the only significant expression of being Afrikaans speaking. These nationalist culture brokers suppressed oppositional and alternative thought within the Afrikaner community. They also minimised the role and place of black Afrikaans speakers in the broader speech community.'[62]

Afrikaans musician Blaq Pearl has said that 'once I embraced where the language came from, I started to feel liberated speaking it.'[63] And non-white Afrikaans speakers have pushed back against all those who attempt to define the language as one of a specific ethnic group. Speaking as part of a series on 'is Afrikaans a white language' hosted by the online platform Coloured Mentality, playwright Amy Jephta said that 'to tell people who've been speaking Afrikaans their whole lives, and who live and breathe in Afrikaans, that by speaking that you're speaking the colonial language or you're partaking in an oppressor's tongue, is also denying how they've found a sense of ownership, or how we as a community have found a sense of ownership.'[64] Despite the dire warnings of groups like AfriForum, the fate of Afrikaans is only bleak if one repeats the historical mistake of looking at it only as a white language. Afrikaans has its roots in non-white South Africa, and it is non-white South Africa which will carry it into the future, not in a form that would be familiar to the architects of apartheid, but a new language for a new country.

PART TWO

Hawaiian

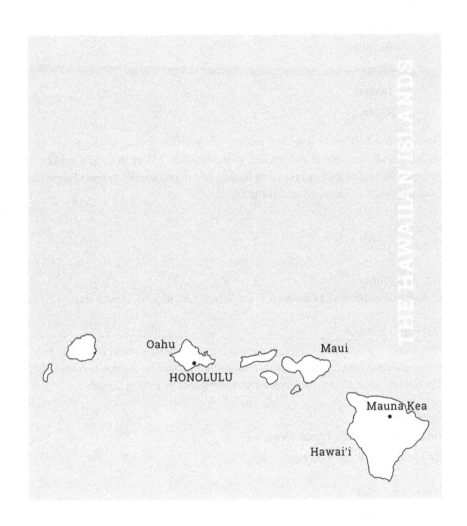

Oahu

HONOLULU

Maui

THE HAWAIIAN ISLANDS

Mauna Kea

Hawai'i

ʻŌlelo Hawaiʻi

(ʔoːˈlɛlo həˈvɐjʔi)

Language family
Austronesian

— Polynesian
    — Eastern Polynesian
        — Hawaiian
        — Māori
        — Tahitian
        — Rapanui

Hawaiian is a Polynesian language, descended from that spoken by the people who settled islands throughout the Pacific. It is related to Māori languages spoken in Aotearoa (New Zealand) and the Cook Islands, and more distantly to other Polynesian languages, such as Tongan, Samoan and Fijian.

Speakers
Hawaiʻi: ~18,000

Writing system
Latin-based alphabet of 13 letters: a, e, i, o, u, h, k, l, m, n, p, w, ʻ (glottal stop)

Distinctive features
Hawaiian is a phonotactic language, in which every syllable ends with a vowel. Every vowel also has a long form, usually indicated with a kahakō, or macron over the vowel. The basic word order is verb-subject-object, compared to SVO in English.

Examples
I'm a native Hawaiian, I speak Hawaiian.
He Kanaka Maoli au, ʻōlelo Hawaiʻi au.

Where is the toilet?
Aia i hea i ka lua?

One language is never enough.
ʻAʻole nō e lawa ka mākaukau ma hoʻokahi wale nō ʻōlelo.

Chapter 5

The princess who was promised

It was the king's birthday, and he was dying. Lot Kapuāiwa turned forty-two on the morning of 11 December 1872; he would not live to see the night.

A round-faced man with a prominent brow and bulbous nose which, combined with his large black moustache, gave him a sober expression that befit his diligent, hardworking personality, Lot had been suffering for months from 'dropsy of the chest', a form of pleurisy which left him short of breath, with a dry cough and sharp chest pains.[1] His illness was not helped by his immense size. Never a thin man, what had been a muscular frame in his youth later had sprawled to fat, and by his death Lot weighed almost 170 kilograms,[2] more than twice the size of an average Hawaiian man in that era.[3]

A descendant of Kamehameha I, the conqueror who had united the eight Hawaiian islands under his rule and begun a dynasty that would dominate their politics for over half a century, Lot had been on the throne for nine years. Unmarried, with no children, as he lay sprawled on his death bed, his chest aching and breath coming shorter and shorter, he had yet to name an heir. Such a situation would be difficult enough for any kingdom, but given the multitude of pressures facing Hawai'i, it threatened all out crisis. Over the course of Lot's life, the decline of the indigenous population, which had begun with the introduction of European diseases following British Captain James Cook's 1788 visit to the islands, had accelerated. Native Hawaiians were increasingly outnumbered by foreigners, both the haoles who poured in from Europe and the United States, and imported labourers from China and Japan who worked the largely white-owned sugar plantations.

While both Britain and France had threatened to annex the islands, it was the Americans who Lot most mistrusted. He was suspicious of the Protestant missionaries who King Liholiho – along with his powerful mother and regent, Ka'ahumanu – had welcomed to Hawai'i in the 1820s, embracing their religion as a path to modernization. In the decades since, the missionaries' power and influence had grown exponentially, and their descendants were among the wealthiest people on the islands. While many had taken Hawaiian citizenship, Lot knew their loyalty remained with their homeland,

and warned of 'hellish conspirators' whose actions would 'lead to the overthrow of the monarchy, annexation to the United States, and ultimate extinction of the Hawaiian race'.[4]

Despite all his concerns however, Lot did not move to shore up native rule by naming a successor who could stand up to haole pressure, both from within the kingdom and without, a decision that would have major ramifications for not only Hawai'i itself but also the Hawaiian language. Lot was the fifth of the Kamehamehas, but the dynasty was poised to end with him unless he took radical action. Finally, hours from death, he turned to a woman sitting at his side, her face already wet with tears, cradling his hand in her own, and asked her to be queen.

'I wish you to take my place, to be my successor,' Lot told Princess Pauahi.[5] Her answer would shape the fate of Hawai'i, and the Hawaiian language, forever.

Pauahi Pākī was born on 19 December 1831, a year and a week after Lot himself. Like many monarchical societies, Hawaiian tradition sets great store by genealogy, and noble children were expected to be able to rattle theirs off by heart.[6] The birth chants recited to mark the birth of Princess Pauahi were long and filled with glory, including both the Conqueror himself and Kānekapōlei, Pauahi's great grandmother, who had been present at the death of Captain Cook.[7]

The augurs of her birth were good, and her lineage was impeccable, but Pauahi was born at a time of crisis. In 1830, the sandalwood trade had collapsed, leaving the crown, which had borrowed heavily against the value of the fragrant wood, very exposed.[8,9] The plunge in the value of sandalwood increased the influence of the Americans, who owned much of King Liholiho's debt, and ruined many ordinary Hawaiians, who were also literally plagued by disease, as they had been since the arrival of the first Europeans.

Smallpox, syphilis and other infectious diseases killed Hawaiians in droves in the decades after first contact. The diseases which struck indigenous Hawaiians cleared the decks for white invasion both literally and spiritually. As American missionaries began to arrive in 1820, they discovered a society where the traditional system of kapu had been recently abandoned. A complex web of rules and rituals which governed all aspects of life, kapu had imploded under the combined pressure of mass death, exposure to foreign ideas and the sight of foreigners themselves, who paid no heed to the restrictions but nevertheless did not face any ill effects.[10] The missionaries, naturally, saw this situation as a gift from God. The 'heathen' nation they had set out to save was already on the path towards saving itself, or as missionary Lucy Thurston put it, a sign of 'the darkness fleeing away from Hawai'i, and that [our] mission family, so hastily fitted out, was going forth to carry the Bible to a nation without a God'.[11]

Disease struck across class lines, with both Liholiho and his queen dying of measles in 1824 during a visit to the UK. That disease would go on to kill tens of thousands more in repeated outbreaks that continued well into the twentieth century.[12]

'In ancient times the land was covered with people. All the lands from Hawai'i to Ka'ula were peopled except the low coral reefs,' historian Samuel Kamakau wrote in the late nineteenth century. 'From the summits of the mountains to the shore are to be found the remains of their cultivated fields and the sites of their houses. Today in some places the ground is white with their bones, and land goes uncultivated because there are none who need it.'[13]

Following Liholiho's death, his brother Kauikeaouli took the throne as Kamehameha III, though their mother, Ka'ahumanu, retained power as co-regent. 'As the tumultous year of 1831 drew to a close it found the Hawaiians sunk in spiritual gloom,' Kathleen Mellen wrote in her biography of Ka'ahumanu. 'Despair had come to the Hawaiians as a sickness comes, moving slowly through the veins and over the spirit. A miasmal melancholy hung listlessly over the land.'[14]

That despair was deepened when Ka'ahumanu followed her older son and daughter-in-law to the grave, at the age of sixty.[15] Free from her influence however, Kauikeaouli emerged as a capable and far-sighted ruler. He rolled back some of the most stringent restrictions on both traditional Hawaiian practices and Catholic worship that his mother, a fierce Protestant convert and strong ally to the American missionaries, had passed.[16] Under his rule, Hawai'i became a constitutional monarchy along the lines of European countries, and Kauikeaouli also gained official recognition for his rule from would-be colonizers, securing the independence of the islands even as more and more of the Pacific was snapped up by voracious imperial powers.[17] While he angered the Protestant missionaries by easing up on the Catholics, Kauikeaouli also backed them in massively expanding the school system throughout Hawai'i, which though it improved literacy, also increased the spread of English.[18]

Initially at least, the missionaries efforts were a boon for the Hawaiian language. Before their arrival, 'Ōlelo Hawai'i was not a written language, and while the missionaries' efforts may have been motivated by a desire to proselytize, it resulted in the creation of both an alphabet and a written grammar. This was a staggering task for anyone to undertake, and the missionaries' ambition may have been aided by a widely shared view among whites that Hawaiian was a 'primitive' or especially simplistic language, and thus did not pose the same challenges a European tongue would when it came to orthography. While James Cook, whose writings on Hawaiian are some of the earliest foreign accounts of the language, took a great interest in the tongue and did not patronize its speakers, later missionary writers found it was 'rude' and 'barbaric,' and often compared Hawaiian unfavourably to more 'sophisticated' languages of their homelands.[19]

Europeans were particularly confused by the Hawaiian pattern, common in Polynesian languages, of ending every syllable with a vowel. A comparative lack of consonants compared to English led many early writers to claim that many Hawaiian words consisted only of vowels. (A similar claim is still made to this day that Welsh has words made up almost exclusively of consonants, ignoring that 'w' and 'y' are vowels in that language.) M.A. Donne, in an early English history of Hawai'i published by the missionary Society for Promoting Christian Knowledge, wrote that 'to our ears Hawaiian sounds feeble, indistinct, and unsatisfying; and no wonder, since it has only seventeen letters, and some of those left out are the ones we could least spare from our own language.'[20]

> The Hawaiians manage to do without c, f, g, j, q, s, x, y, and z. Their syllables are very short, generally having only two letters, and never more than three, and they always end with a vowel. Two consonants are never allowed to come together in any case, and there are many words formed of vowels only; indeed it is possible to make a whole sentence in Hawaiian without using a single consonant.

Manley Hopkins, in another nineteenth-century history, wrote that 'the Hawaiian language is so soft as rather to be compared to the warbling of birds than the speech of suffering mortals. It is usually said to contain but twelve letters, namely, seven consonants, and five vowels.'[21]

This was compared unfavourably to the 'angular teutonic speech' and 'masculine energy and elegant fancy' of the Greek tongue.

Even when foreign observers were not openly disdainful of the sounds and structure of Hawaiian, they nevertheless viewed it as incapable of reaching the rhetorical heights of Old World languages. Laura Fish Judd, whose husband Gerrit would later represent the Hawaiian crown in negotiations with Washington, wrote in 1880 that 'if the Italian is the language of the gods, the French of diplomacy, and the English of business men, we may add that the Polynesian is the dialect of little children.'[22] Few of these observers, even those who spoke passable Hawaiian themselves, seemed to realize that their first impression of Hawaiian as a simplistic language was due in part to Hawaiians simplifying it, in order to make it easier for foreigners to understand.[23] Were Hawaiians to have recorded their own initial impressions of English, they would likely have been similarly unimpressed by the noun and gesture heavy tongue being barked at them by early white colonizers.

Regardless of their opinion about the language, the missionaries were clear on the importance of using it to spread the gospel. An alphabet of twelve Roman letters – made up of five vowels and seven consonants – was adopted in 1826. The 'okina, or glottal stop, though used in Hawaiian printing, was not officially adopted as a letter until much later.

The missionaries' press went into operation on 7 January 1822. One of the first things printed was an eight-page primer on the Hawaiian language itself, covering the alphabet, numbers and a series of simple readings.[24] The press began churning out Christian pamphlets and extracts from the gospels.[25] These were followed by newspapers, in both Hawaiian and English, which would go on to hugely shape the islands' politics, and finally by a 2,700-page Bible in 1839.[26] That Bible was the 'the largest and most demanding single literary project since Hawaiian became a written language', the result of years of work by both missionaries and Hawaiian converts. Here, the missionaries' achievement should not be understated. While translating the Bible into a language that years earlier did not even have an alphabet would have been difficult enough, the deeply pious Hawaiian missionaries chose to base their text not on existing English ones, but on Hebrew, Aramaic and ancient Greek sources.[27]

The Hawaiian written language was a huge success. Supported by the crown and diligently pushed by the missionaries, whose power and influence was growing throughout this period, Hawai'i soon became one of the most literate societies in the world.[28] A written language alone was not enough for this transformation, which was achieved mostly thanks to the expansion of missionary-run schools throughout Hawai'i, again supported by the crown, which saw them as not only a means to gain literacy, but also other benefits of the industrialized nations of Europe and America then taking such an interest in the country.[29]

Pauahi's life would be defined by her years in one of these schools.[30] On 13 June 1839, she entered the Chiefs' Children's School, a brand-new institution founded to give the offspring of the Hawaiian elite the very best education that could be provided. Her cohort included four future kings, the brothers Lot Kamehameha and Alexander Liholiho, William Charles Lunalilo, David Kalākaua, and a future queen, Lili'uokalani.[31] Entrusted with the education of this cream of Hawaiian nobility were two New England Presbyterians with no extensive experience of teaching nor any particular expertise in the subjects they were intended to instruct, Amos and Juliette Cooke.

The Cookes left Boston aboard the *Mary Frazier* in December 1836, arriving in Honolulu after a voyage of one hundred and sixteen days, on 9 April 1837.[32] They were among the eighth company of missionaries sent by the American Board of Commissioners for Foreign Missions, which had also despatched the first crop of Protestant proselytizers, led by Hiram Bingham. The Cookes joined a growing community of Americans in Hawai'i, who had close links to the royals and other segments of the elite. They were soon asked to take on the instruction – in the English language mainly – of several noble children, before, on 3 June 1839, Kamehameha III wrote to the missionary society and asked for 'Mr. Cooke to be teacher for our royal children'.[33]

Amos Cooke was not particularly prepared to run a school. Following a meeting with Gerrit Judd, a senior member of the mission and close advisor to the king, in which he was briefed on his responsibilities, the new schoolmaster came home to find six of the children sitting waiting for him. 'I sent for a desk ... and placed it here in my study and had the children seated,' Cooke wrote in his journal. After an hour, he sent them home again.[34] He does not mention what exactly he taught them, either on the first day or during other hour-long sessions that week, but likely it was lessons from the Gospel, the only thing the Cookes were close to expert on.

For the pampered and often-spoiled children of the Hawaiian elite, the schedule at the Chiefs School was intense. They woke at 5 am for morning devotions, breakfast and then three hours of study from 9 am to midday. During the afternoon, they had another three hours of classwork, studying English, mathematics, religion and, depending on gender, carpentry or needlework, before supper at 5:30 pm, evening prayers, and bed by 7 pm. Each pupil was given three meals a day, with no snacks in between, and anyone late to dinner had to go without. On Sunday, they were expected to attend two church services, responding immediately to the sound of the school bell.[35]

The list of rules was long, stringent and puritanical, with the Cookes especially outraged by any demonstration of teenage sexuality. Amos Cooke likely holds the record for having struck the most number of future kings, and almost all of the boys were thrashed by him at some point, while others were punished by being locked in their rooms or withheld meals.[36]

Aside from religion, English was the most important subject they learned, and soon became the primary language within the school, both during classes and among the children themselves. 'All their studies have been and are still in the English language,' Cooke wrote in a report to the ABCFM in 1843. 'Hitherto they would have learned more if their studies had been pursued in native, but from this time forward they will learn a great deal faster for having the English language. They now use very little native even among themselves in common conversation.'[37]

The Cookes did not disdain Hawaiian, and both spoke the language fluently. The children continued to speak the language with their parents and other Hawaiian visitors, though even older elite Hawaiians were at this time increasingly switching to English as their primary language.

'They have become very much attached to us and would much prefer to stay with us than to run at large as formerly,' Cooke said of the children in his report. Indeed, despite the occasional thrashings and the strict puritan morality employed at the school, almost all the students appear to have valued their time there, and remained close to the Cookes after graduation, increasing the couple's influence, and that of the missionaries in general, over the Hawaiian nobility. Pauahi was particularly close to Juliette Cooke, and the older woman would prove pivotal in helping her reach one of the most important decisions of her young life.

Honolulu in the nineteenth century was a less than welcoming sight for visitors to the Hawaiian Islands. Henry Lyman, son of the missionary David Belden Lyman, who opened one of the largest schools for native children on Hawai'i Island,[38] wrote of a visit to the kingdom's capital in July 1846 that it was 'one of the least inviting spots on the face of the earth.'[39]

'The unlighted streets of the city were destitute of pavement and sidewalks; the shops were low, dark, and repulsive,' he wrote. 'An attractive retail store, a hotel, or any place of refreshment better than a grog-shop for drunken sailors, did not exist.'

To this scene a few months later came William Little Lee and Charles Reed Bishop.[40] Originally from New York, the pair were on their way to Oregon, sovereignty over which had just been hashed out between Washington and London, putting the

American part of the territory on the road to incorporation and eventual statehood.[41] Lee suffered from tuberculosis, the consumption which accounted for between one third and one half of all deaths by disease throughout much of the nineteenth century,[42] and he hoped the clean air of the northwest coast would bring him some relief. While Hawai'i could arguably serve the same purpose, neither man had any intention of visiting the islands, let alone remaining there.[43] But by the time their ship, the *Henry*, cleared Cape Horn and began crawling up the South American west coast, it was in dire need of repairs and its crew, stuck aboard a ship for eight months in some of the worst weather they had ever experienced, were desperate to step onto dry land.

The *Henry* pulled into Honolulu harbour on 12 October 1846, where the two young Americans were warmly welcomed by the missionary community. Lee in particular was a prize the haoles had no intention of letting slip through their fingers. Educated at Harvard, he had practised law in Sandy Hill, where he and Bishop grew up, and was only the second trained attorney to arrive in Hawai'i after then attorney general John Ricord, who quickly recruited the twenty-six-year-old to serve as his deputy and later as appellate judge.[44] Bishop was also convinced to stay, and took a job as a clerk at the US Consulate in Honolulu. Three months after landing, on 25 January 1847, he celebrated his twenty-fifth birthday.

It was the summer of that year when Bishop first met Pauahi. Throughout its existence, the Chiefs' School had been a destination for the Oahu elite, where educated and worldly people could join in conversation with the smart, precocious teenagers who would one day run the islands. In his book, Lyman recounts an evening with the Cookes and 'young princes and princesses of the royal family' who 'received me with great affability'.[45]

As the students at the Chiefs' School grew older, their attraction came to be their eligibility for marriage. In early 1847, Lee and Bishop visited the school for the first time, and it is there the two met Pauahi.[46] Lee may have been the main attraction for the haole elite, but it was Bishop who drew the eyes of the girls at the Chiefs' School. Handsome, with full lips, high cheekbones, and eyebrows that looked like they had been shaped at the salon, Bishop was a breath of fresh air for the young women who were surrounded by relatives, boys they had known for so long they may as well have been, and the austere, excessively bearded missionaries.

Pauahi was no less attractive to Bishop. Delicately featured, with large eyes that dominated her slim, rounded face, framed by carefully arranged ringlets of dark hair falling to the nape of her neck, she had long been remarked on as a great beauty. Writing of her during their school years, the future Queen Lili'uokalani said Pauahi was 'one of the most beautiful girls I ever saw; the vision of her loveliness at that time can never be effaced from remembrance; like a striking picture once seen, it is stamped upon memory's page forever.'[47] Beyond looks, she was, as the Cookes frequently noted in their journals, among the smartest if not the smartest student at the school, and with a charitable, down to earth character which belied her privileged birth.

At a wedding in September 1847, Bishop stood next to Pauahi during the service, she a bridesmaid and him a groomsman; but if there were any murmurings in the crowd about future nuptials, it was to look forward to the joining of Pauahi and Lot, her royal cousin, not Pauahi and Bishop. During her childhood, as was customary for the Hawaiian elite, Pauahi had been fostered by Lot's parents, Kina'u and Kekūanāo'a, who always intended for the two to marry, uniting two lines of the Kamehameha dynasty.[48] Pauahi knew this, and the death of her foster mother Kina'u in 1839 only made the burden of obligation heavier.

Indeed, at first, Pauahi put off Bishop's advances, though whether this was with an eye to duty or simple disinterest is unclear. When he called on her a year after the wedding, he was instead met by Juliette Cooke, who 'answered his inquiry in the negative', her husband wrote in his journal.[49]

Following this apparent refusal, Bishop prepared to quit the islands, taking out an advertisement in the *Polynesian* newspaper that, along with eight others, he intended to 'depart from this kingdom, and request all persons having demands against them to present them immediately'.[50] If this was a gambit to pull at Pauahi's heart strings, it worked, and within two months Bishop had abandoned his plans to leave. In February the following year he became a Hawaiian citizen and renewed his courting of Pauahi. In August 1849, Cooke wrote in his journal that 'Mrs. C received a note from Mr. C. R. Bishop respecting [Pauahi] & today she replied to it & returned it. It will probably lead to the union of those two.'[51] Shortly after responding to his note, the young woman met with Kekūanāo'a, her onetime foster father. Cooke recorded the meeting in his journal:

> Yesterday [Pauahi] had a talk with Governor Kekuanaoa about his desire that she marry Lot. She told him she did not like L. It made her quite unhappy all day & she went to be early with a headache.[52]

Just as she was broaching the subject delicately, Pauahi's parents hit her with a broadside, telling her she was to be engaged to Lot before he departed for San Francisco with his brother, Alexander Liholiho, and Gerrit Judd, and married on their return. Her parents, steeped in both Hawaiian traditions and the assumption of nobility everywhere that marriages are diplomatic rather than romantic matters, had no reason to expect she would defy them, and Pauahi did not want to disappoint both her late foster mother and her natural parents.

On 7 September 1849, Pauahi met with Lot and told him that she would consent to their parents' plans for them, but that doing so would leave her forever unhappy, because he did not love her, nor she him. She also wrote to her parents with the drama befitting a love-struck teenager, that if they 'wished her buried in a coffin, she would submit their authority, & she would as soon have them do so to her, as to promise to marry Lot'.[53]

In the end it was Lot, the one party who had been consulted the least about his own planned marriage, who settled matters. The future Kamehameha V wrote to Pauahi's parents and said that he released her from all 'promises in her youth', and said he 'would not be the means of murdering her, or rendering her unhappy, that he knew he was unworthy of her, but that there was one who was, even the one she loved & he hoped she would be happy with him'. Thus doubly refused, Pauahi's parents and Kekūanāo'a were stymied in their attempt to marry their children, though the matter caused no small strain between them and the Cookes, who they rightly recognized had always preferred Bishop to Lot for Pauahi, and had lobbied for that result.[54]

On 4 June 1850, Pauahi and Charles were married in the parlour of the Royal School. Pauahi wore a gown of white cotton and a lei made of jasmine flowers. The entire ceremony was over in an hour. Neither her parents nor any other members of the Hawaiian elite attended, and Pauahi was given away by Amos Cooke. The following day, the new Mr and Mrs Bishop left for Kauai, an island in the western edges of the archipelago, for a short honeymoon.

Pauahi's refusal of Lot in 1849 dramatically shaped both her future and that of the Hawaiian islands. Were they husband and wife as he lay dying in 1872, there would have been no question but for her to have ruled as sole monarch following his death, continuing the Kamehameha line. As it was, Lot never married, and his designated successor, Crown Princess Victoria Kamāmalu, died six years before him, aged just twenty-seven.[55]

Lot had ignored repeated pleas from his family and advisors to name another successor in the years since his sister's death. This continued on his death bed, where he slapped away Attorney General Stephen Philips, attempting to get the king to write a name on a new will. Lot said he needed space 'to consider so important a subject', and had been taken by surprise at the statement of his physicians that time was running out.[56] Finally, the king looked to Pauahi, his childhood friend who had refused him once in the past but surely would not do so again with the future of their dynasty and the Hawaiian Kingdom at stake.

'I wish you to take my place, to be my successor', he said, straining to breathe as the illness sapped his final strength.

'No, no, not me', she replied. 'Don't think of me, I do not need it.'

Realizing that he was about to be refused again, Lot appeared to notice his audience, and gestured angrily for the crowd to clear the room, leaving just Pauahi and a handful of key ministers to hear what came next.

'I do not wish you to think that I do this from motives of friendship, but I think it best for my people and the nation', he said.

Pauahi again refused, saying that the crown belonged to Ruth Ke'elikōlani, Lot's half sister, 'by right', though her own claim was just as strong.

'She is not fitted for the position', he said.

'We will all help her', Pauahi responded. 'I, my husband, and your ministers; we will all [help] her and advise her.'

'No, she would not answer [to the occasion].'

Lot stopped the exchange, perhaps planning to preserve his strength for another round later, but that would never come. An hour after he spoke with Pauahi, Lot died, and Honolulu, which had been primed to celebrate his birthday, instead marked his death.

'National festivities scattered over many a league were checked and hushed with the ominous warning, and the echoes of the death peal reverberating among the cliffs and crags of the mountains bore to the distant parts of the island a vague hint of the brooding of a public crisis,' the missionary Sanford Dole wrote.

Following Lot's death and failure to name an heir, it fell to the legislature to choose the first non-Kamehameha to rule Hawai'i. They eventually settled on William Lunalilo, a former classmate of Lot and Pauahi's at the Chiefs' School, of equally royal blood. Lunalilo said he would only take the crown if his succession was approved by a plebiscite, and he eventually won a reported 100 per cent of the votes cast, despite a late campaign by David Kalākaua, another Chiefs' School alum with an equal claim to the throne.[57]

As the 'people's King', Lunalilo was hugely popular. At a service to commemorate Lot, one observer wrote that when the crowd spotted Lunalilo in the royal procession, 'they set up a roar of spontaneous and hearty cheers – a strange sound, drowning the funeral march by the band and the wailings of the professional mourners.'[58]

'The people were full of hope and expectation that [his rule] would be long and prosperous,' the observer wrote. These hopes were dashed however, when Lunalilo, aged just thirty-nine, succumbed to pulmonary tuberculosis and died on 3 February 1874, thirteen months after taking the throne.[59] Like Lot, Lunalilo did not name a successor, telling his advisers that since the people had chosen him, so should they choose the next monarch.

That choice again came down to two candidates, though this time the competition was far fiercer and the result more contested. Queen Emma, the widow of Kamehameha IV, put herself forward as the candidate of the native Hawaiians, while David Kalākaua again made a pitch for the throne, appealing largely to the haole and mixed elite, in particular the increasingly powerful plantation owners.[60] Unlike in Lunalilo's case, the legislature, not the wider public, made the decision, and chose Kalākaua. This led to rioting, which eventually had to be put down with the assistance of American troops despatched from a warship moored in Honolulu harbour.[61] This would not be the last time US forces intervened in Hawaiian politics during Kalākaua's reign, and the next time they did would not be in support of him.

Chapter 6

Sandwiched islands

The guests milled around the grounds of 'Iolani Palace, which gleamed in the sun reflecting off its white stone columns and coral-painted concrete exterior.[1] It was 18 November 1889, and King Kalākaua was celebrating his fifty-third birthday.[2] A long grass lawn stretched from the building's steps to the wrought iron gates that guarded the entrance to the grounds, the uniform expanse broken only by tall monkey pod trees, their leafy branches splayed outwards like overly protective mothers encircling a gaggle of children.

Kalākaua had begun work on the palace in 1879, after he tore down the modest one-storey coral brick house that had served as Hawai'i's royal residence since the days of Kamehameha III. The new building was the work of three separate court architects, blending the faux Greco-Roman grandeur of the US Capitol with the intricate and ornate decorative stonework of the Italian renaissance into a style unique to Hawai'i.[3] Four towers stood at each corner of the palace, connected by long porticos supported by rounded stone pillars. In the centre of the building, the main tower rose three storeys to a commanding height of 23 metres, above which fluttered the flag of Hawai'i, the bizarre combination of the British Union Jack and the red and white stripes of the American republic. (The flag was a creation of Kamehameha I, designed to cater to British and US tastes as he expanded trade with both powers.)

From the upper floors of 'Iolani, a visitor could look out on one side across Honolulu Harbour and Quarantine Island to the endless blue of the Pacific Ocean, while on another side the building looked over the city itself, behind which rose the scrub-covered slopes of Punchbowl Crater, the 150-metre tall remnant of a long-dead volcano which was once the site of ceremonial executions.[4]

It was to the crater that the king's guests, munching on refreshments after a morning spent watching a regatta held in the harbour, looked now. Lili'uokalani, the king's younger sister and heir, joined the others in watching a large balloon which had begun slowly climbing into the air from the foot of the crater. For hours, aeronaut Joseph Van Passell had been making final adjustments as he prepared to be carried high above the city, from where he would make a dramatic parachute jump into the palace grounds, to the delight of the distinguished audience which had gathered to watch.[5] Despite a stiff breeze blowing over the lip of the crater, the twenty-six-year-old Van Passell was unconcerned, telling a reporter it wouldn't make a difference. One of his assistants convinced him to put on a life jacket, in case he was blown towards the water, but the aeronaut shrugged it off just before he buckled into the balloon, preferring to be unencumbered.

At seventeen minutes past 2 pm, Van Passell gave the 'let go' signal and there was a cheer and applause as the balloon soared into the air, aided by a strong updraft. Soon the balloon and its cargo were floating some 1,000 metres above the city, and Van Passell, his parachute already unfurled, released himself from the trapeze hanging underneath.[6] Instead of floating gracefully down to the palace however, the wind kept Van Passell aloft and carried him out to sea. Unable to help, the crowd below watched in horror as he was carried out over the harbour, then the reef, to the deep waters of the Pacific Ocean proper, where his chute finally began to sink downwards. As yachts and other boats in the harbour scrambled in Van Passell's direction, the unlucky aeronaut finally hit the water, some 500 metres beyond the edge of the reef. Militia major Charles Gulick, standing on the shore at Kalihi, west of 'Iolani Palace, was perhaps the last to see Van Passell alive, watching through a telescope as the doomed man tried to get his boots off in the seconds before he splashed down. Gulick saw the aeronaut's head bob to the surface twice as he struggled to stay afloat, before he was lost to view. Perhaps he drowned, Gulick thought, though there were worst fates awaiting those who strayed beyond the safety of the harbour: tiger sharks, deadly hunters that could grow to be more than 5 metres long and weigh as much as a grand piano, second only to great whites for their propensity to kill humans.

Lili'uokalani watched in horror with the rest of the guests, as steamships and pleasure craft were despatched to search futilely for Van Passell. Neither he, nor his parachute, was ever found. 'The poor man', Lili'uokalani wrote later, 'probably met his fate at the jaws of the monsters of the deep the moment he touched the water.'

Safe at shore, Lili'uokalani and Kalākaua were nonetheless surrounded by sharks of their own, ones which were just as ravenous. Neither knew it at the time, but the siblings would be the last two people to ever serve as sovereign of the independent state of Hawai'i, and the country itself would cease to exist before the end of the century, drowned in a sea of intrigue and imperialist greed.

Hawai'i was colonized three times, and the third time it took.

In 1843, sixty-five years after James Cook and the crew of HMS *Resolution* made the first documented European contact with the Hawaiian islands, another British frigate sailed into Honolulu harbour.[7] Captain George Paulet, claiming that British citizens were being abused and denied their rights, demanded the islands be ceded to the British crown, and raised the Union Flag over Honolulu. Kamehameha III recognized he was outgunned and agreed to 'yield the breadth of my kingdom', trusting in the 'magnanimity of the British government to redress the wrong and restore my rights.'[8]

Amazingly, given the rapacious behaviour of the British Empire elsewhere, this is what they did. After a five-month occupation by Paulet's forces, Admiral Richard Thomas arrived on his flagship and met with Kamehameha III. Following a brief interview with the king, Thomas reversed his subordinate's actions and restored ownership to the Hawaiians.[9] In a speech marking his return to power, Kamehameha III said the words that would go on to become the motto both of the American state of Hawai'i and of those who seek the islands' independence, 'Ua Mau ke Ea o ka 'Āina i ka Pono,' or 'The sovereignty of the land is perpetuated through justice.'[10]

Perpetuated through justice it might have been, but indigenous sovereignty was a fragile thing. Six years after the Paulet affair, it was the French who invaded and occupied the islands.[11] Following a prolonged dispute over the rights of Catholics in Hawai'i, who had suffered various discriminations and restrictions under the missionary-dominated government and Kamehameha III's stringently anti-Catholic mother and co-regent, Kīna'u, Admiral Louis de Tromelin landed a force in Honolulu and sacked the city, causing an estimated $100,000 worth of damage.[12] De Tromelin's forces left after about a month, but the experience, coming so soon after the British occupation, shook Kamehameha III, who despatched diplomats around the world to seek recognition from and protection of great powers for his continued independent rule.

Following a meeting in Washington with John Clayton, President Zachary Taylor's secretary of state, the king's representative Gerrit Judd, himself a former US citizen, wrote that the republic had agreed that it did 'not want the Islands, but will not permit any other nation to have them'.

'I asked if the US would go to war on our account,' Judd wrote in his journal. 'He replied yes – that is they would send a force and retake the Islands for the King and if that made a war they would carry it out.'[13]

When US troops landed in Honolulu in 1893 however, it was not to support the Hawaiian crown, but a junta led by the descendants of American missionaries, who staged a coup against Lili'uokalani, who had succeeded her brother two years earlier.[14] They declared the Republic of Hawai'i, which four years later was formally annexed by the United States. Sanford Dole, president of the Republic, became the new territory's first governor.[15] Writing ahead of the move, as his junta sought to prevent Lili'uokalani and other indigenous Hawaiians voicing their objections to becoming an American colony, Dole urged Washington seize the Hawaiian islands and make them 'the western outpost of Anglo Saxon civilisation and a vantage ground of American commerce in the Pacific'.[16]

The loss of native sovereignty had a devastating effect on the Hawaiian language. After the putschists seized power and declared a Republic, they promulgated a new constitution to shore up white rule. Their own writings were clear about the purpose of the document. 'I hope', coup leader Lorrin Thurston said, 'that those who are drafting the constitution will not allow fine theories of free government to predominate over the necessities of the present situation.'[17]

Act 77 of the new constitution, signed into law by President Sanford Dole on 15 June 1896, set as grounds for full citizenship in the new Republic of Hawai'i that applicants be able 'to read, write and speak the English language'. More so, they must be 'able intelligently to explain in his own words, in the English language, the general meaning and intent of any article or articles of the Constitution of the Republic of Hawai'i'.[18] A similar requirement was made of prospective voters, that they be able to 'read and write, with ordinary fluency any section or sections of this Constitution'.[19]

To treat native Hawaiians 'with forbearance and courtesy is like trying to disinfect leprosy with rose water', Thurston told Dole, before suggesting voting rights be restricted 'absolutely to those who can speak, read and write the English language'. While the constitution did provide for voters to be able to speak Hawaiian, the language about explaining the constitution was adopted – again on Thurston's suggestion – from post-Reconstruction laws in Mississippi designed to disenfranchise Black voters. 'This limitation of the electorate is of course going to raise a great howl from many of the natives', the coup leader noted.[20]

At the same time as it was restricting the rights of Hawaiian speakers at the polls, the new constitution also introduced restrictions on the language's use in schools. The Department of Public Instruction would oversee all public and private schools, in which 'the English language shall be the medium and basis of instruction'.[21] Schools could apply to teach another language 'in addition to the English language', but such a move would have to be approved by the head of the Board of Education, Henry Cooper, who also served as the Republic's minister of foreign affairs.[22]

Cooper's board was not sympathetic to the Hawaiian language, and schools were instructed to stamp out its use, even in the children's homes. This provoked outrage among opponents of the Republic, with the pro-monarchy, English-language *Independent* writing that 'we are informed that teachers in our public schools have been instructed to remain on the school premises during the noon recess and severely punish all children speaking the Hawaiian language'.

> *Are we living in the Hawaiian Islands yet, or are we living in a conquered province? The Prussians have forbidden the use of the Danish language in Schleswig and of the French language in Alsace-Lorraine, and the civilized world has held up its hands in holy horror and condemned the action of the Prussians. The Prussian Government has at least an excuse by right of conquest. What excuse has Mr. Cooper's Board of Education in its efforts of exterminating the Hawaiian language?*[23]

Teachers who would not go along with the new policies were warned it would result in their termination, while at some private boarding schools, even children's letters to parents were opened to check that they were not written in Hawaiian, and censored if they were.[24] Not all aspects of Hawaiian culture were easily stamped out: in a piece months before Hawai'i's annexation, *The Independent* noted wryly that teenagers had been found performing the hula – a traditional practice much disdained by missionaries and other prissy foreigners for allegedly promoting licentiousness – apparently with the approval of teachers.[25]

> *It is reported that complaints have been made to the Board of Education because a teacher in a Government school has had some big girl pupils dance the hula in all the whirling and twirling gracefulness of that moral and much abused national dance. The Board of Education does not desire to retain the Hawaiian language in public schools. The Hawaiian hula is of course a very different matter. Eh! Brother Cooper?*

But the overall effect was severely deleterious to the language which had been the primary tongue of the islands for hundreds of years. A Reverend Dr Cooper spelled out the purpose of the legislation in a commentary for the missionary newspaper *The Friend* a few months before the constitution was enacted:

> *The English language will be taught in all the public schools. For a time all former methods of mission work have been disarranged; but now there will be adjustments to new conditions … The present generation will generally know English; the next generation will know little else. Here is an element of vast power in many ways. With this knowledge of English will go into the young American republican and Christian ideas; and as this knowledge goes in, kahunaism [a reference to Hawaiian religious figures, known as kahunas], fetishism and heathenism generally will largely go out.*[26]

Indeed, few in the white oligarchy now running the islands lamented this loss. The inspector general of schools A.T. Atkinson noted in a report in 1896 that 'the gradual extinction of a Polynesian dialect may be regretted for sentimental reasons but it is certainly for the interest of the Hawaiians themselves'.[27] The following year, a new curriculum issued to all public elementary schools instructed teachers to tell 'children to express in English what they perceive and what they do in the schoolroom, on the playground, on the way to school, and at home'.[28]

Between 1880 and 1902, the number of schools using Hawaiian as the teaching medium dropped from a high of one hundred and fifty to zero.[29] The following year, the *Paradise of the Pacific*, a magazine, predicted:

> *By the end of this century Hawaiian speech will have as little usage as Gaelic or Irish has now … The native children in the public and private schools are getting a good knowledge of English, and, indeed, it would be doing them an injustice to deny them instruction in English speech.*[30]

It would be decades before a Hawaiian revival would begin to turn the course of the language around. The setting for part of that revival, and one of its primary battlegrounds, would be a chain of schools established by the will of Pauahi Bishop and named for her ancestor, Kamehameha.

Chapter 7
I Mua Kamehameha

Pauahi Bishop's life was bookended by disease and death. In her youth, it was the horrific epidemics that decimated the native population, leaving those living with the terror that they or their family members would be the next to succumb. In adulthood, she watched the deaths of her parents, both biological and adoptive, and then her royal brothers, Alexander Liholiho and Lot Kamehameha. Her difficult refusal of Lot's offer of the crown was made all the more so by the death of his elected successor Lunalilo soon after.

Pauahi was born in a Hawaiian-speaking, Hawaiian-ruled kingdom, she died in an English-speaking country shifting to white rule and mere years away from becoming a republic. Modern Hawaiians have spoken of the heartache of having no connection to one's language and culture, of the alienation and spiritual confusion which results. What must it be like to watch that culture and language, and indeed an entire society, shift and slip away over a lifetime? And then to watch everyone you knew, the people who tied you to the past, themselves weaken and die, to fade away like a wilting flower, replaced by the new, stronger roots of an invasive species?

The final death, before Pauahi's own, was that of her cousin, Ruth Keʻelikōlani. As beautiful as Pauahi in her youth, the adult Keʻelikōlani was cruelly dismissed by many in the white elite for her large size – she stood 1.8 metres and weighed over 180 kilograms at the time of her death[1] – and a face disfigured by a botched operation on her nose which left it splayed across her face like a prize fighter who has gone too many rounds. This, combined with her dark skin and insistence on using her native language despite a more than capable command of English, led some to dismiss her as dull witted, with the United States' minister to Hawaiʻi Henry Pierce describing her as a 'woman of no intelligence or ability'.[2] While even sympathetic observers testified to her difficult personality, Keʻelikōlani was no idiot, and she was beloved by ordinary Hawaiians. In one of her last public actions, she travelled to Hilo, on the far eastern side of Hawaiʻi Island, at the request of locals who were threatened by a rapidly approaching lava flow. In Hawaiian tradition, royalty was tasked with appealing to Pele, the goddess responsible for volcanos, and the people of Hilo asked Keʻelikōlani to pray for them.[3] According to witness accounts, Keʻelikōlani arrived on 4 August 1881, and began traditional sermons and offerings to Pele. The lava stopped flowing five days later, never reaching Hilo.[4]

Soon after this act of myth making, Keʻelikōlani retired from public view as her health declined. She died in her sleep on 24 May 1883, with Pauahi and the dowager Queen Emma at her side.[5] 'Her death will cause one of the last links of the old traditions and memories of the past to the Hawaiian race to be snapped,' an obituary in the *Daily Bulletin* noted, adding that it would be 'universally regretted and by none more than those who have known her intimately'.

The loss of Keʻelikōlani was indeed hard for Pauahi, who was now the last surviving Kamehameha.[6] In that fact was a responsibility to more than just posterity. As the dynasty had died out, its wealth – extensive land holdings dating to the feudal era – had become more and more concentrated. With Keʻelikōlani's death, almost all had passed to Pauahi, who was now by far the largest landowner in Hawaiʻi, with a portfolio worth billions of dollars in today's money.[7]

Pauahi and Charles never had children, so what to do with her vast wealth became an ever more pressing matter as her own end began to near. In her will, completed months after her cousin's death, she made numerous generous bequests to family members and retainers,[8] but the majority of her fortune and landholdings were set aside 'to erect and maintain in the Hawaiian Islands two schools, each for boarding and day scholars, one for boys and one for girls, to be known as, and called the Kamehameha Schools'.[9]

> I direct my trustees to invest the remainder of my estate in such manner as they may think best, and to expend the annual income in the maintenance of said schools; meaning thereby the salaries of teachers, the repairing of buildings and other incidental expenses; and to devote a portion of each year's income to the support and education of orphans, and others in indigent circumstances, giving the preference to Hawaiians of pure or part aboriginal blood; the proportion in which said annual income is to be divided among the various objects above mentioned to be determined solely by my said trustees they to have full discretion.
>
> I desire my trustees to provide first and chiefly a good education in the common English branches, and also instruction in morals and in such useful knowledge as may tend to make good and industrious men and women; and I desire instruction in the higher branches to be subsidiary to the foregoing objects.

The will was signed, with her husband as witness, on 31 October 1883. Within months, as if her body was responding to this release of responsibility, she began showing signs of the illness that would eventually kill her.[10] In March 1884, she was encouraged by her doctor to travel to San Francisco to visit a specialist, who diagnosed breast cancer and advised immediate surgery. Samuel and Harriet Damon, friends of the Bishops, were in California at the time and visited Pauahi in hospital. Harriet later wrote that 'I haven't the least faith in the knife for a cancer'. Indeed, treatment at this time was often horrifically invasive, with doctors taking advantage of developments in anaesthesia to carve out more and more flesh around the tumour in an often-futile attempt to stem its growth.[11] American doctors were particularly fond of the knife, but Pauahi survived the procedure, and at first the cancer appeared to have been defeated, enabling her to return to Hawai'i.

Months later however, the tumour returned with a vengeance. Juliette Cooke visited her in October 1884, and was horrified by the condition she found her old pupil in.

> She is failing. The tumor is again growing with rapid strides. It commenced in the old wound about 2 weeks ago. Now there are several lumps that are very painful. Some lumps under the arm & on the back of the neck! The head, limbs, neck & heart are all painful. She takes opium a half grain once in four hours & still suffers great pain. Says that the medicine does not help her much ... I asked how she was and she replied, 'I do not know how to think of myself!' ... Mrs. Allen feels very bad about B.'s condition. She says the Dr. shakes his head.[12]

Pauahi died on 16 October 1884, a couple of months short of her fifty-third birthday. Flags across the kingdom were lowered to half mast as preparations began for a state funeral. The procession carrying Pauahi's coffin to the Royal Mausoleum was so long it took almost half an hour to go by, with nine hundred people taking part, including large numbers of school children, all of them carried in seventy-five horse-drawn carriages.[13] The procession was escorted by police and a battalion of cavalry.

Beyond the official ceremonies, Pauahi was eulogized in both the press and pulpits. During a funeral sermon the Sunday after Pauahi's death, Reverend J.A. Cruzan, pastor of the Fort Street Church, called her the 'last and best of the Kamehamehas', adding that 'this quiet, modest, true womanly life has been for years, and still is, and will be for years to come, a mighty power for good here in Hawai'i'.[14,15]

'Through the combined influence of birth, wealth, culture and character, she occupied a position not only peculiar but unique. The representative of the most powerful line of chiefs of the olden time, she was also an exponent of the best type of foreign habits and mode of life', The Friend wrote in an editorial. 'The Hawaiian race may yet develop many noble characters, manly, brave, intelligent, patriotic men and loving, devoted and virtuous women, but the peculiar niche occupied by the lady who just passed away, is vacant and must ever remain so.'

The first Kamehameha School opened on 20 October 1887. Per Pauahi's will, it was only for boys, with a girls' school not opened until 1894.[16] In accordance with the increasingly Anglo-centric environment of the last years of the Kingdom of Hawai'i, lessons were taught in English. By the time the girls' school opened, it would be illegal to have it any different. The model for the new institution was that of the boarding schools for indigenous children set up in the American territories, which sought to 'kill the Indian, but save the man'.[17] (Such schools had a devastating effect on indigenous languages in the continental United States, which were often suppressed even more fiercely than Hawaiian.) While it lacked the high walls which had cut off the Chiefs' School students from their families and retainers, Kamehameha sought to nevertheless segregate its native pupils from the wider Hawaiian community. In line with Pauahi's will, Protestant practice was strictly enforced, as was military discipline and the strict English-only policy.

The year of the first Kamehameha School's founding was also that of the Bayonet Constitution, forced upon King David Kalākaua by the white elite and their armed militia, the Honolulu Rifles. The new constitution stripped the monarch, then thirteen years on the throne, of most of his powers, and shifted them to the white-dominated legislature. The vote was denied most Hawaiians by property qualifications which essentially restricted the franchise to the haole elite.[18] Lorrin Thurston, who was involved in both the constitutional putsch and the subsequent overthrow of Kalākaua's successor, Queen Lili'uokalani, in 1893, wrote that 'unquestionably, the constitution was not in accordance with law; neither was the Declaration of Independence from Great Britain. Both were revolutionary documents, which had to be forcibly effected and forcibly maintained.'[19]

Thurston's ancestors and those of other elite haole Hawaiians had arrived in the islands with a desire to help the native population. Their often-patronizing and patrician attitudes notwithstanding, the early missionaries wanted to win the islands to Christ, not Washington, and were often fierce supporters of native rule. They sought to uplift and educate Hawaiians, founding schools and creating the Hawaiian alphabet and many of the early texts printed in the language. This attitude continued through the Chiefs' School, where the haole missionaries crafted the Hawaiian elite in their own image. They might have been cultural imperialists, fully convinced of the correctness of their own religion and way of life, but they did not see the Hawaiian as inherently lesser. In the decades following however, the missionaries' children and grandchildren had become infected by the pervasive white supremacy that was spreading throughout the United States, justifying the genocide of the continent's indigenous population and the continued subjugation of its newly freed Black one.

In an influential 1885 lecture on 'manifest destiny' that was later published in *Harper's*, John Fiske said that 'the work which the English race began when it colonised North America is destined to go on until every land on the earth's surface that is not already the seat of an old civilisation shall become English in its language, in its religion, in its political habits and traditions, and to a predominant extent in the blood of its people'.[20]

For elite haoles in Hawai'i who subscribed to Fiske's views, the attitude to natives shifted from benevolence or indifference to outright hostility. To his critics, King Kalākaua was not merely wanting as a man, he was racially incompetent to rule. This led naturally to the Bayonet Constitution, which itself set the ground for, in 1893, the complete overthrow of the monarchy, and later for the annexation of Hawaiʻi by the United States, the great Anglo-Saxon power and heartland of white supremacy.

Charles Bishop, widower of the last of the Kamehamehas and long-time beneficiary of the largess of the Hawaiian crown, did little to prevent the overthrow of the monarchy, but nor did he voice approval of it. In 1894, a year after Liliʻuokalani was removed from office and following the founding of the Kamehameha Girls School, he left the islands for California, where he remained until his death in 1915.[21] Other trustees of the Bishop Estate, which funded and oversaw the schools, were fierce supporters of both the republic and its eventual annexation by the United States. One, William Smith, even helped draft the Bayonet Constitution and was a member of the 'Committee of Safety' which overthrew the monarchy.[22]

It was natural then that the man they chose to run Kamehameha Schools was in their own mould. William Brewster Oleson was a native of New England and a Protestant minister before he came to Hawaiʻi in 1878 to take over the Hilo Boarding School, which he soon turned into an English-only institution.[23] Oleson 'was a fervent American democrat, with no tolerance for monarchies',[24] and he, like Smith, was part of the committee which drafted the Bayonet Constitution for Kalākaua, whom Oleson loathed, seeing him as a sign of everything that was wrong with Hawaiʻi. While the schools may have been established with the vision of uplifting and educating native Hawaiians, many of the faculty were also adamant annexationists and white supremacists. During the brief and unsuccessful counterrevolution of 1895, which sought to restore Liliʻuokalani to the throne, three Kamehameha teachers took up arms on behalf of the white government. One, Uldrick Thompson, set out his choice in strictly racial terms: 'If I take part in this matter, I must resign and go home. I cannot shoot Hawaiians and then return to teach these boys. But if it comes to a choice between the whites and the Hawaiians I must of course stay with my own race.'[25] Fortunately for his career, Thompson did not fire a shot, and he returned to teach after the rebellion was put down.

Oleson's counterpart at the Girls' School was Ida Pope, a graduate of the missionary-minded Oberlin College and former teacher at a boarding school in Honolulu.[26] 'Much of the success of the venture during the twenty years of Miss Pope's leadership must be attributed to her foresight and indefatigable efforts,' the author of a report into a century of public education in Hawaiʻi noted years later.[27] 'Mother' Pope was beloved by her students and her girls outdid their male counterparts in every measure of academic and other success. She was also less of a rigid disciplinarian than Oleson, allowing girls to learn the waltz and the two-step, even occasionally inviting boys to join in, though the dancers were always kept strictly at arm's length from each other.[28] Despite this, she was still a Puritan at heart, writing that 'constant and consistent restraint is the way to control the careless, joyous, happy-go-lucky nature of the Hawaiian'.

One area in which constant and consistent restraint was always practised was in the use of the native language. 'The anti-Hawaiian campaign at Kaiwi'ula was relentless,' teacher Kawika Eyre said of the atmosphere on the school's original campus.[29]

> *Every teacher was to be a teacher of English. Every incentive was offered, every tactic tried: slogans, 'Better English Weeks,' encouragement to sit in the library and read books, praise and prizes for pronunciation, speech contests, oratory at assemblies, discussion groups, debating societies, drama clubs, off-campus passes, free periods, an 'English holiday' for anyone not caught talking 'native' for a month.*

The only place Hawaiian was used – except in secret – was in recitation of the 'Lord's Prayer' during chapel services. These policies relaxed somewhat when Theodore Richards succeeded Oleson as principal in 1893. That was also the year of the coup, after which many Hawaiians refused to send their children to a school run by staunch annexationists, and attendance at the boys school in particular cratered. Richards responded to this by adding some Hawaiian flavour to the curriculum, encouraging the singing of traditional Hawaiian songs – though the language of the school remained strictly English.

Following the 1898 annexation of Hawai'i and the end of any potential native resistance – which had failed to seriously challenge the Honolulu Rifles, let alone the might of the US empire – there was some relaxation of the restrictions on the Hawaiian language. While Kamehameha remained, in Eyre's words, 'essentially an English immersion school', it became one that acknowledged its Hawaiian heritage, rather than pretending to be a far western offshoot of some New England preparatory college. One key aspect of Hawaiian culture remained banned however, and would be the subject of paranoia and loathing well into the twentieth century: hula.

Like other Polynesian peoples, Hawaiians practised a polytheistic religion that would give an expert in the Greek pantheon pause for its complexity and variety of deities.[30] The Hawaiian nobility, or ali'i, were believed to be descended from the gods, and in possession of great mana, spiritual energy.[31] Interaction between commoners and the ali'i was governed by a web of spiritual rules known as kapu, which covered almost every aspect of an ancient Hawaiian's life, from what they ate and who they ate with, to what they could wear or where they could go. (An equivalent term in Tongan, 'tabu', is the progenitor of the English term 'taboo'.[32]) A priest class, known as kahuna, adjudicated the rules and, when necessary to empower a particularly influential noble, set new kapu. Though later all denounced by the missionaries as wicked sorcerers, many kahuna were more like doctors or courtiers, and considered themselves apart from and superior to the kahuna 'anā'anā, the black magicians who would put curses on people and carry out blood sacrifices.[33]

Without a written language, the islands' history, myths and most importantly genealogy – which established a noble's lineage and therefore right to his or her high rank – were transmitted through chants. Hula developed alongside the chants, giving life to ancient stories and making entertaining dull lists of names stretching back centuries. While the hula did intertwine with the Hawaiian religion, and there were sacred dances, it could also be a secular practice. Dances were held before battles, during celebrations, in memory of a fallen chief or simply for entertainment.[34]

The missionaries loathed the hula. While Cook and other early European visitors wrote appreciatively of the practice,[35] the Americans – steeped in austere Christianity and sexual prudishness – were appalled to see women dancing topless, swaying their hips and moving their hands seductively, chanting all the while in a strange tongue. This antipathy only deepened when they understood hula's connection with traditional religious practices. To the missionaries, the hula was heathen, uncivilized, and immoral – symbolic of everything that was holding the people of Hawai'i back from embracing true Christian civilization.

'The whole arrangement and process of their old hulas were designed to promote lasciviousness, and of course the practice of them could not flourish in modest communities,' wrote missionary leader Hiram Bingham. 'They had been interwoven too with their superstitions, and made subservient to the honor of their gods, and their rulers, either living or departed and deified. Liholiho was fond of witnessing them, and they were managed to gratify his pride and promote his pleasure.'[36]

Liholiho and his stepmother, Queen Regent Ka'ahumanu, had done away with the kapu shortly before the missionaries' arrival, devastating the old religion and clearing the decks for Christianity in a way the New Englanders couldn't help but see as divinely ordained. When Ka'ahumanu converted to Christianity in 1825, she banned the hula along with prostitution and drunkenness, the traditional dance seen as just another vice. For the missionaries it was worse: they saw the hula, kapu and the blasphemy of the kahuna's black magic as all one and the same. They fought a decades-long war to stamp out the hula, as future rulers relaxed or did not enforce prohibitions against it.

Less religious members of the haole elite disapproved of the practice for another reason: it was distracting their Hawaiian plantation workers. As the *Pacific Commercial Advertiser* wrote in an 1857 editorial: 'Natives care little for anything else than witnessing hula by day and night. They are in fact becoming a nuisance, fostering indolence and vice among a race which heaven knows is running itself out fast enough, even when held in check with all the restraints which civilisation, morality and industry can hold out.'[37]

David Kalākaua's support of the hula and other traditional practices helped kickstart the First Hawaiian Renaissance in the 1880s. The 'Merry Monarch' did more than just support the arts, he wrote 'Hawai'i Pono'ī', which became the kingdom's national anthem. Lili'uokalani wrote music too, composing among others songs 'Aloha 'Oe', which would become an iconic musical cue for Hawai'i in many Americans' minds, thanks in large part to its adoption by *Looney Tunes* composer Carl Stalling.[38] But while Kalākaua's encouragement of the hula was welcomed by native Hawaiians, it was seen as characteristic by his haole enemies of the king's backsliding licentiousness, proving the need for more competent white rule.[39] The printer of a Hawaiian-language programme for Kalākaua's coronation ceremony, which included the texts of several hulas to be performed, was even charged by the white-run legislature with 'obscenity'. Robert Grieve only avoided jail because the kingdom's Supreme Court ruled that as he did not understand Hawaiian he could not have intended to commit the offence.[40]

Few haoles, even those not against the practice, understood the true value of the hula, and its importance in preserving not only traditional practices, but the native language itself. For the ancient Hawaiian, Nathaniel Bright Emerson wrote in his 1909 study of the practice, *The Unwritten Literature of Hawaii*, the hula was the equivalent 'of our concert-hall and lecture-room, our opera and theatre, and thus became one of his chief means of social enjoyment'.[41] (A son of missionaries, Emerson's sympathy for the hula and other traditional Hawaiian practices did not stop him taking part in the overthrow of the monarchy.[42])

The suppression of the hula was therefore as detrimental to native Hawaiians as the banning and marginalization of their language. Combined, this served to sever Hawaiians from their heritage and culture, leaving them adrift in a country that was becoming more American every year. While prurience and religious rivalry may have been behind most of the anti-hula invective, the haole elite appears to have also recognized the practice as a stumbling block to assimilation. Following Kalākaua's death in 1891, Reverend Sereno Bishop, editor of the missionary newspaper *The Friend*, blamed the hula for all the problems suffered by the kingdom to that date.[43] In an article headlined 'Why are the Hawaiians dying out?' he wrote that 'one of the foul fluorescences of this great poison tree of Idolatry is the Hula,' the 'chief posturings' of which were 'pantomimes of unnameable lewdness'.

> If it be asked why sixty-eight years of Christian teaching has not availed to lift the Hawaiian people out of the mire of impure living, if it be thus efficacious, its teachers would point to the great increase of adverse influences for the last thirty years, and to the direct fostering of sorcery and hulas by authority during that time, and latterly to the promotion of hardly concealed worship of the gods.

An arch annexationist, Bishop – no relation to Charles – gave the prayer at the opening of the Kamehameha Boys' School, and maintained a strong relationship with the institution throughout his life.[44] It should come as no surprise then that the hula was strictly forbidden at Kamehameha, a rule that was doubly effective due to Pauahi's own rumoured disdain for the practice. More Westernized than many of her royal relatives, unlike them Pauahi never hosted hula performances at her residence, and early Bishop Estate commercial leases banned the practice along with consuming liquor on the premises.[45] Sereno Bishop's complaints about traditional practices went well beyond the hula, though it was clear he saw it as a gateway drug to sin.

He and other conservatives blamed the Hawaiian priest class for keeping the practice alive. The kahuna, another contributor to *The Friend* wrote, was 'the deadly enemy of

Christian civilisation. He and enlightenment are sworn foes, and he does his utmost to create aversion and jealousy toward the haole and particularly the "missionary". We cannot, the writer added, 'be governed by Pulolos, or by people of that turn of mind'.[46]

Pulolo was the name of a kahuna on Lanai who had been convicted in 1892 of flaying her husband alive and murdering her nephew and sister, breaking one's neck and suffocating the other with the assistance of several young male followers.[47] The case caused a sensation both in Hawai'i and the United States and reports of the trial were carried prominently in newspapers across the country. *The Argus Leader* saw in Pulolo a foreboding warning of what was to come when Hawai'i joined the Union. 'With a prospect ahead for the annexation of the Hawaiian Islands there is very little absolute knowledge here of the queer superstitions some of the native islanders indulge in,' the paper quoted a former resident of Honolulu as saying. 'Every one in this country has a general notion that the natives are superstitious, but with the absurd notions entertained and practices that are permitted so far as the common people are concerned, we have but the faintest conception.'

Pulolo's case, this self-appointed expert on Hawaiian religion continued, 'would not be matched, I think, in any superstitions among the North American savages'.[48]

That Pulolo was widely believed among local Hawaiians to have committed the murders of her husband and sister in order to marry her brother-in-law (who assisted her in the crimes), not in pursuance of some evil spirit's approval, was noted in some reports but largely ignored. She was routinely referred to as a 'witch' or 'sorceress' and sentenced to life in prison. When she was released in 1914, one of around a dozen mostly older prisoners granted a Christmas pardon, she had been in jail longer than any other woman at the facility. Then around sixty, Pulolo left prison, a contemporary report noted, 'an aged, broken and deeply-chastened woman.'[49]

She stepped out into what was now the US Territory of Hawai'i, annexation having occurred six years into her sentence. The kingdom had changed far beyond losing its sovereignty. The population was now majority non-Hawaiian, with white and Japanese immigrants making up the largest ethnic groups.[50] It was also by now majority Christian, with the power of the kahunas, such that it was, once and truly broken.[51] But while fear of 'kahunaism' slipped away with the turn of the century, antipathy towards the hula did not.

The person who did perhaps more than anyone else to revive the hula was born in 1923, nine years after Pulolo's release. Winona Kapuailohiamanonokalani Desha Beamer was, by traditional genealogical belief, destined for this role.[52] She was named in part for the Chiefess Manono, who died in 1819 alongside her husband Keaoua Kekuaokalani, nephew of Kamehameha I, when he unsuccessfully led a rebellion against the Conqueror's successor Liholiho after the latter abolished kapu.[53,54] Beamer's great-great-grandmother, Kapuailohia, composed traditional chants and taught the hula in secret when the practice was suppressed, as did her daughter and granddaughter, Beamer's own grandmother, Helen Desha.[55] Helen was a graduate of the Kamehameha School for Girls, and her father in particular encouraged her to focus on more respectable musical endeavours. But though she was recognized during her time in school as a talented pianist,[56] Helen did not stop practising or teaching hula, even when she had to hide the fact of her lessons from her haole husband, Peter Beamer. According to family legend, Mr Beamer was won over when he returned home unexpectedly one day and found his wife performing with a group of neighbourhood women. 'He first fell into a chair, and then under the hula's spell, and finally said, "It's all right".'[57]

Winona Beamer spent much of her early life with her grandmother, from whom she inherited both music and a fierce independent streak. She also became a teacher herself. When the family opened a hula studio in the 1930s, Beamer and the other children worked there part time, helping their mother and grandmother with classes and carrying out errands and basic administrative duties. Beamer's first solo teaching experience was in 1937, aged twelve, when her mother fell sick and asked her to fill in. Her student for the day was Mary Pickford, the actress known as 'America's Sweetheart' (despite being Canadian), who was honeymooning in Hawai'i with her new husband, Buddy Rogers.

'She was tiny – she was smaller than I was,' Beamer remembered later. 'And her little hands, little feet, she was completely charming. Got me over the fear of teaching because we were talking and singing and doing lovely hula hands, graceful as the birds. And I got over my fear.'[58]

The experience, and the effervescent praise of two Hollywood celebrities, solidified her desire to teach. When she enrolled at the Kamehameha Girls' School that September, the third generation of her family to do so, she quickly signed up to volunteer at a local mission school in a deprived area of Honolulu.[59] At the school, Beamer sang and recited traditional chants to the children, and seeing their enthusiastic reaction, she was inspired to form a Hawaiian club, the Hui Kumulipo, at Kamehameha, and began teaching other girls to chant and stand the hula.

As the club grew in size, it attracted the support of school administrators, one of whom invited the girls to perform at a tea for the board of trustees.[60] The esteemed gentlemen were sitting out in one of the school's luxurious gardens, surrounded by bright pink bougainvillea bushes, when a troop of teenage girls entered, swaying their hips and moving their arms to the rhythm of an old chant. The trustees were appalled to see the old 'foul fluorescences' back again.[61] After the girls finished, they bowed uncertainly, not totally sure why their performance had been greeted by stony silence. The school's principal later told Beamer to 'pack your bag and leave this campus'. It was only through the intervention of her grandmother that she was readmitted and able to graduate.[62]

'I went to a Hawaiian school because I wanted to be Hawaiian. Then not to be allowed to be Hawaiian,' Beamer said later. 'Of all things, for a Hawaiian school not to be Hawaiian!'[63]

After graduation, Beamer went to university in the United States, where she majored in anthropology at Barnard College and joined a touring hula group, performing across the east and midwest. There she found a far more welcoming audience than in the garden at Kamehameha. Beginning at the turn of the century, American and Hawaiian entrepreneurs had realized that, despite the objections of the Calvinists in Honolulu, there was a market for hula. At first this was a decidedly crass and commercialized vision of the ancient practice – flyers for the first touring group invited people to see the 'naughty naughty hula dance' – but it helped kickstart a craze for all things Hawaiian among mainland Americans.[64] By the time Beamer arrived in the United States, the hula girl had been adopted by the embryonic Hawaiian tourist industry as the iconic symbol of the islands, and the dance's cultural cache had only risen among Americans thanks to the success of *The Bird of Paradise* and other Hawai'i-themed Broadway musicals.[65] During the Second World War, Hawai'i was flooded by American troops en route to the Pacific theatre. These young men came seeking the grass skirt-wearing, topless hula-dancing beauties they'd been promised by pinups back home, and while they mostly went away disappointed, there was a desire growing among American visitors for Hawaiian culture that, while orientalized, kitschified and commercialized, was nevertheless distinct and exotic.

After touring the mainland, Beamer returned to Hawai'i and resumed teaching hula at the family studio in Waikiki. She saw an opening for greater attention to be paid to other parts of traditional Hawaiian culture as well, and began lobbying for it to enter the general curriculum. At a workshop with teachers from the territory's Department of Public Instruction in 1948, Beamer coined the term 'Hawaiiana' to refer to her intention to 'teach only the best of Hawaiian culture in the classroom'.[66,67] (Hawaiiana is not a reference to Americana, as many assume, 'ana' in Hawaiian means 'to be measured, surveyed, evaluated'.[68])

In 1949, Beamer returned to Kamehameha to found the school's Hawaiian studies department, which would begin life in a former laundry room and go on to transform the school's curriculum.[69] A small, slender woman whose oval face was made striking by a prominent jaw and cheekbones, framed by a mess of black curls, Beamer was a force to be reckoned with, but even she needed help. It was only with the support of Gladys Brandt, the first native Hawaiian woman to run the Girls' School, that the kapu on performing hula at Kamehameha was finally lifted. After lobbying each of the school trustees in turn, Brandt was called by Edwin Murray, the first Kamehameha graduate to sit on the board and a fierce opponent of the hula. 'Woman, if those girls wiggle too much, you know where you'll be,' he said, and hung up on her. She had won, the hula would again be permitted at Kamehameha.[70]

It was far from Beamer's last victory on behalf of the hula. In 1959, a priest in Kona, on the western coast of Hawai'i Island, complained that some of his parishioners were performing an 'idolatrous' hula to the god Pele. Alongside an article on 'What does statehood mean for you?', the Reverend Glen Fisk was quoted as saying hulas which referenced the old gods 'might become a stumbling block to those weak in Christian faith'.[71]

'In the New Testament, Paul says that even if we who are Christian might not be affected by something, if others might be, we should do away with it,' Fisk added. 'I happen to know that there are many folks out here who still hold on to the old superstitious beliefs – like sprinkling salt around the house after a funeral, or placing ti leaves in the house when there are visitors, to drive away evil spirits.'[72]

Fisk, who had previously sparked controversy when he praised God in a sermon for bringing the gospel to Hawai'i and 'supplanting the false gods of the Hawaiians,'[73] blamed one woman in particular for encouraging this religious backsliding, the then thirty-five-year-old Beamer.

Beamer was more than a match for a young firebrand priest, only five years in Hawai'i. Though proudly native Hawaiian, Beamer was also descended from 'missionary stock', and as Christian as they come. She challenged Fisk to a debate on KGMB, Hawai'i's main and for a time only television channel. On air, Fisk returned to the gospel of Paul, and his warnings that the recitation of old chants could cause Hawaiians to waver in their newer faith. 'I suggest you make firmer Christians then,' Beamer responded curtly. And that was that.[74]

At the time of their debate, the seeds that would blossom into the Second Hawaiian Renaissance were being planted throughout the islands. Two years earlier, in 1957, Mary Kawena Pukui and Samuel H. Elbert published their Hawaiian dictionary, containing some thirty thousand words, all marked with their 'okina (glottal stop) and kahakō (macron) in the right place.[75] Two years later, when Hawai'i became the fiftieth American state, the government funded the creation of the Committee for the Preservation of Hawaiian Language, Art, and Culture at the University of Hawai'i. Schools, including Kamehameha, soon began offering Hawaiian as an elective language.

All of this could be traced back to the hula. Pukui and Elbert consulted with hula teachers on ancient terms and traditional sayings, and the continuation and growing popularity of the practice – both in a classical form and the modern, commercialized variety – helped reawaken interest in learning the Hawaiian language and connecting with traditional culture. Without the hula, said one teacher years later, 'we would have nothing to hold us to our identity.'

That identity had been almost lost completely following Pauahi's death, with even the schools she founded pushing assimilation and cultural catabolism. That it was not was thanks to the work of Kamehameha graduates like Winona Beamer. Now that the identity had been rediscovered, the job of defending it and expanding it would pass to a new generation of Hawaiians.

Chapter 8
Ke Ea Hawai'i

On Instagram and in glossy travel spreads, Hawai'i is lush and verdant, overflowing with greenery damp from generous tropical rain, waterfalls and pools. But Maui, the second-largest island in the chain, is dry.[1] So dry there are wildfires and water shortages during which the government bans people from washing their cars or watering the lawn.[2] The island was formed by two overlapping volcanoes: Mauna Kahalawai, in the west, and Haleakalā in the east, whose magma-produced mountains are linked by a large, flat isthmus.[3] This central plain is arid and hot, with dark brown earth and sparse, sun-bleached vegetation, reminiscent more of Navajo country or the Australian outback than the rest of Hawai'i. In the past, plantations diverted streams and rivers to water sugar cane or pineapple fields, and residents still look suspiciously on any project that threatens to further denude the area of water, pumping it to tourist-filled resorts or swanky golf courses.[4]

At the northwestern edge of this dry plain sits Kahului, Maui's main port and largest town, its houses, churches and strip malls sprawling up the sides of Kahalawai. Every morning during the school year, and many other days besides, 'Ekela Kani'aupio-Crozier leaves the town and drives east across the valley to Kamehameha Schools Maui, on the slopes of Haleakalā. Her husband, a conservationist, heads in the opposite direction, and the two joke that they could wave to each other at lunch time from their respective mountains.

A large woman with an easy, broad smile and long, flowing grey-black hair that she pulls up into a bun atop her head, when we met in 2019, 'Ekela was on her third stint working for Kamehameha. In the past she'd quit out frustration with the bureaucracy and the slow pace of progress, but the potential of the schools kept pulling her back. Kamehameha had the money, the resources and the influence to do something great for Hawai'i and the Hawaiian language, as well as a literal royal edict to do so.

'Ekela is hardly alone in having mixed feelings about Kamehameha. The school is immensely rich, with an endowment of over $12 billion in 2019,[5] more than half the universities in the Ivy League. The trust which owns the schools is Hawai'i's largest private landowner, with sprawling holdings throughout the islands. While tuition is relatively cheap as far as US private schools go, Kamehameha is, on the face of it, exactly the kind of elite institution that is often blamed for entrenching privilege and exacerbating class divides. Thanks to Pauahi Bishop's will however, the school is obliged to focus its immense wealth on providing for the children of Native Hawaiians, which has a major redistributive effect. Kānaka maoli, as Hawaiians call themselves, are almost twice as likely as whites to live in poverty,[6] and up to 25 per cent of spaces at Kamehameha are also reserved for applicants identified as either orphaned or indigent.[7] Courts have repeatedly upheld Kamehameha's selective admissions policy against legal challenges from non-natives on the grounds that they serve a 'legitimate remedial purpose by addressing the socioeconomic and educational disadvantages facing Native Hawaiians'.[8] One former student has written that Pauahi's 'educational legacy [is] a lifesaver for Native Hawaiians'.[9]

Despite these noble goals, Kamehameha is far from perfect. In the late 1990s, a scandal engulfed the school system and its parent trust, then called the Bishop Estate. Trustees were accused of paying themselves extortionate salaries, rigging the selection process for their successors and lining their own pockets at the expense of the institution itself.[10] In 1999, after almost two years of court battles between trustees and a coalition of activists, parents and teachers, the Internal Revenue Service intervened by threatening to revoke the trust's tax-exempt status if the board was not dismissed. Multiple trustees were eventually charged with corruption, as were several state legislators, and Hawai'i's entire charity oversight system was reformed.[11,12,13]

Prior to the scandal, trustees once argued that they had inherited the absolute power of Hawaiian royalty, precluding any challenge to how they controlled the trust's land or spent its vast endowment.[14] As the trust entered the new millennium, it was considerably more humble.[15] Hawaiians were also far more ready to make themselves heard. Winona Beamer, who helped lead protests against the corrupt board, called on the native community to speak out against injustice and embrace confrontation, even if it was uncomfortable. 'The way the Kamehameha 'ohana rallied and worked together as a family to defend Princess Pauahi's legacy says much about how to live effectively and righteously in a fast-changing world,' she wrote. 'It demonstrates the power of informed people unified by moral conviction, and should always be a source of pride and inspiration.'

One thing it inspired was a redoubling of the school's focus on Hawaiian language and culture. Kamehameha, which had once banned the speaking of Hawaiian and sought to Americanize its students, would now be among the language's foremost defenders, inculcating a new generation of speakers. The endorsement of people like 'Ekela was key to this new approach, and to maintaining Kamehameha's reputation as a true steward of Pauahi's legacy.

Growing up on Oahu in the 1960s, 'Ekela's world was one that for most of Hawai'i, no longer existed. Her grandparents were preachers at a nondenominational church which maintained Hawaiian-language services throughout the coup, annexation and the suppression which followed. They made sure to teach their children the language, regardless of the fact they were banned from speaking it in school. As a child, 'Ekela's home remained thoroughly Hawaiian, even as the world outside was becoming more American. But this disconnect eventually made 'Ekela uncomfortable, and as she grew older, she began to speak the language less and less, responding in English to her grandmother and rolling her eyes at the old woman's insistence on speaking in Hawaiian.

But her tutu had a plan for her. Out of her several dozen grandchildren, she had decided that 'Ekela would be the one to carry on her own legacy of Hawaiian-language activism. She sent her to after school classes at the church, where 'Ekela was often the only child in a room full of adults trying to reconnect with their language. Even in the face of pre-teen obstinacy, she would tell 'Ekela over and over that she was going to be a Hawaiian-language teacher.

When 'Ekela enrolled at 'Aiea High School, in the suburbs of Honolulu, there were no Hawaiian-language courses on offer, and she happily switched to Spanish. After years of studying Hawaiian, she was keen to try a new language, and she adored her Spanish teacher, Marjorie Woodrum.

'She was just an awesome teacher, she brought culture alive for me,' Ekela said. 'I felt like I was in Spain, she just took me to all these places that they spoke that language and just made it real.'

Woodrum was a talented linguist as well as a good teacher, speaking English, French and Spanish along with her parents' native tongue, Czech.[16] She moved to Oahu from the US mainland in 1968,[17] and soon began taking evening classes in Hawaiian at the university. Woodrum had been lobbying for Hawaiian to be taught at 'Aiea as well, and when administrators failed to hire anyone, she took it upon herself to begin teaching the language, despite her own very rudimentary grasp of it. 'Ekela's grandmother, with a parent's knack for learning something a child wants to conceal, soon heard about the lessons being offered, and signed 'Ekela up. On joining the class however, the fifteen-year-old, probably the most fluent Hawaiian speaker in the school, was nonplussed. All of a sudden, this teacher she had loved, who had helped her discover a foreign culture and language, was just another haole butchering the Hawaiian tongue.

'She'd speak in this terrible accent and everything was just so bad,' 'Ekela said. 'I saw her whiteness. It just didn't connect. And so for the first quarter, I just gave her the hardest time.'

Finally, after weeks of seeing her most enthusiastic Spanish pupil start rolling her eyes and snorting with derision during Hawaiian lessons, Woodrum pulled her aside. She brought out a globe and spun it, asking if 'Ekela knew where Czechoslovakia was? She didn't. What did she know about the country? Nothing.

'Well I do,' Woodrum said. 'I know the customs, I know the traditions, I know how people dress, what they eat, and more importantly, I know how they think. I know this because I speak their language.'

'Ekela looked on impassively, confused about what this had to do with Hawaiian.

'And I know that you've grown up with this language, and you feel it more than you speak it, and we have to recognise that there's something valuable about that,'

Woodrum said. 'You don't like the fact that I'm teaching it, and really, I don't like the fact that I'm teaching it either. But there's no one else on this campus who believes that language is important to someone's identity.'

She pointed out that there were Hawaiian children in the school, in class alongside 'Ekela, who unlike her, had little connection to their culture or identity. Woodrum told 'Ekela that she should be the one teaching these children, helping them understand where they came from.

By this point, both women were crying, and 'Ekela became emotional telling the story years later.

'She knew she didn't sound right or anything, but she wanted to bring it there for us Hawaiians in this school,' 'Ekela told me. 'So many of my friends who are Hawaiian didn't have the experience I had, didn't have the opportunity to hear the language growing up, except maybe in music. That's where the language sat for many people, in music. Whereas for me, it was a real language that people actually spoke all the time, they preached in it, they prayed in it, they taught in it, they scolded you in it'.

The conversation with Woodrum changed 'Ekela's attitude completely. She came home and told her grandmother that she would become a Hawaiian teacher, as the old woman had always predicted.

'She just nodded. She never said I told you so,' 'Ekela said. 'Instead, she told me the stories that would change my life, about what she had gone through to save this language for me.'

Her tutu explained how the language had been suppressed, how when she was a child, a teacher had covered her mouth with tape and told her she couldn't speak until she learned English. 'She told me these stories about being abused and mistreated because she spoke Hawaiian, I didn't know anything about this,' 'Ekela said. 'I was always in a place of this being such a regular thing. It was such a blessing to able to learn Hawaiian in a way that was so normal.'

In the 1970s, the language movement which had grown out of the Second Hawaiian Renaissance scored several key successes. The University of Hawai'i began offering degrees in Hawaiian for the first time, and in 1978, it was made an official state language, alongside English.[18] But the overall trend was not positive, as the last generation to grow up speaking Hawaiian was increasingly dying off, and many of their children did not have a sufficient grasp to pass it on, threatening the language with extinction. Even in 'Ekela's church, the number of people competent enough to preach in Hawaiian had fallen such that sermons were increasingly held in English.

'None of my cousins, none of my brothers or sisters could speak Hawaiian, even when [our grandmother] spoke to them in that language,' 'Ekela said later. 'Our church was all in Hawaiian, but it didn't seem to matter. Nobody was teaching people so that they could understand the prayers, the songs, the sermons. It was just disappearing, disappearing.'

When she graduated, 'Ekela threw herself into the nascent language movement. In 1984, the first Hawaiian immersion kindergarten had opened on Kaua'i, and more began popping up throughout the islands.[19] Two years later, a bill allowing Hawaiian to be used as a medium of instruction in public schools passed, and pressure grew on the state government to do more to support the language. In 1988, the Native Hawaiian Education Act provided funding and an edict to do so, establishing a council to support Native Hawaiian education programmes and grants for language courses and immersion schools.[20] In 1990, this progress went nationwide, when the US Congress passed the Native American Languages Act, sponsored by Daniel K. Inouye, senator for Hawai'i, and lobbied for by Pūnana Leo, a network of immersion preschools. In 1999, for the first time in over a century, a class of students educated entirely in Hawaiian from the age of four to eighteen graduated, and at the turn of the millennium, Kamehameha Schools introduced new requirements for all students to receive some instruction in Hawaiian.[21]

It cannot be overstated how close Hawaiian came to extinction. Many of the immersion preschools had to bring in elderly people to act as teachers, as so few in the intervening generation spoke the language. Had the Hawaiian renaissance come a decade later, many of these people would have been dead, and the process might have been closer to reviving an extinct language than revitalizing one under threat, a far, far harder task.

Today, 'Ekela is one of Hawaii's foremost language activists and teachers. At Kamehameha Maui, she acts as an advisor on cultural and language issues, ensuring that the school is as Hawaiian an environment as possible, normalizing both the language itself and traditional practices, in a way completely at odds with the institution's onetime assimilationist policies. Kamehameha is still not a leader in the language movement, but it is a symbol of how far it has come.

'For the last fifty years, the primary goal of most Hawaiian parents was to get their kids into Kamehameha Schools,' said Kū Kahakalau, one of Hawaii's foremost language experts. 'When Kamehameha Schools say something it is listened to, in the legislature and in the state house, and they have finally been looking at the rest of Hawaiians, and understanding they also have a responsibility to those children who are not admitted, but who are also the descendants of the Princess Pauahi who established the trust.'

Chapter 9

Road closed due to desecration

The summit of Mauna Kea, the highest mountain in Hawai'i, is stark and cold. Little vegetation grows this high, some 4,200 metres above sea level, leaving the landscape rocky, brown and barren, almost Martian in appearance. Above the clouds, during the day a person can look up into a painfully blue sky, the air thin enough to make breathing difficult, the sun an intense, white glare. At night, the ancient volcano offers almost unparalleled views of the stars, making it among the best places in the world for astronomy. Beginning in 1970, the summit has become dotted with large telescopes peering into the sky above, their gleaming metal exteriors and spheroid shapes giving them an appearance as alien as the landscape itself.

On 7 October 2014, dignitaries gathered atop the summit, seated in white folding chairs to watch a groundbreaking ceremony for what promised to be the biggest observatory yet, the Thirty Metre Telescope (TMT). Delegations from the universities of Hawai'i and California, as well as representatives of the Indian, Chinese and American governments were in attendance. Many wore garlands of green leaves tied around their necks; baseball caps pulled low over their eyes to protect from the sun.[1] Getting to the summit had not been easy. A caravan of cars ferrying guests to the ceremony had been blocked by protesters, who objected to yet another massive engineering project on top of the mountain. Native Hawaiians consider Mauna Kea to be sacred,[2] and have long lobbied against the telescopes, which they argue are being built on indigenous land without the consent of its people.[3] Environmental concerns have also been raised,[4] both about the effect of the construction work on the fragile, lofty ecosystem, and the potential threat to the Mauna Kea aquifer, a major source of water on Hawai'i Island.

More than an hour after the ceremony was due to begin, many seats were still empty, including those belonging to Hawai'i governor David Ige, and the mayor of Hawai'i County, Billy Kenoi, who was still arguing with protesters on the access road up to the summit. A live stream set up to broadcast the groundbreaking online showed only a static image.

After hurried consultations by satellite phone with those lower down the mountain, who warned that the protests were growing in size and becoming increasingly disruptive, organizers decided to press on regardless, or risk the ceremony being derailed completely.[5] As a few more stragglers took their seats, Danny Akaka stepped forward to conduct a traditional blessing for the site. The son of a former US senator, his presence served to reassure the worried guests that not all Native Hawaiians objected to the plan. But before he could begin, someone screamed his name.

'Akaka!' Lanakila Mangauil shouted like a war cry. 'This is wrong, this is wrong.'

Twenty-eight years old, muscular and bare chested, Mangauil was dressed only in a traditional loin cloth and a cloak of patterned, light brown kapa, a fabric made of tree bark. His hair was shaved into a mohawk, a long plait falling down his back, and his feet, despite the rocky surface of the mountaintop, were bare. Mangauil's voice was loud and clear, his handsome face locked in an expression of almost theatrical outrage. As he strode towards the site of the groundbreaking, guests could have been forgiven for thinking Mangauil was part of the performance, before he turned and denounced them, in English, as 'slithering snakes', each syllable dripping with scorn.

Addressing himself to Akaka, Mangauil said protesters had been told, after they succeeded in blocking the main caravan of guests, including Mayor Kenoi, that the ceremony was being called off. A small group of people had left the stranded vehicles and walked towards a set of portable toilets. Assuming they were just going to use the facilities, the protesters ignored them, noticing too late that they had continued past the toilets to another set of vehicles beyond the roadblock, waiting to pick them up and take them to the summit.

'The forked tongue mayor told us they would leave. The forked tongue police told us they would leave. So we allowed them through,' Mangauil shouted. 'They came in like slithering snakes to come up and desecrate our sacred land!'

As Akaka and other organizers looked on helplessly, unsure what to do, Mangauil continued to berate the shocked dignitaries.

'We gave all of our aloha to you guys over there. We sang and we gave you our deepest hearts, and you slithered by us like snakes,' he said. 'For what, for your greed to look into the sky? You guys can't even take care of this place.'

By this time, more protesters had begun appearing at the summit, singing and beating drums. Finally, event organizers were forced to accept defeat, and began packing up, the ground unbroken.

'Obviously there are a number of people who have showed up who have contrasting opinions about the construction of the Thirty Meter Telescope,' the live stream host told viewers around the world. 'We'll have to conclude this broadcast at this point and we do hope that we would be able to find a common ground and proceed with this in the future.'[6]

It was a victory for the protesters, but one that seemed doomed to ultimate futility. The ceremony had been spoiled but the $1.4 billion project was steaming ahead, with construction due to begin in early 2015. Press coverage outside of Hawai'i portrayed the protests with bemusement at best, outright scorn at worst.[7] Often the story was framed as one of a battle between cutting-edge science and indigenous religion,[8] with astronomer Tom Kerr capturing this patronizing attitude when he described the argument as 'about returning to the stone age versus understanding our universe'.[9] Even within Hawai'i, where the public was more aware of long-standing objections to TMT, the over a century of exploitation of native land, and the environmental concerns, the assumption was that the resistance would come to nought. After all, previous protests had failed to stop twelve other observatories being built on the mountain, and the TMT project had the full weight of the Hawaiian and US establishment behind it, including the University of Hawai'i, the governor and much of the local media.

But just as in Wales, where Tryweryn was not the first dam to flood a Welsh village, or the first time Welsh rights had been superseded by English needs, TMT was the right outrage at the right time. It caught a growing wave of discontent with the continued marginalization of indigenous people, one that was led by a new generation of Hawaiian activists, many of whom had been involved in the language movement or come up through Hawaiian-language schools. Revolutions occur not when oppression is at its worst, but when a relaxing of controls creates a window for radical change. The seeds for this had been sown decades before, as schools were freed to teach in Hawaiian and the islands underwent a cultural renaissance, and now the government was reaping. When the construction trucks arrived in April 2015, they were met by another protest blockade. Mangauil was among eight arrested in April that year, and the youngest by far. The sight of elders, or kūpuna, being handcuffed and led into police cars outraged many Hawaiians, and swelled the numbers of protesters the following month. Pu'uhuluhulu, a volcanic cone which sits opposite a junction where the Mauna Kea access road leads off the highway, became a permanent protest camp, with food tents, recycling stations, traffic wardens and a university holding lectures on Hawaiian culture and history. Celebrities, including actors Jason Momoa and Dwayne Johnson, visited the site and offered words of support for the protesters, many of whom had begun living at Pu'uhuluhulu full time, as the camp spread across almost 3 kilometres of highway.[10] Protests expanded across the islands, with posters, graffiti and signs opposing TMT becoming a common sight.

In January 2020, over five years after the initial Mauna Kea protests, I drove up from Hilo to Pu'uhuluhulu. Hawai'i Island is a land of immense lushness and sudden desolation, as thick forests give way to bare, volcanic rock or red, sun-baked dirt. The Daniel K. Inouye Highway, which stretches across the island, is beautifully smooth and fast, and Mauna Kea rises up so gradually that you don't notice how high you are until the vegetation begins to disappear and the temperature plummets. As I passed a sign for the Pu'uhonua o Pu'uhuluhulu, the Pu'uhuluhulu sanctuary, a traffic warden waved and gestured where to park. It was the day after the new year, and the camp was quiet but happy. Governor Ige, who had in mid-2019 issued an emergency order for the protest camp to be cleared, sparking another round of demonstrations, this time the biggest yet, had backed down, and construction appeared to be delayed for at least another year. Support for the TMT, once widespread, had taken a major hit, with many scientists joining the clamour against the project and some sponsors beginning to express doubts.[11] On Oahu, one local had summarized it to me as 'enough is enough'. He was sympathetic to the scientific goals of the telescope, but argued that the actual project itself was irrelevant, coming on the back of over a century of marginalization of native people and exploitation of the land.

At Puʻuhuluhulu, I was joined by Kū Kahakalau, the Hawaiian-language expert. Kū's life spans the revitalization project: her grandparents spoke fluent Hawaiian but her father had basically lost the language when she was growing up, and the family spoke in English. She grew up largely in Germany, where her father worked as a jazz musician. Returning to the islands in 1978, she enrolled in language courses, and was among the first to graduate from the University of Hawaiʻi with a degree in the Hawaiian language. Even then, after Hawaiian had been declared an official state language, 'I was told I was a fool, asked why was I wasting my time studying Hawaiian.'

She graduated in 1985 and became a certified Hawaiian teacher, working first in a public school, teaching a few hours a week, before shifting to an immersive programme and finally founding her own charter school, completely focused on teaching through Hawaiian. 'It has been an extremely slow process,' Kū said, and she was still frustrated with the lack of support from the government and the severe shortage of qualified teachers, but the programmes begun in the 1990s and 2000s are beginning to bear fruit.

'We have a third generation coming through now,' she said. 'My grandson, his parents both speak Hawaiian, his grandparents both speak Hawaiian, that didn't happen twenty years ago.'

In 2017, Kū helped found Kanaeokana, whose name translates loosely as 'a network of extraordinary strength', and includes dozens of schools across Hawaiʻi, including the Kamehameha institutions.[12] The purpose of the network is to develop and promote the Hawaiian language and education system, and work to normalize Hawaiian across the islands. 'This idea [of a network of schools] had been suggested as early as 1987,' said Kū, who now sits on the steering committee of Kanaeokana, alongside ʻEkela Kaniʻaupio-Crozier. 'Kamehameha has that funding to make this kind of transition happen and foster a coming together of very independent camps who are far stronger by working together.'

While the Kamehameha trust bankrolls Kanaeokana, the organization is independent, enabling it to be more radical than many of its individual members, such as the firm stance it has taken against TMT.

Another key focus is the normalization of Hawaiian, of making the islands a truly bilingual place by encouraging businesses to use the language and lobbying for its use in the public sphere, similar to how Welsh activists once fought to have the language on road signs and tax forms. This has had some success. Shops have begun printing labels and signs in Hawaiian. The state's main airline gives safety announcements in both languages. Both radio and TV use the language more often, and many haoles increasingly pepper their English with Hawaiian words or phrases.

The Mauna Kea movement supercharged this shift, and Pu'uhuluhulu provided both a venue for advocacy and education, and proof of concept for a truly Hawaiian, native-run society. Classes given in the camp university focused on Hawaiian language and culture, and traditional ceremonies involving chants and hula were held three times a day. Hawaiians, both native and not, could visit the camp and feel connected with the islands' indigenous culture and language.

'This is the first time many Hawaiians see this traditional community,' said Pua Case, one of the driving forces behind the camp. 'This is the first time some people have felt loved in this way.'

Like many involved in the Mauna Kea project, she felt there had been a tipping point in favour of the native protectors, as the protesters describe themselves. Polls showed support for the telescope project was lowest among native communities and young people,[13,14] who connected indigenous rights to activism around Black Lives Matter and other nationwide US civil rights issues. This went both ways, and like the 2016 protests against the Dakota Access Pipeline protests in Standing Rock, led by Lakota people, Mauna Kea had attracted expressions of solidarity from mainstream US society too, with politicians, actors and human rights groups speaking out against TMT.[15] 'Ekela Kani'aupio-Crozier said many of her students at Kamehameha had, like young native and non-native people across Hawai'i, been radicalized by the protests.

They are not the first generation of Hawaiian youth to fight for their rights, and likely won't be the last. But they have a connection with their identity, language and culture that has been lacking from the islands for almost a century. This creates a level of confidence that leads to situations like that seen on Mauna Kea, where a small group of protesters has held off a billion dollar project supported by the state's most powerful entities for years now, and may see it defeated altogether. And that activism fed back into the language movement: enrolment in immersion programmes spiked in 2019 as protests at Mauna Kea intensified, with some schools having to turn away parents for the first time in their history.[16]

Back on Maui, 'Ekela told me a story about her daughters. Living on Oahu, the girls had gone to an immersion elementary in Honolulu, where everything was taught in Hawaiian, but when they were ten and eleven, the family moved islands. The Maui school offered classes in both English and Hawaiian, separated into language streams, and it was the first time the girls had experienced such a mix of languages, or the disdain some non-Hawaiian speakers had for their native tongue.

'They were looked down upon, and my kids had never experienced that, they'd never experienced anyone telling them their language wasn't cool, you know?' 'Ekela said. 'I remember on the first day, my eldest daughter came home and she was like, "I just told them off".'

When 'Ekela asked what had happened, the eleven-year-old explained calmly that some boys had heard her speaking Hawaiian with her sister and begun mocking them, saying they couldn't read English, that they were stupid.

'And she turned around and say, "I'm not stupid, I can read in Hawaiian and in English. I can read in both. I can speak in both languages. What can you do? You only speak in one language, which means you only know one way".'

'Ekela was pleasantly surprised, for all her encouragement of her kids to learn Hawaiian and be proud to be Hawaiian, this degree of self-confidence and assurance 'was just not something we'd taught her'.

'Her worldview was totally different,' she said, tears in her eyes. 'So I would say, that's my gift back to my grandmother, you know, these kids that when they get together, they can talk to each other and they have their language that binds them and binds them to us as parents.'

Interlude: The old, new tongue

Around the middle of the nineteenth century, in the western reaches of the Russian Empire, two babies were born. They grew up 200 kilometres apart, in devout Jewish families, and would both for a time become ardent Zionists. Both men were also instrumental in creating two new languages that persist to this day, with millions of speakers between them, a remarkable achievement that was inspired in part by the equally unlikely success of a language they both shared: Yiddish.

Eliezer Ben-Yehuda and Ludovik Zamenhof, the progenitors of Modern Hebrew and Esperanto respectively, started from similar origins and beliefs but ended up staking out wholly different, even diametrically opposed positions on some of the most important questions for the Jewish community of their day. Living during the heyday of political Zionism, as the winds of antisemitism grew stronger in Europe ahead of the storm that was the Holocaust, both Ben-Yehuda and Zamenhof sought linguistic solutions for a debate that has bedevilled Jews for centuries: whether to pursue greater assimilation into the societies in which they found themselves, or to stake out a distinct Jewish national identity, in either their countries of origin or a Jewish homeland.

Ben-Yehuda would play a pivotal role in reinvigorating Hebrew to create a language that could, he hoped, sustain a new Jewish state. With Esperanto, Zamenhof sought to create a wholly new tongue that would aid assimilation and remove barriers between Jews and Gentiles, before going on to refashion Judaism itself to open the religion up to anyone. But even as they split on the question of Zionism, Ben-Yehuda and Zamenhof shared a difficult and eventually disdainful relationship with Yiddish, a language that could have served both their purposes and was all the more remarkable for arising organically. This disdain was common among many Jews of their era, particularly those who would found and build the state of Israel, and helped drive Yiddish's decline in the new country. Decades on, that attitude has metastasized into a cultural chauvinism that has driven a wedge between Hebrew-speaking Israelis and many Jews in the diaspora, who see in Yiddish a link to an identity that is not dependent on

Israel, nor the aggressive nationalists who have dominated its politics for much of the country's modern existence.

Eliezer Ben-Yehuda was born Eliezer Perelman on 7 January 1858 in Luzhki, a village in what is now northern Belarus but was then part of Russian-controlled Lithuania.[1] At the time, almost all Jews in Russia were confined to the Pale of Settlement, an area which roughly conforms with modern-day Belarus, Lithuania and Moldova.[2] In some parts of the Pale, Jews made up over 60 per cent of the population, and Ben-Yehuda was raised in a close-knit, highly religious community.[3] He began learning Biblical Hebrew at a young age, before being sent to a yeshiva – a religious school – in the hope he would become a rabbi.[4] He dropped out instead, and switched to a secular secondary school in the nearby town of Dynaburg. There he joined the Narodniki, an early socialist movement. As well as their interest in emancipatory economics, the Narodniks were also Russian nationalists, and Ben-Yehuda increasingly came to identify as a Russian himself, except in one area. 'Even when everything Jewish had become strange to me, almost repugnant,' Ben-Yehuda wrote later, 'I could not separate myself from the Hebrew language, and, from time to time, wherever and whenever I happened to chance upon a book of Modern Hebrew literature, I could not summon enough will-power to overcome my desire to read it.'[5]

Though Hebrew had existed for thousands of years and remained a key part of all observant Jews' lives, the language itself was in a dormant state, not quite dead but by no means alive either. It was used as a written language primarily for religious purposes, and few people used it in daily lives, or spoke it much beyond reciting the Torah.[6] By the time Ben-Yehuda was a teenager however, the process of reviving Hebrew was already underway, emboldened and increasingly intertwined with Jewish nationalist and Zionist thought. Ben-Yehuda was also inspired, writing at seventeen of a vision he had of a 'national revival' in Palestine of the Jewish people, a new, Hebrew-speaking country.[7]

Ben-Yehuda finished his schooling in 1877, the year Russia declared war on the Ottoman Empire in support of Bulgaria's revolt against Turkish rule. Nationalist sentiment was on the rise across Europe as the old empires began to unravel, and Ben-Yehuda felt these stirrings in himself, this time not for Russia, but for Israel:

> *Thirstily I read about these events in the press without realizing at first the connection between them and myself ... and suddenly, like lightning before my eyes, my thoughts flew across the Balkans ... to Palestine, and I heard a ... voice calling to me: the revival of Israel and its language in the land of its forefathers!*[8]

In 1878, Ben-Yehuda left Russia and moved to Paris to study medicine.[9] At the Sorbonne, he attended classes in Middle Eastern history, as well as advanced Hebrew-language courses.[10] He also began writing on the topic of Hebrew, and the year after he arrived in Paris, he published an article entitled 'A Serious Question'. In it, Ben-Yehuda discussed not only the future of Hebrew in Europe, but also the Jews themselves.[11]

Only in Palestine, he argued, in this and later writings, could Jews finally have a secure home of their own free from both aggression and assimilation, and only in such a state could Hebrew truly be revived.

Around the time Ben-Yehuda was travelling west to Paris, another Lithuanian Jew was headed east, to begin his studies in Moscow. Like Ben-Yehuda, Ludovik Lazarus Zamenhof was born in the Pale, and grew up in a predominantly Jewish area.[12] Though primarily Russian speaking,[13] Zamenhof's father was a talented linguist, and worked as the official imperial censor for newspapers and publications in German, Yiddish and Hebrew.[14] The elder Zamenhof was also fluent in French and Polish, and much in demand as a Torah leyner, or reader.[15] It was in this multilingual, religious context that Zamenhof, like Ben-Yehuda, put his mind to the 'Jewish question'. Aware of growing antisemitism throughout Europe, and that both Hebrew and Yiddish were indelibly linked to Jewishness, Zamenhof thought that a new language, one that had no ties to ethnicity or nationality, could help reduce strife between the peoples of the Russian Empire. He became obsessed with the idea, such that his father described him as being beset by an 'incurable madness'.[16]

In this he was by no means alone. For as long as we have been aware of the breadth of linguistic diversity and the difficulties of translation, there have been people who sought a solution, either via a search for an 'original' ur-tongue, or by creating a new, superior language that could replace or supplement all others. Many early Christian scholars saw Hebrew as a potential original language,[17] but this fell out of fashion, due to both the complexities and inefficiencies of Biblical Hebrew and the antipathy some had to adopting a language that was so linked to Judaism. For a time, empires solved this problem by simply forcing all subjects to learn the imperial tongue, but as they began to fracture and nations were revived or formed in the nineteenth century, some began to fret about the difficulties of communicating and desire a practical solution. 'The search for a cure for Babel was as old as the story of Babel, but the cure proposed before this point usually involved the discovery of the original language of Adam as crafted by God,' Arika Okrent writes in her book, *In the Land of Invented Languages*. 'Now, in the throes of the scientific revolution, people started to think that perhaps a solution could be crafted by man.'[18]

As Okrent documents however, 'the history of invented languages is, for the most part, a history of failure'. This was something Zamenhof was highly conscious of. In 1879, as he was beginning to think about creating his own language, a German priest named Johann Schleyer introduced the world to Volapük, received, he said, in a vision from God.[19] The language was greeted with enthusiasm and Volapük societies sprang up, mainly within the German-speaking Catholic community that Schleyer hailed from, but some as far afield as China.[20] The success of the language itself was more limited however, mostly due to Volapük's intense complexity – one verb might take thousands of forms – and at its first two conferences, the primary language spoken was German.[21] George Orwell, who lived with some constructed language enthusiasts during his time in Paris, once wrote that 'for sheer dirtiness of fighting, the feuds between the inventors of various of the international languages would take some beating',[22] and it was this disunity that ultimately wrought Volapük's downfall, as the community which had formed around Schleyer's original vision fell out over how to interpret it.

In 1879, Zamenhof enrolled at the Imperial Moscow University, promising his father that he would not publish anything about his language obsession until after he graduated. In Moscow, just as Ben-Yehuda was becoming more convinced in his Zionism – and the importance of Hebrew – and making plans to travel to Palestine at the earliest opportunity, Zamenhof convened a group of some dozen or so fellow Jewish students and 'unfolded to them a plan [to found] a Jewish colony in some unoccupied part of the globe'.[23] If he had any doubts about the need for a Jewish homeland these were erased in 1881 when, following the assassination of Tsar Alexander II and false rumours of Jewish involvement, violent pogroms broke out across the western empire. Growing antisemitism also intensified Zamenhof's desire to invent a new international language, which he was convinced would have 'enormous usefulness to humanity'.[24]

'I was taught that all men were brothers, and, meanwhile, in the street, in the square, everything at every step made me feel that men did not exist, only Russians, Poles, Germans, Jews and so on,' Zamenhof wrote.[25] In 1887, determined to solve this problem, he published *Lingvo Internacia*, sketching out a language that could be 'unconditionally accepted by everyone, and the common property of the whole world'.[26] He signed his pamphlet not with his own name, but the pseudonym Doctor Esperanto, the name of his new language and its word for 'hopeful'.

Six years before Zamenhof introduced Esperanto as a way to help save Europe from the divisions of nationalism and antisemitism, at least one Jew had run out of hope for the continent. In October 1881, Ben-Yehuda arrived in Ottoman-controlled Palestine, determined to help build a Jewish state and with it, a new and living form of Hebrew.

Nineteenth-century Palestine was at least as linguistically chaotic as the Russian Empire, even within the small Jewish community. In their daily lives, people might have come across various European tongues, multiple forms of Arabic, Turkish and two Jewish languages, the predominantly Ashkenazi Yiddish and Sephardic Ladino. 'In a small group of twenty persons, ten languages are spoken and no-one understands the language of his neighbour,' Ben-Yehuda wrote. However, to his delight, this lack of cohesion actually played in his favour, because the one language that all Jews living in Palestine had in common was Hebrew, albeit the old-fashioned tongue of the Torah. 'When for example a Sephardi from Aleppo would meet a Sephardi from Saloniki or a Sephardi from Morocco would come into the company of a Jew from Bukhara, they were obliged to speak in the Holy Tongue.'[27]

Ben-Yehuda, along with a few friends, had already committed to only speaking Hebrew whenever he could, and as more Jews travelled to Palestine – both enticed by the emergence of political Zionism under Theodor Hertzl, and driven there by the pogroms and rising antisemitism in their home countries – he became determined to inculcate the language in the new arrivals, thus proving it could be the official tongue of a future Jewish state. This was not a universally popular idea. Many more religious Jews in Palestine saw blasphemy in Ben-Yehuda's project, which involved both modernizing and secularizing the holy tongue, and for some he became a figure of loathing.[28]

To prove his point that Hebrew could be the tongue of daily life once again, Ben-Yehuda made his own family an example. When his son, Ben-Zion Ben-Yehuda, later better known as Ittamar Ben-Avi, was born in 1882, Ben-Yehuda committed, with the somewhat reluctant agreement of his Russian-speaking wife, to raise the child purely in Hebrew.[29] According to Ben-Avi's own account, his father went to extremes to create a Hebrew-only environment, sending him to bed when visitors came so he would not hear them speak another language, and angrily remonstrating with the boy's mother when he found her singing Russian lullabies.[30] Whether this draconian approach was actually needed, Ben-Yehuda's experiment was successful, and his son grew up with Hebrew as his first language, becoming a sensation in Jerusalem as strangers flocked to the house to see this 'miracle' of language revival.[31] In an unexpected side effect of teaching his son Hebrew, Ben-Yehuda found he also had to modernize the language. Because he had committed to only speaking Hebrew with his son, when Ben-Avi asked, as any child does, what objects were called, his father had to find a Hebrew answer for him. Thus Ben-Yehuda began creating a modern Hebrew lexicon, a task that would occupy the rest of his life, researching old texts to rediscover words that had fallen out of fashion or could be co-opted for modern purposes, or creating entirely new words out of ancient Hebrew roots.[32] Like a Hebraic Milton or Shakespeare, Ben-Yehuda is credited with creating or rediscovering hundreds of words, in areas from colours (brown, pink) to foods (cream, cauliflower, truffle, strawberry), to military terms (cannon, dynamite, gunpowder) and diseases (cancer, a cold, measles).[33]

Once he had proven Hebrew could be imparted in this manner, Ben-Yehuda set about ensuring that all Jewish children in Palestine were taught the language, which he hoped would 'go from the synagogue to the house of study, and from the house of study to the school, and from the school it will come into the home and ... become a living language'.[34] Invited to teach at the Alliance Israélite Universelle School in Jerusalem, Ben-Yehuda adopted a system of teaching Hebrew through Hebrew, with no translation into other tongues, thus ensuring that children became comfortable using it faster and regarded it as their first language.[35] He was not a pioneer of this method, but his success at home and his growing fame helped popularize it in schools across Palestine, which quickly began churning out scores of Hebrew-speaking graduates. He was also helped by the timing: the first mass migration of Jews to Palestine began in 1883. Some twenty thousand new immigrants arrived in what is known as the First Aliya, or 'ascent', and they brought with them a host of different languages, making the need for a universal tongue – Hebrew – all the more important.[36] Many did share a Jewish language, Yiddish, but this was far less welcome than the immigrants themselves, and Hebrew proponents actively sought to repress Yiddish in favour of their new language. Ben-Yehuda was not involved in the worst of that repression, but he recognized the importance of creating as much as possible a monolingual environment for promoting

Hebrew as a living language. In 1884, he founded his own Hebrew newspaper, *Hatzvi*, 'to serve as an instrument for teaching adults, both via its content and its language', in the words of one historian.[37] He also founded the Hebrew Language Council, the supreme authority on all language matters,[38] and began work on a seventeen-volume 'Complete Dictionary of Ancient and Modern Hebrew', the first edition of which published in 1910.[39]

As Ben-Yehuda was finding success in the Middle East, back in Europe, Zamenhof's fortunes were more mixed. In the first edition of *Lingvo Internacia*, which outlined his basic proposal for a new language, he had printed coupons which readers could fill out, promising to learn Esperanto if ten million others also committed to doing so.[40] Only a few hundred coupons were ever returned, and Zamenhof soon realized that if there was to be widespread interest in Esperanto he would have to spark it himself. As well having the unua libro, or 'first book', translated into English, Hebrew, Yiddish, Swedish and a host of other languages, he began writing his most important work, *Fundamento de Esperanto*.

Despite being active in Zionist circles in Russia, by the turn of the century, Zamenhof had undergone a complete reversal. Not only was Palestine, in his view, a wholly inappropriate place to build a new Jewish state, the idea that the 'Jewish problem' could be solved in this way was itself mistaken.[41] He rejected the concept of Jews as a people unto themselves, saying that they were only a religious grouping, one that was regarded as more than this only by a quirk of history. To move beyond the difficulties and antipathy this merging of religion with ethnicity had created, Zamenhof said Judaism itself needed to change, becoming a faith open to all peoples and races, one that would not define its practitioners in ethnic terms. For spiritual support, Zamenhof looked to the teachings of Hillel the Elder – coiner of the Golden Rule, 'do not do unto others that is which hateful to you'[42] – and sought to simplify the vast canon of Mosaic law down to a few basic principles:

1. *We feel and acknowledge the existence of the highest Force that rules the world, and we name this Force God.*

2. *God placed his laws in every person's heart in the form of the conscience. Always obey the voice of your conscience, therefore, because it is the never silent voice of God.*

3. *The essence of all laws given to us by God can be expressed by the following formula: Love thy neighbour and do unto others as you would have them do unto you and never commit acts openly or in secret that your inner voice tells you would not be pleasing to God. All other instructions that you may hear from your teachers and leaders and that do not fit into the three main points of religion are merely human commentaries, which could be true, but which could also be false.*[43]

In 1901, he published *Hillelism: A Plan for Solving the Jewish Problem*, under the pseudonym Homo Sum, Latin for 'I am a human being'.[44] The new faith was not a complete departure from his language work, however, Zamenhof envisioned that his modern form of Judaism would use instead of Hebrew his new international language as its primary tongue, thus creating a stable base for Esperanto for generations to come. 'An international language will become forever strong only if there exists a group of people who accept it as their family, hereditary language,' Zamenhof wrote around this time. 'One hundred such people are hugely more important to the idea of a neutral language than a million other people. The hereditary language of even the smallest and most insignificant human group has a much stronger guarantee of a continued existence than a language without a people even if it is used by millions.'[45]

In 1905, *Fundamento* was published, establishing the grammatical and linguistic rules of Esperanto. That year, it was adopted by the first world Esperanto conference as the 'single foundation of the language'.[46] The conference, held in Boulogne-sur-Mer on the French side of the English Channel, was attended by 668 people,[47] and marked not only the beginning of Esperanto's success as an international language, but also the shifting of gravity around it from Russia to France. While French Esperantists would play an important role in the language's development and growing popularity, the country was not necessarily any friendlier to its Jewish creator than his homeland. This was the France of the Dreyfus affair, in which a Jewish army captain was convicted on trumped-up treason charges, and whose trials and eventual exoneration unleashed a torrent of antisemitism.[48] At the encouragement of French Esperantists, including some who were Jewish themselves, Zamenhof downplayed or hid this side of his identity, even as he was undergoing a religious awakening that he would come to see as more important even than the creation of his language.

Esperanto's growing popularity in France and other parts of western Europe was based largely on Zamenhof's nods to Enlightenment thinking and the desire for scientific efficiency. As he wrote in the introduction to *Lingvo Internacia*, 'Were there but an international language, all translations would be made into it alone, as into a tongue intelligible to all, and works of an international character would be written in it in the first instance.'[49] His French followers were horrified to find, ahead of the Boulogne-sur-Mer congress, that Zamenhof's new obsession was not linguistic efficiency but Judaic mysticism. In a letter to one of the organizers, Zamenhof wrote that Hillelism would be a 'moral bridge by which all peoples and religions could unite in brotherhood without the creation of any new dogmas and without the need for people to throw away their own religion, up to this point'.[50] Organizers insisted that he let them approve a speech he intended to give, and persuaded him, after great argument, to remove a couple of the more explosive lines, such as 'Christians, Jews or Mahometans, we are all children of God.' The French followers also worked hard behind the scenes to ensure that any press coverage of the event did not mention Hillelism at all or even that Zamenhof was a Jew.

The Boulogne conference was a 'phenomenal success',[51] and it boosted the profile of Esperanto even further. The success of the French faction in hiding Zamenhof's religious leanings did not put him off Hillelism, and in 1906, spurred in part by a wave of deadly pogroms which had erupted in Russia, he published the twelve-point 'Dogmas of Hillelism', written in Esperanto.[52] One precept was that Hillelists were to abandon all country names based on ethnicity, choosing new Esperanto terms fashioned from the name of their capital, so that Russian Hillelists would be Peterburgregnaj-Hilelistoj, and Poles Varsovilandaj-Hilelistoj.[53] At the same time, Zamenhof worried that the name of the faith itself was overly ethnic, and decided to drop the reference to an ancient Jewish scholar for Homaranismo, from the Esperanto word for humanity. In Boulogne, Zamenhof had spoken of 'the creation of a brotherhood of human beings from diverse ethnic groups', and Homaranismo would embrace universalism even more than Hillelism, which Zamenhof had seen as aimed primarily at Jews.[54] If Hillelism was Reform Judaism, Homaranismo was Christianity, and Zamenhof pictured its following being diverse as that faith.

At the second international Esperanto conference in Geneva in 1906, Zamenhof had planned to introduce Homaranismo as the 'inner idea' driving the language, and he fiercely criticized those, including French practitioner Louis de Beaufront, who argued against 'linking Esperantism with any sort of spiritual concept, even in private'.[55] Beaufront's faction won out in persuading Zamenhof not to openly frame Esperanto as a religious language, likely dooming its public perception in antisemitic Europe, and so though he spoke in Geneva and elsewhere of an 'inner idea' behind the language, he did not publicly identify that as Homaranismo.[56]

Zamenhof and his followers' attempts to distance Esperanto from its founder's Judaism were only of limited success. Ahead of the eighth international conference in Krakow in 1912, the Polish press ran a series of openly antisemitic articles about Zamenhof. As the language marked its twenty-fifth anniversary that year, with some ten thousand speakers around the world,[57] Zamenhof announced he was giving up any formal role in its future development so that his political and religious ideas would not be seen as representing the wider Esperanto movement.[58] He did not give up his universalism however, nor his belief that language could unite rather than divide fractious ethnicities. As Europe sank into war in 1914, he wrote an open letter to the continent's leaders, urging them to create a 'United States of Europe', and guarantee that 'each sovereign state shall belong morally and materially to all its natural and naturalised inhabitants regardless of their language, religion or supposed origin'.[59] Anticipating the League of Nations, Zamenhof saw that after the war finished, there would be space to create a new order and relationship between states themselves and between states and their people. Any future peace conference, he urged, should ensure that 'no ethnic group in the state shall have greater or lesser rights than the other groups'.

All citizens shall have the full right to use whatever language or dialect and to practise whatever religion they please. Whichever language is accepted by common consent of the citizens to be the state's official language shall be used only in public institutions that are not designed to serve one particular ethnic group.[60]

He did not live to see the end of the war. Zamenhof died of a heart attack in German-occupied Warsaw on 14 April 1917, aged just fifty-seven. His children continued to promote Esperanto and Zamenhof's philosophy until their own deaths,[61] at the hands of the Nazis, despite a last-ditch attempt by Esperantists around the world to get them out of Poland.[62,63] Hitler's regime denounced Esperanto and its Jewish creator, who represented everything – pacifism, universalism, a world beyond ethnicity and race – that the Nazis stood in opposition to. A book on the life of Lidja Zamenhof, who promoted her father's language around the world along with Homaranismo and her own Bahai'i faith, is dedicated to the 'memory of thousands of Jewish Esperantists, friends, and co-workers murdered by the Nazis'.[64]

Despite the death of its founder, Esperanto persisted, and in the 1920s, as the constructed language grew in popularity worldwide, several societies dedicated to Esperanto popped up in Palestine, including in Tel Aviv.[65]

The fact this coastal settlement was known as the 'First Hebrew City' demonstrates just how far the situation in Palestine had changed by the end of the First World War. Ben-Yehuda, who had done more than anyone to revive and popularize Hebrew, seeing success beyond his expectations, died in 1922 aged sixty-four. That same year, the British, who now controlled the region, established that 'English, Arabic, and Hebrew shall be the official languages of Palestine'.[66] Ben-Yehuda's wife and son continued working on his dictionary, the seventeenth and final volume of which was published in 1959.[67] Today, more than 95 per cent of Israelis speak Hebrew, and more than 50 per cent speak it as their first language.[68] In 2018, the Israeli Knesset passed a new law declaring 'Israel as the Nation State of the Jewish People',[69] and holding that 'the right to exercise national self-determination' in Israel is 'unique to the Jewish people'. Among other things, the law defined the state's sole official language as Hebrew, and downgraded Arabic to 'special status', English having long been set aside. The law, part of a general rightward shift in Israel under Prime Minister Benjamin Netanyahu, was denounced by Arab lawmakers and Palestinian groups, and by Jewish organizations overseas, for moving the country further towards an 'apartheid'-like system in which Arabs throughout Israel and the occupied territories are made second-class citizens.[70]

That the nation state law would include such a language-policy reflects how, in the years since Ben-Yehuda's death, Hebrew has transformed from a minority tongue struggling to survive into a dominant, even hegemonic language. Arabic is only the latest loser in this game, and while there is no risk of the language going extinct in Israel due to its strong base among Palestinians and all of the country's neighbours, Arab Israelis have seen their language continually downgraded and marginalized,[71] and used as a way to attack them or portray them as disloyal and threatening to Hebrew-speaking Israelis.[72] This muscular, aggressive Hebrewism started before the language was even fully revived, and its first target was not Arabic, but Yiddish, the language which had tied parts of the Jewish diaspora together for centuries, maintaining a link between them and their culture and religion even as they underwent assimilation and antisemitism.

Yiddish evolved along the Rhine in the western reaches of the Holy Roman Empire around the eleventh century,[73] when Jews living in the free imperial cities of Worms and Speyer mixed Hebrew with Middle High German, the language of trade, to form a pidgin that eventually spread throughout Jewish communities in Europe, reaching as far east as Russia.[74] During the Enlightenment, Yiddish blossomed as a literary language and by the turn of the nineteenth century it was the primary tongue of European Jews.[75] Yiddish means 'Jewish', and for both its speakers and critics that is what it was, the language of the Jews. This did not, in an antisemitic continent, win it much praise from outsiders, unlike Hebrew which could be at least partially redeemed by its connection with biblical revelation. 'To foes of the Jews, Yiddish was the chicken-squawk gibberish of a historically chickenhearted people literally demonised as horned Christ killers with yellow stripes down their back,' Neal Karlen writes in his history of the language.[76] But unlike Hebrew, Yiddish also did not gain much respect from its speakers, who until almost the twentieth century referred to it as 'jhargon', and did not regard it as a full language equal to those spoken around them.[77] Such denigration would be out of place in most linguistic areas, but even more so in western Europe, with its mix of bastardized Latin, Germanic and Celtic tongues. The origins and sources of English are at least as mixed and confused as Yiddish, it was simply lucky enough to become the language of one of Europe's strongest powers, instead of one of its most marginalized peoples.

Jewish embarrassment over Yiddish came in part from the location in which it was spoken for most of its history: the ghetto. For centuries in some parts of Europe, Jews were confined to separate areas of cities and deprived of political and social rights. Ghettos could be overcrowded and dirty, and many residents were unemployed and on the verge of destitution.[78] Even for those with wealth, having to live among squalor was a daily reminder of their marginalization. Following emancipation, while Yiddish became the dominant language of the Jewish press,[79] and the lingua franca for some two-thirds of the world's Jewish population,[80] it still bore with it the stain of the ghetto for many Jews.

Not all observers saw this as a negative. For members of the Bund, a Jewish socialist party founded in Russia in 1897, Yiddish was the more authentic Jewish tongue, the language of the Jewish worker, as opposed to the Hebrew of rabbis and bourgeois intellectuals.[81] 'He who scoffs at Yiddish, scoffs at the Jewish people; he is only half a Jew,' one Bund member wrote.[82] The push for emancipation had helped create an active Jewish political force, and left-wing thinkers saw Yiddish as the tool to maintain this solidarity and keep the community together, a 'weapon of national struggle in place of fallen ghetto walls', historian Simon Dubnow writes.[83] In their attachment to Yiddish, leftist Jews were joined by the ultra-Orthodox, many of whom were appalled at the revival – debasement as they saw it – of Hebrew then underway in Palestine.[84] To this day, Haredim in Israel and elsewhere prefer to use Yiddish rather than denigrate the 'language of holiness' by engaging it for everyday tasks.[85]

The true enemies of Yiddish were the secular Zionists who were leading both the settlement of Palestine and the advancement of Hebrew there.[86] While the Bund and other left-wing groups sought modernization and emancipation through embracing Yiddish, many Zionists saw the language as an anchor tying Jews forever to the ghetto.[87] Oppressed peoples internalize the criticisms of their oppressors, and some Zionists looked for the causes of antisemitism among their own people. While Theodor Hertzl, the father of modern Zionism, preferred German over Hebrew, he had even less time for Yiddish, which he regarded as a 'gutter dialect', unfit for a cultured nation.[88] David Ben-Gurion, first prime minister of the state of Israel, also possessed a deep loathing of Yiddish,[89] and openly insulted the 'foreign, grating language' on multiple occasions.[90] The New Hebrew Man would be the antithesis of the Diaspora Jew, the weak, ghettoized, Yiddish-speaking creature who had no place in the future state of Israel.[91]

Hebrewist opposition to Yiddish was not just rhetorical. At the same time as Ben-Yehuda's programme was achieving massive success in the early twentieth century, and Hebrew was becoming the medium of choice for Zionist schools in Palestine and new publications,[92] Hebrew-language extremists bombed Yiddish printing presses, burned kiosks selling Yiddish newspapers, and hassled and intimidated Yiddish speakers and writers.[93] Theatre productions in Yiddish were shut down, and rabbis preached that the language was treif, or non-kosher, with one going so far to say that it was 'more treif than pork'.[94] In 1914, a mob prevented Chaim Zhitlowsky,[95] the socialist and Yiddish advocate, from delivering a lecture in Jaffa by cutting off the building's power and pelting the audience with stones.[96] A newspaper later published the text of Zhitlowsky's aborted speech, in which he argued that adoption of Hebrew 'should not force us to cut out the living tongue of the masses and uproot their language-soul'. While he approved of the teaching of Hebrew in schools, Yiddish, he said, was a 'supreme, natural and national force, that transcends ideologies and creeds', and should be preserved at all costs.[97] By contrast, around the same time, a leading Hebrew proponent wrote that 'there is room for at most one of the two languages. If this is so, one can hardly speak about an alliance. All that is possible is an aggravated, life-and-death struggle between the two languages.'[98] In 1930, a group calling itself the Army for the Defense of the Hebrew Language attacked a screening of one of the first feature-length Yiddish-language films, *My Jewish Mother*. They broke into the theatre in Tel Aviv, threw ink at the screen and smoke bombs into the audience. Even after the police intervened, the mob returned a second time and succeeded in forcing the screening to end.[99]

The Holocaust was the final blow to Yiddish as the leading Jewish language.[100] Of the six million Jews murdered by the Nazis, a great proportion were Yiddish speakers, and this ended any chance of there being a majority Yiddish-speaking population in Israel.[101] Those Yiddish speakers who did make it to the new Jewish state found an environment more hostile to the language than ever before. Yiddish already bore with it the shame of the ghetto, now it carried the stench of the death camps. 'The struggle against Yiddish was rooted in a hatred of anything that was connected with the "Diaspora," considered to be marked by self-deprecation and cringing submission to non-Jews, a culture that was thoroughly second-rate, lacking in any estimable qualities, counterfeit and meretricious,' writes Yiddish preservationist Abraham Brumberg.[102] There was no suggestion of Israel working to sustain a language that the Nazis had almost succeeded in wiping out, quite the opposite, many in Palestine saw their diaspora fellows as an embarrassment, 'inferior human beings who went "like lambs to the slaughter"', in the words of one historian. 'Only the Zionist undertaking in Palestine had succeeded in raising a courageous and resourceful new generation of Jewish youth, the very antithesis of Diaspora Jews.'[103] That such a generation had been raised in Hebrew proved that Yiddish should be done away with. This was not an attitude felt only among those who had avoided the Shoah, survivors travelling to Israel around this time willingly ditched Yiddish in favour of Hebrew for the express purpose of distancing themselves from the horrors they had experienced. Yiddish was the language of a people nearly exterminated, Hebrew was the language of a new country, and a people rising from the ashes of destruction, and many sought to abandon any link to their former diasporic past.

Writing in 1951, Israeli prime minister David Ben-Gurion said that while 'Yiddish was one of the important spiritual assets of the Jewish people', it had no official place in the state of Israel, and belonged 'to the Jewish past, not the present and certainly not the future'.[104] It was not until the 1960s, with Hebrew's ascension secure, that Israel began to lift restrictions on the use of Yiddish. Just as assimilationist imperial powers across the world have willingly turned indigenous languages into museum artefacts after they are dead or weakened to the point of no return, wringing their hands at the destruction they oversaw, the Israeli state's attitude began to shift in favour of preserving Yiddish as a flavour of historical Jewish life,[105] 'like an asset that every nation keeps in its pantheon of culture, as a positive feature of the past', but one that could in no way threaten the Hebraic hegemony.[106] On 26 May 2009, seventy-four years to the day that rioters had prevented Zhitlowsky's speech in Tel Aviv, the Israeli Knesset observed Yiddish Language and Culture Day, and published a Yiddish–Hebrew parliamentary lexicon for the occasion.[107]

American rabbi and Yiddishist Benjamin Weiner said that for the current generation of Israeli Jews:

The language is either morose or hysterical, either the melody of a 'Holocaust song' or the buffoonery of the Wise Men of Chelm, into whose antics ... the entirety of Ashkenazic achievement has been distilled. For their part, some middle-aged Israelis now long for Yiddish with a dewy-eyed nostalgia. And the State has acknowledged its neutralization of the language by enshrining it in the pantheon of 'our proud Diasporic heritage.'[108]

This attitude is prevalent in the United States too, with Yiddish often seen not as the living language it is, but a quirk of the past, spoken by Jewish grandmothers in punchlines or anti-assimilatory Haredim.[109] Rokhl Kafrissen, a New York-based playwright, has spent years documenting media coverage of supposed Yiddish 'revival' programmes, which ignores the awkward fact the language still has hundreds of thousands of speakers and is far from dead, even if it is increasingly vulnerable.[110] There is hostility among both Hebrew- and English-speaking Jews to a more active, muscular Yiddish culture, which tends to be anti-Zionist, or at least critical of Israel, and seeks to build a Jewish identity outside that prescribed by the right-wing Israeli state. Writing in 2015, British-Israeli academic Avi Lang said that for many Jews, learning Yiddish can be a political statement:

> *Just as Modern Hebrew represents Zionism and nationalism, and echoes the often unpleasant and unpopular policies of the Netanyahu government, Yiddish has come to represent its opposite. While Hebrew is the language of a nation, Yiddish is the language of the diaspora; where Hebrew is the language of power, Yiddish is the language of pacifism, and where Hebrew stands for Zionism, Yiddish stands for internationalism. It is precisely this semiotic dichotomy that has led so many left-wing Jews in recent years to embrace the study of Yiddish.*[111]

Lina Morales, another younger Jewish writer, said that for her, 'Yiddish held the promise of a Jewishness not defined by Zionism or any specific political project.'

> *Modern Israeli Hebrew, a language whose revival was a definite goal of the Zionist movement, makes me think of the tanned soldiers and women wearing bikinis that I saw on a Tel Aviv beach as a teenager on my Birthright trip. Most of my Birthright peers found the idea of tanned, buff, and militaristic Jews fulfilling and exciting, but I found them alienating and more than a little problematic, since I knew what cruelties some of those buff soldiers were committing against the Palestinian people. Yiddish, on the other hand, offered a real and deep Ashkenaziness, an alternative to the endless caricaturization. To learn Yiddish was to go against the current of assimilation and Zionism, to reclaim the nebbish shtetl Jew that most Jews found an embarrassing relic. Learning Yiddish was almost contrarian, and that sounded to me like the theme of my life.*[112]

Morales's article was subtitled, 'An alternative to assimilation and Zionism', and this is what in many ways Yiddish has always represented. It is what tied together Zamenhof and Ben-Yehuda. Before he sought to create both a language and a religion that surpassed Judaism, Zamenhof worked on modernizing Yiddish and wrote a detailed grammar of the language. Ben-Yehuda grew up surrounded by Yiddish and was at least in part inspired by that language's success in launching his effort to revive Hebrew. Yiddish has persisted for centuries, and while Hebrew, along with Esperanto, English, German, Russian and other languages, has challenged it as the primary tongue of the Jewish people – and the Holocaust devastated its first-language population – it has managed to survive. While it may never challenge Hebrew for dominance in Israel, Yiddish may yet become stronger than it is today, as diaspora Jews once again seek to carve out their own identity separate to that prescribed by Zionism. In this, they may take inspiration from Esperanto, which now claims a speaker base of some two million people worldwide, as well as a few thousand native speakers, whose determined parents, like Ben-Yehuda before them, made sure their children grew up speaking a new language.[113]

PART THREE

Cantonese

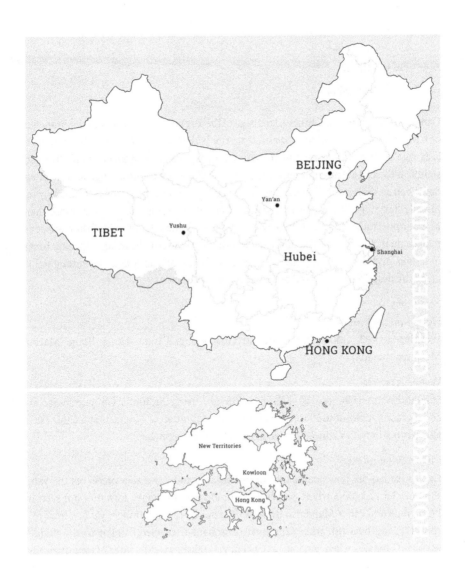

Gwóngdūng wá 廣東話

(kʷɔːŋ³⁵tʊŋ⁵⁵ wäː²²⁻³⁵)

Language family
Sino-Tibetan

— Sinitic

— Yue

— Cantonese

— Mandarin

— Putonghua

Cantonese is a Sinitic, or Chinese, language of the Yue family. Like other major branches of Chinese, including Mandarin and Wu, Yue is descended from Middle Chinese, a language spoken during the fourth century. Today, all three branches have diverged significantly, and are not mutually intelligible. While many Chinese languages are often described as 'dialects' in English, this is a mistranslation of the Chinese term fangyan, literally 'language of a place' or topolect. Cantonese is not a dialect any more than Mandarin is, rather both are languages within the Chinese family. Confusion arises as many actual dialects, such as different varieties of Mandarin, have large speaker bases in China, and because for political reasons, only the official tongue of Putonghua is given the descriptor 'language' by the Chinese government.

Speakers
Hong Kong: ~7 million
Worldwide: ~73 million (primarily in Guangdong, China; Hong Kong; Macao; Malaysia; Canada)

Writing system
Standard Written Chinese (書面語, syūmihnyúh), using traditional Chinese characters and a grammar closer to Putonghua than spoken Cantonese. Vernacular Cantonese is also written in both Chinese characters and the Latin alphabet.

Distinctive features
Cantonese has six tones compared to Putonghua's four, and also preserves the yahp sīng, or checked tone, where words end in plosive consonants, a feature not seen in Putonghua and other Mandarin dialects. Examples are the numbers yāt (1), luhk (6), chāt, (7), and baat (8), where the final consonant is clipped, similar to the middle letters of 'butter' when said in a Cockney English accent: 'bu'er'. Grammatically, spoken Cantonese also differs from Putonghua, for example in the use of direct object–

indirect object word order rather than indirect object–direct object, 'give water me' in Cantonese, instead of 'give me water' in Putonghua.

Examples

I'm a Hong Konger, I speak Cantonese.
Ngóh haih Hēung Góng yàhn, ngóh sīk góng Gwóngdūng wá.

Where is the toilet?
Chisó hái bīndouh a?

How much is this egg tart?
Nī go daahn tāat géi chìhn a?

Chapter 10
Dialectics

Hugh Monk stood on the deck of the HMS *Wellesley*, the seventeen-hundred tonne, seventy-four-gun flagship of the British fleet in China. It was 7 January 1841, and two empires were at war.[1]

He watched as, ahead, the HMS *Nemesis* ploughed through a crowd of smaller Chinese ships. A rocket fired from the British steamship found the gunpowder storage of one of the diminutive junks, igniting a huge explosion which sent bodies and debris flying into the air. Soon afterward, another junk was disposed of the same fashion, killing nearly all on board, and the crews of the surviving Chinese vessels began leaping into the water in a desperate bid for safety.

'The empty junks were then set on fire, and produced a series of magnificent bonfires … finishing with stunning explosions, superior to every thing of the sort ever exhibited at Vauxhall,' Monk wrote in a letter to his sister, back in Guernsey, a British island in the English Channel. The twenty-three-year-old had been despatched to the East Indies two years earlier, taking up the position of assistant surgeon aboard the *Wellesley*. Following the battle, his team established a hospital for the wounded Chinese, 'and I had the satisfaction of saving a poor devil's life by a successful amputation of the arm, for which he was apparently grateful.'

Not a single British soldier or sailor lost their lives in the engagement,[2] while more than five hundred Chinese troops were killed, around a dozen ships destroyed, along with almost two hundred guns, and the forts of Chuenpi and Taikoktow. It was a dramatic demonstration of the might of the Royal Navy, and the complete inability of the Qing Empire to resist it. Just over two weeks later, British forces landed on an island in the mouth of the Pearl River Delta, and raised the Union Flag, seizing Hong Kong for the crown.[3] Monk himself reached the new colony in August, from where he wrote to his father, reporting the Navy's great successes and his own brush with military glory. A year later, he was aboard the *Wellesley* as the fleet arrived at Nanjing, where a formal treaty was signed, opening up China to trade and ceding Hong Kong to the British crown in perpetuity. 'The Chinese war is I think at last concluded, I thank God!' Monk wrote to his sister from Nanjing. 'Yesterday the treaty was signed by Elipoo [a top Qing official] and the emperor's uncle, and is gone to Peking for the emperor's seal.' He expressed hope that the treaty would hold, 'for I am getting heartily sick and tired of the war.'[4]

Monk would not make it back to Guernsey. He died of dysentery at sea, en route for the British colony of Singapore.[5] In total, less than a hundred British soldiers died in over two years of fighting.[6] Chinese casualties were at least thirty times as high.

British troops who did return to the UK did not necessarily do so draped in glory. The Opium War, as it would come to be known, had been fought 'in order to advance the interests of [Britain's] national drug dealers, who for years had been smuggling opium to China's coast against the laws of the country', writes historian Stephen Platt.[7] The conflict was greeted with disgust even by the jingoistic British public, who, while they happily supported imperial adventurism elsewhere, drew the line at invading a sovereign state to help pushers of a product that was illegal in the UK. During a parliamentary debate that narrowly failed in stopping the conflict, a young William Gladstone said, 'a war more unjust in its origin, a war more calculated in its progress to cover this country with permanent disgrace, I do not know, and I have not read of'.[8]

In the opulent halls of the Forbidden City in Beijing, the embarrassing defeat of the Qing military at the hands of a far smaller British force was an ugly wake up call for an empire that had been resting on its laurels as smaller rivals, once dismissed as insignificant, outstripped it technologically and militarily. It was also a portent of what was to come: the so-called century of humiliation, during which first European powers, and then even tiny Japan, inflicted military defeat and unequal treaties on the Qing.[9]

The Opium War, while ostensibly fought for trade rather than conquest, also gave the British a new imperial property, Hong Kong, which officials grandly claimed had been occupied 'not with a view to colonisation, but for diplomatic, commercial, and military purposes'.[10] While this did little to change the reality for those being forcibly ruled by a foreign power, it did influence some policies of the new colonial administration, particularly towards language. Unlike other British properties, Hong Kong did not see the kind of forced Anglicization that characterized colonial education in much of India and Africa. While English was made the colony's only official language, marginalizing non-speakers – cutting them out of government and the court system, except as defendants, when they were at a severe disadvantage[11] – there was also no attempt to force the language on Chinese schools, which continued to teach in Cantonese. Many British officials were largely ignorant of the Chinese language, and made no distinction between Cantonese, as spoken in the colony and across the border in southern China, and Mandarin, the main language spoken in northern China, despite the two being mutually unintelligible. But while this undoubtedly caused communication issues, there was no great desire to teach English to the crown's new Chinese subjects, reflective of an attitude among some colonial officials in Asia that doing so was counterproductive. As one administrator wrote in a report from Malaya during this time, 'Pupils who acquire an edge of English are invariably unwilling to earn their livelihood by manual labour, the immediate result of affording an English education to any large number of [people] would be the creation of a discontented class who might become a source of anxiety to the community.'[12]

As Hong Kong expanded in population and importance, particularly following the seizure of Kowloon in 1860, during the Second Opium War, the British authorities began to pay more mind to their Chinese subjects. John Pope Hennessy, who became governor of Hong Kong in 1877, was among the first of the city's leaders to believe in the 'importance of encouraging an English speaking community of Chinese in Hong Kong'.[13] To that end, he argued, he would 'like to see no Government School whatever in this Colony in which the children are not taught English'. Other officials had also begun to look askance at the Chinese schools, which were viewed with widespread disdain among the colonial elite. The author of an 1889 report wrote that 'when a Chinaman goes to school he is given a little book, and he just simply sits and pores over it, not understanding the meaning of a character, and he goes on growing and getting other books which he does not understand at all'.[14] The Reverend S.R. Brown, former headmaster of a mission school which taught Chinese pupils, complained that his charges came 'with a mind to be emptied of a vast accumulation of false and superstitious notions that can never tenant an enlightened mind, for they cannot coexist with truth'. The principal characteristic of Chinese students, Brown added, was 'an utter disregard of truth, obscenity, and cowardliness'.[15]

But while these views may have been motivated by bigotry as much as anything, concerns about the quality of Chinese education were also being voiced in Beijing. In the Qing capital, the successive defeats at the hands of foreign forces had created space for previously verboten suggestions, such as scrapping the imperial examination system, focused as it was on Confucian texts and classical Chinese writing, or even reforming the language itself in order to increase literacy nationwide. Actually doing so, however, would be a task that bedevilled multiple Chinese governments to come.

The men stood in a row outside a small riverside temple in southern Hubei province. Down their backs hung the long, plaited cues every man in the Qing Empire was required by law to wear, while around their necks were red sashes or kerchiefs.[16] From a ferry on the river, eight-year-old Yuen Ren Chao watched intently as the men moved in unison, one fist punching forward with an exhale of breath, the other cocked tight by their side, their faces locked in expressions of intense focus.

It was 1900, and the men he watched were members of the Society of Righteous and Harmonious Fists. Two years earlier, disgusted by the repeated humiliations China had suffered at the hands of various foreign powers, who had carved up the country into a checkerboard of legations and colonies, they had launched a rebellion against the Qing Empire.[17,18] The Boxers, as they came to be known, targeted corrupt local officials, Western missionaries, and Chinese Christians, destroying churches and massacring and burning parishioners. As the rebellion spread throughout northeastern China, so did lurid tales of Boxer atrocities and supposed magical powers, such as superhuman strength or imperviousness to bullets.

Despite being the grandson of an imperial official, Chao was not scared as he watched the men doing their strange exercises with such fierce determination. By the time he saw them, the Society had undergone a bizarre transformation, from a potential challenge to the Qing to one of the imperial throne's strongest defenders, co-opted and manipulated by conservative elements at court to go after their foreign enemies.[19]

He did not know it then, but the Boxers would change Chao's life forever. For the Qing court's alliance with the peasant rebels who had once sought to overthrow them turned out to be a catastrophic mistake for the dynasty. In July 1900, after Boxer forces laid siege to foreign concessions in the port city of Tianjin, and torched churches and embassies in Beijing, an international force of tens of thousands of troops from eight countries invaded northern China.[20] A multinational army under the command of British general Alfred Gaselee stormed the capital, overwhelming a force of Boxers and Qing regulars and lifting the siege of the city's foreign quarter. Troops under Gaselee and other foreign commanders, including large Russian and Japanese contingencies, matched the Boxers atrocity for atrocity,[21] carrying out revenge massacres and public executions. In September 1901, the defeated and humiliated Qing sued for peace.

The ensuing Boxer Protocol, in which the Qing ceded yet more territory to the foreign powers and agreed to pay a massive indemnity,[22] was another entry in the long list of defeats suffered during the century of humiliation. Those at the hands of Japan particularly stung, with China's neighbour to the east easily defeating the Qing in 1895, ending the imperial throne's influence over Korea and Taiwan. Japanese forces also took part in suppressing the Boxers, cementing the county's position as a modern power equal to those of Europe. By comparison, China was severely lagging behind, held back by a creaking imperial bureaucracy that was stuck in the previous century.

The Guangxu Emperor, who had come to power in 1875, had attempted to remedy matters, launching a radical reform programme in 1898 that would have modernized the military, established a constitutional monarchy, and abolished the traditional examination system which controlled who entered the all powerful civil service.[23] Before the year was out however, Guangxu's aunt, the Dowager Empress Cixi, along with conservative elements in the Qing court, launched a coup against him, leaving the emperor sidelined and ineffectual, his reforms abandoned.[24]

The need for change was recognized far beyond Beijing however, and agitation for reform continued even as Cixi and her conservative faction took control of the country. In particular, the education system, geared towards the imperial examinations, was in dire need of improvement. Far from the meritocracy it was intended to cultivate, it had calcified into a system which rewarded those who could afford to laboriously study and memorise the Confucian classics, while not encouraging innovation or independent thought. This model was made all the more difficult by the way Chinese was written at the time, which could itself be a bar to upward mobility for many people.

This was a difficulty Chao was intimately familiar with. He was born in Tianjin on the coast of the Bohai Sea in 1892, and spent much of his early life in what is now Hebei, as the family followed his grandfather's imperial postings around northeastern China.[25] Despite their northern travels, their roots were in Changzhou, a city in Jiangsu province between Shanghai and the future republican capital of Nanjing, and the Chaos considered themselves 'southerners'. At the time, China did not have an official national spoken language, and the Chao household was a mix of the Changzhou dialect of Wu, the language most of the elders had grown up speaking, and Mandarin, the dominant northern tongue.[26] While both are Sinitic, or Chinese, languages, Mandarin is not mutually intelligible with Wu, and Chao's grandfather and father's Mandarin abilities were limited, though Chao later boasted his mother spoke 'pure Pekingese'. She was fanatical about literacy, and began drilling her son on Chinese characters at age four.[27] From practising character flashcards with his mother, Chao graduated to reading the *Great Learning*, the first of the four Confucian classics that made up a key part of the imperial civil service examinations. At age six, Chao and two of his cousins began lessons with a teacher hired from 'the south' (again, the central-eastern Chinese seaboard around Jiangsu), called Lu Ko-hsuan. He continued to drill them on the classics, introducing them to Confucius's *Analects* and the writings of Mencius. In the evenings, Chao's mother taught them poetry, 'which was really learning to run before we could crawl,' he said later.[28]

At the time, there was no crawling if one wanted to be literate in Chinese; everything was a marathon, run at a punishing pace. The written tongue was still the classical language: wenyan, an archaic and highly stylized way of writing based on a fossilised spoken form of Chinese that hadn't been used in centuries. Understanding wenyan was not simply a matter of learning an old-fashioned but familiar tongue, like reading Chaucerian English, or even an ancient language like Latin; it also required a deep textual knowledge, like having to memorize the entire works of Shakespeare before you could understand a simple poem. Because wenyan texts relied so much on allusion to other works, they could often be literally unintelligible for someone who had not done the required reading. For example, the *Three-Character Classic*, a thirteen stanza primer for children written during the Song dynasty, contains allusions to the early life of the philosopher Mencius, a classical tale about filial piety, and the actions of a descendant of Confucius, all of which make little sense without knowing the context.[29] Another stanza reads 'Dou Yanshan, had the right method / He taught five sons, each of whom raised the family reputation,' an oblique reference to a tenth-century family's success in the imperial examinations.[30]

Lexically, classical Chinese was also far removed from any of the languages spoken in the country, and had an extremely compact style, with nearly all words confined to a single syllable, an almost complete aversion to punctuation, and the use of honourifics and other terms that had mostly fallen out of fashion in spoken Chinese languages. Many words that were historically pronounced differently had also become homophones in modern tongues, creating additional confusion for readers. Chao would encapsulate this point adeptly later in life with his poem, 'Lion-Eating Poet in the Stone Den', or '施氏食獅史', pronounced in Mandarin as 'shi shi shi shi shi'. Because it bore little relation to what people spoke in their daily lives, wenyan required intense study and 'was almost perversely difficult to learn and master', in the words of historian David Moser.[31] This worked to the advantage of many in the imperial court. Along with other byzantine traditions that governed elite culture, wenyan acted as a form of gatekeeping, preventing all but the most determined from improving their class situation or challenging those in power.

Then there was the matter of the writing system itself. Despite a common misconception among non-Chinese speakers that characters are pictograms, only a small number fit this description. The technical term for this type of writing system is logographic, with each character representing a word or concept, as opposed to alphabetic and syllabic systems, in which the various characters represent the sounds of the language itself. (Some linguists disagree with classifying Chinese as logographic, as some characters include phonetic clues or serve phonetic functions.) When Chao was growing up, and for generations before, the path to literacy in Chinese was a years-long slog of rote memorization, learning the meaning and pronunciation of thousands of characters, as well as the particular brush order in which they had to be written.

For decades, some in China had recognized the problems these bars to literacy were causing for the country, and advocated for reform. In particular, they argued, replacing or supplementing characters with a phonetic alphabet or syllabary would make them easier to learn. Christian missionaries had, since the nineteenth century, been printing Chinese Bibles written in the Latin alphabet, to great success. And although abandoning or diluting characters was so revolutionary as to be deemed unthinkable in some quarters, there were models for such a transformation. Japan and Korea, which historically used Chinese characters for their writing systems, had both undergone a similar shift, with Korea largely replacing characters with Hangul, beginning in the thirteenth century, and Japan supplementing kanji with kana during the late 1800s.[32] Resistance to a similar move in China was profound however, as evidenced by the centuries between the development of Japanese and Korean syllabaries and similar conversations even beginning in China. There were many reasons for this, including natural conservatism, when something has been in place for so long, we are often loathe to change it, particularly when it comes to language.[33] There was also undeniable affection and loyalty to characters, one of the oldest forms of writing, with a deep pedigree that stretched back throughout Chinese history. When the country was successful, this pedigree could serve to blind people to any issues with characters or the language itself, such as when the Song-era historian Zheng Qiao dismissed Sanskrit as 'very simple', even while noting it could be used to represent endless sounds with just a few strokes. 'The world is of the opinion,' he asserted, 'that people who know ideographs are wise and worthy, whereas those who do not know ideographs are simple and stupid.'[34]

Conveniently for the wise and worthy like Zheng and his successors, by maintaining the complex character system and classical writing style, they also reduced competition for positions that required literacy, and made it more difficult for an illiterate peasantry to organize against them. As William Brewster, an American protestant missionary working in Fujian province, wrote during the late Qing era:

> *Where the ability to read and write in any nation is confined to a literary caste, it follows as the night the day, that the members of this caste obtain and permanently hold the reins of government. Such a class of men would be something more than human if they did not fashion the government, so that they would obtain all the political plums and enjoy every possible privilege at the expense of the ignorant and almost helpless masses. So China has a government of the literati, for the literati, and by the literati.*[35]

'The illiterate classes have opinions,' Brewster continued.

> *They know they are oppressed. They resent it. But they cannot be heard, because they cannot speak through the press. They cannot organise a reform without educated leaders. As long as the masses endure in sullen silence, or break out only in an occasional abortive uprising that is easily crushed, these privileged men will go on as near as possible in the ways of their fathers, oppressing the people whom they despise because they can neither read nor write.*[36]

Such resentment and anger would soon fuel the Boxer Uprising, which originally targeted many among the Qing literati.

It took the humiliation suffered in the last decades of the Qing, particularly at the hands of the Japanese in 1895, for anyone in a position of power to seriously consider breaking with Chinese characters. 'The leaders of the New China had learned that one chief element in the amazing efficiency of the Japanese soldier lies in the fact that he can read,' wrote another missionary, Arthur Smith. 'The Chinese soldier is generally illiterate, and with the hieroglyphics only he will be so always.'[37]

A 'Movement for a Phonetic Alphabet' began lobbying for just that,[38] and in 1898 the Guangxu Emperor even gave his imprimatur to a phoneticization scheme developed by Lu Kan-chang, which would have supplemented Chinese characters with an alphabet partially based on Roman characters, and could be used for multiple Chinese languages and dialects. This plan was dashed however, along with the rest of Guangxu's reforms, when Cixi's coup rendered the emperor just a powerless figurehead.[39]

Despite myriad criticisms of wenyan and the character system as it existed, one advantage classical Chinese had was in ensuring a degree of linguistic uniformity across the vast Qing Empire. Imperial officials writing in Beijing could be sure that their edicts would be legible to subordinates in as far-flung paces as Guangdong and Xinjiang, even if in person, the men might have struggled to make themselves understood. The phonetic flexibility of Chinese characters, which can be read in any language (even non-Chinese ones in theory, though grammar is a major issue), meant that anyone versed in wenyan could understand it on the page, whether they spoke Beijing Mandarin, Suzhou Wu or Cantonese. By opening up space for the vernaculars to take over, reformers risked undoing the linguistic uniformity which helped tie the vast empire together. While the court itself used a dialect of Mandarin known as guanhua, or 'official speak', as its lingua franca, in parts of central and southern China, where the dominant language was not closely related to Mandarin, proficiency in the court tongue could be very low, and even in Mandarin-speaking areas, local dialects were often far more widely spoken than guanhua.[40] Writing in Hong Kong in the early 1900s, then-governor Frederick Lugard, who favoured using English as the language of education for the colony, also suggested it could be a potential national tongue for all of China, 'since the populations of the various provinces in China speak no common language, and the Chinese vocabulary has not yet adapted itself to express the terms and conceptions of modern science.'[41]

Throughout his highly mobile childhood – the family moved seven times in as many years – the young Chao got a glimpse of China's vast linguistic diversity, and the problems that came with it. When his grandfather died in 1902, and the family escorted his body south to their ancestral home, Chao was shocked to find the servants in his relatives' household could not speak Mandarin. Given his own limited ability in Changzhou dialect at that time, he found, to his great frustration and embarrassment, that he was largely unable to communicate with them.

The death of Chao's grandfather was only the start of the family's tragedies. In 1904, when Chao was not yet thirteen, his mother succumbed to tuberculosis after a years-long fight with the disease. Just six months later, his father died of dysentery.[42] Chao was put into the care of relatives, and in 1906 moved to the family home in Changzhou. Having lost his grandfather, mother, father and been uprooted multiple times in a matter of years, Chao might have been expected to suffer a breakdown, but instead he threw himself even more vigorously into his studies. At school in Changzhou, he began studying English for the first time, along with mathematics and science.[43] In 1907, he was sent to boarding school in Nanjing, where he added more languages and dialects to what was already becoming an impressive arsenal. It was also in Nanjing that he had his first taste of revolutionary fervour, albeit in a very minor form, when he and other boys burst out laughing at the command to 'commence lamentations' during a ceremony to mark the death of Dowager Empress Cixi.[44]

In Nanjing, Chao met his first American, a southerner named David John Carver, who helped the teenage Chao improve his English but left him with a distorted impression as to the average American accent: visiting the country years later he was surprised to find that 'most people did not talk quite the way Mr. Carver did'.[45]

Chao's journey to the United States came about as a result of the Boxer Rebellion. After the war, the foreign powers had forced yet another treaty on the Qing, including a large indemnity to be paid to the various powers involved.[46] Washington had used this money to establish the Boxer Indemnity Scholarship to fund promising young Chinese to study at American universities, and in August 1910, Chao travelled with seventy-one other young scholars to Shanghai, where they boarded a postal steamer, the appropriately named SS *China*, for the long trip to the United States.[47] Before they left, they were toasted at a reception in the American consulate, on the banks of the Huangpu River. There, their hosts briefed them on the basics of US culture and high society, such as the need to buy a bowler hat to wear on all formal occasions (advice Chao ignored).

The well-educated scion of a wealthy, upper-class family, Chao was as worldly as perhaps any Chinese man his age, and yet he was still vastly unprepared for the culture shock he experienced on arrival in the United States. He came from a pre-industrial, largely rural society, where women still bound their feet, men wore the cue – Chao cut his off, with some trepidation, days before departing – and electric lights were rare. He landed in the most technologically advanced country in the world, with a booming economy, that was on track to become the next superpower. Arriving in San Francisco after a brief stopover in Hawai'i, Chao and his fellow students were dazzled. No matter that the city was still showing the effects of the 1906 earthquake and fire which reduced much of it to rubble, it was grand and impressive and every bit the picture postcard American metropolis. Travelling east to take up his studies at Cornell University, Chao was somewhat less impressed – why had all the tall buildings been replaced by rundown shacks? – but he soon settled in. It was at Cornell, majoring in mathematics, that he received word of the Chinese revolution and fall of the Qing in 1911, when another student ran through the campus shouting, 'Good news! Good news!'[48]

The revolution opened the door to reform that Cixi's coup had slammed shut, including on the issue of language. In 1913, the new Republican government established a Commission on the Unification of Pronunciation.[49] The hope was that the commission could craft a new lingua franca for the whole country, similar to the guanhua of the Qing court, that would preserve the uniformity and cohesiveness provided by wenyan, while opening the door for script and linguistic reform that could improve access to literacy. Republican leaders were inspired both by the new nation-states of Europe, founded on the principle of 'one country, one people, one language',[50] and by Japan, which had undergone a similar linguistic reform during the Meiji era, one that some credited with allowing that country to leapfrog the Qing and become a colonial aggressor. The term for the proposed new national language, Guoyu, was itself borrowed from Japanese, Kokugo.

Representatives from every province, as well as Mongolia, Tibet, and overseas Chinese groups, convened in Beijing to hash this out, with the intention of establishing a standard way of pronouncing 6,500 Chinese characters, forming the basis of a new Guoyu.[51] The meeting, a collection of some of the biggest egos in Chinese linguistics, almost immediately fell into acrimony. In the words of chair Wu Zhihui, 'It was the desire of almost every delegate to go down in history as the originator of a great reform in the written language,'[52] but no two persons agreed on what this would entail. On the matter of choosing an existing language to form the basis of the new Guoyu, the commission split into two broad camps, one favouring Mandarin, the dominant northern language, the other made up of representatives of southern languages, including Wu and Cantonese. While Mandarin was by far the largest of the Chinese language families, the southerners had a strong argument in favour of adopting one of their tongues: even with its four tones, Mandarin possesses a smaller number of phonemes, the distinct sounds which make up a spoken language, than other Chinese languages, particularly those spoken in the south. Cantonese has some 1,800 syllables, compared to just 1,300 for Mandarin, which means there are far more homonyms in Mandarin and potential for confusion when it is spoken out loud (though context provides many clues and actual confusion is very rare).[53]

The debate soon turned ugly. In a move that was not particularly conducive to compromise, the Mandarin faction adopted the slogan, 'Force the South to follow the North,' while those opposing them were led by Wu Zhihui, the commission chairman, a polarizing figure with a quick temper. During an earlier debate on Confucianism, Wu had called for China to 'flush all classical literature down the toilet', referred to the Manchus who ran the Qing as a 'dog-fucked race', and called the late Empress Dowager a 'withered old hag'.[54] He particularly clashed with his deputy, Wang Zhao, who led the pro-Mandarin camp. Eventually, after several intense arguments, Wu resigned his position in frustration, declaring 'I can't stand this!'

Wang was no less intemperate. At one point after he assumed the chairmanship, he attempted to end the stalemate by calling for a vote in which each province would get to cast one ballot, a clear attempt to stack the decks in favour of the numerically superior Mandarin representatives.[55] He also nearly came to blows with another delegate when, in a neat encapsulation of the problem they were all trying to solve, the man used a colloquial Shanghainese expression for 'rickshaw', which Wang misheard as a Mandarin insult and angrily chased him from the hall.

In the end, Wang and the other northerners gained the upper hand, and it was agreed that Beijing Mandarin would be the basis of the new national lingua franca. In a sop to the southerners however, Guoyu would incorporate a fifth tone common in many non-Mandarin Chinese languages, as well as some grammatical aspects from other dialects. The commission urged the Ministry of Education to promulgate the new standard and encourage officials across the country to aid in its promotion, along with a new Guoyu course that would be taught in primary and middle schools.[56]

In addition, the commission also endorsed a phonetic system to represent the new Guoyu standard. Despite the success of missionary publications that used the Latin alphabet, the widespread use of the Wade–Giles system in English-language textbooks and newspapers, and the support of many academics for such schemes, there was widespread hostility towards any Romanization of Chinese, seen as too radical, and foreign, a change for many.[57] Instead, the commission settled on a syllabary of thirty-nine symbols based on a system created by attendee Zhang Binglin, who in turn had been inspired by seal script, one of the oldest forms of Chinese writing. This gave Zhuyin, as it would become known, a pleasing historical sheen, modernizing while also remaining true to the country's great literary past,[58] though proponents of a Romanised system expressed concern that it would be too alien and difficult for foreigners to learn, holding the Chinese language back in an increasingly globalized economy.[59] (That this concern was even being voiced was something of a radical reversal from the Qing era, when preventing foreigners from learning Chinese was the stated goal of some bureaucrats.[60])

Like most things agreed upon by the 1913 commission, Zhuyin was an awkward compromise that left few feeling satisfied. Ignoring complaints from southern attendees, the new syllabary was restricted to the hybrid Mandarin chosen for the national standard, and not adapted for use with other dialects or languages. Conservatives also insisted that it could only be presented as an adjunct to characters, not a potential replacement, going so far as to dropping 'alphabet' from the official name, for fear that they could be viewed as a system independent of characters.[61] Apathy over Zhuyin prevented it from being effectively promoted by the government in Beijing or widely adopted by the public, and one Japanese observer spoke for many Chinese-language reformers when he asked in 1922, 'Why does China even now continue to insist on creating such a script when we already have a universal and very convenient Roman alphabet?'[62] This didn't stop others from finding even Zhuyin a step too far however. Zhang Zuolin, a Manchurian warlord, saw the new writing as a malicious plot intended to undermine his regime, and in 1924 he banned it in territory he controlled as part of a decree that ordered the use of only the classical literary style in school textbooks, forbade scholars from visiting the countryside, and outlawed the Boy Scouts.[63]

Political strife also dashed any hopes for Guoyu catching on. As the commission met in Beijing, the Republican state was increasingly coming under the sway of Yuan Shikai, the former Qing general who was instrumental in forcing Puyi's abdication, Yuan had been declared the country's first president in a power-sharing deal with revolutionary leader Sun Yat-sen. In office however, Yuan marginalised his liberal allies and cultivated a monarchical form of government, eventually declaring himself the Hongxian Emperor in 1915. Sun and others fled overseas, from where they attempted to launch a second revolution to overthrow Yuan, who was also facing rebellions from ambitious warlords throughout the country. Clearly, this was not the ideal time for far-reaching educational reforms, and the movement stalled. It would take another Republican government, and a new generation of language reformers, Yuen Ren Chao among them, to restart it.

Chapter 11

A Chinese alphabet

English	Chinese	Pinyin	Wade-Giles	Latinxua	Gwoyeu Romatzyh
Beijing	北京	Běijīng	Peking	Beiging	Beeijing
China	中國	Zhōngguó	Chung-kuo	Zhongguo	Jonggwo
I speak Putonghua	我說普通話	Wǒ shuō Pǔtōnghuà	Wo shuo p'ut'unghua	Wo shuo Putongxua	Woo shuo Puutonghuah

Yuen Ren Chao sighed, as the man in front of him switched into broken, heavily accented Mandarin. It was October 1927, and Chao, accompanied by his assistant Yang Shifeng, had been traipsing around southeastern Jiangsu province for days, interviewing hundreds of people about their knowledge of the Wu language and its various dialects.[1]

While their subject was not itself politically sensitive, field work at this time carried with it great potential danger, from both bandits roaming the countryside to the various armed groups struggling for control of China. In the twelve years after Yuan Shikai's death in 1916, there were twenty-six prime ministers and nine heads of state,[2] as the rump administration left in the Hongxian Emperor's wake, known as the Beiyang government, struggled to hang on in the face of challenges from various warlords and the Kuomintang, the Nationalist Party founded by Sun Yat-sen. The year before Chao began his study in Jiangsu, the new KMT leader, Chiang Kai-shek, had launched his Northern Expedition that would, in 1928, result in the overthrow of the Beiyang regime and resumption of Kuomintang rule.

In this environment, two men walking around asking people questions, recording them and taking notes, were liable to get shot for being spies, and so Chao and Yang were careful to describe their trips as 'study tours'. Their main problem was not with officials however, but the interviewees themselves. Hearing that the two men were from an important Beijing university, they often switched from the languages Chao and Yang were trying to record, into the Mandarin they assumed people from the capital would be accustomed to (even if often their mastery of this language was less than competent). Others thought they were there expressly to test their language ability, and the constant encouragement to speak their local dialect merely an attempt to catch them out. It was only Chao's own familiarity with the languages of the region that salvaged his work. He wrote later that, it was 'important to put them at ease by trying to speak their own dialect to set the tone right, literally, in the interviews'.[3]

Chao's polyglottal abilities had saved more projects than just his own. In 1919, following agreement on the new national pronunciation, or Guoyu, by the Commission on the Unification of Pronunciation in Beijing, attention had turned to how to propagate it around the country (ideally in a way that did not rely too heavily on the creaking Beiyang state). Linguist Wang Pu was tasked with producing a set of phonograph records, reading out the most common 6,500 Chinese characters in their Guoyu pronunciation.[4] In a development that did not augur well for the future, Wang, a Beijinger, found himself unable to properly capture the southern phonetic elements that had been added to the commission's hybrid form of Mandarin, and the attempt had to be abandoned. Chao, with his roots in both northern and southern China, and mastery of multiple languages, proved the perfect person to take up the task. In 1921, he flew to New York and at the Columbia Phonograph Company laid down a series of Guoyu records.[5] Not everyone had his linguistic abilities however, and despite the efforts of Chao and other members of the commission, the hybrid standard never took off. Years later, Chao would joke that he was probably the only person who ever spoke a language intended to be the daily tongue of half a billion people.

When he first travelled there, Chao had intended to spend just four years in the United States, but ended up staying for the best part of a decade. He was made for academia, the type of twentieth-century polymath that does not exist today. After arriving at Cornell, he learned passable German and French, achieved degrees in mathematics and philosophy, published a set of piano compositions and was a founding member of the Chinese-language journal *Science*.[6] A photo from 1916 shows him looking every inch the American intellectual, in a double-breasted suit and tie, small rimless glasses perched on a round, youthful, somewhat imperious face, his dark hair slicked back and the slightest hint of a smile on his lips.

Developments in China eventually became too interesting to stay away any longer however. The fall of the Qing had given rise to a questioning of all the old orthodoxies, including on the subject of language. The New Culture Movement was in full swing, and one of Chao's former Boxer classmates, Hu Shih, was leading a revolution in literature. Along with Chen Duxiu, who would go on to help found the Chinese Communist Party, Hu advocated for abandoning classical Chinese, which he argued cut off whole swaths of the country from the written language and propped up a small intelligentsia of people with the time and money to master the key texts. Instead, Hu and his fellows argued, written Chinese should match the spoken language.

'What we call our literary language is an almost entirely dead language,' Hu wrote in a 1916 article:

Dead it is, because it is no longer spoken by the people. It is like Latin in medieval Europe; in fact, it is more dead (if mortality admits of a comparative degree), than Latin, because Latin is still capable of being spoken and understood, while literary Chinese is no longer auditorily intelligible even among the scholarly class except when the phrases are familiar, or when the listener has already some idea as to what the speaker is going to say.[7]

In Chen's journal *New Youth* the following year, Hu laid out his vision for literature reform. Authors should write with substance and emotion, he argued, in a style and language that was modern and colloquial, and not weighed down by old clichés and allusions to ancients texts.[8] In 1918, he boiled his argument down to four points:

1. *Speak only when you have something to say.*
2. *Speak what you want to say and say it in the way you want to say it.*
3. *Speak what is your own and not that of someone else.*
4. *Speak in the language of the time in which you live.[9]*

Vernacular writing was not a wholly new idea – the most famous Chinese novel of all time, Cao Xueqin's *Dream of the Red Chamber*, was written in the Beijing Mandarin dialect; Christian missionaries also published Bibles written in various Chinese languages and dialects – but Hu and other reformers sought to popularize the practice at a time when the country was crying out for modern ideas and to move away from the often-stifling conventions of the imperial era. 'No dead language can produce a living literature,' Hu said later.[10]

For some reformers, this provided the opportunity to abandon Chinese altogether. Esperanto went through a brief craze in China, and two of Chao's Cornell classmates were big proponents.[11] While Chao was not an avid Esperantist, he was attracted to the idea of a scientifically crafted language, and saw this as a potential solution to China's linguistic morass.[12] To Chao, the obvious solution to the problem of literacy was not only to write in the vernacular, but also to introduce a phonetic system to accompany characters that would, at least, give a clue to their pronunciation, connecting the language on paper with that spoken by the reader.

Zhuyin, the syllabary endorsed by the 1913 language commission, was supposed to fill this role, but the system had struggled to catch on in the political turmoil of that decade. By the time Chao and other language reformers met in Beijing in 1925 for a new Committee on Unification of the National Language, the window had reopened for Romanization.

The primary focus of that committee was Guoyu, and members discussed how to improve upon the efforts of the previous commission and succeed where they had failed. In the end, they did so largely by throwing out much of what had previously been agreed. With far less rancour than their predecessors, the new committee decided to ditch the hybrid pronunciation standard and adopt instead the dialect of Mandarin spoken in Beijing as the new national language, to be propagated by an educational campaign supported by the KMT government, as well as a new set of phonographs, again recorded by Chao.[13]

After that, they turned to the topic of Romanisation, something Chao was deeply invested in personally, having begun work on a new way to write Chinese using the Latin alphabet while still in the United States. Whether because he was ensconced in the English-speaking world, or because Zhuyin had not, at that time, taken hold, or because of an instinct, shared by many young language reformers, particularly of the scientific bent, to propose their own system, but Chao did not share the hostilities towards Romanization that had led to it being dismissed by the 1913 commission. 'Whatever symbols we use, of course we pronounce them in the Chinese way,' he wrote in a 1916 article attacking common objections to the use of the Latin alphabet. 'A Chinese Alphabet may be derived from any source, but it must be of the Chinese, by the Chinese, and for the Chinese.'[14]

While Zhuyin had a certain historical resonance and aesthetic appeal, it required the learning of an entirely new system before it could be used. The Latin alphabet was already widely used around the world, including within China, and was familiar to the educated classes, particularly those who spoke a European language. Romanization therefore started off from a stronger base than Zhuyin ever had, even if, for completely illiterate speakers, it would still require them to learn a new alphabet. In the name of familiarity and ease of adoption, Chao was also opposed to using diacritics or other marks to indicate tones, preferring a change in spelling rather than the introduction of something the reader might not understand and could find alienating. The system he eventually developed, along with author Lin Yutang, was called Gwoyeu Romatzyh – an 'epoch-making innovation', in the words of one Western admirer.[15] Others were less impressed, finding the new alphabet and its rules around tones confusing and the words that resulted difficult to pronounce (such as 'Beeijing,' for China's capital, or 'Shanqhae' for its largest city). Despite some opposition however, Chao's system was adopted in 1928 as a second National Phonetic Alphabet,[16] alongside Zhuyin, and published in an official dictionary – Gwoin Charngyonq Tzyhhuey – put out to popularize the new Beijing Mandarin-based Guoyu standard.[17] There were still those, particularly within the KMT state, who felt that any departure from characters, even if for the purposes of aiding literacy, risked breaking up the country. Chen Guofu, a senior KMT leader, warned that 'China's ability to achieve unity is entirely dependent on having a unified written language', and even criticized those Chinese who used a Western script for signing their names.[18]

At the same time as Chao and his fellows were meeting in Beijing, another Chinese language reform programme was underway almost 6,000 kilometres away, in Moscow. In the 1920s, the Soviet Union had decreed that all 'nationalities' had the right to primary instruction in their own language.[19] To that end, multiple Romanization programmes were launched for languages spoken across the Soviet Empire, with Lenin himself allegedly remarking that 'Latinisation is the great revolution of the East' after Azerbaijan became the first of the republics to do away with Arabic in favour of the Roman alphabet.[20] (Future Soviet leaders were less enamoured, and in 1930 Stalin put a stop to the Latinization programmes and restored Cyrillic to prominence.[21])

In Moscow, the task of Latinizing Chinese – on behalf of the some one hundred thousand ethnic Chinese living in the USSR, mainly in the far east – was taken up by Soviet linguists and several Chinese Communists studying in the capital. Chief among these was Qu Qiubai, who from 1929 onwards worked alongside V.S. Kolokolov and later A.A. Dragunov to develop what would become Latinxua, or Sin Wenz, the 'new writing'.[22] Qu dismissed common concerns that an alphabetical system would make it impossible for people of various regions to understand each other, or that doing away with characters would undermine national unity. 'In the first place, if the various regional "dialects" are very different from each other, then basically they cannot be forcibly unified but must be provided with several different scripts,' he wrote. 'In the second place, China now has a p'u-t'ung hua [common language] which can serve as a general standard and can be used provisionally in creating a common script.'[23] (Qu's use of the term 'Putonghua' was a reference to the way people were used to code switching and using different languages and dialects to communicate as required, not the Beijing Mandarin-based standard that would be adopted later.) Most strikingly, Qu's system also did away with tones altogether, not bothering with diacritics or the gymnastic spelling of Gwoyeu Romatzyh, on the grounds that 'tones are nothing but stress', and that any confusion between homonyms was rare and easily solvable by the writer. Moreover, while Gwoyeu Romatzyh and Zhuyin were limited to representing Guoyu, the intention of Latinxua was to develop phonetic alphabets for all Chinese languages and dialects, allowing people to write in their own tongue for the first time, and eventually to do away with characters altogether.

In 1931, a *Latinised Chinese Reader for Workers* was published, followed by the *Latinised Chinese-Russian Dictionary* (1933) and *Mathematics Exercises for Partial Literates* (1936), as well as a translation of Tolstoy's *The Prisoner of the Caucuses*, in 1937.[24] The chief Chinese newspaper published in the Soviet Union, *The Worker's Way*, also adopted the new alphabet alongside characters, while the all-Latinxua journal *Support the New Writing* dedicated itself to promoting the system.[25] More than three hundred teachers were trained in the alphabet, and by 1938 it was reported that most of the Chinese living in the Soviet Union had become literate in the new script.[26]

The success of Latinxua in the USSR did not go unnoticed by language reformers in China. Lu Xun, the famed writer and poet, said approvingly that 'it is not a plaything of the study or library'.

'It is a thing of the streets and the alleys. Its connection with the old writing is tenuous, but its relation to the people is close,' Lu wrote. 'There are some reformers, who are very fond of talking about reform, but when a real reform reaches them it throws them into a panic.'[27]

And panic they did. Conservatives loathed Qu's alphabet, seeing in the new writing every worst fear they had about a phonetic system. After the Chinese Civil War broke out in the late 1920s, following the collapse of the first United Front between Chiang's Kuomintang and leftist forces, it was also tainted by association with communism. Qu himself was put to death by a KMT firing squad in 1931, having slipped back into the country to take up the position of Commissioner of Education in the Jiangxi Soviet, the Communist Party territory in southern China.[28] His script was banned in many KMT-controlled areas, and publications promoting or written in Latinxua were confiscated. When the Committee for the Promotion of the National Language Romanisation met in 1934, it attributed Latinxua to 'the meddling of foreigners' and described one aim of the conference as 'to investigate how to resist destruction from abroad'.[29]

Younger, more progressive Chinese embraced Qu's system however. During student protests in December 1935 to demand the KMT resist growing Japanese aggression, the left-wing Shanghai Society to Study the Latinisation of Chinese Writing issued a declaration in support of Qu entitled 'Our Views on Promoting the New Writing'.[30]

> *China has reached the critical point of life or death, and we must therefore organise and educate the masses in order to resolve our national difficulties. But at the very outset this task of educating the masses runs into an enormous difficulty, namely the Chinese ideographs. It is necessary to expend several years' time and several tens or hundreds of dollars before it is possible to acquire even a superficial knowledge of them. The masses, who work hard for twelve or thirteen hours a day, lack the time and the money to divert themselves with this pastime.*

The declaration had little time for either Zhuyin, which it described as 'simply auxiliary' to characters, or Gwoyeu Romatzyh, which 'venerates the speech of [Beijing] as the National Language; nominally it advocates the unification of the National Language, but actually it sets up a dictatorship of the [Beijing] speech.'

> *What the masses need in the way of a new script is a new phonetic writing, a new writing without the nuisance of tone indication, a new writing that deals with regional dialects. Such a writing has already appeared. Our brothers in Vladivostok were the first to create the new Latinised script, and with very good results. But let us make no mistake about it the Chinese in Vladivostok were also Chinese. So this scheme, though created outside the country, is still the creation of Chinese.*

> *Experience in Shanghai shows that people can learn to read and write Sin Wenz by spending one hour a day for half a month, or, if they are somewhat dull, for a month. The cost is three cents per person. This is much more economical in time and money than any other means of becoming literate.*

> *The fear that Sin Wenz will disunite China is unjustified. The ideographs are only nominal unifiers and the National Language is suited only to a few intellectuals. The*

unity which we need must be neither abstract, illusory, nor artificial, but one derived from real life. Sin Wenz will enable the masses within a region to communicate with each other internally. Items of local significance need be written up only in the local Sin Wenz, whereas items of nation-wide interest can be translated and given wide distribution by intellectuals. Thus more intellectuals will be produced and culture will be further developed. This will aid the unity of China.

Within months, more than a thousand people had signed a document supporting the declaration, including Lu Xun, Hu Shih and other prominent literary reformers. Faced with this overwhelming support, promoters of Gwoyeu Romatzyh and other systems sued for peace, calling for a 'halt to all internecine warfare'.[31] Restrictions on Latinxua were dropped, and dozens of periodicals and textbooks, the majority in Mandarin but also in Shanghainese, Cantonese, Hakka and other languages, were published in Hong Kong, Shanghai and Beijing before they fell to the Japanese in the late 1930s.[32]

But this output was as nothing compared to the success seen in Communist-controlled parts of the country, where Latinxua was the basis of the Party's literacy programme. The benefits of this programme to the Communists were twofold, not only did they begin building the educated workforce necessary to transform what was still then a pre-industrial country, but their education programmes also helped generate goodwill and spread propaganda. When the American journalist Edgar Snow visited Yan'an, the remote mountain base where the Red Army had retreated to following the Long March of 1934, he observed one rural study group, remarking later:

When farmers and farmers' sons and daughters finished the book they could not only read for the first time in their lives, but they knew who had taught them, and why. They had grasped the basic fighting ideas of Chinese communism.[33]

'It was a dramatic thing to see: the ideograph in revolt,' Edgar's wife Helen Foster Snow wrote later. 'The Chinese language liberating itself from its ancient tomb.'[34] Writing of Latinxua-focused classes in Yan'an, she described it as a revolution 'of as great a significance as the Renaissance of Europe'.[35]

It means more than the emancipation of thought and the quickening of new intellectual life among the illiterate masses of China. It means laying the foundation for a new cultural and political democracy.

'What a disgrace not to know how to read,' went the refrain of 'Song of the Graduates,' a Communist anthem promoting Latinxua. 'Impossible to describe the depth of our sorrow. For four millennia we lived like oxen and horses, And life had become unbearable to us.'

Wanting to read, to live, and to sustain ourselves,
Now we have learned the New Writing.
We have made use of Latin letters to write.
This is a new life for the Chinese language.
This is the great revolution of the East![36]

In late 1936, the civil war was paused as the Communists and KMT again joined in a united front, this time against Japan, which had invaded Manchuria and was threatening to take over all of China. But while this succeeded in stalling the Japanese advance, it did little for the cause of language reform, which was halted once again. Following Japan's surrender in 1945, fighting quickly renewed between the two Chinese factions, but this time the Communists came out on top. And when the dust had settled in 1949 and the People's Republic had been declared, opinion was already beginning to shift on the issue of language.

Having won a bitter civil war and entered the deepening Cold War, China's new rulers shied away from testing the assertion that a flowering of linguistic diversity would not lead to disunity. Instead, almost immediately, they began a programme that would see Putonghua, 'the common language', become the country's unified tongue, both spoken and written, to a degree never before seen in China. Legally, Putonghua was defined as having the 'Beijing phonological system as its norm of pronunciation, and Northern dialects as its base dialect, and looking to exemplary modern works in baihua "vernacular literary language" for its grammatical norms'.[37] Essentially, the Guoyu settled on by the KMT government in 1925.

By this time, Yuen Ren Chao had returned to the United States. He had been in Shanghai when the Japanese attacked in 1937, and the family fled first to western China, and then to Hawai'i, where they remained for two years, leaving for the mainland before the 1941 attack on Pearl Harbour pulled America into the war.[38] Chao ended up at Harvard, where he began teaching Chinese, first to regular students and then increasingly to members of the US military, as Washington allied with Chiang Kai-shek in fighting Japan.[39] Because his charges were expected to go overseas soon after they finished the course, Chao focused on teaching spoken Chinese by way of Romanized transliterations, a vindication of his years-long advocacy of such systems. At the time, the assumption was that US troops landing in China would do so in the south, and so Chao taught his students Cantonese, eventually adapting his course into a primer in that language that was published after the war, followed soon after by a similar book on Mandarin. ('Few people know that the Mandarin Primer was a translation from my Cantonese Primer,' Chao remarked years later.)[40]

At the time, if foreigners had exposure to a Chinese language, it was more likely to be Cantonese than Mandarin or any other. Centuries of trade, and later European colonialism, meant that many Cantonese-speaking Chinese, living on the southern coast, were among the first to emigrate from China. Cantonese soon became the dominant tongue among the Chinese diaspora throughout

Asia, Europe and the United States,[41] a position it would hold until the 2000s.[42] Throughout this period of mass migration, the principal city of Chinese foreign trade was Guangzhou, on the edge of the Pearl River Delta. The Portuguese called it Cantão, which in English became muddled with the name of the surrounding province, Gwongdung, resulting in Canton, from which we get 'Cantonese' (廣東話, Gwóngdūngwá, literally, 'Gwongdung speak').[43]

Cantonese had the population, some seventy million, and the prestige, through the wealth of the Hongs, the millionaire merchants of Guangzhou, to challenge Mandarin as one of the primary languages of China. But it was looked down upon by the country's rulers in Beijing. Southern China had once been home to the Yue, an indigenous people who spanned much of southwest China and Vietnam, but were regarded as 'barbarians' by Chinese rulers to the north.[44] Beginning in the first century BCE, the Han dynasty pressed south, and waves of Chinese colonizers began moving into the area, killing, displacing or assimilating the indigenous Yue. Well into the modern era, while ethnically Han for centuries at this point, the region was still seen as less trustworthy and less Chinese than the Mandarin-speaking heartlands. Beyond politics, there was also a general antipathy towards the Cantonese language itself. The Yongzheng Emperor, who ruled during the height of the Qing dynasty in the eighteenth century, was 'exasperated by the unintelligible speech of officials from Fujian and Guangdong'.[45] He established special institutions in the south to teach them the 'correct pronunciation' of Guanhua, the Mandarin-derived lingua franca of the imperial court.[46,47] The language reformers of the Republican era spoke of forcing 'the south to follow the north', despite the fact that Sun Yat-sen and other revolutionary icons were themselves Cantonese speakers.

Even the British administrators of Hong Kong, who didn't really have any stake in the Chinese language rivalries, viewed Cantonese as inferior to the Mandarin they were accustomed to speaking with imperial, and later Republican, officials. In a 1935 report on the state of education in Hong Kong, the authors wrote that it would have to be 'very carefully considered whether the Chinese medium of instruction should be Cantonese, as at present, or Kwok Yu [sic], which, it is understood, the Government of China wishes to establish as the universal spoken language throughout China'.[48]

Following the Chinese civil war, the country's new Communist leaders, despite their stated commitment to linguistic diversity, remained wary of the 'localism' and 'clan outlook' in the Cantonese-speaking south.[49] One Mandarin-speaking cadre transferred to the region in 1950 warned that efforts at reform were being stymied by the 'feudal personal relations' between local officials and their subjects, who insisted that outsiders learn Cantonese before they would have any dealings with them.[50]

This attitude would have major ramifications when it came to advancing the People's Republic new language policy, which became increasingly assimilationist in the face of international insecurity, particularly the Sino-Soviet split of 1956, after which the country's leaders focused on ensuring national unity and territorial integrity above all else. When Pinyin, a successor to Latinxua, was officially adopted by the Communist state in 1958,[51] the more radical goals of Latinxua advocates were abandoned, including plans for further phonetic alphabets, and for the eventual abolition of characters. Just as the Shanghai students had feared Gwoyeu Romatzyh would, Pinyin increasingly shored up the 'dictatorship' of Putonghua, threatening other Chinese languages and dialects, including Cantonese.

Chapter 12
Common tongue

On the morning of 4 April 1966, commuters jostled each other as they waited for the Star Ferry at a pier in downtown Hong Kong.[1] Opened in 1888, the ferry was the primary means of getting from Hong Kong Island to Kowloon, across the harbour, transporting some four million passengers each month.[2] As they waited for the boat that morning, many in the crowd were likely venting over a proposal to increase the cost of the ferry by ten cents a trip, at a time when many low-wage workers were only making a couple of dollars per day.[3] The increase came amid similar price hikes for buses, and rising rents for public housing; for poor Hong Kongers it felt like wherever they turned they were being squeezed for extra cash.

So Sau-chung, a twenty-five-year-old translator, understood this feeling, and had decided to do something about it. Wearing a black turtleneck, sunglasses and a black leather jacket, his hair swept into an Elvis-style pompadour, he jumped up onto the ferry concourse, shouting for attention. On his jacket, in thick white letters, he had written 'Staging hunger strike, Opposing fare increase.'[4] Above that, in both English and Chinese, was 'Support Elsie!' a reference to Elsie Tu, the lone member of the government-run Transport Advisory Committee who had voted against the fare hike. Tu had also launched a petition drive, attracting twenty-thousand signatures against the plan, and even travelled to London to lobby the British government directly on behalf of impoverished Hong Kongers.[5]

But this did little to sway the colonial authorities, or the monopoly which controlled the ferries. Despite widespread public anger, a protest like So's was unprecedented at the time, and took many observers by surprise. 'A Chinese man who pledged to go on a hunger strike in protest against the proposed "Star" Ferry fare increase, yesterday attracted the attention of many passers-by,' the *South China Morning Post* reported on 5 April 1966, the second day of So's protest, by which time several others had joined him on the ferry pier, holding signs and shouting slogans.[6]

At around 4 pm that day, police officers demanded So leave the concourse, and arrested him for 'obstruction' when he refused to do so.[7] Small groups of protesters gathered outside Government House and at the ferry pier in Tsim Sha Tsui, on the Kowloon side of the harbour. The crowd marched north, and by the evening had grown to include some four thousand people. Police fired tear gas in an attempt to disperse them, leading to a riot. This proved to be the spark that lit the tinder colonial authorities had been blindly stacking for years. Violent protests broke out across the city, which were met with heavy force by police and the British army. Some fourteen hundred people were arrested in the resulting disturbances, in which one person died and twenty-six were injured.[8] But while the unrest alarmed the government, officials did not take any deeper lessons from it. A report on the riots released in December 1966 found police actions had 'generally been characterised by restraint', and concluded 'we do not believe that political, economic and social frustrations were the direct causes of the 1966 riots'.[9] Another lesson would be needed.

In May 1967, amid sweltering, record-high temperatures, workers at the Hong Kong Artificial Flower Works factory in San Po Kong went on strike, after management announced it was slashing wages and bonuses.[10] At the time, plastics manufacturing was one of the biggest industries in Hong Kong, and there was money to be made in fake flowers, which in 1967 counted for over 12 per cent of all Hong Kong's industrial output, employing around thirty thousand workers in more than nine hundred factories across the colony.[11] Li Ka-shing, who would go on to become Hong Kong's richest man, made his start in the plastic flower game, and many other factory owners became wealthy during this time.

But the gains were not shared equally.[12] There was scant legal protection for workers, many of whom toiled in factories that were 'reminiscent [of] Dickensian England'.[13] Before 1960, the government ran virtually no social welfare programmes, letting the burden fall on charities. Reforms in that decade were largely cosmetic, as colonial officials shied away from passing any legislation that might anger business or risk the territory's economy.[14]

The San Po Kong strike was one of many worker actions that year, and it attracted widespread support, not only from leftists and student radicals, but also from the press and even some government lawmakers, who criticized factory owners for their handling of the matter.[15] Had bosses reacted quickly, things might have ended there, but as they dithered, more and more workers joined the strike, and the unrest attracted the attention of Chinese Communist Party-linked unions and newspapers, who soon began promoting it as a revolutionary struggle against British imperialism.

At the time, China was a year into the Great Proletarian Cultural Revolution, a campaign launched by Mao Zedong to shore up his control of the country by purging supposed 'rightists' and revisionists from the Party. His actions plunged much of China into chaos, as hard-left factions seized control in many cities, ousting local officials and staging show trials of their enemies. Many had been advocating for the revolution to spread to Hong Kong, with Red Guards in Guangdong referring to it as 'Expel-the-Imperialists City' in all their official communications.[16] At first however, Beijing urged caution on its representatives in Hong Kong, unwilling to risk a confrontation with the British at a time when much of China was in disarray. But with the neighbouring Portuguese colony of Macao already engulfed by pro-Communist demonstrations by the end of 1966, and worker discontent growing in Hong Kong, this could only last so long. After police moved to arrest the striking San Po Kong workers on 6 May 1967, Communist newspapers in the city denounced the government and accused officers of attacking unarmed protesters.[17]

Leftist organizations and Communist front groups began staging sympathy protests across the city, many of which turned violent. These were egged on and exaggerated by the left-wing press, most of which was controlled by local Communist agents, who colonial authorities increasingly believed were hoping to prompt a military intervention by Beijing. On 15 May, China's Ministry of Foreign Affairs demanded the Hong Kong government stop all 'fascist atrocities', free those who had been arrested and accept the workers' demands. *The People's Daily*, mouthpiece of the Communist Party, warned colonial authorities to 'stop before it is too late'.[18]

Protests continued into July, growing in size and ferocity, and the police response became increasingly violent. Local Communist groups attempted to organize a general strike, and tens of thousands of students joined the protests. On 8 July, an armed militia crossed the Chinese border at Sha Tau Kok and attacked a police guard post, killing five officers and injuring eleven others.[19] Soon, violence spread throughout the city, as anti-government militants began a bombing campaign, targeted at first but increasingly indiscriminate. More than fourteen hundred bombs were planted around the city, killing fifty-one people and injuring hundreds more.[20] This was a severe tactical misjudgement, and even as the British authorities deployed the military and used emergency powers to suppress the protests, public opinion turned hard against the Communists. Two incidents in particular provoked widespread disgust: the death of a seven-year-old girl and her two-year-old brother in a bombing in North Point,[21] and the brutal murder of radio commentator Lam Bun, who was set alight and burned to death in his car on 24 August.[22]

The violence did not fully subside until October 1967, when authorities in Beijing signalled they would not support further unrest and had no intention of invading Hong Kong. Unlike after the Star Ferry riots, the protests of 1967 did prompt the colonial administration to act. Over the next five years, numerous social and political reforms were introduced, building a substantial safety net for the poor, improving worker conditions, expanding public housing and providing free education to all primary-aged children.[23]

Education policy in Hong Kong had always been crafted with one eye towards the border. Around the time of the Chinese revolution of 1911, as a wave of nationalism swept through Hong Kong, colonial officials warned that schools could become 'breeding grounds for sedition'.[24] Rather than strip schools of their Chinese identity however, they instead sought to promote 'ultraconservative values and Confucian orthodoxy in the local school curriculum', which the British saw as a useful counterweight to the increasingly left-wing, revolutionary sentiment across the border.[25]

In the wake of the 1967 riots, education again became a key battleground, and a new 'special bureau' was established, dedicated to rooting out potential left-wing influence in schools.[26] Officials also looked for easy ways to gin up public support. One obvious concession was on the issue of language: since the establishment of the colony over a century before, English had been the only official language, and discontent had been growing in recent decades over the lack of legal recognition for Chinese and continued marginalization of Cantonese speakers in the courts and government.[27]

In 1972, members of the Legislative Council were permitted to use Cantonese for the first time. The historic moment, when it came, was during an otherwise stultifyingly dull debate on 18 October over modifications to the Peak Tram, the small train which ports passengers up and down a mountain on Hong Kong Island.[28] Chung Sze-yuen, a square-jawed former engineer, rose to note that 'for the first time in 130 years since Hong Kong was founded, a member of this council as from today may ... address the council in either the English or the Cantonese language'.

'With your permission, Sir, I would like to speak in Cantonese in support of this Peak Tramway (Amendment) Bill 1972', he said, and so he did. Responding for the government, Financial Secretary Charles Philip Haddon-Cave congratulated Chung for the 'historic privilege of being the first to speak in this Council in Cantonese'. He added that 'I have the honour of being the first to reply to such a speech, but I fear it will be in English'.

Two years later, in 1974, the Official Language Ordinance was passed, giving people the right to use Cantonese in court and mandating that all ordinances and laws be published in both English and Chinese. This law did not, however, define what 'Chinese' meant, a pattern that would be repeated in the 1980s when negotiations began for the city's handover to Chinese rule.

The deadline for that handover had been set almost a century before, in 1898, when, following the Qing's defeat at the hands of Japan, the British had moved to expand Hong Kong by acquiring a vast swath of land north of Kowloon. Unlike the previous treaties enforced on the Qing however, the agreement which created the New Territories was a lease, not an absolute cession. The period agreed upon was 99 years, effectively setting a countdown to the end of British control over Hong Kong, as it soon became apparent that the land acquired could not simply be sloughed off in future, nor could the city function without the New Territories. In December 1984, after months of secret negotiations, to which no Hong Kongers were party to or consulted about, British prime minister Margaret Thatcher and Chinese premier Zhao Ziyang signed an agreement that would end over 150 years of colonial rule; establishing a timeline for China to assume sovereignty over the city on 1 July 1997.[29]

As Hong Kong prepared to become part of China, experts from both sides of the border set about drafting the Basic Law, a document that would serve as the Chinese

Special Administrative Region's de facto constitution. Here again however, the wording chosen regarding official languages only referred to 'Chinese', making no reference to Cantonese or Putonghua.[30] In the words of one observer, 'The potentially contentious issue of the relationship between [Putonghua] and Cantonese in Hong Kong after 1997 was deftly sidestepped.'[31]

Ironically, as the city moved closer to Chinese rule, a new, distinct Hong Kong identity began to be established, one that was rooted in the Cantonese language. Through the 1970s and '80s, Cantonese-language cinema, particularly kung-fu movies, achieved global success, and many Chinese actors and directors strove to work in the Hong Kong film industry. Cantonese was the dominant language of pop music and television too, with Hong Kong broadcasters pumping out soap operas that were the K-dramas of their day, consumed throughout China and Asia, as Cantopop records sold out across the region. In publishing too, Cantonese was thriving, with newspapers and paperbacks published in Chinese characters written to match Cantonese vernacular.[32] Any competition from Putonghua-language movies during this era was scant, as widespread censorship and propaganda edicts meant that mainland Chinese cinema often had little appeal within China, let alone beyond its borders. 'As the curtain closed on Hong Kong's colonial tenancy in 1997,' linguists Robert Bauer and Paul Benedict wrote at the time, 'Cantonese stood at the peak of its prestige and at the same time on the threshold of a new historical period.'[33]

There was reason for concern about what the future might bring however. Hong Kongers were not blind to Beijing's language policies across the border, nor the effect they had had on non-Mandarin-speaking communities in recent decades.[34] In neighbouring Shenzhen, the tiny fishing village Deng Xiaoping had turned into China's first special economic zone in 1980, Cantonese-speaking locals had been swamped by new arrivals from across the country, and Putonghua had become the dominant language of the 'instant city'.[35] In Guangzhou, the city which gave Cantonese its English moniker, the language was also under threat: Bauer and Benedict reported struggling to find a young person with whom to speak that language in 1997, writing, 'they seem quite reluctant to do so and prefer to use Putonghua.'[36]

Not everyone in Hong Kong was opposed to such a linguistic change: Tin Siu-lam, a professor at the city's Lingnan University, argued as early as 1992 for the aggressive promotion of Putonghua. She also had harsh words for defenders of Cantonese.[37] 'If one insists that the position of Cantonese is above that of Putonghua, or even seeks to prove that Cantonese is a language independent of the Chinese language, then, in the narrow view, this does not conform to elementary linguistic knowledge; in the broad view, this does not accord with Hong Kong's interests or the nation's righteous cause,' Tin wrote.[38] Cantonese speakers, she argued, needed to get with the programme and accept that the language of government, business and education post-1997 would naturally be Putonghua, and forget any concerns that this could lead to the denuding of Cantonese.

Chapter 13

'Cantonese gives you nasal cancer'

Whenever she was away from home – at her all-girls boarding school in South Carolina, visiting family in far-flung Sichuan province, or anywhere else outside the sprawling metropolis where she had grown up – the sound of Shanghainese always brought Jenny Wu a sense of comfort, of belonging, even though she couldn't understand what anyone was saying. Growing up, Wu had always been jealous of those who spoke the local language.[1] It felt like they had a connection to the city's culture and history that she lacked, leaving her always on the outside. Her parents had moved to Shanghai soon after she was born, just two of the some seven million people who migrated to the metropolis in the early 2000s.[2] While neither of her parents' native tongue was Putonghua, that was the language they used at home, and it was also the language of Wu's school, and so it was the only language she learned. When she would return to her parents' hometowns for Lunar New Year or family get togethers, Wu would listen to her relatives speaking their native tongues, struggling to follow the conversation. In her mother's hometown of Chengdu, in Sichuan province, she could understand more, because her relatives spoke a Mandarin dialect, but even then, she could often only say a few words or phrases before breaking into standard Putonghua. With her friends, it was the only language they used, but Wu was aware that when the others went home, many spoke a different tongue with their parents. There was an unspoken ranking to these various languages. Shanghainese carried with it the romance and cool of the city's golden age, the 1920s, when it was the 'Paris of the East', home to gamblers and gangsters, Hollywood's foothold in China. Cantonese had a similar panache, associated with Hong Kong cinema and pop music. Some dialects, those with links to imperial history – such as that spoken in neighbouring Suzhou – were romantic, hinting at days spent in grand palaces and beautiful, ornate gardens. Others were best not mentioned, peasant tongues that exposed someone as a recent migrant, a country bumpkin gawping at the skyscrapers of the most futuristic city in China. Even these, though, had a personality that Wu felt her own mother tongue lacked. Her life was all in one language, Putonghua. Someday, all of China's might be.

Soon after the People's Republic officially adopted Putonghua as the national language, in 1956, it began promoting the new standard tongue around the country. Putonghua was made the mandatory medium of education for schools throughout China, other than in 'autonomous' minority areas. Slogans such as 'love the national flag, sing the national anthem, and speak Putonghua' proliferated, and it was made clear that to be a citizen of the New China was to be a Putonghua speaker. In 1982, an update to the constitution, while nominally protecting the use of other languages, also made Putonghua's primacy official, with a new Article 19 reading 'the State promotes the nationwide use of Putonghua (common speech based on Beijing pronunciation)'.[3]

Jenny Wu is part of the Putonghua generation, those children born after the mass migrations that accompanied the economic boom beginning in the 1980s, when their parents left hometowns and home languages for the big cities, which have increasingly become Putonghua outposts amid a sea of other languages, dramatically changing China's linguistic map. Of the three largest cities outside traditional Mandarin-speaking areas – Shanghai, Guangzhou and Shenzhen – all are either already, or well on the way to becoming, majority Putonghua-speaking.[4,5] In Shanghai, some 50 per cent of the population, around ten million people, claimed to speak the local language in 2010, but when researchers looked into the matter, they found the actual rate of fluency was far, far lower, with only a tiny percentage of mostly older residents actually able to speak fluent Shanghainese.[6] According to researcher Fang Xu, herself a native Shanghainese speaker, there has been a 'rapid language shift taking place since the end of the twentieth century, when Shanghai absorbed astonishing amounts of foreign direct investment, and allowed in millions of internal migrants who do not speak the local lingua franca, but rather the vastly different Putonghua Mandarin Chinese'.[7]

'In the current global Shanghai, one rarely hears the Shanghai dialect in public,' Xu writes. Her assessment is backed up by reports in state media, though these must be taken with a pinch of salt, given their potential bias towards promoting the supposedly inevitable dominance of Putonghua. 'I have seen parents ask questions in Shanghai dialect while their kids respond in Putonghua,' one parent told a Shanghai-based newspaper. 'In the end, both switched to speaking Putonghua for convenience.'[8] Those children could understand Shanghainese, but lacked enough of a grasp on the language to respond.[9] As they become adults, it's unlikely they will pass the language on to their own kids, who, with schools using Putonghua alone, will have no other means of learning Shanghainese.[10,11] The language is already seen as a bygone artefact to some: when the local government, responding to concerns about its survival, agreed to add announcements in Shanghainese to public transport (after Putonghua and English) there was pushback from some residents. 'A lot of people from other cities criticised this action,' Wu said, 'because they viewed it as an exclusion of those who can't understand Shanghainese, instead of as preservation of the dialect.' Today, announcements in Shanghainese are only made on buses and one subway line, out of eighteen in total.[12]

In Shenzhen, across the border from Hong Kong, the situation is even more acute, and Putonghua is by far the dominant language, despite the city being in the centre of the traditional Cantonese heartland. With hundreds of thousands of migrants pouring in from across China, Shenzhen was the type of city the national lingua franca was designed for, one that appears to buttress official arguments in favour of a state-promoted standard language. It was perhaps inevitable that it would undergo a linguistic transformation therefore; that the same situation would play out 8 kilometres to the north, in Guangzhou, was anything but. That city's fate is due far more to public policy than to the inexorable momentum of migration.

In 1990, apparently frustrated at the lack of progress Putonghua was making in these areas, the national government identified both Guangdong and Shanghai as in need of 'extra effort' in promoting the national tongue.[13] Two years later, authorities in Guangdong issued a directive making Putonghua the province's official language, a technically redundant move that nevertheless heralded a raft of policies further marginalizing Cantonese. New Putonghua tests were introduced for teachers and other public sector employees, who faced being sacked if they weren't up to scratch, and broadcasting in Cantonese was massively scaled back.[14]

By the turn of the millennium, it would have been difficult to find someone in Guangzhou who did not speak at least some Putonghua, while any person born after 1980 was likely to be fluent. On paper, the government's drive to promote Putonghua, even in one of the country's most recalcitrant regions, was successful. It had transformed Guangdong from an overwhelmingly Cantonese-speaking region to a bilingual Putonghua–Cantonese province, where the former language was in the ascent. Only the existence of Hong Kong, which, outside of the national government's direct control, had continued to pump out movies, literature and music in Cantonese, keeping its cultural cache high, likely prevented the language from entering the same spiral of decline as other tongues, such as Shanghainese. That consecutive provincial and national governments have continued to actively push Guangdong towards this fate suggests an agenda that goes far beyond simply promoting Putonghua. The constant chipping away at Cantonese, the hostility towards bilingualism, is indicative of the deep suspicion those in power have towards the language and the 'localism' and 'feudal' attitudes it might cultivate. Just as with Tibetan or Uyghur languages, which have been heavily suppressed in recent decades, Cantonese connects a speaker with an identity, history and culture that is outside the government's control, and is therefore seen as a potential threat to the Communist Party's grip on power.

As Putonghua's position in Guangdong has improved, the government has actually become more aggressive in its denuding of Cantonese, not less. This has not gone unopposed. As people have become more aware of the intention to wipe the language out, they have begun organizing and demonstrating in its defence. In 2010, mass

protests erupted in Guangzhou over a proposal for the city's main television channel
– the last redoubt of public Cantonese broadcasting – to switch to Putonghua.[15] The
level of resistance and anger took officials by surprise, and one local politician told
state media that promoting Putonghua 'does not mean Guangzhou has to eliminate
its dialect. The city government has never had such a plan to abandon or weaken
Cantonese.' Two years later however, that was exactly what the Guangdong authorities
did, introducing new regulations mandating that Putonghua alone was to be used
by government employees, schools and broadcasters, effectively banning Cantonese
from most public spheres.[16] The protests likely only emboldened the government to
move more forcefully against Cantonese, having demonstrated exactly the type of
independent identity that they were trying to stamp out in the first place. Propaganda
authorities have also launched a campaign against the language, demeaning it as a
'dialect' or 'regional tongue' and accusing its proponents of standing in the way of
progress or even seeking to break up the country. In Guangzhou, posters encouraging
the use of Putonghua bore the slogan 'use civilised language – Be a civilised person'.[17]
Kong Qingdong, a jingoistic Chinese academic who claims to be descended from
Confucius and is known for his bombastic outbursts on national TV, publicly mocked
the sound of Cantonese, and called those who refuse to speak Putonghua 'bastards'.[18]
In the most outlandish example, state media even reported on a study that was claimed
to show that speaking Cantonese could 'cause nasal cancer'.[19] The researchers involved
were actually looking into whether foods preferred in Cantonese-speaking regions
could result in higher frequencies of certain types of cancer. That thesis, like the
language link, was also later debunked.

These campaigns have had an effect, particularly on those of Jenny Wu's generation,
who have always lived in a Putonghua society, with Cantonese only spoken at home or
heard in Hong Kong movies. 'The schools and the government have been discouraging
Cantonese in the community for a long while,' one Guangzhou parent told a newspaper
in 2018. 'Most kids nowadays don't like speaking Cantonese even though they were
born and are growing up here.'[20] Why would they? Study after study has shown the
effects on a language when its cultural cache is denuded, and it is confined to the home,
spoken only by parents and elderly relatives. While Hong Kong artists and musicians
have continued to put out work in Cantonese, for the Putonghua generation, whatever
pop culture the city creates has been dwarfed by the behemoths of Mando-pop and
Putonghua-language television.

Online too, they are increasingly living in a Putonghua world. Linguist Gretchen
McCulloch has argued that 'the internet and mobile devices have brought us an
explosion of writing by normal people [and] writing has become a vital, conversational
part of our ordinary lives',[21] but for Cantonese speakers in mainland China, this has
become yet another sphere in which their native tongue is being replaced by Putonghua.

Pinyin, as well as being a medium for learning Chinese characters, is also by far the
most common input method for writing them on electronic devices (users type Pinyin
on a Latin-based keyboard, and the text is converted into Chinese characters on the

screen). So Cantonese-speaking kids, when they're texting with friends, are mostly doing so in Putonghua via Pinyin. What they're reading, too, is closer to Putonghua than any other Chinese language. While written Chinese can be read in any tongue, the development of the modern written language has meant it is far closer, grammatically and in vocabulary, to Putonghua. In Hong Kong, kids read in Cantonese, but to do so they use a more formal version of the language, Modern Standard Chinese, which differs to that spoken outside the classroom. This is similar to the diglossia in many Arabic-speaking countries, where the high version of the language on paper can differ greatly from that of the streets. For example, while the phrase 'she is my sister' is written in Modern Standard Chinese following Putonghua grammar, the same sentence spoken in vernacular Cantonese uses a completely different pronoun for 'she', a different verb for 'is' and a different noun for 'my sister'. The word for 'I' is the only similarity between the phrases. Written vernacular Cantonese is used in Hong Kong in some areas, such as online and in tabloid newspapers, with the text more closely resembling what is spoken thanks to the adoption of archaic characters not used for writing Putonghua, co-opting of homonyms and the occasional Latin letter. Cantonese speakers across the border are mostly cut off from this however, thanks both to the Great Firewall of China, the country's vast online censorship apparatus – those newspapers using vernacular Cantonese tend to be anti-government publications – and that Hong Kong uses traditional characters, which can be a stumbling block for some more used to the simplified system introduced in the PRC in 1956.

Even new forms of entertainment, less restricted than state-run TV or media, have limitations on language. In early 2020, Cantonese users on Douyin, the Chinese version of video sharing app TikTok, were suspended and asked to 'please speak Putonghua' because the company's moderators, largely based in Beijing, could not understand enough Cantonese to police the platform to the degree required by Chinese law.[22] Instead of finding Cantonese-speaking censors, the company decided it was easier to just force users to all speak Putonghua.[23] Some Cantonese creators online have found more followers outside of Guangdong than within the language's home region. Heyson, a YouTuber who makes content about Cantonese, said he has been contacted by teachers elsewhere in China who use his videos to help teach the language to their students. With no political concerns or threat that it could challenge Putonghua, these schools outside of the Cantonese heartland are free to experiment with the language, while in Heyson's native Guangzhou, Cantonese is barely heard in schools. 'Seeing the next generation in Guangdong, I feel hopeless,' the YouTuber said in July 2020. 'But I do see some hope in other places where people are learning Cantonese.'[24]

The Putonghua generation in Guangdong are increasingly facing a situation like that of children born in the Cantonese diaspora. While they may be able to speak the language with their parents, or at least understand what is being said to them; like Jenny Wu's parents, they are less likely to pass it on to their own kids, using instead the dominant national language, be it Putonghua in China or English in countries like Canada and the United States.

Chapter 14
Sounds of separatism

Inside the tiny antechamber to the Legislative Council, Hong Kong's parliament, the air is hot and muggy. What little oxygen remains is sucked up by the mass of people crammed into the tight space. The lingering smell of pepper spray and sudden surges forward by the crowd intermittently prompt me to put on my gas mask, pulling it up and over my face, the rubber squeaking and yanking my hair as I tighten the straps. Minutes later, the feared for tear gas having failed to arrive, I take it off, dripping with sweat, unable to bear the additional limits on my breathing, slightly disgusted at the lack of nerve I displayed. I repeat this process three more times as the clang of metal on metal and smashing glass continues around me. It is 1 July 2019. Dozens of protesters, helmets on heads, faces covered, hands inside heavy gloves, arms wrapped in cling film to protect against pepper spray, are attempting to force open a large metal shutter that bars the way into LegCo. Earlier, they broke through the reinforced glass that led into the tiny antechamber from the square outside, where thousands more protesters, having spent the day besieging the building, wait to storm it.

Then, suddenly, a gust of cool air. Blessed relief. The protesters at the front have managed to break through part of the shutter, bending a corner upwards, allowing the climate controlled air inside the building to seep out into the antechamber. Earlier breaches – small holes smashed in reinforced windows elsewhere on the building – had been met from inside with blasts of pepper spray and yelled demands to get back, but now, here, there is nothing. It takes almost another hour to find out why, as the shutter is finally forced up and open, and protesters pour into the legislature. The police have left, surrendering the building – intentionally some will say later – to the destruction to come.

LegCo sits overlooking Victoria Harbour, with Hong Kong's financial district to its rear and the mass of the population, across the water in Kowloon and the New Territories, in front. It forms part of the Central Government Complex, a collection of glass and chrome buildings of seemingly random heights and shapes that were, nevertheless, planned, with the main office block, a twenty-six-storey building which houses the city's vast civil service and is shaped like a lowercase n, straddling Tamar

Park. That a public park runs through the complex is a testament to the original concept of it as an open and welcoming space for the city's residents, one that consecutive administrations have, since the complex opened in 2011, slowly chipped away at, frustrated at the public's ability to confront them at their doorstep. Despite these rollbacks however, the complex remains difficult to fortify, bordered both by the park and three roads, including a major highway.

On 12 June, lawmakers had been due to hold a second reading of an extradition bill with China. The proposed law was hugely controversial; many feared it could lead to activists being ferried across the border to face prosecution, and days earlier, hundreds of thousands had marched to demand it be shelved. Despite the widespread opposition to the bill, police seemed taken by surprise when, in the middle of morning rush hour, protesters seized the roads around LegCo. I was standing outside on an upper level of the complex, waiting for the inevitable scuffle as lawmakers attempted to enter past crowds of protesters, when, at 8 am, small groups began running into Harcourt Road, an eight-lane highway, dragging with them barriers and fencing that police had helpfully erected around the complex. Thousands of protesters soon flooded Harcourt and the other streets around the complex, cutting it off to traffic and lawmakers alike. By 11 am, the second reading had been called off, and protesters declared victory, with many hailing the start of a second Umbrella Movement, the pro-democracy demonstrations that saw parts of the city occupied by protest camps for months in 2014, which also began with an occupation in the LegCo area.

A lengthy sit-in seemed inevitable, but hours later police initiated a major clearance operation, firing tear gas into the crowd and launching baton charges to force them away from the complex. The roads around LegCo quickly became a battleground, as protesters continued to fight with police, throwing bricks, bottles and helmets, and turning barricades into makeshift battering rams to charge into police lines. More police reinforcements poured in, and they stepped up the use of tear gas, along with rubber bullets, pushing the crowd back, the fight turned into a rear-guard action as police pursued the remnants of the initial protest into the city.

The violence that day, initiated to an extent by the protesters but escalated massively by police, changed the tone of the protests, and expanded their demands. What had been a largely peaceful movement to block the extradition bill, similar in tone and tactics to a successful effort in 2003 to stymie the passage of an anti-sedition law, sprawled. Officially, the movement adopted five demands: drop the bill, reverse a categorization of the 12 June protest as a 'riot', launch an independent inquiry into police brutality, grant amnesty to arrested protesters, and universal suffrage for the election of the chief executive and LegCo. In reality, the protests were an expression of something even larger, of years of growing frustration and anger at the direction the city was headed under Chinese rule, the fear that Hong Kong was growing more authoritarian, not more democratic, as promised by its constitution, which set various deadlines for political reform, all of which were ignored by the government. If 12 June was an escalation in police tactics, with major ramifications, 1 July and the storming of LegCo was the counterpunch by the protesters, with its own unforeseen consequences.

I step under the wrecked folds of the shutter in a slight daze, and look around at an environment both familiar and alien. While I've been to LegCo many times before, the context is so different that at first, nothing is recognizable, like returning to school long after graduation. The protesters have no such hesitation. Around me is an orgy of destruction. They had been pounding at the doors of the building for hours in the heat and noise and tear gas, and the adrenaline and pent up aggression are now running free. One man near me picks up a metal pole from the floor and begins striking television screens set into the wall, but they are protected by reinforced glass that does not even chip as a result of his ministrations, and he quickly moves on, sheepish behind his mask and goggles. Others find easier things to break: glass doors leading to a seating area, a display of various pamphlets, a reception desk, throwing the contents of its drawers over the floor. I have been on my feet for hours, running with the crowd, dodging tear gas, standing and waiting for something to happen, and I take a moment to sit on the desk, watching the chaos and stealing sips of water from a bottle stuffed into a pocket on the side of my backpack. My gas mask hangs off my arm, ready to be thrust onto my face once again if the police storm the building. While I'm sitting, the reception area less crowded as the invaders spread through the building, a protester comes up to the desk and begins another ransacking of its contents. He finds scissors and begins cutting any wires or cables in sight, including one that gives off a loud bang and sparks as the metal meets the electricity within. Thankfully, he stops after this.

I proceed up two sets of escalators, past a colleague on the phone to our bureau. He is white, middle aged, his face uncovered. He looks out of place, but utterly calm. Later, a photo of him, taken around the time I pass, will be used to claim that CIA agents were on the ground coordinating the protests. The photo is carefully cropped above the word 'PRESS' emblazoned across his chest. On an upper floor, I enter the legislative chamber itself. The room is seething with people, as protesters spray slogans on the wall and look for things to break. A large seal showing the Hong Kong flag behind the speaker's podium has been defaced; it will become a symbol for those who hate the protests. There are few other satisfying targets in the room, it is mainly a collection of seats, most filled with journalists taking a break, helmets on desks, using the building's Wi-Fi to file updates. By now, several legislators, sympathetic to the cause but not the destruction, have arrived, and they persuade, beg, the protesters not to do more damage. They are only somewhat successful. Later some protesters, keyboard warriors rather than those here now, will point to this limited restraint as a sign that the night's events were strategic, planned, not an explosion of angry chaos.

The few protesters who remain in the legislative chamber have gathered around the speaker's table, where they have erected a display of protest signs, along with large portraits of the city's leader, and the two officials responsible for the proposed extradition law. One protester takes off his mask. His name is Leung Kai-ping. He does not want to hide his identity anymore. 'I took off my mask because I want to let everyone know that we Hong Kongers have nothing more to lose,' he tells the room, speaking in Cantonese, as reporters frantically snap photos. 'The more people here, the safer we are. Let's stay and occupy the chamber, we can't lose anymore.' Leung is twenty-five, handsome, with short dark hair and skinny arms, which he thrusts into the air to emphasize his point. A surgical mask is slung under his chin, atop his head is a yellow builder's helmet. He is instantly iconic. Later he will flee to the United States.

Leung is not alone in calling for an occupation, but as police announce their intention to retake LegCo, sentiment among the protesters changes – they have no leaders, decisions are made by popular will, for bad or worse – and they flee the building. Those who disagree, who want to stay, are forcibly carried out by their fellows. I take one final tour of the building as it empties, before following the last of the protesters out onto a darkened side street. By the time I emerge, the police have arrived. There are pops of tear gas canisters going off, and clouds of white, choking smoke rise, illuminated by street lights. The protesters have little fight left in them though, and nothing to defend any longer, so they retreat easily enough, fleeing onto Harcourt Road, the highway they occupied on 12 June, as police march across debris left by the hours-long siege. I stay to watch the police advance, protected by my fluorescent press vest, my gas mask on and helmet strapped tightly to my head. Eventually, I decide the night is over. I begin walking out of the protest area, looking for a road unaffected by the chaos from which I can call a cab. It's approaching 1 am. As I'm leaving, I come across the portrait of former Legislative Council president Jasper Tsang, which had been pulled from its frame inside the building and carried here. It's bent in half, abandoned on the street next to the remnants of a barricade. I snap a photo. Tsang was born in Guangdong in 1947, shortly before his family moved to Hong Kong. As a university student in 1967 he took part in the Communist-backed riots that were put down by the British army.[1] Later, he cofounded the Democratic Alliance for the Betterment and Progress of Hong Kong, the city's largest pro-Beijing political party. Despite this, he was seen as a moderate figure, well liked even by many among the democratic opposition. When he announced plans to retire from the legislature, it was hoped that he would stand to become the city's leader, that Beijing might choose a man who would be willing to stand up to his bosses. He decided not to run. The woman who got the job, Carrie Lam, spearheaded the extradition bill.

While they may not have been at the forefront of the minds of those who stormed the Legislative Council, concerns about Cantonese were one of many underlying issues and grievances fuelling the 2019 protest movement. Like the tiny screw that wiggles loose and causes a rocket to explode, the extradition bill had unleashed all this pent up energy that would eventually see the city tear itself apart. From housing policy to growing inequality, everything came back, eventually, to the issue of democracy, to the lack of trust in leaders who were, by and large, chosen by Beijing. The Hong Kong chief executive is appointed by a pro-Beijing committee representing less than 0.1 per cent of the city, while around half of seats in the legislature were for so-called functional constituencies, industry and business groups that invariably favoured Beijing; some candidates regularly ran unopposed. The language issue, while it might have seemed detached from the wider fight for democracy, was part and parcel with this lack of representation. The city's constitution stated only that 'both the Chinese and English languages are to be official languages',[2] and while in practice this generally meant trilingualism in English, Putonghua and Cantonese, there was no legal protection for the latter tongue, and many feared that it was being gradually superseded by Putonghua, especially in schools. Government reassurances to the contrary meant nothing when trust in officials was so low, and proponents of Cantonese could do little to protect the language apart from lobby lawmakers, the majority of whom were dependent on Beijing for their positions and unwilling to go against central government policy.

'In many ways, Hong Kong is just like a foster child who was raised by a white family and, without his consent, returned to his Chinese biological parents,' activist Joshua Wong wrote in 2019. 'Mother and son have very little in common, from language and customs to the way they view their government. The more the child is forced to show affection and gratitude toward his long-lost mother, the more he resists. He feels lost, abandoned and alone.'[3]

As the protests continued that summer, they eclipsed the 2014 Umbrella Movement – previously the largest pro-democracy protests in Hong Kong's history – in both size and importance, and consumed opposition politics from the inside out, leaving many long-term pro-democracy figures peripheral to the new, mostly young, leaderless movement. At the same time, the issue of language took on increasing importance, characterizing both the protests themselves and those they were in opposition to. Cantonese, shouted from the streets or daubed across signs and buildings, often gloriously profane and layered with innuendo, became a means of both generating solidarity and differentiating the city from Putonghua-speaking China.

When Hong Kong was handed over from British to Chinese rule in 1997, though Cantonese was at the height of its cultural prestige internationally, there were soon calls to switch the language of education to Putonghua. These were made both on economic grounds, given the ballooning of the Chinese economy as the country became the world's second superpower, and educational, with some arguing that, since the written language used in classes, Modern Standard Chinese (MSC), was closer to Putonghua in grammar and vocabulary, it made more sense to teach it in that tongue. Proponents claimed that students performed better when Putonghua is used, but defenders of Cantonese argue the data does not bear this out, and that statistics which do appear to favour Putonghua-medium schools are reflective of the greater funding and support they receive as a result of switching languages.[4,5] Switching to Putonghua has been heavily promoted by the education bureau, responding to national rather than local-level priorities.[6] In 2012, Putonghua overtook English as the second most widely spoken language in Hong Kong,[7] and two years later, a survey found that some

70 per cent of primary schools and 40 per cent of secondary schools had switched to using Putonghua for teaching the Chinese language, though Cantonese remained the language used to teach other subjects.[8] In 2014, the bureau sparked outrage when it published an article on the subject which described Cantonese as 'a Chinese dialect which is not a statutory language'.[9] While officials apologized for the gaffe, it confirmed for many that government policy was becoming increasingly slanted in favour of Putonghua. A similar attitude was seen in a bizarre promotional video put out by the bureau, in which two young children find themselves at home during a robbery and use 'Putonghua knowledge to fight against the gangsters with wisdom and bravery'.[10] The gangsters, of course, speak Cantonese.[11] In 2018, the bureau again courted controversy by quoting in a pamphlet on medium of instruction a mainland Chinese scholar arguing that Cantonese was a 'dialect' and therefore could not be considered someone's mother tongue.[12] Asked that year about tension with Putonghua, Chief Executive Carrie Lam said that 'we are speaking Cantonese every day, so this is a non-issue'. Pushed by a reporter to say what her native language was, she responded, 'Sorry, I don't answer silly questions.'[13]

The figures would seem to support Lam's dismissal of the issue. Statistically, Cantonese in Hong Kong is in good health. In 1996, the year before the city was handed over from British to Chinese rule, 88.7 per cent of people said they spoke Cantonese at home.[14] At the last census, in 2016, that figure had risen to 88.9 per cent.[15] By comparison, the number of native Putonghua speakers in the city stood at just 1.9 per cent of the population, less than English, which had almost a century as Hong Kong's sole official language. There are some 6.2 million native Cantonese speakers in Hong Kong, and tens of millions more in the wider Cantonese diaspora, a position that would be envied by speakers of most languages, let alone those considered endangered. And yet, since the transition to Chinese rule in 1997, concerns around its future have dogged Cantonese, with a popular perception that the language is headed for terminal decline. 'How can a language appear robust on paper, yet inspire death knells from the general public?' one writer asked in 2017, in a piece titled, 'Cantonese isn't dead yet, so stop writing its eulogy.'[16]

As the situation in Guangdong has demonstrated however, there is reason to be concerned. Language decline happens very quickly, in a generation or two, and can be exceptionally hard to stop once the process is underway. Moreover, the factors which lead to this decline are largely out of the hands of most speakers. In a society like Hong Kong, which does not elect its leaders, the ability to push back against government policy is limited.

In June 2020, I met Andrew Chan, chairman of Societas Linguistica Hongkongensis, which advocates in favour of Cantonese, inside a cluttered office shared with a branch of the pro-democracy Civic Party. Chan founded the group in 2013, by which point a majority of primary schools had shifted to using Putonghua as the medium of instruction.[17] Chan saw the motivation for this as political, and was concerned by what he felt was a widespread complacency among Cantonese speakers in Hong Kong about the state of the language, despite the rapid transformation that Guangdong was undergoing from a Cantonese-speaking province to a Putonghua one.

'I met with people in Guangzhou and they told me that it can change very quickly, that language can be replaced very quickly,' Chan said. 'They started in the kindergartens, telling children that if you want to be civilised, you have to speak in Mandarin, and that Cantonese is an uncivilised language.'

Chan had experienced personally how language politics could become heated. In 2018, then a fifth-year student of traditional Chinese medicine, Chan had been interning at a hospital in Guangzhou, when he had to rush back to Hong Kong.[18] Chinese state media had picked up on a video of Chan taking part in a protest at Baptist University, in opposition to the Hong Kong school's requirement that all students pass a Putonghua proficiency test to graduate.[19] Chan and another student, Lau Tsz-kei, were eventually suspended over the protests, during which they got into a shouting match with university staff.[20]

Chinese media accused those objecting to the Putonghua test of being pro-Hong Kong independence, and encouraged the school to expel them.[21] One nationalist website had singled out Chan and accused him of being 'anti-China', combing through his Facebook to find alleged evidence of anti-government or pro-independence sentiment.[22] Soon, Chan was receiving death threats online, and details about his internship were posted on social media. On Tianya, a popular forum, he was called a 'comrade of Joshua Wong', the prominent pro-democracy activist, and a 'Baptist University anti-Mandarin thug'.[23]

This scandal was reflective of a growing politicization of the language debate on both sides of the border. What once would have been a spat between university administrators and students had been subsumed by the wider debate around Hong Kong's position within China, and increasing paranoia in Beijing over support for independence in the city. Regina Ip, a pro-government lawmaker who is nevertheless critical of Hong Kong's language policy, noted in 2018 that even distinguishing Cantonese and Putonghua as separate languages 'while technically justifiable … would no doubt be deemed unacceptable by those cagey about the advocacy of Hong Kong as a separate political entity'.[24]

With the outbreak of the protests in 2019, the role of Cantonese in fostering a Hong Kong identity in opposition to China was once again thrust to the forefront. 'Cantonese is a language of the resistance,' Lian-Hee Wee, a professor at Hong Kong Baptist University who studies Cantonese phonology, said at the time. 'Movements like this have the side effect of revitalising the language because we suddenly need the language to express the intensity of emotions.'[25]

Slogans, posters, graffiti and even a de facto Hong Kong national anthem proliferated,[26] all drawing on a deep well of Cantonese idioms, puns and profanity, much of which is unintelligible to Putonghua speakers. Mary Hui, a young Hong Kong journalist, wrote that 'Cantonese is closely connected with the protests' spirit of reclaiming and restoring'.[27] Just as protesters wanted to reclaim the city itself for the people, they also re-appropriated insults thrown at them, such as when a police officer was videoed yelling 'jih yàuh hāi' or 'liberal cunt' at a protester. As the footage went viral, a Chinglish translation, 'Freedom Hi' ('jih yàuh' can mean freedom or liberty) quickly became popular among protesters, seen on t-shirts and phone cases.

'Wordplay and puns strip the language down to its constituent parts (its basic tones), then reformulate them into a new language of protest,' Hui wrote. 'Protesters take ownership of the language and the message. They even create new composite characters.'

Both sides recognized the role Cantonese was playing in the protests, with signs popping up saying 'support Cantonese, Hong Kong people', and hostility to the language growing in China. One anchor for Chinese state TV, Liu Xin, complained online that while she was reporting on the protests in Hong Kong, a security guard she asked for directions 'couldn't understand Chinese', by which she meant Putonghua. 'I had to [use] English,' Liu said. 'Twenty-two years after handover, this is not what it should be. "One Country, Two Systems" doesn't mean one can live in the past.'[28] Responding to her on Twitter, one Chinese language scholar wrote that 'this has been the position on all non-Mandarin languages for decades: people's mother tongues are "backwards," "uncivilised," "low-quality," and so on. What makes this case special is that the coloniser had to address the colonised in the language of a different coloniser.'[29]

When users on LIHKG, the largest anti-government forum in Hong Kong, became worried that Putonghua-speaking state security agents were attempting to spy on them, they took linguistic experimentation a step further, abandoning Chinese altogether to write Cantonese in Latin characters, creating posts that were completely unintelligible to anyone not completely fluent in the language, including Hong Kong-specific slang.[30] The interspersal of Latin and Chinese characters in art, as well as the mixing of Cantonese with English, also became a key emblem of the protests, evidence of the city's multicultural, outward-looking personality, in contrast to the nationalistic monoculture that many felt China was becoming.[31]

Inevitably, this pro-Cantonese attitude also carried with it an undercurrent of hostility towards Putonghua, which could sometimes turn ugly. Several men were accosted and assaulted by protesters, accused of being agents of Chinese security simply based on the fact they were Putonghua-speaking, or spoke Cantonese with a mainland accent. Restaurants sympathetic to the protests began refusing to take orders in Putonghua, saying the establishments were for 'Hong Kongers only'.[32] This was self-defeating for many reasons, not least, as some pointed out, that the city's leader Carrie Lam and her entire cabinet spoke Cantonese, and were from Hong Kong, meaning they were in theory welcome at these avowedly anti-government businesses. The bigotry against Chinese immigrants, while ugly enough on its own, was also particularly bizarre given that several prominent protest figures, including Edward Leung, the imprisoned pro-independence leader who coined the slogan 'liberate Hong Kong, the revolution of our times', and Nathan Law, who co-founded the political party Demosisto with Joshua Wong, were born in China. While many Chinese immigrants to the city were pro-government, others, including students, also took part in the protests, seeing in them a chance to protect what drew them to Hong Kong in the first place.

One protester I interviewed several times, who I will call Daniel, was born in a city in Guangdong. Like Jenny Wu, he was part of the Putonghua generation, whose education was wholly in that language, only using his parents' native Cantonese at home. Daniel came to Hong Kong at nineteen, to study at one of the city's universities, where he became increasingly involved in politics. In 2019, he took part in the anti-extradition bill marches and the LegCo siege, and grew increasingly radical, shifting from being a peaceful protester to what Hong Kongers called a 'frontliner', those who regularly clashed with police, dodging tear gas and rubber bullets, and responding with petrol bombs and rocks. Daniel spoke coldly of the logic of violence, saying that only escalation could make the government listen to the protesters' demands.

While he was born in China and bilingual in Putonghua and Cantonese, he was not particularly disturbed by the hostility towards Chinese migrants among some strands of the protest movement. For Daniel, what mattered was how you positioned yourself with regard to the movement, which was intimately connected with the language. 'Putonghua is not Hong Kong's culture,' he said. 'The first step is to use Cantonese to identify with Hong Kong people, but this is not just about language or nationality, it's also about the value system. Someone can be born in Hong Kong and spend their whole life living in Hong Kong, and yet think like a mainlander. Or they can be a non-Hong Kong permanent resident yet totally support Hong Kong's value system.'

That value system took another major blow in 2020, when, in response to the protests the previous year, the Chinese government announced it was imposing a new security law on the city. The law, which banned the loosely defined crimes of sedition, secession and collusion with foreign forces, was written behind closed doors in Beijing, and promulgated in Hong Kong without the approval or consultation of the city's legislature. Within hours of its passage, multiple political parties disbanded, and some anti-government figures began fleeing the city. Online, self-censorship was widespread, as people deleted social media profiles full of anti-government invective, and scrubbed photos of protests. Shops and businesses previously covered in anti-government paraphernalia, themselves examples of Cantonese-language resistance, pulled their displays down, or replaced them with blank sheets of paper.

While the legislation was openly geared towards stemming the protests, which prior to its passage had been ramping back up, following a break forced by the coronavirus pandemic, the scope of the security law was vast. It included an obligation for the city's government to 'promote national security education in schools and universities',[33] and officials made clear that an overhaul of the city's education system was on the cards, pro-Beijing lawmakers long having blamed Hong Kong's teachers for cultivating a generation of anti-China youth.

What this will mean for Cantonese remains to be seen, but the pattern that China has established in other territories on its periphery is not an encouraging one. As Putonghua is increasingly promoted by the government, it seems likely that any defence of Cantonese will be seen as akin to promoting Hong Kong independence, now illegal under the new security law. Just as language advocates in China have been charged with secession and subversion, Cantonese defenders could find themselves locked up. In both Xinjiang and Tibet, as well as throughout China proper, the government has seen promoting Putonghua as a key tool for binding the country together and fostering a sense of national identity. Almost everywhere, this has been at the expense of local languages, and there seems to be no reason to assume Cantonese will be any different. Speaking in mid-2020, Dominic Lee, a young pro-government politician who had built a substantial following online for his openly nationalistic, anti-protester rhetoric, dismissed concerns about Putonghua replacing Cantonese. 'Many trends and cultures come and go,' he told an interviewer. 'Just as there is no Qing Dynasty culture today, things will change.'[34]

Much of this book has focused on the resurgence of languages once oppressed and marginalized. Cantonese is at the opposite end of this cycle. To talk of the potential loss of a language with millions of speakers may seem hyperbolic, but the rapid decline of languages across China since the rise of Putonghua does not leave room for complacency. While the large diaspora community will undoubtedly help preserve the language even if it is suppressed in Hong Kong, losing the city as a hub of Cantonese culture and literature will take a major toll, as diaspora speakers face their own pressures to assimilate, particularly in English-speaking countries. Cantonese is facing rough decades ahead, and its speakers may find themselves fighting for the survival of their language sooner than they expect.

At the height of the 2019 protests, a popular meme in Hong Kong, sprayed on walls and shared on social media, looked to China's other border regions for a warning of what might be to come. In its simplest form, it read '1949 Xinjiang, 1951 Tibet, 2019 Hong Kong', referring to the years those respective places had come under Beijing's full control. While Hong Kong has experienced nowhere near the levels of oppression that Xinjiang or Tibet have, the latter region in particular is instructive in how future language policies may play out in Hong Kong, as use of Cantonese is increasingly politicized and suppressed. Unfortunately however, the warnings from Tibet for Cantonese advocates are dire ones.

Chapter 15
Language plateau

Chen Zuoru woke up early, as he did almost every day in 2017, leaving the house while it was still dark. Winter on the Tibetan plateau is bitterly cold, the temperature far below freezing. Icicles form wherever there is a drip, and snow on the ground crunches beneath every step, or sends walkers slipping and sliding. As Chen stepped outside, the biting wind turned any uncovered patch of skin red, and he felt his heart rate increase and his breathing growing more laboured, the lack of oxygen making a short walk seem like an arduous hike. Of all the hardships of life on the plateau, altitude sickness was the worst, bringing with it headaches, dizziness, and a nausea that could be crippling, sapping the spirit and leaving the sufferer trapped in bed, unable to do anything but stare blankly at the ceiling and try not to vomit. Chen had been through it several times himself, but it did not dissuade him from his task. He had a calling.

'To walk on the roof of the world is a dream that grew from my heart,' he wrote in his journal. 'No one can shake my footsteps, and children will always be my highest purpose.'[1]

Chen had arrived in Tibet a year earlier, one of a cohort of around eight hundred teachers from the Chinese interior, sent to the plateau to provide 'educational aid' to one of the country's poorest, least literate territories.[2] Like his fellows, most of whom were in their forties, born during a period when Tibet was seen as both impossibly remote and embarrassingly backward, Chen regarded his mission as a civilizing one, that required considerable personal sacrifice but brought with it rewards in 'the innocent eyes and desire for knowledge of the Tibetan children'.[3] The programme had launched in 2016, following a speech by Chinese president Xi Jinping, in which he said that 'changing the appearance of Tibet and Tibetan-inhabited areas fundamentally depends on education'.[4] The new 'group form' educational aid system replaced a hodgepodge of other, mostly short-term, volunteer-based programmes, with a comprehensive, three-year placement, designed to attract some of China's best teachers and create in their new students 'patriotic builders and successors of the nation and the Chinese Communist Party for the socialist project'. Authorities offered higher wages and benefits to those teachers who signed up – overwhelmingly Han Chinese men from the wealthy east –

and state media hailed the 'sacrifice' of those that did, emphasizing the difficulties of working in remote parts of the plateau, wracked by altitude sickness, far from their families.[5] There was even a song. 'Big Sisters Whose Husbands Are Aiding Tibet' told the story of a wife left behind in the east, who overcomes her desire to keep her partner home by embracing the value of his work 'for ethnic unity' and 'happiness for the great [Chinese] family'.

The biggest problem Chen and his fellow teachers faced was that parachuting a qualified educator in from the big city didn't magically improve standards in the mostly rural, poorly funded schools on the plateau. Many of the teachers were appalled to discover just how low these standards were, and even rhapsodical official accounts could not hide how powerless they felt in trying to achieve their goals. 'Compared to students in the interior, Tibetan students' educational foundations … are generally weak, but the children themselves don't consider this to be so because they are surrounded by classmates who are also like this,' wrote Zhong Qiuming, a senior Hunanese education official, in a report summarizing his experiences in Tibet.[6] 'Education is a cause of love that can transcend … barriers,' Zhong said, but 'due to the lack of common life experiences, cultural foundations, and even religious beliefs … there are major cultural divides' between teacher and student. The teachers were particularly shocked at the level of Putonghua, or lack thereof, among their Tibetan students. Zhong wrote that his charges' ability 'to express themselves in Chinese is poor'.

Teachers express themselves very well and in a lively manner, but the students are indifferent. Not only is communication poor, the teachers are also frustrated. Bilingual education in Tibet is now basically universalised at pre-school, and for a high-school student, daily communication in Chinese should not be a problem.

Zhong recommended that the authorities should 'expand the scope of bilingual education' to improve the students' skills in Chinese. At the same time, he said, teachers should carry out 'home visits' and 'joint school-home education efforts' in order to 'cultivate strong nationality sentiments' and 'heart-to-heart dialog' with the students.[7]

Cultivating a sense of nationality among those on the plateau has been a key goal of the Chinese state since the People's Liberation Army marched into Tibet in 1951. At that time, according to Chinese sources, literacy was rare and only a tiny number of children were in formal schooling.[8] Since then, the government has made great efforts, and expended considerable capital, in raising educational standards across the Tibetan Autonomous Region (TAR) and Tibetan-majority areas in other provinces. Despite this, the educational level of Tibetans has consistently ranked last among all ethnic groups in China, with the average number of years spent in formal education at 5.4 per the 2010 census, over three years less than the national average.[9] While today, the number of children enrolled in elementary and middle school is nearly 100 per cent, by high school age this begins to drop off, and just 40 per cent of Tibetans attend college or university, compared to over 80 per cent nationally.[10]

There are numerous explanations for these statistics. Tibet has the smallest economy of any Chinese territory,[11] among the lowest average salaries, and is the least urbanized part of the country, with just 30 per cent of Tibetans living in cities, half the national average. (Unless otherwise noted, 'Tibet' here refers to the TAR, the Chinese-controlled territory which constitutes much of the western and central plateau, but does not include parts of other provinces that were historically Tibetan and have large Tibetan populations.) The responsibilities of rural farming life, as well as the comparatively large distances children may be required to travel to attend school, all have an effect on attendance.[12] And while parents in these areas are often very encouraging of their children, and desperate for them to get a quality education, having been denied such opportunities themselves, they can find it harder than their counterparts in the interior to assist their children in learning or navigate the bureaucracy needed to get them into the best schools. There is also a scarcity of qualified teachers, due to both the lack of access to training and the brain drain caused by the economic disparity between Tibet and the rest of China. Parachuting highly qualified educators in for a year or two may seem like a solution to this issue, but it often isn't long enough for them to have an effect, nor do outsiders necessarily understand or sympathize with the unique situation on the plateau in order to effectively connect with their students and communities. But just as in Wales, where the British government looked not to its own policies but instead blamed the Welsh language for educational failure, Tibet's rulers have found an easy scapegoat of their own.

Tibetan languages are not closely related to Chinese, and differ greatly in terms of grammar, phonology and syntax. Tibetan languages also have a number of writing systems separate to that used for Chinese, the most common of which is a thirty-letter syllabic alphabet or abugida, that is written left-to-right and bears a visual similarity to Devanagari, the main script used for writing Hindi.[13,14]

Despite a stated commitment to preserving Tibetan languages and promoting 'bilingual education', recent decades have seen a major increase in the amount of Chinese used in education across the region, at the expense of local tongues, with Putonghua replacing Tibetan languages as the medium of instruction at almost all levels, from primary through high school.[15,16] Mass immigration by Han Chinese, as well as large numbers of tourists from the interior, has also increasingly made Putonghua a requirement for employment, marginalizing adults who don't speak the language and placing additional pressure on their children to learn it. This has put Tibetan languages, in the words of one observer, under 'real threat of extinction … within two – or at the most three – generations'.[17]

For many languages in Tibet, the situation is already desperate. While 'Tibetan' is often discussed, by commentators and even activists, as if it were a single language spoken throughout the plateau, there is in fact great linguistic diversity within Tibet, and many minority tongues face pressure both from more dominant local languages and the advance of Putonghua.[18] The future that speakers of major Tibetan languages fear – no schooling, no publishing, no presence in the public sphere or in broadcasting – is already the situation for many minoritized languages on the plateau, such as Manegacha, Ngandehua, Minyag, Khroskyabs, Rta'u, Lamo and Tibetan Sign Language.[19] And while some of these have been replaced by Amdo Tibetan or other more dominant local tongues, most speakers have instead switched to Putonghua. Some minority languages, such as Duoxu, are already on the verge of extinction, the first victims of a language policy that now threatens all tongues on the plateau.[20]

Following the 'peaceful liberation' of Tibet by the PLA, Beijing promised that the 'religious beliefs, customs, and habits of the Tibetan people shall be respected.'[21] At first, this was largely the case, at least in the TAR, where the government led by the Dalai Lama retained some degree of control. But in the eastern half of the plateau, annexed to Chinese provinces, 'democratic reforms' connected to Mao Zedong's disastrous Great Leap Forward saw Tibetan communities uprooted, nomads and farmers stuffed into cooperative farms, their animals and crops given over to Han control.[22] This policy was a failure, as government officials hoarded food and tried to grow crops unsuitable for the plateau, ignoring centuries of local knowledge. Famine and misery spread, and many traditional communities were devastated, with thousands of refugees fleeing to Lhasa. In 1959, as unrest grew throughout the plateau and the PLA prepared to crack down, the Dalai Lama fled across the Himalayas to India. Communist control ramped up everywhere, as did restrictions on Tibetan culture, language and religion. This reached its apogee during the Cultural Revolution, when Mao's Red Guards smashed Buddhist temples and humiliated, beat, and killed monks and nuns.

After Mao's death in 1976, his successors reversed many of the policies of the previous decade, and Tibetan language education was actively encouraged as the best way to improve educational standards across the region.[23] This was codified in the 1982 Constitution, which said that 'the people of all nationalities have the freedom to use and develop their own spoken and written languages, and to preserve or reform their own ways and customs'. In keeping with the pro-'dialect' writings of the old Latinxua advocates, slogans such as 'learn Tibetan, use Tibetan, and develop Tibetan' sprang up on the streets of Lhasa.[24] Programmes were developed which took note of the 'special characteristics of the nationalities', and Tibetans were encouraged to be proud of their ethnic and linguistic identity.[25] (Though this was confined by the idea of 'one ethnicity, one language', and speakers of minority languages across Tibet missed out on even this limited multiculturalism.)

Gradually however, as proficiency in Putonghua became linked to employment and the Tibetan economy further tied to that of the rest of China, government support for Tibetan languages decreased and it was seen as more important to teach children Chinese. As with other minoritized tongues, the pressure to drop Tibetan languages in favour of Putonghua came from multiple directions. Many Tibetan parents are fierce advocates of Chinese-medium teaching, seeing it as the best means of their children gaining employment after graduation or going to a good university in the interior. As the language of schooling has changed, it has also become harder for teachers who speak a Tibetan language to find work, with Putonghua-speaking candidates given preference. The government often claims there is a deficit of 'qualified teachers' in the region, but this generally means a lack of candidates who can teach in Chinese, rather than cannot teach at all. Tibetan-language resources are also far scarcer and of poorer quality than the vast supply of high-quality Chinese-language textbooks produced for the country as a whole. With the migration of more Han Chinese to Tibet, there are also many more mixed schools, where students speak both Tibetan and Chinese languages at home but Putonghua is the shared tongue, though Tibetans still dominate demographically in most classrooms. But while these factors certainly contribute towards a shift from Tibetan languages to Putonghua, the speed and scale of the transformation in recent years has been largely down to a deliberate policy of assimilation, with language seen as the primary means of inculcating patriotism and 'strong nationality sentiments' among those on the Tibetan plateau.

With Tibet stubbornly failing to repeat the GDP busting growth of the southern and eastern provinces, and as ethnic strife continued and overseas criticism grew particularly loud around the 2008 Olympics, attitudes in Beijing hardened. Since the late 2000s, the state has effectively reversed its previous pro-Tibetan policy, seeing a lack of Putonghua as a key reason for any unrest on the plateau. Already the language of most high schools, Putonghua increasingly replaced Tibetan languages in primary schools and even kindergartens, meaning that the majority of children, particularly in urbanized areas, spoke a Tibetan language only at home. 'Tibetan [is] used only in classes where the Tibetan language is the topic of the class, if it is taught at all,' a state media report noted in 2016, adding 'many Tibetan parents have found that their kids are not learning how to speak their mother-tongue.'[26] Now, the posters outside schools in Tibet read: 'I am a Chinese child; I love to speak Putonghua.'[27]

Spring in Beijing. The season is fleeting, a brief interlude between the oppressive, choking smog and bitter cold of winter, and the oven the city turns into during summer. Cherry blossoms, white, pink and yellow, bloom across the city's parks, where crowds flock to take selfies and bask under the newly blue skies. In 2015, the Chinese capital's breakneck expansion, which began in the run up to the 2008 Olympics, was showing no signs of slowing, and the seventh ring road, still then under construction, was set to create millions of new Beijingers, thrusting the borders of the city far out into surrounding Hebei province.[28] Closer to the city centre, poorer neighbourhoods and ancient towers were being torn down in the name of progress, replaced by gleaming skyscrapers and personality-deprived corporate erections. The year before, President Xi Jinping had called for an end to the 'weird architecture' that had come to dominate the city's skyline in the economic boom following the Olympics,[29] and the massive stimulus programme launched in the wake of the 2008 global financial crash. That period saw Beijing's economy double in size, as it overtook London to become the city with the fourth highest number of billionaires in the world.[30] All that money sloshing around had been accompanied by a corresponding spike in corruption that was hard to miss, both in the capital and far beyond, as even county-level officials in rural backwaters began sporting designer watches and driving expensive cars. Xi came into office promising to stamp out graft, and his anti-corruption campaign made him hugely popular with ordinary people and sent a ripple of terror through the Communist Party. With few officials not tainted in some way, the campaign proved an ideal way to clear out any rivals as he shored up control of the levers of power, and in early 2015 he claimed his biggest scalp yet, when Zhou Yongkang, a one-time Politburo member and former security tsar, was officially charged with bribery and abuse of power. Later that year, Zhou would be sentenced to life in prison, the highest-ranking Chinese official ever convicted of corruption.[31]

Xi's firm hand was not limited to the Party, and by 2015, any hopes that he might reveal himself as a closet liberal had long been dashed. Instead, Xi had emerged as the most authoritarian, and most powerful Chinese leader since Mao Zedong, cracking down on the internet and civil society, locking up human rights lawyers and activists, and advancing a forceful, aggressive foreign policy.[32] In particular, Xi took a hard line on Xinjiang and Tibet, two non-Han majority regions which had both seen major ethnic unrest at the end of the previous decade and were still the site of sporadic protests and incidents of violence, from self-immolations in Tibetan regions, to militant attacks in parts of Xinjiang. Their distinct religious, racial and linguistic identities were seen as the root of the problem, and efforts were stepped up to bind the far west closer to the Chinese interior. This included nakedly assimilationist policies, such as cracking down on religious practice, encouraging interethnic marriage and Han migration, and an influx of development funds to Han-owned businesses as part of Xi's signature Belt and Road infrastructure and trade mega project. Speaking in 2014, Xi emphasized the need to 'bind the people of each ethnic group into a single strand of rope',[33] while the following year he would call for greater efforts to ensure ethnic minorities identified with 'the motherland, Chinese nationality, Chinese culture, the CCP [Chinese Communist Party] and socialism with Chinese characteristics'.[34]

In Tibet, language policy was seen as key to this transformation, with one government report noting that the purpose of bilingual education was to 'better integrate the Chinese language [as] a means of eliminating elements of instability in Tibetan regions'.[35] Just as practice of Islam has increasingly been viewed as suspicious and potentially dangerous by authorities in predominantly Muslim Xinjiang, promotion and use of Tibetan languages has become politically fraught, viewed not as preserving cultural diversity but seeking to separate the region from the rest of China. Any pushback against assimilationist policies is cast as justification for them: people would not complain if they better understood they were part of one big happy Chinese family.

As the securitization of Tibet and Xinjiang was ramping up, and word was beginning to leak out of human rights abuses and crackdowns on indigenous religion and culture, access to both regions became increasingly difficult for foreign reporters, and those who did manage to travel to the far west were met with intense surveillance and harassment from local authorities.[36] So when, in early 2015, a contact of *New York Times* journalist Jonah Kessel's recommended he meet with a Tibetan man who had a story worth telling, Kessel readily agreed.[37]

Still, it was not without scepticism that Kessel let Tashi Wangchuk into his apartment in Beijing for their first interview. Anyone who works as a reporter in China for an extended period will hear plenty of accounts of human rights abuses, or frustrations with the often arbitrary and unfair nature of the Chinese justice system, of legal and constitutional protections ignored or undermined by corruption. Particularly in Beijing, where petitioners from across China travel to seek recourse from the central government for the failings of local officials, people will sometimes turn to the foreign press, expecting journalists not only to share in their outrage but, somehow, fix their problems. More often than not, they go away disappointed. This is not because journalists are unsympathetic or uninterested, but that the stories being told are often impossible to independently verify, or are unfortunately so routine that they would be difficult to tell in a way that would rise to the level of international news. Often even those who approach journalists directly are not actually willing to speak on the record, or shy away from doing so once the potential risks are explained. For video journalists like Kessel, these difficulties are compounded: he needed not only a subject willing to tell their story on camera, but for the story itself to have additional visual elements not necessary for a print article in order to make an effective documentary. Soon after meeting Tashi however, Kessel felt relieved. The short, sad-faced man in front of him, with acne-scars on his cheeks, a sparse moustache, and dark, overgrown hair, had a compelling story to tell, and seemed to understand and be willing to bear the potential risks of speaking out.

Tashi Wangchuk was born in 1985 in Chindu, a small town of mostly one or two-storey whitewashed brick buildings, topped with bright blue or red metal roofs, clustered at the base of a valley, around a river that cut through the mountains at the eastern edge of the Tibetan plateau. Chindu was part of the Yushu Tibetan Autonomous Prefecture, a majority-Tibetan region within Qinghai province, which neighbours Tibet to the north. In theory, autonomous prefectures – in which some 60 per cent of Tibetans in China live – are run by their own 'organs of self-government', which use 'one or more commonly used local languages when they are performing official duties', including in setting educational policy.[38] In practice however, such areas are anything but autonomous, and are highly controlled by Han Chinese provincial and regional officials.[39] In 2012, Qinghai, despite once being a great producer of Tibetan-language culture and academia within China,[40] phased out Tibetan as a language of instruction in primary and secondary schools, laying off teachers who could not speak Putonghua, and issuing new Chinese-language textbooks which focused on Han history and culture and did not cover Tibet. In March of that year, a Tibetan student in neighbouring Gansu province, which adopted similar policies, set herself alight and died after her high school switched to teaching in Chinese.[41] Hundreds of other Tibetans, mostly young monks and nuns, have self-immolated since 2009, the majority in Tibetan regions outside the TAR, many citing controls on the practice of their religion, culture and language as their reason for doing so.[42] By one tally, some 13 per cent of self-immolators said that 'protecting the national language' was their primary motivation.[43] The government however responded to these gruesome protests with more repression, cracking down on monks accused of encouraging self-immolators and blaming the Dalai Lama and other exiled Tibetan leaders, who have never promoted the practice. When high school students protested against language policies in Qinghai in early 2015, the local government accused 'hostile Western forces' of tricking students to 'defy the law, disrupt society, sabotage harmony and subvert the government'.[44]

Tashi was a precocious child, and Chindu was always too small for him. As a seventeen-year-old, he travelled to a nearby town and tried to hitch a ride on a train to Shanghai, the glittering eastern metropolis, but he was caught and thrown off.[45] Instead, he took a train to Lhasa, the Tibetan capital, which at the time was undergoing a transformation, becoming more and more commercialized as tourists poured in from the Chinese interior, and Han-owned businesses opened to cater to them. Tashi also looked into moving to India, where a large Tibetan exile community has lived since the Dalai Lama fled there in 1959. But as tensions within Chinese-controlled Tibet grew, the government cracked down on the flow of emigration, banning most Tibetans from holding passports and heavily policing who could travel to towns on the border.[46] Being trapped in Tibet didn't stop Tashi looking outward however, he just moved online. He opened an account on Weibo, a Chinese social media platform, where he posted about Tibetan culture and life on the plateau, but also dabbled in dicier political issues, asking pointed questions about the government's response to an earthquake which struck the Yushu region in 2010. For this, Tashi received his first visit from the authorities, and a warning to keep his mouth shut, but it did little to dissuade him.[47]

Despite growing tension between Tibetans and Han Chinese during the early 2010s, as well as the often crippling poverty in much of rural Qinghai, Tashi also found economic success online. He switched from herding sheep to selling craft goods via Taobao, the Chinese e-commerce site, to customers across the country. In 2014, he even appeared in a flashy promotional video produced by Taobao's parent company, Alibaba, hosted by founder Jack Ma, who explained that his company – soon to go public at a value of $231 billion[48] – fought 'for the little guy, the small businessmen and women and their customers'.[49] In the video, Tashi is seen wearing a brown woollen coat, its bright red trim decorated with white flowers. Speaking Putonghua, he explains that 'before, living in Yushu, I felt isolated from the outside world'.

'A physical shop can only reach local customers,' he says. 'But a Taobao shop is open to customers around the world. As long as I have a mobile phone, I can manage my shop anytime. My hometown [Chindu] is even more remote. My nephew has a soccer team, they bought all their jerseys and shoes from Taobao.' The video then cuts to a scene of a group of Tibetan boys playing football on a field in front of snow-capped mountains, as an upbeat piano track playing in the background.

Like the moderate Uyghur academic Ilham Tohti, who was imprisoned for life in 2014 on charges of separatism, Tashi fit precisely what the government wanted an ethnic minority in the People's Republic to be.[50] He was enterprising, successful, keen to establish links with the rest of China, and not remotely radical in his religious or political beliefs. The problem came when, like Ilham, he asked the government to live up to its own commitments to him as a citizen, to actually follow through on the grand promises made in the Chinese constitution and other laws to preserve ethnic minority culture, language and autonomy.

Even growing up in the 1990s, before the government had fully abandoned the pro-minority language policies adopted in the wake of the Cultural Revolution, Tashi's Tibetan education was severely limited.[51] He learned the basics of reading and writing in primary school, and from older brothers who had studied with a monk, but when he switched to a nominally bilingual middle school, all classes were in Putonghua, and as an adult, he was more comfortable in that language than in what Tibetans call their 'father tongue'. After graduation, he also studied with a monk for several years, but he was always worried his language was 'slipping away' and would spend hours laboriously copying out texts in Tibetan.[52]

Until 2015, classes offered by monasteries and individual monks and nuns, of the sort Tashi and his brothers attended, had largely filled the gap created by the shift towards 'bilingual' education in government-run schools. That year however, as part of a wider crackdown on Tibetan activism and alleged 'criminal gangs connected to the separatist forces of the Dalai Lama', the government banned the practice. 'Illegal associations formed in the name of the Tibetan language, the environment and education' were listed on a government notice as one of twenty illegal pro-independence activities that should be reported to the authorities.[53]

Tashi was the youngest in his family, and doted on his siblings' children. After the monks were forced to stop teaching, he set about trying to find his nieces a school they could transfer to. At considerable cost, he visited five different schools across Tibetan-majority regions of Qinghai, Sichuan and Yunnan provinces, but none were offering Tibetan except as a separate language class, similar to how English or other foreign languages were taught.[54]

This experience was the start of Tashi's political awakening. As he paid more attention to the supposed autonomous Tibetan region he called home, he noticed how rare it was to see anything written in that language. In 2015, he posted a series of photos on Weibo showing Chinese-language school textbooks, shop signs and adverts, writing 'here, the Tibetan language is like a foreign language'.[55] One sign hanging over an Agricultural Bank of China ATM didn't even go that far, it included instructions in Chinese and English only. 'I don't think the local government is protecting the Tibetan language or the culture of the Tibetan people,' Tashi wrote. So he set about trying to force them to do so. On the basis of the constitutional provision that 'all nationalities have the freedom to use and develop their own spoken and written languages', Tashi began crafting a lawsuit against local and regional officials in Yushu to compel them to provide Tibetan-medium education.

It was around this time that Tashi came onto Kessel's radar. The Tibetan had travelled to Beijing to meet with lawyers and attempt to get press coverage – initially from state media but failing that foreign journalists – for his lawsuit.[56] After meeting with ten lawyers in the Chinese capital, Tashi could not find anyone willing to take his case, or offer him advice on how to sue the government. Several commented that he should be grateful that China's language policies brought 'great benefit' to the Tibetan people. This kind of patronizing dismissal was a common response from Han Chinese. In one scene in the documentary Kessel eventually made about Tashi, the Tibetan phones China Central Television, the state broadcaster, and tries to pitch his story. The woman on the other end of the line says that 'China Mobile and other companies are all using Chinese language right? So what's the problem?'

'This is devastating. It's destroying our ethnicity's culture,' Tashi responds. 'So I'm about to file a lawsuit and I want to ask if China Central Television will report this?'

'I can only put down your request and report to the program. They will decide whether to interview you about this.'

They didn't. Having failed to get any help from Chinese lawyers or media, Tashi decided to go directly to the Supreme People's Court himself and see if he could lodge a case. Kessel filmed from a discrete distance as Tashi, dressed in a black suit and white shirt, walked up to the heavily guarded gates of the court, just off Tiananmen Square in central Beijing. 'If they can't take the case,' he told Kessel, 'it proves one point, which is that the whole Tibetan issue cannot be solved through the law. At least this will be clear.'

Tashi's case was not accepted by the court that day, or any other time he attempted to file it. In November 2015, Kessel's documentary 'Tashi Wangchuk: A Tibetan's Journey for Justice' was posted online. Two months later, Tashi was detained in Yushu and held without charge for almost a year.[57]

In January 2018, Tashi appeared before the Yushu Intermediate People's Court. The major piece of evidence against him was the New York Times documentary, which was played several times in court. Tashi's lawyer, Liang Xiaojun, said his client was calm, pushing back on the prosecution's claims that he was advocating for Tibetan independence, and reiterating that all he wanted was to protect the Tibetan language. 'The debate during the hearing was very passionate,' Liang told me. 'There was a female Tibetan prosecutor, she was very good at debating. Her Putonghua was better than that of her colleagues.'

Chinese trials are more often than not a foregone conclusion, and in May 2018, Tashi was found guilty of 'inciting separatism' and sentenced to five years in prison.[58] According to court documents, prosecutors accused Tashi of 'distorting the facts, attacking the state's policies on ethnic minorities, making remarks that undermine ethnic unity and national unity', and cited his appearance in the New York Times documentary as one reason for his imprisonment.[59] 'After the video was uploaded, numerous websites and media outlets redistributed it, spread it, commented on it, and reported on it, damaging the national image,' the court documents said.

When we first spoke in August 2020, Liang had not seen his client for over two years. Tashi was finally released in January 2021, but remains under government surveillance in Qinghai. Human rights activists in China are often tightly limited in their movements and who they communicate with, even after leaving prison, and especially if they previously spoke to foreign media. Following his release, Liang has struggled to reach Tashi, and expressed skepticism about whether he was 'truly free.'

Liang admired Tashi, describing him as bright eyed and 'very smart', but the veteran human rights lawyer – who has been barred from leaving China and seen dozens of his colleagues locked up for their work[60] – couldn't help thinking his client was somewhat naive about the Chinese legal system. 'I think he didn't understand what the risks were,' Liang said. 'This originated from a very humble wish, to want people to care about the lack of education for Tibetans. He tried all different ways to solve this problem, but when he found that there was no way to do so [through the Chinese system] he went to the foreign media. But I don't think he imagined that the consequences would be so serious.'

Kessel, who has since left China, is still conflicted about his potential role in Tashi's arrest. While it's likely the Tibetan would have found another foreign outlet to tell his story to if it wasn't the *New York Times*, and repeatedly insisted on speaking on the record, despite having the potential danger explained to him, Kessel was nevertheless torn over his decision to include a section in the documentary where Tashi discusses self-immolation. 'So many people have self-immolated,' Tashi says. 'I can understand them now, because we have very few ways to solve problems. No one wants to live in an environment that's full of pressure and fear.' Later, as he and Kessel sit on a train to Yushu, where part of the documentary was filmed, Tashi says 'they didn't just set themselves on fire because of family issues or something. I believe they also saw culture disappearing and other cultural problems.' He adds, 'But I want to try to use the People's Republic of China's laws to solve the problem.'

'I always wonder if we cut that, if he'd be in jail,' Kessel said. 'It's really tough. You want [the film] to be as powerful as possible. You want to show reality, but to simultaneously do so in a way that doesn't destroy people's lives.'

Almost certainly, Tashi would have ended up in prison with or without the film. He was testing a system that has moved further and further away from its stated commitments to promoting and protecting minority languages, while growing more sensitive to any criticism of this. Just as the government has connected self-immolation protests to separatism, regardless of the stated goals and desires of those setting themselves alight, it has increasingly tied any promotion of Tibetan languages, let alone an aggressive defence such as launched by Tashi, to being pro-independence. Ironically, in cracking down so hard in this instance, the Chinese government spread Tashi's message far beyond what he would ever have achieved by himself. 'One of the saddest things I struggle with now is that had the Chinese government done nothing, Tashi would be [free], and probably nothing would have happened,' Kessel said. 'There would be no change [in language policy]. But we also wouldn't be having this conversation.'

'But they did do something. They arrested him. They took away his rights and took away his ability to see his family, his lawyers, they forcefully disappeared him, allegedly tortured him, all before a sham trial. And because of that, they have made this case a global topic. And that point I'm happy about. I'm happy that people are talking about this as an issue because it is an issue. At the same time the cost of this conversation is and has been Tashi's freedom.'

Speaking in August 2020, President Xi Jinping called for China to build an 'impregnable fortress' in Tibet to fight against separatism. Key to this, he said, was strengthening political and ideological education to 'plant the seeds of loving China in the depths of the hearts of every youth'.[61]

'It is necessary to dig out, sort out and publicise the historical facts of the exchanges and integration of all ethnic groups in Tibet since ancient times, guide the people of all ethnic groups to see the direction and future of the nation, deeply realise that the Chinese nation is a community of destiny, and promote exchanges and integration of all ethnic groups,' Xi said, adding that the government would 'actively guide Tibetan Buddhism to adapt to the socialist society and promote the sinicisation of Tibetan Buddhism'.

Similar policies have been applied in Xinjiang with even more ferocity than in Tibet, with the Uyghur language and traditional culture tightly restricted, and growing suspicion of increasingly any expression of Islamic faith. As of late 2020, hundreds of thousands of ethnic Uyghurs had passed through a series of re-education camps established by the government in the name of fighting 'extremism'. Former internees have spoken of political indoctrination and abuse, and many face tight monitoring even after they are released. In September 2020, despite growing international criticism, Xi described the policies pursued in Xinjiang as 'completely correct', and said that 'we must also continue the direction of Sinicizing Islam to achieve the healthy development of religion'.[62]

Nor would such policies be limited to Tibet and Xinjiang either, Beijing made clear around this time, as authorities announced educational reforms in Inner Mongolia – the only other region with a large non-Han population – making Putonghua the language of instruction for key subjects in elementary and middle schools across the region.[63] For over seventy years, Inner Mongolian students had all classes taught in their native tongue, apart from a Chinese language and literature course which began at age eight, and English class from age ten. The new arrangement essentially flipped this, with Putonghua replacing Mongolian as the default language, and that tongue confined to two classes focused on the language itself. The new Chinese textbook would be called 'Language and Literature', while the Mongolian text was renamed '*Mongolian* Language and Literature', making clear which was to be seen as the primary tongue, a shift some Mongols compared to 'the step-father taking the place of the father'.[64]

The announcement sparked widespread protests across Inner Mongolia, demonstrations that were all the more surprising given they involved an ethnic group that historically has not objected to Beijing's rule to the level seen in the two other majority non-Han regions.[65] Officials were clearly unprepared for the level of anger and paranoia the language reforms would spark. One Mongolian protester told a newspaper that 'if we accept teaching in Chinese, our Mongolian language will really die out'.

While they might have been unprepared for the backlash, the protests did little to change the government's mind. A statement on the rollout of new Chinese-language textbooks said they showed 'the loving care of the Party and the state towards ethnic regions' and benefitted 'the promotion of ethnic unity, the development and progress of ethnic regions, and the building of a strong sense of community for the Chinese nation'.[66] Top officials in Beijing dismissed reports of the protests as 'political speculation with ulterior motives'.

'The national common spoken and written language is a symbol of national sovereignty', foreign ministry spokesperson Hua Chunying told reporters in the Chinese capital. 'It is every citizen's right and duty to learn and use the national common spoken and written language.'

The model being followed in Inner Mongolia matches that applied in Tibetan regions of the country a decade ago.[67] There too, moves to replace Tibetan languages with Putonghua were met with anger and protests, but these were suppressed via mass arrests and denounced as the work of foreign actors, and the changes went ahead regardless. As Xi himself said in 2014, the intention of the government is to bind all of China's ethnic groups, be they Tibetan, Mongolian, Uyghur, Cantonese or Han, 'into a single strand of rope'. This requires a more assimilationist policy, and no longer will ethnic and linguistic diversity be protected or allowed to undermine a push towards 'national unity'.

And while language did not stand in the way of Mongolians becoming a 'model ethnic minority' in the New China, that is no guarantee that it will not in future. In fact, Beijing's hard hand in the region is likely motivated by changes across the border, in Mongolia proper. Under Soviet influence, Mongolia, which split from China in 1921, abandoned the traditional script and switched to writing Mongolian in the Cyrillic alphabet. In Chinese-ruled Inner Mongolia, the script did not change, preserving a key piece of linguistic heritage but also serving to divide Mongols on either side of the border. That situation could change in 2025, when Mongolia plans to reintroduce the traditional script, 'a situation China fears will foster dangerous cross-border loyalties', in the words of one observer.[68] Better to Sinicize the region now, while resistance is likely to be lower, and Mongolia itself is less likely to intervene.

In September 2020, almost a month after the first protests broke out in Inner Mongolia, students began returning to class, as the authorities launched a manhunt for protest leaders and suggested parents who kept their children from school could lose their jobs.[69] 'The students are back in school, [there are] no more complaining parents or students,' one teacher told a Western newspaper. 'We are officially using the new textbooks.'

Epilogue

In his pivotal 1962 speech on the 'fate of the language', Welsh activist and writer Saunders Lewis warned that 'there is nothing in the world more comfortable than to give up hope. For then one can go on to enjoy life.'[1]

Language revitalization and reclamation can often feel hopeless. Preservation or promotion of a minority tongue is hard, while language death is so easy it often takes place while no one is looking. Lewis was speaking at the nadir of Welsh-language activism, when terminal decline and eventual extinction appeared inevitable. 'The political tradition of the centuries and all present-day economic tendencies militate against the continued existence of Welsh,' he said, words that could apply to any minoritized language. 'Nothing can change that except determination, will power, struggle, sacrifice, and endeavour.'

His call for action inspired just that, setting the stage for a hugely successful Welsh revival that has not only revitalized the language to levels not seen since the early twentieth century, but put it on track to reach a million speakers within the next decade.

Lewis recognized that for a language to survive, it must be used in all aspects of life, from education, to government and the law, to culture. Of these, the former is the most vital for the long-term health of the language, but all three are important. Without modern culture, a language stagnates, its prestige fades and transmitting it to the next generation is all the harder. Cut out of government or the law, speakers of minority languages are marginalized, and less likely to get into positions of power from where they can influence the fate of their tongue and others. As the authors of a handbook on language revitalization write:

> A 'healthy' language is one that is supported at home, at school, in the community, on the job, and in the media. We have seen that attention to only one of these venues is never enough. Acquisition must be accompanied by continued use of the language if revitalisation is to flourish. Thus for a community to reach their goal depends on the provision of opportunities for both language learning and language use in many and hopefully all of these venues. People who are in communities whose languages are endangered or no longer spoken natively may see this as an impossibility, but the presence of the language in all venues need not be in place before language revitalisation begins. Instead, it is a bottom-up process that grows over time.[2]

Small successes beget larger ones, and even apparently minor improvements in language use can help popularize or normalize a minority tongue's position within society, setting the stage for greater acceptance and promotion. Linguist Miquel Strubell has put forward a circular model for language revitalization, which traces the interrelationship between language learning, demand for and supply of goods and services in that language, consumption of goods and services in the language, perception and prestige of the language, and motivation to learn and use it.[3]

In education, decades of work in language revitalization has provided a clear model for minority tongues around the world. Work begins at home, encouraging and supporting parents to use their native languages, and in pre-schools, with immersion kindergartens or 'language nest' schemes showing success in numerous countries, including New Zealand, Wales and Hawai'i. Such programmes can rely to an extent on existing language speakers who are not trained educators, but beyond pre-school age, investment must be made in teacher training in order to expand minority language use throughout the education system. For communities who do not have government support, after school programmes, language camps, language play groups and at home teaching have shown success, as have classes focused on improving adult proficiency, enabling more parents to transmit the language to their own children more effectively.[4]

While other languages provide guidance, there is not a one-size-fits-all model, and in particular, what works in a society where there is one primary indigenous or minority language – such as Wales, New Zealand or Hawai'i – may not work in a multilingual one. Australia, for example, has dozens of mutually unintelligible indigenous languages spoken across the continent. A national programme to promote Wiradjuri, a language of New South Wales, would not do much to help speakers of Yolŋu, in the Northern Territory. But there is no reason a policy could not be crafted to identify and support a given region's indigenous languages, building on existing programmes developed by local communities and activists. Government support for a language can happen at multiple levels, from local to national, and may differ from region to region as the requirements dictate. In all areas, government should follow the lead of indigenous communities and grassroots activists, but even partial official recognition for a language, whether through education or via adoption as a state or national language, can have a major effect in boosting a tongue's prestige and encouraging its use.[5] Within multilingual communities, special attention must be paid to ensure that the promotion of one minority language does not lead to the marginalization and endangerment of another. Instead, policies should be crafted to support all language communities, building on existing programmes and providing funding and resources to expand them, rather than imposing a top-down model that risks over-emphasizing any particular language.[6]

Beyond education, money should also be set aside for cultural programmes, either within existing arts budgets or as separate, dedicated funding for indigenous language art and literature. This is vital not only for prestige, but also for making the language a living, vibrant tongue, and for increasing its visibility among both native and non-speakers. Visibility and legitimacy are also strong arguments in favour of widespread translation of official documents, from government forms and announcements, to street signs and place names. These may seem like small steps, but they make a major difference for the communities affected, and help bring new potential speakers to the language. In particular, such visibility makes non-speakers and non-native people aware of a language and helps get them invested in its future, often a vital step towards revitalization for minority communities.

This book has largely focused on the politics and history around minority languages and the movements to protect and revive them, rather than the specific scientific and linguistic models for doing so. That is in part because on a practical level, how to go about the process of revitalization is fairly established, building on the work of Welsh, Hawaiian, Māori, Lakota, Navajo, Wiradjuri, Sami, Cornish and countless other minority-language speakers in creating a framework that can apply to nearly any tongue. But while language activists have pulled off miracles around the world, revitalization cannot only be from the ground up. Governments must enable communities to exercise self determination, empowering and supporting them to promote their indigenous culture and language. Space must be made within education systems to support minority languages, not as some sop to tradition, but as living, vibrant tongues that can be used in and outside of class. Colonial and postcolonial governments owe a particular debt in this regard, as many were responsible for the marginalization and suppression of indigenous languages in the past, or inherited a legacy of destruction. All people living in postcolonial societies should be encouraged to learn indigenous languages and to be given a stake in supporting and sustaining those tongues in the future. Most nominally monoglot countries are in fact multilingual, and should embrace this and promote language diversity, in education, government and culture.

Inevitably, minority-language movements will face pushback from those within the majority who see such work as either a threat to the dominant tongue or a waste of money. In the United States, there have been numerous setbacks for minority languages, as conservative national governments have cut funding for bilingual programmes or focused on promoting English use among indigenous and immigrant populations.[7] Convincing governments to support minority languages is not easy. By their very nature, oppressed and marginalized peoples do not have much political power or influence, nor are politicians always susceptible to arguments about correcting historical wrongs. Lewis argued that 'success is only possible through revolutionary methods,' and in Wales, mass civil disobedience and even violence was part of the Welsh revitalization project. Other language movements have found success through less radical protest, though some degree of civil disobedience is usually required to get the attention of those in power. Hawaiian activists have been adept at cultivating solidarity with other oppressed groups in the United States, from the Black Lives Matter movement to other indigenous peoples, such as the Standing Rock tribe and their allies who organized around protesting the Dakota Access Pipeline.

At a governmental level, work promoting minority languages can be justified to less supportive parts of the population in the context of reparations, or as an investment in the country's future. Mother tongue teaching has been shown time and again to improve educational attainment, which feeds into economic success and uplifts minority communities. Bilingualism and multilingualism bring a host of cognitive and health benefits, including improved learning outcomes and delaying the onset of dementia and other neurodegenerative diseases.[8] Minority languages also contain within them new ways of thinking and new solutions to the problems that we face, solutions that are desperately needed in the face of climate catastrophe and other global challenges. Culturally, we are also richer when we can engage with art and literature from around the world, whether in translation or the original language, inspiring each other to do better and be better. As Hinton, Huss and Roche write:

> *It is important to bear in mind that language revitalisation is not really about language. It is about many other things: autonomy and decolonisation, knowledge of traditional values and practices, a renewed understanding and care of the land, a sense of community togetherness and belonging, and a strong identity that children can grow into. Language is one of the keys to all of this, and language revitalisation is about all of these things. We do not know what the future of language revitalisation will look like, but it is clear that a new era exists for endangered languages. Indigenous and minoritised groups now have renewed relationships to their languages, whether it is in the form of archives being put to use by communities to research their languages or in the form of new generations of speakers, however small, who speak new varieties of their ancient languages and are putting them to use in new and creative ways.[9]*

Minority movements can shape policy and revolutionize whole political systems. In the decades after Lewis' speech, the number of Welsh speakers continued to shrink, before rebounding in the late 1980s, and yet, through the work of those he inspired, and organizations like Plaid Cymru and Cymdeithas yr Iaith, language preservation became a key issue in Welsh politics. Today, despite Welsh speakers still being a minority, all major political parties support the goal of a million speakers. Like the work of Welsh activists, the roadmap created by the government in Cardiff for achieving that goal offers important lessons for other languages. Key priorities identified include expanding the amount of Welsh used in education, and offering greater resources for those coming to the language as adults, from increasing the use of Welsh in the workplace and in government services, and providing funding for culture, media and digital technology to ensure that Welsh is a language of the twenty-first century. The digital realm in particular offers both new challenges and opportunities for minority languages and those who speak them.

*

As a teenager in Dublin in the mid-2000s, Noah Buffini Higgs was obsessed with the Irish language, but he hated how it was taught. He hated the overly formal lessons that seemed disconnected from people's day-to-day lives, and most of all, he hated the effect the lessons had on his fellow students' willingness to speak Irish outside of class.

Higgs, who has blond hair, prominent ears, and light grey eyes, had been using an app on his phone to learn French, and it occurred to him that there was no reason it couldn't also be used for Irish. This was Duolingo, the app my father uses to study Welsh, along with hundreds of thousands of other users. That course might not have existed however, had Higgs and others like him not inundated the app's makers with emails enquiring about adding support for Irish.

'It was this kind of crazy teenage idea, that they'd pay any attention to me,' Higgs said about his first email. 'I didn't get a reply.'[10] But his pleas weren't ignored. Inside the company's open plan, Silicon Valley-style headquarters in Pittsburgh, Pennsylvania, change was afoot. Within five years, the US start-up would build a library of over thirty languages, including some of the most endangered on the planet.

At its core, Duolingo is a flashcards app. Users are presented with a variety of words, phrases and sounds, and then are tested on how well they remember them. The process is gamified, with users earning points for completing lessons and competing in daily and weekly leaderboards. The company's lofty mantra is very Silicon Valley – 'Making language education free, fun and accessible for everyone in the world' – but it initially focused on the most profitable, and largest, languages in the world, such as English and Spanish.

Higgs's email arrived at the perfect time however, when some in the company were questioning the focus on such languages, and wondering whether they could expand the app to include smaller tongues. Their overflowing inboxes demonstrated a clear demand for such courses, and not only that, but they were also being inundated with offers to volunteer to build them, if only they would provide a way.

In October 2013, Duolingo launched its 'incubator', a programme for anyone to begin building language courses. Even this, however, was mainly viewed as a way to add new major languages – Russian was an early candidate – rather than minority tongues. But Higgs's 'heartfelt plea' had struck a chord inside the company, said Myra Awodey, a language and community specialist. Duolingo founder Luis von Ahn 'was like, "why not? This guy sounds cool. He's serious, let's just do it"', she told me.

Irish became the first endangered or minority language added to the platform, though Higgs would not join the team for another year or so. 'They didn't choose me in the first round,' he said ruefully. But he was part of the team by the time Irish president Michael Higgins commended them at a public ceremony in 2016 for their contributions in preserving the Irish language, which Higgins called 'an act of both national and global citizenship'. By then, millions of people – more than the population of Ireland itself – had tried the Irish course, according to company data. Today, the language has around a million active weekly users, around the same as Polish and Greek, languages with 40 million and 13 million speakers worldwide, respectively.[11,12,13]

'Its been a massive, massive benefit to the language,' said Oisín Ó Doinn, a learning technologist at Dublin City University and one of the original creators of the Duolingo Irish course. He said that many language learners in schools had begun using the app to supplement their studies, and that it has been a huge success in the United States thanks to pickup from the Irish diaspora. The success of the Irish course also cultivated a mini revolution inside Duolingo, which now employs 190 designers, developers, linguists, computer scientists and other staff.

'We had to focus in the beginning on the courses that had the most demand and largest audience served,' said product manager Conor Walsh. 'But the cool thing about technology is that the incremental cost decreases. Now that we have all these courses, and we've ironed out a lot of the technical complexity, now adding a new course, in many ways, doesn't cost us that much.'

The internet and smartphone revolutions have not always been a positive development for minority languages. Hungarian linguist András Kornai, among others, has warned that the digital revolution presents a potential nail in the coffin for many endangered tongues, as they fail to transition to a digital environment, becoming more and more detached from daily life, increasingly conducted on screens and devices.[14] But while the risk of 'digital language death' is still widespread, the internet has also facilitated language preservation, such as in the work of the Endangered Language Alliance in New York, as well as helping to popularize and normalize minority languages, both in their traditional communities and within the diaspora.

'It's really important that people see a language like Welsh as something they can interact with and use on modern devices,' said Jonathan Perry, a language teacher who works on Duolingo's Welsh course. 'It brings the language up to date with modern technology usage which is absolutely so essential that a language feels fresh and used.'

Beyond apps like Duolingo, which are specifically focused on learning a language, Welsh speakers can increasingly operate in that language online, switching their Facebook, Google and smartphone to Welsh.[15] Wicipedia, the Welsh-language online encyclopaedia, covers some 130,000 entries, from the history of the Welsh flag, to a biography of Gwenno Saunders, the Cardiff born musician who sings in both Welsh and Cornish. Podcasts, videos and even video games offer new means of interacting with a heritage or minority language, including for speakers living elsewhere around the world. As well as Welsh, other languages are seeing a flowering of offerings online as well, and many minority-language speakers actively campaign companies like Amazon, Apple and Google to expand their services.

'Even if people aren't becoming entirely fluent [in this manner], it's hugely beneficial in terms of raising visibility and that's incredibly important,' said Ó Doinn, the Irish Duolingo course creator.

'Status and support are the most important things for facilitating a language's usage. My phone is in Irish because I have an Android and I'm able to make that decision. My Gmail is in Irish. These things are done for free by the community for the community. If we open up those resources that people can modify themselves, that's really important for preserving minority languages online.'

Cost was once thought to be a major driver of digital language death, as why would companies that cater to millions around the world spend money to support a language spoken by only tens or hundreds of thousands? But improvements in artificial intelligence, as well as the work of thousands of volunteers, has seen the cost of such translation plummeting. Projects also feed into each other: the existence of Welsh Wikipedia has given Google Translate a huge, open source library to draw upon, substantially improving its results. And like at Duolingo, once a company has built out support for one minority language, this makes it easier to add others in the future. Governments too have got involved: since 2018, Iceland has spent millions of dollars supporting public and private initiatives to digitize the Icelandic language and assist in the creation of technologies to support it, such as providing a database of hundreds of thousands of words to assist in Google voice search.[16] The country expects to spend some $20 million in five years on the language, an amount Higgs, the Irish advocate, said was absolutely value for money. 'Twenty million dollars is nothing,' he said. 'How many millions of Euro a year do you think France invests in the Alliance Française or the Académie to keep French alive and perfect?' (Paris budgeted around $475 million in 2020 for promoting the French language around the world, including subsidies for the Alliance and the Institut Français.[17])

The coronavirus pandemic accelerated many online language learning projects, forcing teachers and activists to find new ways to connect with their various communities online. In August 2020, North Island College, on Canada's Vancouver Island, moved its 'elder in residence' programme to video-chat, allowing students to more easily connect with language speakers from indigenous communities and ask them questions about grammar, history and cultural practices in Kwak'wala and other local languages.[18]

Ambitious revitalization projects do not always benefit the language they are trying to defend however. In late 2020, it emerged that much of Scots Wikipedia, a version of the online encyclopaedia purportedly written in that language... wasn't.[19] An American user, who began contributing to the project in 2013, when he was just twelve years old, had made thousands of edits, and written many pages, despite not speaking a word of Scots, a language used in parts of Scotland that is related to English. The linguistic house of cards came crashing down after a Reddit user noticed that much of the supposed Scots was in fact just English written in a pseudo-Scottish accent. When they checked who had created these pages, they all traced back to one user, AmaryllisGardener, who was also an administrator of the whole Scots Wikipedia project.

'The problem is that this person cannot speak Scots,' the Reddit commenter wrote. 'I don't mean this in a mean spirited or gatekeeping way where they're trying their best but are making a few mistakes, I mean they don't seem to have any knowledge of the language at all.'

For years, Scots speakers had been complaining about the poor quality of language on Wikipedia, which they felt was contributing to an impression, widespread in England and parts of Scotland, that the language is simply English spoken with an accent, and not worthy of protection. And while other contributors to the Wiki rapidly set about trying to undo Amaryllis's work, the ramifications of his contributions could be far reaching. Just as Welsh Wikipedia is used to train artificial intelligence systems, the lousy Scots content created by AmaryllisGardener may have spread well beyond its original pages, something the Redditor who exposed the debacle called 'cultural vandalism on a hitherto unprecedented scale'.[20]

Early in the reporting for this book, I interviewed David Hand, then president of the St. David's Society of Hong Kong, a group for Welsh people living in the city.[21] Hand grew up in Porth Tywyn on the south Wales coast, in a Welsh-speaking family. He also attended a Welsh-language school, a rarity at the time. But as he got older, 'English really took over,' particularly as he began his career and moved abroad.

By the time we talked, Hand had been living in Greater China for the best part of two decades. And yet, his household, in rural Hong Kong, was a Welsh-speaking one, despite being thousands of kilometres away from the only place the language is widely spoken. Hand's three children – Arwen, Huw and Tomos – had never lived in Wales, but all three speak Welsh fluently, and only spoke that language with their father. (Dai died, tragically and far too young, in late 2019. He was described in an obituary as 'passionately Welsh, a Welsh-speaker and champion of our cause'.)

'As the kids were growing up until the age of five we always had a Welsh speaker at home in addition to me,' Hand told me. The couple hired a string of Welsh nannies, usually young women taking time out between high school and university, to come live with the family in Beijing. 'It's about the mindset of thinking of yourself as Welsh and a Welsh speaker, and compare yourself to a French person or a Spaniard or a German,' Hand said. 'They wouldn't contemplate not teaching their children their own language.'

Apps like Duolingo, and Welsh-language services online, make such a task infinitely easier for families today, while, in Wales itself, Welsh-medium education is expanding every year as the country builds towards the goal of a million speakers. This is not yet the norm for many minority languages, and many tongues endure ongoing marginalization and suppression, while others, such as Cantonese, face an uncertain future and potential decline, but successes are becoming less and less rare, and the model for revitalization is clearer than ever. What is required, and what unfortunately remains a battle to achieve, is the political will and power to pursue it.

– *James Griffiths, Hong Kong, March 2021*

Author's Note

In writing a book about language, especially one about the way languages have been oppressed and marginalized, it is important to treat other tongues with respect. I have endeavoured to do so, while also aiding readers who do not have any familiarity with the languages being discussed to get a feel for them as much as one can in print. To this end, I use diacritic marks for all languages that use them when written in the Latin alphabet. The exception to this is when words in these languages are commonly used in English, such as the Chinese names for cities and provinces. One of the arguments of this book is that multilingualism and multiculturalism are positives for society, and should be protected and prized, and so I have followed the lead of other postcolonial writers in avoiding italicizing non-English words, and thus needlessly exoticizing them. However, in the interests of readability, I have avoided for the most part the use of languages other than English in quotes and excerpts, in favour of just providing a translation. In the case of names, particularly in Chinese, I have chosen to follow the lead of the subjects themselves, even if this sometimes leads to inconsistency in terms of Romanization. For historical figures, I have used the most common transliteration, so Mao Zedong but Sun Yat-sen.

Aside from English, I only speak one of the languages covered in this book fluently (Welsh), and so the risk of inadvertent errors in discussing other tongues is high. To avoid this, I have relied on the advice of native speakers and experts who viewed the manuscript at various stages. Any mistakes that remain are mine alone.

Any work of journalism is done standing on the shoulders of those who went before, and I am eternally grateful for the work of those reporters, writers and historians cited in this book for helping me understand and pointing the way. That anyone is willing to speak to a journalist, let alone for extended periods of time, sometimes at potential risk to themselves, is a constant surprise and joy. Thank you to everyone who agreed to be interviewed for this book, from the characters in it to the many academics and language experts who spoke to me during my reporting.

If no one bought my first book, *The Great Firewall of China*, I likely wouldn't have had a chance to write a second, and so I am forever grateful to those that did. I am thankful too for the continued support of Zed/Bloomsbury, particularly Kim Walker, who bought this book based largely on a phone call and a hastily written outline, and to David Avital, who ably guided it to publication. My agent Clare Mao supported and championed this work, while Catherine Griffiths, Paul Griffiths, Gerald Roche, Gina Tam, Lindsey Ford and Ella Wong all offered advice and feedback during the drafting stage. Erik Crouch went above and beyond with his assistance, going through multiple revisions with me, for which I am in his debt.

This book grew out of an article on language rights I wrote for CNN. That article was edited by Steve George, who suggested, as he slashed chunks out of my text, that it could make a good book. He was right. For years, I was jealous of writers who developed close partnerships with their editors, and in Steve I finally found that myself. He made my work better every time, and most of my best story ideas were either developed in collaboration with him, or suggested by him in the first place. CNN supported me through the writing of two books, and I am hugely grateful in particular to Brett McKeehan and Inga Thordar for their endless encouragement and cheerleading. Thanks too to my colleagues at CNN in Hong Kong and around the world, both past and present.

Thanks to Natasha Steinberg for helping with research in the UK; Catrin Sion and Nia Thomas for assistance with Meibion Glyndŵr documents; Gina Tam for sharing an advance copy of her own book on language; Brendan O'Kane for classical Chinese advice; and Jeff Wasserstrom for constant guidance and encouragement. In Hawai'i, 'Ekela Kani'aupio-Crozier and Kū Kahakalau were generous hosts and guides. Sam Dalsimer hosted me in Pittsburgh, and responded to my endless requests for Duolingo contacts. In Hong Kong, friends supported and encouraged me during the reporting and writing of this book, even if they didn't realize it.

Thanks too to my family, who made sure I got an education in Welsh and encouraged me to learn not only that language but any others I had a mind to.

Finally, thanks to my wife, Ella Wong, who is a far better linguist than I could ever be. This book is for her.

Notes

Introduction

1   D. Everett, *How Language Began: The Story of Humanity's Greatest Invention*, Liveright Publishing, 2017.

2   M. Tallerman and K. Gibson (eds.), *The Oxford Handbook of Language Evolution*, Oxford, 2012, p.2.

3   Ibid., p.4.

4   C. Kenneally *The First Word: The Search for the Origins of Language*, Penguin Books, 2008.

5   M. Arbib, 'Evolving the Language Ready Brain and the Social Mechanisms That Support Language', *J Commun Disord*, Vol. 42, No. 4, July-August 2009, pp.263–71 https://www.ncbi.nlm.nih.gov/pmc/articles/PMC3543814/

6   J. McWhorter, *The Power of Babel: A Natural History of Language*, Arrow Books, 2003.

7   K. Kerenyi, *The Gods of the Greeks*, Thames and Hudson, 1951, p.222.

8   Captain W. E. H. Barrett, 'Notes on the Customs of the Wa-Giriama, etc., of British East Africa' *Journal of the Royal Anthropological Institute*, xli. (1911) p.37, in J. G. Frazer, *Folk-lore in the Old Testament: Studies in Comparative Religion, Legend and Law*, Macmillan, 1919, p.384.

9   J. Teit, 'Kaska Tales', *The Journal of American Folklore*, Vol. 30, No. 118, October–December 1917, pp.442–3.

10   J. McWhorter, *The Power of Babel: A Natural History of Language*.

11   B. Bryson, *The Mother Tongue: English and How It Got That Way*, HarperCollins, 1990.

12   'Why Does a Cow Become Beef?' *Dictionary.com* https://www.dictionary.com/e/animal-names-change-become-food/

13   J. Mason, 'The Languages of South America', in J. Steward, *Handbook of South American Indians*, Vol. 6, 1950, Smithsonian, p.303.

14   D. Brinton, *The American Race: A Linguistic Classification and Ethnographic Description of the Native Tribes of North and South America*, Cambridge University Press, 26 November 2009, p.170.

15   M. Camp and A. Portalewska, 'The Electronic Drum: Community Radio's Role in Reversing Indigenous Language Decline', *Cultural Survival Quarterly Magazine*, March 2013 https://www.culturalsurvival.org/publications/cultural-survival-quarterly/electronic-drum-community-radios-role-reversing-indigenous

16 *'Chinese, Yue'*, Ethnologue, 2019.

17 'How Many Languages Are There in the World?' *Ethnologue* https://www.ethnologue.com/guides/how-many-languages

18 'UNESCO Atlas of the World's Languages in Danger', UNESCO http://www.unesco.org/languages-atlas/index.php

19 M. Walsh, '"Language Is Like Food …": Links between Language Revitalization and Health and Well-being', in L. Hinton, L. Huss and G. Roche (eds.), *The Routledge Handbook of Language Revitalization*, Routledge, 2018, p.5.

20 A. Taff et al., 'Indigenous Language Use Impacts Wellness', Oxford Handbooks Online, September 2018 https://www.oxfordhandbooks.com/view/10.1093/oxfordhb/9780190610029.001.0001/oxfordhb-9780190610029-e-41

21 R. Perlin, 'Capitalism, Colonialism and Nationalism Are Language Killers', Al Jazeera, 28 December 2014 http://america.aljazeera.com/opinions/2014/12/language-diversityeconomy.html

22 R. Perlin, 'Radical Linguistics in an Age of Extinction', *Dissent Magazine*, Summer 2014 https://www.dissentmagazine.org/article/radical-linguistics-in-an-age-of-extinction

23 "2019 International Year of Indigenous Languages', *United Nations*, 12 January 2019 https://www.un.org/development/desa/dspd/2019/01/2019-international-year-of-indigenous-languages/

Chapter 1

1 R. R. W. Lingen et al., *Reports of the Commissioners of Inquiry into the State of Education in Wales*, Appointed by the Committee of Council on Education, 1848, p.37.

2 P. Higginbotham, 'Introduction', Workhouses.org.uk http://www.workhouses.org.uk/Wales/

3 '1834 Poor Law', *The National Archives* http://www.nationalarchives.gov.uk/education/resources/1834-poor-law/

4 P. Higginbotham, 'The Workhouse in Wales', Workhouses.org.uk http://www.workhouses.org.uk/Wales/

5 R. R. W. Lingen et al., *Reports of the Commissioners of Inquiry into the State of Education in Wales*, pp.136–7.

6 Ibid., Appendix, p.238.

7 C. Lucas, 'Lingen, Ralph Robert Wheeler Lingen, Baron', Encyclopædia Britannica, 1911, Vol. 16.

8 R. R. W. Lingen et al., *Reports of the Commissioners of Inquiry into the State of Education in Wales*, p.25.

9 Ibid., p.27.

10 Ibid., pp.25–6.

11 Ibid., p.27.

12 Adapted from third-person account of Williams's speech. W. Williams, 'Education In Wales', *Hansard*, 10 March 1846, Vol. 84, pp.845–67 https://api.parliament.uk/historic-hansard/commons/1846/mar/10/education-in-wales

13 D. Williams, *'WILLIAMS, WILLIAM (1788–1865), Member of Parliament'*, *Dictionary of Welsh Biography* https://biography.wales/article/s-WILL-WIL-1788

14 Description based on a contemporary portrait of Williams held by The National Library of Wales.

15 Adapted from W. Williams, 'Education In Wales', pp.845–67.

16 G. Clement Boase, *'Symons, Jelinger Cookson'*, Dictionary of National Biography, 1885–1900, Vol. 55.

17 W. Lubenow, *The Cambridge Apostles, 1820–1914: Liberalism, Imagination, and Friendship in British Intellectual and Professional Life*, Cambridge University Press, 29 October 1998, p.420.

18 R. Dod, *The Peerage, Baronetage, and Knightage of Great Britain and Ireland*, Whittaker and Co, 1864, p.685.

19 G. Moody, *The English Journal of Education, volume 4*, Darton & Co, 1846, p.381.

20 R. R. W. Lingen et al., *Reports of the Commissioners of Inquiry into the State of Education in Wales*, pp.309–10.

21 Ibid., p.4.

22 Ibid., p.297.

23 Ibid., p.310.

24 Ibid., p.452.

25 Ibid., p.312.

26 P. Morgan, 'From Long Knives to Blue Books', in *Welsh Society and Nationhood*, edited by R. R. Davies et al., University of Wales Press, 1984.

27 R. Marsden, 'The Treachery of the Blue Books', in *'Methodism in Wales, 1730–1850'*, Open University https://www.open.edu/openlearn/history-the-arts/methodism-wales-1730-1850/content-section-8

28 G. Roberts, *The Language of the Blue Books*, University of Wales Press, 2011, p.209.

29 P. Morgan, 'From Long Knives to Blue Books', p.205.

30 Ibid., p.213.

31 Quoted in W. Williams, *A Letter to Lord John Russell on the Report of the Commissioners appointed to inquire into the State of Education in Wales*, James Ridgway, 1848, p.31.

32 G. Roberts, *The Language of the Blue Books*, p.220.

33 W. Brooks, *Welsh Print Culture in y Wladfa: The Role of Ethnic Newspapers in Welsh Patagonia, 1868–1933*, Cardiff University Press, 2012, p.27.

34 E. James, 'The Argentines Who Speak Welsh', BBC, 16 October 2014 https://www.bbc.com/news/magazine-29611380

35 G. Roberts, *The Language of the Blue Books*, p.220.

36 E. Humphreys, *The Taliesin Tradition: A Quest for the Welsh Identity*, Black Raven Press, 1983, p.182.

37 Quoted in M. Arnold, *On the study of Celtic literature*, p.x.

38 Ibid., p.12.

39 G. Jenkins and M. Williams, *'Let's Do Our Best for the Ancient Tongue': The Welsh Language in the Twentieth Century*, University of Wales Press Cardiff, 2000, p.19.

Chapter 2

1   T. Pennant, *Tours in Wales, vol. ii*, H. Humphreys, 1883, pp.368–74.

2   Ibid., p.368.

3   S. Baring-Gould and J. Fisher, *The Lives of the British Saints: Vol II*, C. J. Clark, 1908, p.423.

4   Ibid., pp.1–10.

5   T. Price (ed.), *Iolo Manuscripts: A selection of ancient Welsh manuscripts*, William Rees, 1848, pp.150–1.

6   T. Pennant, *Tours in Wales, vol. ii*, pp.368–75.

7   R. Jones, *The North Wales Quarrymen, 1874-1922*, University of Wales Press, 1982, p.78.

8   The Editors, 'League of Nations: Second Period (1924–31)', *Encyclopedia Britannica*, 2017 https://www.britannica.com/topic/League-of-Nations/Second-period-1924-31

9   H. Steiner, 'The Geneva Disarmament Conference of 1932', in *The Annals of the American Academy of Political and Social Science*, Vol. 168, pp.212–19.

10   A. C. Temperley, *The Whispering Gallery Of Europe*, Collins, 1938, pp.273–4.

11   I. Kershaw, *Making Friends with Hitler: Lord Londonderry, the Nazis, and the Road to War*, Penguin, 2005.

12   Lord Londonderry, 'Imperial Defence', Hansard, House of Lords, 22 May 1935, Vol. 96, c.1017.

13   Tan-y-Llŷn is a pivotal moment in the history of Welsh nationalism and the Welsh language. My account of it is based partially on newspaper accounts of the time and the writings of Saunders Lewis and his co-conspirators. It would not have been possible however, without Dafydd Jenkins's definitive recounting of the fire and its aftermath, *Nation on Trial: Penyberth 1936*, translated by A. Corkett, Welsh Academic Press, 1999.

14   D. Jenkins, *Nation on Trial: Penyberth 1936*, translated by A. Corkett, Welsh Academic Press, 1999, p.8.

15   G. Jenkins and M. Williams, *'Let's Do Our Best for the Ancient Tongue": The Welsh Language in the Twentieth Century*, pp.123–35.

16   I. Peate, '*The Llyn Peninsula: Some Cultural Considerations*', letter to the Council for the Preservation of Rural Wales, 27 July 1935, cited in ibid.

17   S. Lewis, 'The Case for Welsh Nationalism', *The Listener*, Vol. XV, No. 383, 13 May 1936, p.915.

18   An Acte for Laws & Justice to be ministred in Wales in like fourme as it is in this Realme, 27 Henry VIII c. 26, 1535.

19   D. Jenkins, *Nation on Trial: Penyberth 1936*, pp.12–13.

20   Ibid., p.39.

21   '*Three to Be Tried on Charges of Firing R.A.F. Camp*', *Manchester Guardian*, 17 September 1936.

22   D. Jenkins, *Nation on Trial: Penyberth 1936*, p.40.

23 *'Trial of Welsh Nationalist Leaders'*, *Manchester Guardian*, 14 October 1936.

24 *'Three to Be Tried on Charges of Firing R.A.F. Camp'*, *Manchester Guardian*, 17 September 1936.

25 Currency conversion done using UK Inflation Calculator, Official Data Foundation. Contemporary sterling value as of September 2019. https://www.officialdata.org/uk/inflation/1936?amount=2500

26 D. Jenkins, *Nation on Trial: Penyberth 1936*, p.41.

27 Malicious Damage Act 1861, 24 & 25 Vict c 97, pp.766–7.

28 *'Trial of Welsh Nationalist Leaders'*, *Manchester Guardian*, 14 October 1936.

29 D. Jenkins, *Nation on Trial: Penyberth 1936*, p.55.

30 My account of the trial and verbatim quotes come from an extensive contemporary report in the *Manchester Guardian*, checked against other sources. *'Trial of Welsh Nationalist Leaders'*, *Manchester Guardian*, 14 October 1936.

31 D. Jenkins, *Nation on Trial: Penyberth 1936*, p.87.

32 Lloyd George to Megan Lloyd George. 1 December 1936, Lloyd George: Family Letters, pp. 212–13, cited in K. Morgan, *Rebirth of a Nation: Wales, 1880-1980*, Oxford University Press, 1981.

33 *'Nine Months' Imprisonment for Welsh Nationalists'*, *Manchester Guardian*, 20 January 1937.

34 *'Welsh Nationalists Sentenced to Prison'*, *Manchester Guardian*, 20 January 1937.

35 *'Penhros'*, Airfields of Britain Conservation Trust https://www.abct.org.uk/airfields/airfield-finder/penrhos

36 G. Davies, 'The Legal Status of the Welsh Language in the Twentieth Century', in G. Jenkins and M. Williams (eds), *'Let's Do Our Best for the Ancient Tongue': The Welsh Language in the Twentieth Century*, University of Wales Press Cardiff, 2000, pp.218–48.

37 Hansard, Administration Of Justice (Wales) Bill, HC Deb, 26 February 1937, Vol. 320, c.2428.

38 Welsh Courts Act 1942, 1942 C.40.

39 G. Davies, 'The Legal Status of the Welsh Language in the Twentieth Century', p.234.

40 R. Jones, *The Fascist Party in Wales?: Plaid Cymru*, Welsh Nationalism and the Accusation of Fascism, University of Wales Press, 2014.

41 S. Lewis, *'Tynged Yr Iaith'*, BBC Radio Cymru, 13 February 1962, translated by G. Aled Williams.

Chapter 3

1 J. Beckett, *City Status in the British Isles, 1830–2002*, Routledge, 2017.

2 'Capital of Principality (Cardiff)', *HC Deb* 20 December 1955, Vol. 547 cc310-1W https://api.parliament.uk/historic-hansard/written-answers/1955/dec/20/capital-of-principality-cardiff

3   Historical weather for 17 November 1967, Met Office.

4   'Statement of Major Clifton Melville JEFFERIES, M.B.E., *ASSI* 84/577, National Archives.

5   Evening Post Reporter, 'Bomb Blast at Royal Talks HQ', *Reading Evening Post*, 17 November 1967.

6   'Central Chancery of the Orders of Knighthood', *The London Gazette*, 8 November 1968, No. 44713.

7   Evening Post Reporter, 'Bomb Blast at Royal Talks HQ', *Reading Evening Post*, 17 November 1967.

8   'Statement of Major Clifton Melville JEFFERIES, M.B.E., *ASSI* 84/577, National Archives.

9   J. Davies, *A History of Wales*, Penguin Books, 2007.

10 '1967: Moves to Curb Spread of Foot-and-mouth', *BBC* http://news.bbc.co.uk/onthisday/hi/dates/stories/november/18/newsid_3191000/3191938.stm

11 D. Harari, '"Pound in Your Pocket" Devaluation: 50 Years On', *House of Commons Library*, 17 November 2017 https://commonslibrary.parliament.uk/economy-business/economy-economy/pound-in-your-pocket-devaluation-50-years-on/

12 J. Humphries, *Freedom Fighters: Wales's Forgotten 'War', 1963–1993*, University of Wales Press, 2009, p.4.

13 '"Save Our Homes" Procession Marches in Vain', *The Guardian*, 22 November 1956.

14 'Tryweryn Appeal to the Queen', *The Guardian*, 27 September 1957.

15 E. Crump, 'Tryweryn: Jeers Cause the Reservoir's Opening Ceremony to Be Cut Short', *Daily Post*, 20 October 2015 https://www.dailypost.co.uk/news/north-wales-news/tryweryn-jeers-cause-reservoirs-opening-10287234

16 D. O'Neill, 'Charge of the White Brigade', *The Guardian*, 22 October 1965.

17 'Welsh Fighting Talk', *The Guardian*, 18 April 1966.

18 N. Evans, 'The Investiture of the Prince of Wales', *BBC*, 25 June 2009 https://www.bbc.co.uk/wales/history/sites/investiture/pages/investiture-background.shtml

19 Associated Press, 'Welsh Greet Lord Snowden at Cardiff with Bomb, Jeers', *Fort Lauderdale News*, 18 November 1967.

20 Evening Post Reporter, 'Bomb Blast at Royal Talks HQ', *Reading Evening Post*, 17 November 1967.

21 W. Thomas, *John Jenkins – The Reluctant Revolutionary?* Y Lolfa, 2020.

22 DPP 2/4471 Regina vs Owen Williams et al.

23 J. Humphries, *Freedom Fighters: Wales's Forgotten 'War', 1963–1993*, p.26.

24 W. Thomas, *John Jenkins – The Reluctant Revolutionary?* Y Lolfa, 2020.

25 PREM 13/1801.

26 CAB 164/389.

27 J. Humphries, *Freedom Fighters: Wales's Forgotten 'War', 1963–1993*, pp.226–7.

28 W. Thomas, *John Jenkins – The Reluctant Revolutionary?*

29 Ibid.

30 'Statement of Ian SKIDMORE', *ASSI* 84/577, National Archives.

31 'Statement of Harold Pendlebury', *ASSI* 84/577, National Archives.

32 W. Thomas, *John Jenkins – The Reluctant Revolutionary?*

33 Ibid.

34 Ibid.

35 PREM 13/2903-Royal Family.

36 'Statement of Major Clifton Melville JEFFERIES, M.B.E', *ASSI* 84/577, National Archives.

37 ASSI 84/577.

38 N. Constable, 'A Welsh Bomber and the Little Boy He Crippled', *Daily Mail*, 22 June 2019 https://www.dailymail.co.uk/home/event/article-7162353/Charles-Investiture.html

39 W. Thomas, *John Jenkins – The Reluctant Revolutionary?*

40 'A speech by HRH The Prince of Wales replying to the Loyal Address by Sir Ben Bowen Thomas, President of the University College of Wales, Aberystwyth, The Investiture of The Prince of Wales, Caernarfon Castle, North Wales', *Prince of Wales* https://www.princeofwales.gov.uk/speech/speech-hrh-prince-wales-replying-loyal-address-sir-ben-bowen-thomas-president-university

41 R v John Barnard Jenkins and Frederick Ernest Alders, County of Denbigh Assize, 3 March 1970.

42 ASSI 84/577.

43 W. Thomas, *John Jenkins – The Reluctant Revolutionary?*

44 J. Humphries, *Freedom Fighters: Wales's Forgotten 'War', 1963–1993*, p.155.

45 N. Brooke, *Terrorism and Nationalism in the United Kingdom*, Palgrave Macmillan, 2018, pp.60–1.

46 G. Jenkins and M. Williams, *'Let's Do Our Best for the Ancient Tongue': The Welsh Language in the Twentieth Century*, p.252.

47 '*An Act to* Make Further Provision with Respect to the Welsh Language and References in Acts of Parliament to Wales', *Parliament*, 27 July 1967 https://www.legislation.gov.uk/ukpga/1967/66/introduction/enacted

48 G. Jenkins and M. Williams, *'Let's Do Our Best for the Ancient Tongue': The Welsh Language in the Twentieth Century*, p.243.

49 Ibid., p.272.

50 Ibid., p.273.

51 J. Gower, 'The Story of Wales', *BBC* Digital, 2012.

52 J. Osmond, *Accelerating History – the 1979, 1997 and 2011 Referendums in Wales*, Institute of Welsh Affairs, 2011, p.5.

53 Martin Johnes, 'The Welsh Devolution Referendum, 1 March 1979', *Hanes Cymru*, 26 February 2019 https://martinjohnes.com/2019/02/26/the-welsh-devolution-referendum-1-march-1979/

54 C. Betts, 'Freed Bomber Says He Fears Exile from Wales', *The Western Mail*, 15 July 1976.

55 Welsh nationalist extremism: discussion papers; meetings with Secretary of State for Wales National Archives https://discovery.nationalarchives.gov.uk/details/r/C16310826

56   N. Brooke, *Terrorism and Nationalism in the United Kingdom*, p.73.

57   J. Humphries, *Freedom Fighters: Wales's Forgotten 'War', 1963–1993*, p.162.

58   Ibid., p.164.

59   D. Wigley, Letter to Prime Minister Margaret Thatcher, PREM19/395, House of Commons, 11 July 1980.

60   *Cabinet: Minutes of Full Cabinet CC(80) 23rd*, CAB128/67, Margaret Thatcher Foundation, 11 June 1980.

61   *Record of a Meeting Held at 10 Downing Street*, PREM19/395 f63, Margaret Thatcher Foundation, 15 September 1980.

62   J. Davies, *A History of Wales*.

63   M. Jones, *The Welsh Language in Education in the UK*, pp.11–13.

64   Welsh Language Act 1993.

65   J. Davies, *A History of Wales*.

66   M. Johnes, 'Margaret Thatcher: An Unlikely Architect of Welsh Devolution', *BBC*, 8 April 2013 https://www.bbc.com/news/uk-wales-politics–16315966

67   M. Sutton, 'An Index of Deaths from the Conflict in Ireland', *Conflict Archive on the Internet* https://cain.ulster.ac.uk/sutton/tables/Status.html

68   Gordon Wynne JONES witness statement, ASSI 84/577.

69   J. Gower, 'The Story of Wales'.

70   M. Johnes, 'Margaret Thatcher: An Unlikely Architect of Welsh Devolution'.

71   'The Devolution Debate', *BBC*, 28 February 1979 https://www.bbc.com/news/av/uk-scotland-scotland-politics-29147146/scottish-independence-devolution-79-john-smith

72   'Dissent within the Welsh Labour Party', *BBC* https://www.bbc.co.uk/news/special/politics97/devolution/wales/briefing/dissent.shtml

73   'Welsh Referendum Live – The Final Result', *BBC*, 12 September 1997 https://www.bbc.co.uk/news/special/politics97/devolution/wales/live/index.shtml

Chapter 4

1   R. Harries, 'The Dialects of Wales: How One Country Has Five Different Words for the Same Thing', *Wales Online*, 30 September 2018 https://www.walesonline.co.uk/news/dialects-wales-how-one-country–15194987

2   Named for, much less splendidly, the colonial military hero Redvers Buller.

3   'Welsh Language Results: Annual Population Survey, 2001–2018', *Welsh Government*, 29 May 2019, p.3.

4   'Welsh Language Data from the Annual Population Survey: July 2018 to June 2019', *Welsh Government*, 25 June 2020 https://gov.wales/welsh-language-data-annual-population-survey-july-2018-june-2019

5   'Cymraeg 2050: A Million Welsh Speakers', *Welsh Government*, 2018 https://gov.wales/sites/default/files/publications/2018-12/cymraeg-2050-welsh-language-strategy.pdf

6   S. Brooks, *Why Wales Never Was: The Failure of Welsh Nationalism*, University of Wales Press, 2017.

7   '26,581 Children Every Year Denied Welsh Language Fluency', *Cymdeithas*, 1 January 2020 https://cymdeithas.cymru/news/26581-children-every-year-denied-welsh-language-fluency

8   'The Cornish Language Revival', *Go Cornish* https://gocornish.org/about-go-cornish/the-cornish-language-revival/

9   A. Pennycook, *Language and Mobility: Unexpected Places*, Multilingual Matters, 2012, p.164.

10 'Welsh Language Inspires New Gaelic Campaign in Scotland', 15 October 2019 https://nation.cymru/news/welsh-language-inspires-new-gaelic-campaign-in-scotland/

11 A. Rolewska, 'The Implications of Brexit for the Welsh Language', *Welsh Language Commissioner*, 22 January 2019 http://www.comisiynyddygymraeg.cymru/English/News/Pages/The-implications-of-Brexit-for-the-Welsh-language.aspx

12 A. Lewis, 'Why Wales' Most Pro-Brexit Town Doesn't Care about European Money', *Wales Online*, 3 February 2019 https://www.walesonline.co.uk/news/wales-news/wales-most-pro-brexit-town–15767233

13 F. Perraudin, 'English People Living in Wales Tilted It towards Brexit, Research Finds', *The Guardian*, 22 September 2019 https://www.theguardian.com/uk-news/2019/sep/22/english-people-wales-brexit-research

14 R. Awan-Scully, 'With Welsh Independence Polling Higher than Ever It Is No Longer a Fringe Movement', *Nation.cymru*, 5 June 2020 https://nation.cymru/opinion/with-welsh-independence-polling-higher-than-ever-it-is-no-longer-a-fringe-movement/

15 A. Price, 'A Letter to the People of Wales on the Subject of Welsh Independence', *Nation.cymru*, 17 July 2020 https://nation.cymru/opinion/a-letter-to-the-people-of-wales-on-the-subject-of-welsh-independence/

Interlude

1   L. Thompson, *A History of South Africa*.

2   Ibid.

3   P. Warwick, *Black People and the South African War 1899–1902*, Cambridge University Press, p.4.

4   'Women and Children in White Concentration Camps during the Anglo-Boer War, 1900–1902', *South Africa History Online*, 21 March 2011 https://www.sahistory.org.za/article/women-and-children-white-concentration-camps-during-anglo-boer-war–1900–1902

5   Peace Treaty of Vereeniging, 31 May 1902.

6   L. Thompson, *A History of South Africa*.

7   H. Giliomee, 'The Rise and Possible Demise of Afrikaans as a Public Language', *PRAESA Occasional Papers No. 14*, University of Cape Town, 2003, p.5.

8   Ibid., p.6.

9   Editorial in *The Cape Argus*, 19 September 1857, cited in H. Giliomee, 2003.

10 J. de Waal, *My Herinneringe van ons Taalstryd*, Nasionale Pers, 1932, p. 21, cited in H. Giliomee, 2003.

11 Quoted in F. van Coetsem, '*Loan Phonology and the Two Transfer Types in Language Contact*', Walter de Gruyter GmbH & Co KG, 25 April 2016, p.132.

12 L. Thompson, *A History of South Africa*.

13 I. Evans, *Bureaucracy and Race: Native Administration in South Africa*, University of California Press, 29 September 1997, p.227.

14 L. Thompson, *A History of South Africa*.

15 Ibid.

16 S. Ndlovu, 'The Soweto Uprising', in *The Road to Democracy in South Africa, Volume 2*, South African Democracy Education Trust, 2011, pp.342–3.

17 Hastings Ndolvu's age is given alternatively as 15, 16 and 17 depending on the source. I have chosen to use the older age as it is the one which appears on a commemorative plaque unveiled by his family in Soweto in 2012.

18 'The June 16 Soweto Youth Uprising', *South African History Online*, 21 May 2013 https://www.sahistory.org.za/article/june-16-soweto-youth-uprising

19 B. Hirson, *Year of Fire, Year of Ash: The Soweto Schoolchildrens Revolt That Shook Apartheid*, Zed Books, 15 June 2016.

20 R. Malan, *My Traitor's Heart: A South African Exile Returns to Face His Country, His Tribe, and His Conscience*, Grove Atlantic, 2012, p.59.

21 A. Brink, *A Fork in the Road*, Random House, 2010.

22 '*The June 16 Soweto* Youth Uprising', *South African History Online*, 21 May 2013 https://www.sahistory.org.za/article/june-16-soweto-youth-uprising

23 D. Tutu et al., 'Truth and Reconciliation Commission of South Africa Report', *TRC*, 29 October 1998, p.558.

24 Ibid., p.558.

25 L. Thompson, *A History of South Africa*.

26 K. Prah, 'The Challenge of Language in Post-apartheid South Africa', *LitNet*, 22 March 2018 https://www.litnet.co.za/challenge-language-post-apartheid-south-africa/

27 J. Bester, 'Protesters Throw Poo on Rhodes Statue', *IOL*, 10 March 2015 https://www.iol.co.za/news/south-africa/western-cape/protesters-throw-poo-on-rhodes-statue-1829526#.VSAM3fmUdJc

28 Y. Kamaldien, 'Rhodes Statue: Students Occupy Offices', *IOL*, 21 March 2015 https://www.iol.co.za/news/south-africa/western-cape/rhodes-statue-students-occupy-offices-1835276#.VSEO86g0WSo

29 E. Fairbanks, 'Why South African Students Have Turned on Their Parents' Generation', *The Guardian*, 18 November 2015 https://www.theguardian.com/news/2015/nov/18/why-south-african-students-have-turned-on-their-parents-generation

30 S. Masondo, 'Rhodes: As Divisive in Death as in Life', *City Press*, 22 March 2015 https://www.news24.com/SouthAfrica/News/Cecil-John-Rhodes-As-divisive-in-death-as-in-life-20150322

31 N. Mandela, *Long Walk to Freedom*, Hachette UK, 25 April 2013.

32 Quoted in A. Albuyeh, 'Regime Change Succession Politics and the Language Question', in M. Nyamanga Amutabi and S. Wanjala Nasong'o (eds), *Regime Change and Succession Politics in Africa: Five Decades of Misrule*, Routledge, 4 January 2013, p.180.

33 A. Krog, 'As Afrikaners We Were Scared of What Mandela Would Do to Us – How Wrong We Were', *The Independent*, 13 December 2013.

34 A. Krog, *Country of My Skull: Guilt, Sorrow, and the Limits of Forgiveness in the New South Africa*, Crown/Archetype, 2007.

35 The Constitution of the Republic of South Africa, 1996, p.4.

36 A. Albuyeh, 'Regime Change Succession Politics and the Language Question', p.181.

37 R. Davies, *Afrikaners in the New South Africa: Identity Politics in a Globalised Economy*, Tauris Academic Studies, 2009, p.94.

38 A. Brink, 'A Long Way from Mandela's Kitchen', *New York Times*, 11 September 2010 https://www.nytimes.com/2010/09/12/opinion/12brink.html

39 A. Brink, *A Fork in the Road*.

40 D. Roodt, 'Old Split over Afrikaner Identity Fuels New Terror', *Business Day*, 28 November 2002 https://web.archive.org/web/20021203135532/ and https://allafrica.com/stories/200211290230.html

41 H. Giliomee, 'The Rise and Possible Demise of Afrikaans as a Public Language', p.24.

42 Open Stellenbosch Collective, 'Open Stellenbosch – Tackling Language and Exclusion at Stellenbosch University', *Daily Maverick*, 28 April 2015 https://www.dailymaverick.co.za/article/2015-04-28-op-ed-open-stellenbosch-tackling-language-and-exclusion-at-stellenbosch-university/

43 'Students in South Africa Win Language Victory', *DW News*, 13 November 2015 https://www.dw.com/en/students-in-south-africa-win-language-victory/a-18848432

44 H. Giliomee, 'The War against Afrikaans at Stellenbosch', *Politics Web*, 28 April 2016 https://www.politicsweb.co.za/opinion/the-war-against-afrikaans-at-stellenbosch

45 W. Visser, 'From MWU to Solidarity – A Trade Union Reinventing Itself', *South African Journal Labour Relations*, Vol. 30, No. 2, 2006, p.39.

46 T. Bell, 'Wherefore Art Our Unions in SA?' *City Press*, 8 April 2018 https://www.fin24.com/Economy/Labour/wherefore-art-our-unions-in-sa-20180408-2

47 P. du Toit, 'AfriForum And Solidarity's "Parallel State"', *Huffington Post*, 31 January 2017 https://www.huffingtonpost.co.uk/2017/01/31/afriforum-and-solidaritys-parallel-state_a_21704173/?ncid=other_saredirect_m2afnz7mbfm

48 'About Us', *AfriForum* https://www.afriforum.co.za/en/about-us/

49 M. Du Preez, 'The Problem AfriForum Is Causing the DA', *News 24*, 15 May 2018 https://www.news24.com/Columnists/MaxduPreez/the-problem-afriforum-is-causing-the-da-20180515

50 J. Pogue, 'The Myth of White Genocide', *Harper's*, 15 February 2019 https://pulitzercenter.org/reporting/myth-white-genocide

51 E. Roets, *Kill the Boer: Government Complicity in South Africa's Brutal Farm Murders*, Kraal Uitgewers, 2018.

52 J. Burke, 'Murders of Farmers in South Africa at 20-Year Low, Research Shows', *The Guardian*, 26 June 2018 https://www.theguardian.com/world/2018/jun/27/murders-of-farmers-in-south-africa-at-20-year-low-research-shows

53 Reality Check, 'South Africa Crime: Police Figures Show Rising Murder and Sexual Offences', *BBC*, 12 September 2019 https://www.bbc.com/news/world-africa-49673944

54 'Global Study on Homicide', *United Nations Office on Drugs and Crime*, 2019, p.25.

55 K. Wilkinson, 'FACTSHEET: Statistics on Farm Attacks and Murders in South Africa', *Africa Check*, 8 May 2017 https://africacheck.org/factsheets/factsheet-statistics-farm-attacks-murders-sa/

56 D. McKenzie and B. Swails, 'They're Prepping for a Race War. And They See Trump as Their "Ray of Hope"', *CNN*, November 2018 https://edition.cnn.com/interactive/2018/11/africa/south-africa-suidlanders-intl/

57 'AfriForum v University of the Free State: Media Summary', *Constitutional Court of South Africa*, 29 December 2017 http://www.saflii.org/za/cases/ZACC/2017/48.html

58 'General Household Survey 2018', *Statistics South Africa*, 28 May 2019, pp.8–9 http://www.statssa.gov.za/publications/P0318/P03182018.pdf

59 S. Gordon et al., 'South Africans Prefer Their Children to Be Taught in English', *Quartz*, 2 October 2019 https://qz.com/africa/1720174/south-africans-prefer-their-children-to-be-taught-in-english/

60 'Afrikaans: The Language of Black and Coloured Dissent', *South Africa History Online*, 20 September 2017 https://www.sahistory.org.za/article/afrikaans-language-black-and-coloured-dissent#endnote-217-ref

61 D. Attridge, 'The Triumph of Afrikaans Fiction', *Public Books*, 16 February 2018 https://www.publicbooks.org/the-triumph-of-afrikaans-fiction/

62 H. Willemse, 'More than an Oppressor's Language: Reclaiming the Hidden History of Afrikaans', *The Conversation*, 27 April 2017 https://theconversation.com/more-than-an-oppressors-language-reclaiming-the-hidden-history-of-afrikaans–71838

63 R. Brown, 'In South Africa, a Push to Reclaim an Afrikaans as Diverse as Its Speakers', *Christian Science Monitor*, 23 March 2018 https://www.csmonitor.com/World/Africa/2018/0323/In-South-Africa-a-push-to-reclaim-an-Afrikaans-as-diverse-as-its-speakers

64 'Coloured Mentality: Is Afrikaans a White Language?' *YouTube*, 19 January 2017 https://www.youtube.com/watch?v=x4A8NRsgNpc

Chapter 5

1 G. Kanahele, *Pauahi: The Kamehameha Legacy*, Kamehameha Schools Press, 1986, p.110.

2 'Kamehameha V', *Encyclopaedia Britannica* https://www.britannica.com/biography/Kamehameha-V

3 M. Hathaway, 'Trends in Heights and Weights', *Yearbook of Agriculture* 1959 https://naldc.nal.usda.gov/download/IND43861419/PDF

4 G. Kanahele, *Pauahi: The Kamehameha Legacy*, p.109.

5 Ibid., p.110.

6 E. McKinzie, *Hawaiian Genealogies: Extracted from Hawaiian Language Newspapers, Volume 1,* University of Hawai'i Press, 1983, p.2.

7 J. King, *A Voyage to the Pacific Ocean,* W. and A. Strahan, 1784, p.43.

8 D. Rhodes, 'Overview of Hawaiian History', *National Parks Service* https://www.nps.gov/parkhistory/online_books/kona/history5e.htm

9 'Sandalwood Trade', *Hawai'i History* http://www.hawaiihistory.org/index.cfm?fuseaction=ig.page&PageID=274

10 S. Vowell, 'Unfamiliar Fishes', *Penguin,* 22 March 2011.

11 L. Thurston, *Life and Times of Mrs. Lucy G. Thurston,* S. C. Andrews, 1882, p.29.

12 ST Shulman et al., 'The Tragic 1824 Journey of the Hawaiian King and Queen to London: History of Measles in Hawaii', *Pediatr Infect Dis J.,* Vol. 28, No. 8, August 2009, 728–33.

13 S. Kamakau, *Ruling Chiefs of Hawaii,* Kamehameha Schools, 1992, p.235.

14 K. Mellen, *The Magnificent Matriarch: Kaahumanu, Queen of Hawaii,* Hastings House, 1952, p.254.

15 'Kaahumanu', *Encyclopaedia Britannica* https://www.britannica.com/biography/Kaahumanu

16 J. Haley, *Captive Paradise: A History of Hawaii,* St. Martin's Press, 2014, p.79.

17 N. Silva, *Aloha Betrayed: Native Hawaiian Resistance to American Colonialism,* Duke University Press, 2004, p.54.

18 Ibid., p.55.

19 A. Schutz, *The Voices of Eden: A History of Hawaiian Language Studies,* University of Hawai'i Press, 1994, pp.2–16.

20 M. A. Donne, *The Sandwich Islands and Their People,* Society for Promoting Christian Knowledge, 1866, p.84.

21 M. Hopkins, *Hawaii: The Past, Present, and Future of Its Island-kingdom,* Longmans, Green, and Company, 1866, p.352.

22 L. Fish Judd, *Honolulu: Sketches of Life,* ADF Randolph, 1880, p.25.

23 A. Schutz, *The Voices of Eden: A History of Hawaiian Language Studies,* pp.25–6.

24 J. Haley, *Captive Paradise: A History of Hawaii,* p.91.

25 Ibid., p.55.

26 J. Lyon, *No ka Baibala Hemolele: The Making of the Hawaiian Bible,* Palapala, 2017, p.113.

27 Ibid., p.114.

28 N. Silva, *Aloha Betrayed: Native Hawaiian Resistance to American Colonialism,* p.55.

29 H. Bingham, *A Residence of Twenty-One Years in the Sandwich Islands,* H. D. Goodwin, 1855, p.160.

30 G. Kanahele, *Pauahi: The Kamehameha Legacy,* p.21.

31 Ibid., p.23.

32 Hawaiian Mission Children's Society, *Portraits of American Protestant Missionaries to Hawaii,* Hawaiian Gazette Co, 1901, p.54.

33 M. Richards (ed.), *The Chiefs' Children's School a Record Compiled from the Diary and Letters of Amos Starr Cooke and Juliette Montague Cooke*, Honolulu Star-Bulletin, 1937, p.26.

34 Ibid., p.27.

35 G. Kanahele, *Pauahi: The Kamehameha Legacy*, pp.27–8.

36 Ibid., p.31.

37 M. Richards (ed.), *The Chiefs' Children's School a Record Compiled from the Diary and Letters of Amos Starr Cooke and Juliette Montague Cooke*, p.173.

38 J. Hewitt, *Williams College and Foreign Missions*, Pilgrim Press, 1914, p.155.

39 H. Lyman, *Hawaiian Yesterdays: Chapters from a Boy's Life in the Islands in the Early Days*, A. C. McClurg & Company, 1906, p.123.

40 G. Kanahele, *Pauahi: The Kamehameha Legacy*, p.58.

41 Office of the Historian, 'The Oregon Territory, 1846', *United States Department of State* https://history.state.gov/milestones/1830-1860/oregon-territory

42 T. Goetz, 'When TB Was a Death Sentence: An Excerpt from "The Remedy"', *The Daily Beast*, 4 April 2016 https://www.thedailybeast.com/when-tb-was-a-death-sentence-an-excerpt-from-the-remedy

43 B. Dunn, 'William Little Lee and Catherine Lee, Letters from Hawai'i 1848–1855', *The Hawaiian Journal of History*, Vol. 38, 2004, p.59.

44 G. Kanahele, *Pauahi: The Kamehameha Legacy*, p.60.

45 H. Lyman, *Hawaiian Yesterdays: Chapters from a Boy's Life in the Islands in the Early Days*, p.46.

46 M. Krout, *The Memoirs of Hon. Bernice Pauahi Bishop*, The Knickerbocker Press, 1908, p.82.

47 Liliuokalani, *Hawaii's Story by Hawaii's Queen*, Lee and Shepard, 1898, p.10.

48 'Kinau (c. 1805–1839)', *Women in World History: A Biographical Encyclopedia*, Gale Research, 2002.

49 A. Cooke, 'Sat. Sept. 2 '48', *Amos S. Cooke's Diary No. 8*, p.178.

50 G. Kanahele, *Pauahi: The Kamehameha Legacy*, p.62.

51 A. Cooke, 'Thursday Aug. 16 '49', *Amos S. Cooke's Diary No. 8*, p.303.

52 A. Cooke, 'Aug. 30, 1849', *Amos S. Cooke's Diary No. 8*, p.312.

53 A. Cooke, 'Sept. 7, 1849', *Amos S. Cooke's Diary No. 8*, p.316.

54 G. Kanahele, *Pauahi: The Kamehameha Legacy*, p.69.

55 'Kamamalu, Victoria (1838–1866)', *Women in World History: A Biographical Encyclopedia*, Gale Research, 2002.

56 M. Krout, *The Memoirs of Hon. Bernice Pauahi Bishop*, p.208.

57 F. Judd, *Forty-Fourth Annual Report*, Hawaiian Historical Society, 1936, p.39.

58 Ibid., p.40.

59 P. Galuteria, *Lunalilo*, Kamehameha Schools, 1993, pp.58–9.

60 J. Haley, *Captive Paradise: A History of Hawaii*.

61 T. Coffman, *Nation within: The History of the American Occupation of Hawai'i*, Duke University Press, 2016, p.62.

Chapter 6

1   Description of 'Iolani Palace in the 1880s based on photos published by the Library of Congress. 'Distant View, Palace and Grounds', *Library of Congress Prints and Photographs Division Washington*, 1886 https://www.loc.gov/pictures/item/hi0047. photos.058131p/resource/

2   Liliuokalani, *Hawaii's Story by Hawaii's Queen*, Charles E. Tuttle Company, 1964, p.204.

3   *Iolani Palace*, National Register of Historic Places Inventory Nomination Form, United States Department of the Interior, National Park Service, 1966 https://npgallery.nps.gov/NRHP/GetAsset/NHLS/66000293_text

4   V. MacCaughey, 'The Punchbowl: Honolulu's Metropolitan Volcano', *The Scientific Monthly*, Vol. 2, No. 6, June 1916, pp. 607–13.

5   'Dropped to Death', *Evening Bulletin*, 18 November 1889.

6   'His Last Leap', *The Honolulu Advertiser*, 18 November 1889.

7   J. Haley, *Captive Paradise: A History of Hawaii*, p.128.

8   Ibid., p.131.

9   N. Silva, *Aloha Betrayed: Native Hawaiian Resistance to American Colonialism*, p.47.

10   'Hoʻokahua Examines Other Interpretations of State Motto', *Hawaiian Cultural Center*, July 2014 https://apps.ksbe.edu/kaiwakiloumoku/uamaukeeaokaainaikapono

11   T. Coffman, *Nation within: The History of the American Occupation of Hawaiʻi*, p.56.

12   R. Kuykendall, *The Hawaiian Kingdom 1778–1854, Foundation and Transformation*, University of Hawaiʻi Press, 1938, p.395.

13   G. Judd, 'Private Journal', 4 June 1850, cited in R. Kuykendall, *The Hawaiian Kingdom 1778–1854, Foundation and Transformation*, University of Hawaiʻi Press, 1938, p.397.

14   D. Itsuji Saranillio, *Unsustainable Empire: Alternative Histories of HawaiʻI Statehood*, Duke University Press, 2018, p.66.

15   T. Coffman, *The Island Edge of America: A Political History of Hawaiʻi*, p.29.

16   Ibid., p.16.

17   T. Coffman, *Nation within: The History of the American Occupation of Hawaiʻi*, p.155.

18   *Constitution of the Republic of Hawaiʻi and Laws Passed by the Executive and Advisory Councils of the Republic*, Hawaiian Gazette Company's Print, 1895, pp.265–7.

19   Ibid., p.103.

20   S. Vowell, *Unfamiliar Fishes*.

21   *Constitution of the Republic of Hawaiʻi and Laws Passed by the Executive and Advisory Councils of the Republic*, p.183.

22   J. Hunt, *Hawaiʻi Department of Education Historical Development and Outlook*, Department of Education, 1969, p.297.

23   'Topics of the Day', *The Independent*, 16 October 1896.

24   'A Timeline of Revitalization', *ʻAha Pūnana Leo* http://www.ahapunanaleo.org/index. php?/about/aha_puunana_leo_in_the_spotlight/

25 'Topics of the Day', *The Independent*, 26 October 1898.

26 'Rev. Dr. McArthur on Hawaii', *The Friend*, December 1895, p. 96.

27 *The Biennial Report of the President of the Board of Education*, Hawaiian Gazette, 1896, pp.6–7.

28 P. Lucas, 'Hawaiian Language Policy and the Courts', *The Hawaiian Journal of History*, Vol. 34, 2000, p.9.

29 A. Schutz, *The Voices of Eden: A History of Hawaiian Language Studies*, p.352.

30 Ibid., pp.354–5.

Chapter 7

1 K. Zambucka, *The High Chiefess, Ruth Keelikolani*, Mana Publishing, 1977, p.5.

2 P. Spickard et al., *Pacific Diaspora: Island Peoples in the United States and across the Pacific*, University of Hawai'i Press, 2002, p.244.

3 K. Silva, *Princess Ruth Ke'elikōlani*, Center for Biographical Research University of Hawai'i, 2003, p.3.

4 J. Haley, *Captive Paradise: A History of Hawaii*.

5 'Death of Her Highness Princess Ruth Keelikolani', *The Daily Bulletin*, 28 May 1883, p.1.

6 M. Krout, *The Memoirs of Hon. Bernice Pauahi Bishop*, p.218.

7 'About Pauahi', Kamehameha Schools https://www.ksbe.edu/about_us/about_pauahi/

8 G. Kanahele, *Pauahi: The Kamehameha Legacy*, p.174.

9 'Pauahi's Will', *Kamehameha Schools* https://www.ksbe.edu/about_us/about_pauahi/will/

10 G. Kanahele, *Pauahi: The Kamehameha Legacy*, p.184.

11 N. Hawkes, 'History of Cancer Treatment', Raconteur, 4 June 2015 https://www.raconteur.net/healthcare/history-of-cancer-treatment

12 G. Kanahele, *Pauahi: The Kamehameha Legacy*, p.186.

13 'Funeral of Bernice Pauahi Bishop', The Pacific Commercial Advertiser, 4 November 1884.

14 G. Kanahele, *Pauahi: The Kamehameha Legacy*, pp.191–2.

15 M. Krout, *The Memoirs of Hon. Bernice Pauahi Bishop*, p.228.

16 Ibid., p.239.

17 'A Timeline of Revitalization', '*Aha Pūnana Leo* http://www.ahapunanaleo.org/index.php?/about/aha_puunana_leo_in_the_spotlight/

18 T. Coffman, *Nation within: The History of the American Occupation of Hawai'i*, p.82.

19 Ibid., p.86.

20 J. Fiske, 'Manifest Destiny', *Harpers*, March 1885 https://harpers.org/archive/1885/03/manifest-destiny-2/

21 D. Dela Cruz, 'The Life and Legacy of Hawaii's Influential Charles Reed Bishop', *Hawai'i Magazine*, 14 January 2011 https://www.hawaiimagazine.com/content/life-and-legacy-hawaiis-influential-charles-reed-bishop

22 D. Forbes (ed.), *Hawaiian National Bibliography, 1780–1900: 1881–1900*, University of Hawai'i Press, 1998, p.232.

23 R. Canevali, 'Hilo Boarding School: Hawaii's Experiment in Vocational Education', *Hawaiian Journal of History*, Vol. 11, 1977, p.85.

24 S. King and R. Ro, *Broken Trust: Greed, Mismanagement & Political Manipulation at America's Largest Charitable Trust*, University of Hawai'i Press, 2006.

25 Ibid.

26 S. Bonura, *Light in the Queen's Garden*, University of Hawai'i Press, 2017.

27 B. Wist, 'A Century of Public Education in Hawaii', *The Hawai'i Educational Review*, 1940, p.113.

28 S. King and R. Ro, *Broken Trust: Greed, Mismanagement & Political Manipulation at America's Largest Charitable Trust*.

29 K. Eyre, 'Suppression of Hawaiian Culture at Kamehameha Schools', *speech given in January 2004* https://apps.ksbe.edu/kaiwakiloumoku/makalii/feature-stories/suppression_of_hawaiian_culture

30 V. Valeri, *Kingship and Sacrifice: Ritual and Society in Ancient Hawaii*, University of Chicago Press, 1985, p.12.

31 M. Pukui and S. Elbert, 'Mana', *Hawaiian Dictionary*, Ulukau, 2003 http://wehewehe. org/gsdl2.85/cgi-bin/hdict?a=q&j=pk&l=en&q=mana&a=d&d=D12710

32 J. Cook, *The Three Voyages of Captain James Cook Round the World*, Longman, Hurst, Rees, Orme, and Brown, 1821, p.348.

33 V. Valeri, *Kingship and Sacrifice: Ritual and Society in Ancient Hawaii*, p.138.

34 M. J. Harden, *Voices of Wisdom: Hawaiian Elders Speak*, Aka Press, 2014.

35 J. Cook, *Voyages Around the World*, S. Russell, 1806, p.488.

36 H. Bingham *A Residence of Twenty-One Years in the Sandwich Islands*, H. Huntington, 1848, pp.124–5.

37 N. Silva, *Aloha Betrayed: Native Hawaiian Resistance to American Colonialism*, p.63.

38 L. Hix, 'How America's Obsession with Hula Girls Almost Wrecked Hawai'i', *Collector's Weekly*, 22 March 2017 https://www.collectorsweekly.com/articles/how-americas-obsession-with-hula-girls-almost-wrecked-hawaii/

39 T. Coffman, *Nation within: The History of the American Occupation of Hawai'i*, p.68.

40 P. Lucas, 'Hawaiian Language Policy and the Courts', pp.7–8.

41 N. Emerson, *The Unwritten Literature of Hawaii*, Mutual Publishing, 1998, p.vii.

42 R. Kuykendall, *The Hawaiian Kingdom, vol. 3, 1874–1893, The Kalākaua dynasty*, University of Hawai'i Press, 1967, p.347.

43 S. Bishop, 'Why Are Hawaiians Dying Out?', *The Friend*, April 1889, pp.26–7.

44 K. Eyre, 'Suppression of Hawaiian Culture at Kamehameha Schools'.

45 S. King and R. Ro, *Broken Trust: Greed, Mismanagement & Political Manipulation at America's Largest Charitable Trust*.

46 A. Schutz, *The Voices of Eden: A History of Hawaiian Language Studies*, p.349.

47 'Cruelty of a Witch', *The San Francisco Examiner*, 29 June 1892.

48 'An Hawaiian Sorceress', *Argus Leader*, 26 April 1893.

49 'Woman Is Freed after 23 Years Spent in Prison', *Honolulu Star Bulletin*, 24 December 1914.

50 R. Schmitt, *Historical Statistics of Hawaii*, University of Hawai'i Press, 1977, p.27.

51 R. Schmitt, 'Religious Statistics of Hawai'i,1825–1972', *Hawaiian Journal of History*, Vol. 7, 1973, pp.41–7.

52 H. Trask, 'Feminism and Indigenous Hawaiian Nationalism', *Signs*, Vol. 21, No. 4, Feminist Theory and Practice, Summer, 1996.

53 S. Kamakau, *Ruling Chiefs of Hawaii*, Kamehameha Schools Press, 1961, p.228.

54 J. Molnar, 'For the Love of Hawaii', *The Seattle Times*, 12 September 1993.

55 J. Hopkins, 'The First Family of Hawaiian Song', *Ha'ilono Mele*, Vol. 4, No. 10, October 1978.

56 1995 Hall of Fame Honoree, 'Helen Desha Beamer', *Hawaiian Music Hall of Fame*. https://web.archive.org/web/20080511173248/ and http://www.hmhof.org/honorees/1995/beamer.html

57 J. Hopkins, 'Hula City', *Los Angeles Times*, 17 October 1993.

58 PBS Hawai'i, 'Long Story Short with Leslie Wilcox: Aunty Nona Beamer', *PBS*, 23 October 2007 https://www.pbshawaii.org/long-story-short-with-leslie-wilcox-aunty-nona-beamer/

59 J. Arthur Rath, *Lost Generations: A Boy, a School, a Princess*, University of Hawai'i Press, 2006, p.80.

60 PBS Hawai'i, 'Long Story Short with Leslie Wilcox: Aunty Nona Beamer'.

61 J. Arthur Rath, *Lost Generations: A Boy, a School, a Princess*, p.80.

62 PBS Hawai'i, 'Long Story Short With Leslie Wilcox: Aunty Nona Beamer'.

63 M. J. Harden, *Voices of Wisdom: Hawaiian Elders Speak*.

64 L. Hix, 'How America's Obsession with Hula Girls Almost Wrecked Hawai'i'.

65 Ibid.

66 PBS Hawai'i, 'Long Story Short With Leslie Wilcox: Aunty Nona Beamer'.

67 G. Cartwright, 'Winona Beamer', *The Guardian*, 2 June 2008 https://www.theguardian.com/world/2008/jun/02/usa

68 J. Hopkins, 'The First Family of Hawaiian Song'.

69 Ibid.

70 S. King and R. Ro, *Broken Trust: Greed, Mismanagement & Political Manipulation at America's Largest Charitable Trust*.

71 'Kona Pastor Brands Pele Hula', *The Honolulu Advertiser*, 2 April 1959.

72 'The Hula – Idolatry?', *Honolulu Star-Bulletin*, 2 April 1959.

73 B. Krauss, 'In One Ear', *The Honolulu Advertiser*, 6 April 1959.

74 J. Rath, *Lost Generations: A Boy, a School, a Princess*, University of Hawai'i Press, 2006, p.128.

75 'A Timeline of Revitalization', *'Aha Pūnana Leo* http://www.ahapunanaleo.org/index.php?/about/a_timeline_of_revitalization/

Chapter 8

1   'Rainfall Atlas of Hawaii', *University of Hawai'i* http://rainfall.geography.hawaii.edu/

2   'Water Conservation and Control of Water Usage during Water Shortage', Maui County Code, Title 14, Article 1, Chapter 14.06A.

3   S. Fisher, 'The Story of Waihe'e: The Source of the Land', *Hawaiian Islands Land Trust*, 23 April 2019 https://www.hilt.org/hawaiian-islands-land-trust/2019/3/25/ka-moolelo-o-waihee-ke-kumu-o-ka-aina

4   S. Russell, 'Water Rights Bills Are Unconstitutional', *Honolulu Civil Beat*, 2 April 2019 https://www.civilbeat.org/2019/04/water-rights-bills-are-unconstitutional/

5   'Endowment', *Kamehameha Schools Annual Report* 2018/19, p.21 https://www.ksbe.edu/assets/annual_reports/KS_Annual_Report_2019.pdf

6   'Profile: Native Hawaiians/Pacific Islanders', *Office of Minority Health Resource Center, OMH* https://www.minorityhealth.hhs.gov/omh/browse.aspx?lvl=3&lvlid=65

7   'About', *Kamehameha Schools* https://apps.ksbe.edu/admissions/about/

8   Doe v. Kamehameha Schools/Bernice Pauahi Bishop, 295 F. Supp. 2d 1141 (D. Haw. 2003), US District Court for the District of Hawai'i – 295 F. Supp. 2d 1141 (D. Haw. 2003) December 2003.

9   J. Rath, *Lost Generations: A Boy, a School, a Princess*, p.59.

10 S. King and R. Ro, *Broken Trust: Greed, Mismanagement & Political Manipulation at America's Largest Charitable Trust*.

11 P. Barrett, 'At Bishop Estate, Scandal Widens as Powerhouse's Chair Is Indicted', *Wall Street Journal*, 19 April 1999 https://www.wsj.com/articles/SB924469946310962758

12 S. King and R. Ro, *Broken Trust: Greed, Mismanagement & Political Manipulation at America's Largest Charitable Trust*, p.8.

13 J. Wisch, 'Atg News Release: 20 Years Ago, Bishop Estate Scandal Led to Strict Charities Oversight in Hawaii', *Hawai'i Governor's Office*, 14 August 2017 https://governor.hawaii.gov/newsroom/latest-news/atg-news-release-20-years-ago-bishop-estate-scandal-led-to-strict-charities-oversight-in-hawaii/

14 S. King and R. Ro, *Broken Trust: Greed, Mismanagement & Political Manipulation at America's Largest Charitable Trust*, p.4.

15 Ibid., p.296.

16 H. Verploegen, '7 District Teachers of the Year Honored', *Honolulu Star-Bulletin*, 31 October 1984, p.33.

17 H. Verploegen, 'Snake Teaches Hawaiian', *Honolulu Star-Bulletin*, 20 October 1976, p.28.

18 'A Timeline of Revitalization', *'Aha Pūnana Leo* http://www.ahapunanaleo.org/index.php?/about/aha_puunana_leo_in_the_spotlight/

19 'A Timeline of Revitalization'.

20 'History', *Native Hawaiian Educational Council* http://www.nhec.org/about-nhec/history/

21 'A Timeline of Revitalization'.

Chapter 9

1   Big Island News, 'TMT Opponents Halt Groundbreaking Ceremony', *YouTube*, 8 October 2014 https://www.youtube.com/watch?v=SZ4Gt35hs-s

2   D. Herman, 'The Heart of the Hawaiian Peoples' Arguments against the Telescope on Mauna Kea', *Smithsonian Magazine*, 23 April 2015 https://www.smithsonianmag.com/smithsonian-institution/heart-hawaiian-people-arguments-arguments-against-telescope-mauna-kea–180955057/

3   T. Kehaulani Watson-Sproat, 'Why Native Hawaiians Are Fighting to Protect Maunakea from a Telescope', *Vox*, 24 July 2019 https://www.vox.com/identities/2019/7/24/20706930/mauna-kea-hawaii

4   K. Grable, 'Why Mauna Kea Needs Your Protection', *Greenpeace*, 14 August 2019 https://www.greenpeace.org/usa/why-mauna-kea-needs-your-protection/

5   'VIDEO: Full Coverage of Thirty Meter Telescope Disruption', *Big Island Video News*, 9 October 2014 https://www.bigislandvideonews.com/2014/10/09/video-full-coverage-thirty-meter-telescope-road-block/

6   J. Kelleher, 'Protesters Halt Mauna Kea Telescope Groundbreaking', *Honolulu Star Advertiser*, 7 October 2014 https://www.staradvertiser.com/2014/10/07/breaking-news/protesters-halt-mauna-kea-telescope-groundbreaking/

7   'Episode 90: How Western Media's False Binary between "Science" and Indigenous Rights Is Used to Erase Native People', *Citations Needed*, 16 October 2019 https://citationsneeded.libsyn.com/episode-90-how-western-medias-false-binary-between-science-and-indigenous-rights-is-used-to-erase-native-people

8   M. Peryer, 'Native Hawaiians on Coverage of Mauna Kea Resistance', *Columbia Journalism Review*, 29 July 2019 https://www.cjr.org/opinion/mauna-kea-telescope-protest-hawaii.php

9   D. Herman, 'The Heart of the Hawaiian Peoples' Arguments against the Telescope on Mauna Kea'.

10 T. Kehaulani Watson-Sproat, 'Why Native Hawaiians Are Fighting to Protect Maunakea from a Telescope'.

11 M. Speier, 'Scientists Voice Their Support for Native Hawaiians Protesting the Thirty Meter Telescope', *Pacific Standard*, 25 July 2019 https://psmag.com/news/scientists-voice-their-support-for-native-hawaiians-protesting-the-thirty-meter-telescope

12 'Kahua', *Kanaeokana* http://kanaeokana.net/kahua/

13 KITV Web Staff, 'Results Are In: New Poll Shows Steep Decline in TMT Support', *KITV*, 26 September 2019 https://www.kitv.com/story/41101740/results-are-in-new-poll-shows-steep-decline-in-tmt-support

14 C. Blair, 'Civil Beat Poll: Strong Support for TMT but Little Love for Ige', *Honolulu Civil Beat*, 9 August 2019 https://www.civilbeat.org/2019/08/civil-beat-poll-strong-support-for-tmt-but-little-love-for-ige/

15 'Allies', *Puʻuhuluhulu* https://www.puuhuluhulu.com/learn/allies

16 S. Lee, 'TMT Protest Movement Spurs Enrollment in Immersion Schools', *Civil Beat*, 29 August 2019 https://www.civilbeat.org/2019/08/tmt-protest-movement-spurs-enrollment-in-immersion-schools/

Interlude

1 J. Fellman, *The Revival of a Classical Tongue Eliezer Ben Yehuda and the Modern Hebrew Language*, Mouton, 1973, p.17.

2 The Editors of Encyclopaedia Britannica, 'Pale', *Encyclopædia Britannica*, 20 July 1998 https://www.britannica.com/topic/pale-restricted-area#ref285758

3 A. Korzhenkov, *Zamenhof The Life, Works, and Ideas of the Author of Esperanto*, translated by I. Richmond, Esperantic Studies Foundation, 2009, p.2.

4 J. Fellman, 'Hebrew: Eliezer Ben-Yehuda & the Revival of Hebrew', *Jewish Virtual Library* https://www.jewishvirtuallibrary.org/eliezer-ben-yehuda-and-the-revival-of-hebrew

5 J. Fellman, *The Revival of a Classical Tongue Eliezer Ben Yehuda and the Modern Hebrew Language*, p.18.

6 Ibid., p.11.

7 Y. Rabkin, *Language in Nationalism: Modern Hebrew in the Zionist Project*, Holy Land Studies, November 2010.

8 The Editors of Encyclopaedia Britannica, 'Treaty of San Stefano', *Encyclopædia Britannica*, 24 February 2019 https://www.britannica.com/event/Treaty-of-San-Stefano

9 J. Fellman, *Hebrew: Eliezer Ben-Yehuda & the Revival of Hebrew*.

10 J. Fellman, *The Revival of a Classical Tongue Eliezer Ben Yehuda and the Modern Hebrew Language*, p.20.

11 Ibid., p.13.

12 A. Korzhenkov, *Zamenhof The Life, Works, and Ideas of the Author of Esperanto*, p.1.

13 Ibid., p.2.

14 Ibid., p.4.

15 E. Schor, 'Esperanto: A Jewish Story', *Pakn Treger*, Winter 2009 https://www.yiddishbookcenter.org/language-literature-culture/pakn-treger/esperanto-jewish-story

16 A. Korzhenkov, *Zamenhof The Life, Works, and Ideas of the Author of Esperanto*, p.5.

17 L. Halperin, 'Modern Hebrew, Esperanto, and the Quest for a Universal Language', *Jewish Social Studies: History, Culture, Society n.s.*, Vol. 19, No. 1, Fall 2012, p.6.

18 A. Okrent, *In the Land of Invented Languages*, Spiegel & Grau, 2009.

19 E. Schor, *Bridge of Words: Esperanto and the Dream of a Universal Language*, Henry Holt and Company, 2016.

20 A. Okrent, *In the Land of Invented Languages*.

21 E. Schor, *Bridge of Words: Esperanto and the Dream of a Universal Language*.

22 G. Orwell, 'As I Please', *Tribune*, 28 January 1944 http://www.telelib.com/authors/O/OrwellGeorge/essay/tribune/AsIPlease19440128.html

23 E. Schor, 'Esperanto: A Jewish Story'.

24 A. Korzhenkov, *Zamenhof The Life, Works, and Ideas of the Author of Esperanto*, p.12.

25 E. Schor, 'L.L. Zamenhof and the Shadow People', *New Republic*, 30 December 2009 https://newrepublic.com/article/72110/ll-zamenhof-and-the-shadow-people

26 L. L. Zamenhof, *Dr. Esperanto's International Language*, R. H. Geoghegan (translator), Balliol College, Oxford, 1889, G. Keyes (editor), Verkitsa, 2006 https://www.genekeyes.com/Dr_Esperanto.html

27 J. Fellman, *The Revival of a Classical Tongue Eliezer Ben Yehuda and the Modern Hebrew Language*, p.29.

28 Y. Rabkin, *Language in Nationalism: Modern Hebrew in the Zionist Project*.

29 J. Fellman, 'Hebrew: Eliezer Ben-Yehuda & the Revival of Hebrew'.

30 Ibid.

31 J. Fellman, *The Revival of a Classical Tongue Eliezer Ben Yehuda and the Modern Hebrew Language*, p.37.

32 D. Green, '1858: Hebrew's Reviver Is Born', *Haaretz*, 7 January 2013 https://www.haaretz.com/jewish/.premium-1858-hebrew-s-reviver-is-born-1.5289349

33 J. Fellman, *The Revival of a Classical Tongue Eliezer Ben Yehuda and the Modern Hebrew Language*, p.65.

34 J. Fellman, 'Hebrew: Eliezer Ben-Yehuda & the Revival of Hebrew'.

35 Ibid.

36 J. Fellman, *The Revival of a Classical Tongue Eliezer Ben Yehuda and the Modern Hebrew Language*, p.31.

37 J. Fellman, 'Hebrew: Eliezer Ben-Yehuda & the Revival of Hebrew'.

38 Ibid.

39 D. Green, '1858: Hebrew's Reviver Is Born'.

40 E. Schor, 'L.L. Zamenhof and the Shadow People'.

41 A. Korzhenkov, *Zamenhof The Life, Works, and Ideas of the Author of Esperanto*, pp.37–8.

42 Ibid., p.36.

43 Ibid., p.39.

44 Ibid., pp.35–6.

45 Ibid., p.40.

46 P. Janton, *Esperanto: Language, Literature, and Community*, SUNY Press, 1 January 1993, p.42.

47 Ibid., p.28.

48 E. Schor, *Bridge of Words: Esperanto and the Dream of a Universal Language*.

49 L. L. Zamenhof, *Dr. Esperanto's International Language*.

50 E. Schor, *Bridge of Words: Esperanto and the Dream of a Universal Language*.

51 Ibid.

52 Ibid.

53 Ibid.

54 A. Korzhenkov, *Zamenhof The Life, Works, and Ideas of the Author of Esperanto*, p.43.

55 Ibid., p.31.

56 E. Schor, *Bridge of Words: Esperanto and the Dream of a Universal Language*.

57 'Membronombroj de UEA', *Vikipedio* https://eo.wikipedia.org/wiki/Membronombroj_de_UEA#Diagramo_kaj_tabelo_de_la_suma_membraro_ekde_1908

58 A. Korzhenkov, *Zamenhof The Life, Works, and Ideas of the Author of Esperanto*, p.33.

59 Ibid., p.47.

60 Ibid., pp.47–8.

61 N. Berdichevsky, 'Esperanto and Modern Hebrew – "Artificial" Languages That Came to Life', *New English Review*, February 2014 https://newenglishreview.org/custpage.cfm/frm/160333

62 E. Schor, *Bridge of Words: Esperanto and the Dream of a Universal Language*.

63 L. Halperin, 'Modern Hebrew, Esperanto, and the Quest for a Universal Language', p.24.

64 N. Berdichevsky, 'Esperanto and Modern Hebrew – "Artificial" Languages that Came to Life'.

65 L. Halperin, 'Modern Hebrew, Esperanto, and the Quest for a Universal Language', p.16.

66 League of Nations: The Mandate for Palestine, 24 July 1922.

67 D. Green, '1858: Hebrew's Reviver Is Born'.

68 'Hebrew', *Ethnologue* https://web.archive.org/web/20190927074706/ and https://www.ethnologue.com/language/heb

69 'Full Text of Basic Law: Israel as the Nation State of the Jewish People', *Knesset*, 19 July 2018 https://web.archive.org/web/20180719173434/ and https://knesset.gov.il/spokesman/eng/PR_eng.asp?PRID=13978

70 A. Carey and O. Liebermann, 'Israel Passes Controversial "Nation-State" Bill with No Mention of Equality or Minority Rights', *CNN*, 19 July 2018 https://www.cnn.com/2018/07/19/middleeast/israel-nation-state-legislation-intl/index.html

71 'The Status of Arabic-Speakers in Israel', *The Economist*, 27 November 2016 https://www.economist.com/the-economist-explains/2016/11/27/the-status-of-arabic-speakers-in-israel

72 A. Sikseck, 'How Arabic Became a Foreign Language in Israel', *YNet*, 5 September 2017 https://www.ynetnews.com/articles/0,7340,L-4959477,00.html

73 A. Lang, *The Politics of Hebrew and Yiddish: Zionism and Transnationalism*, The Federalist Debate, Number 2, July 2015.

74 B. Mitchell, 'Yiddish and the Hebrew Revival: A New Look at the Changing Role of Yiddish', *Monatshefte*, Vol. 90, No. 2, Summer 1998, pp.190–1.

75 A. Lang, *The Politics of Hebrew and Yiddish: Zionism and Transnationalism*.

76 N. Karlen, *The Story of Yiddish: How a Mish-mosh of Languages Saved the Jews*, p.12.

77 Ibid., p.13.

78 M. Richarz, 'The History of the Jews in Europe during the Nineteenth and Early Twentieth Centuries', *The Holocaust and the United Nations Outreach Programme*, pp.77–80 https://www.un.org/en/holocaustremembrance/docs/pdf/Volume%20I/The_History_of_the_Jews_in_Europe.pdf

79 B. Mitchell, 'Yiddish and the Hebrew Revival: A New Look at the Changing Role of Yiddish', pp.190–1.

80 E. Schor, 'Esperanto: A Jewish Story'.

81 J. Shanes, 'Yiddish and Jewish Diaspora Nationalism', *Monatshefte*, Vol. 90, No. 2, Summer, 1998, p.180.

82 W. Laqueur, *A History of Zionism*, Tauris Parke, 2003.

83 J. Shanes, 'Yiddish and Jewish Diaspora Nationalism', p.179.

84 Y. Rabkin, *Language in Nationalism: Modern Hebrew in the Zionist Project*, p.8.

85 Ibid., p.9.

86 Ibid., p.3.

87 B. Mitchell, 'Yiddish and the Hebrew Revival: A New Look at the Changing Role of Yiddish', p.192.

88 J. Shanes, 'Yiddish and Jewish Diaspora Nationalism', p.185.

89 N. Karlen, *The Story of Yiddish: How a Mish-mosh of Languages Saved the Jews*, p.146.

90 R. Rojanski, 'The Status of Yiddish in Israel, 1948–1951: An Overview', in J. Sherman (ed.), *Yiddish after the Holocaust*, Boulevard, 2004.

91 Y. Rabkin, *Language in Nationalism: Modern Hebrew in the Zionist Project*, p.3.

92 Ibid., p.5.

93 B. Mitchell, 'Yiddish and the Hebrew Revival: A New Look at the Changing Role of Yiddish', p.192.

94 E. Freeburg, *The Cost of Revival: The Role of Hebrew in Jewish Language Endangerment*, Yale University, 1 May 2013, p.38.

95 A. Pilowsky, 'Yiddish alongside the Revival of Hebrew Public Polemics on the Status of Yiddish in Eretz Israel, 1907–1929', in J. Fishman (ed.), *Readings in the Sociology of Jewish Languages*, Brill Archive, 1 January 1985, p.106.

96 L. Bush, 'May 26: In Israel, Yiddish Language and Culture Day', *Jewish Currents*, 26 May 2016 https://jewishcurrents.org/may-26-in-israel-yiddish-language-and-culture-day/

97 A. Pilowsky, 'Yiddish alongside the Revival of Hebrew Public Polemics on the Status of Yiddish in Eretz Israel, 1907–1929', p.107.

98 J. Shanes, 'Yiddish and Jewish Diaspora Nationalism', p.186.

99 L. Bush, 'September 27: Anti-Yiddish Riots', *Jewish Currents*, 26 September 2012 https://jewishcurrents.org/september-27-anti-yiddish-riots/

100 B. Mitchell, 'Yiddish and the Hebrew Revival: A New Look at the Changing Role of Yiddish', p.193.

101 Ibid., p.194.

102 A. Brumberg, 'Yiddish and Hebrew – End of a Feud?' *Haruth* http://haruth.com/YiddishHebrew.html

103 D. Porat, 'The Blue and the Yellow Stars of David, Harvard University Press, 1990, p.239.

104 R. Rojanski, 'The Final Chapter in the Struggle for Cultural Autonomy', *Journal of Modern Jewish Studies*, 2007, 6:2, p.200 http://dx.doi.org/10.1080/14725880701423071

105 B. Mitchell, 'Yiddish and the Hebrew Revival: A New Look at the Changing Role of Yiddish', p.195.

106 R. Rojanski, 'The Status of Yiddish in Israel, 1948–1951: An Overview', p.54.

107 L. Bush, 'May 26: In Israel, Yiddish Language and Culture Day'.

108 B. Weiner, 'The Return of the Repressed: Yiddish in Israel', *Jewish Currents*, 2 April 2009 https://jewishcurrents.org/the-return-of-the-repressed-yiddish-in-israel/

109 J. Young, 'Down with the "Revival": Yiddish Is a Living Language', *Yivo Institute*, 12 September 2014 https://yivo.org/down-with-the-revival-yiddish-is-a-living-language

110 R. Kafrissen, 'Oy Gevalt! Yiddish Is Definitely Alive. Or Dad. Or in Purgatory. Or Hiding in Switzerland for Tax Purposes.', *Yiddish Praxis*, 31 December 2011 http://rokhl.blogspot.com/2011/12/oy-gevalt-yiddish-is-definitely-alive.html

111 A. Lang, 'The Politics of Hebrew and Yiddish: Zionism and Transnationalism'.

112 L. Morales, 'Yiddish in the Age of Identity', *Jewish Currents*, 11 May 2017 https://jewishcurrents.org/yiddish-in-the-age-of-identity/

113 'Esperanto', *Ethnologue*, 2019.

Chapter 10

1 Monk is a distant ancestor of mine; I found his letters in our family archives. H. Monk, *Letter to Isabella Monk*, 16 July 1841, Monk family private collection.

2 J. J. Bremer, *Admiralty Dispatch, 6 March 1841*, Bulletins of State Intelligence, p.225.

3 Ibid., p.273.

4 H. Monk, *Letter to Isabella Monk*, 30 August 1842, Monk family private collection.

5 H. Shea, *Letter to H. Monk, Esquire, Guernsey*, 6 October 1843, Monk family private collection.

6 R. Martin, *China; Political, Commercial, and Social: An Official Report*, James Madden, 1847, pp.80–2.

7 S. Platt, *Imperial Twilight: The Opium War and the End of China's Last Golden Age*, Alfred A. Knopf, New York, 2018, p.xxiii.

8 War with China—adjourned debate, *HC Deb*, 08 April 1840, Hansard, Vol. 53, c.818 https://api.parliament.uk/historic-hansard/commons/1840/apr/08/war-with-china-adjourned-debate

9 S. Platt, *Imperial Twilight: The Opium War and the End of China's Last Golden Age*, p.xxiii.

10 S. Tsang, *A Modern History of Hong Kong: 1841–1997*, p.20.

11 Ibid., p.60.

12 A. Pennycook, 'Language Policy as Cultural Politics: The Double-Edged Sword of Language Education in Colonial Malaya and Hong Kong', *Discourse: Studies in the Cultural Politics of Education*, Vol. 17, No. 2, 1996, pp.138–9.

13 Ibid., pp.138–9.

14 Ibid., p.143.

15 Ibid., p.143.

16 R. Levenson, 'Chinese Linguist, Phonologist, Composer and Author, Yuen Ren Chao', *China Scholars Series*, The Bancroft Library, University of California, Berkeley, 8 August 1974.

17 J. Fenby, *The Penguin History of Modern China*, Penguin, 2018, pp.83–5.

18 The Editors of Encyclopaedia Britannica, 'Boxer Rebellion', *Encyclopædia Britannica*, 22 November 2019 https://www.britannica.com/event/Boxer-Rebellion

19 J. Fenby, *The Penguin History of Modern China*, pp.87–8.

20 Ibid., pp.91–2.

21 L. Thompson, *William Scott Ament and the Boxer Rebellion: Heroism, Hubris and the 'Ideal Missionary'*, McFarland, 2009, p.168.

22 H. Franke and B. Elman et al., 'China', *Encyclopædia Britannica*, 4 February 2020 https://www.britannica.com/place/China/The-Hundred-Days-of-Reform-of-1898#ref590596

23 J. Grasso and M. Kort, *Modernization and Revolution in China*, M.E. Sharpe, 2015, p.55.

24 J. Fenby, *The Penguin History of Modern China*, pp.87–8.

25 R. Levenson, 'Chinese Linguist, Phonologist, Composer and Author, Yuen Ren Chao'.

26 P. Chen, *Modern Chinese: History and Sociolinguistics*, Cambridge University Press, 2004, p.12.

27 Y. Chao, *Aspects of Chinese Sociolinguistics*, A. Dil (ed.), Stanford University Press, 1976, p.24.

28 Ibid. pp.25–6.

29 Translation via 三字经 *The Three-Character Classic: A Confucian Roadmap for Kids*, Yellow Bridge https://www.yellowbridge.com/onlinelit/sanzijing.php

30 'A Right Way to Raise Children Demonstrated by Mr. Dou Yan Shan', *The Collection of Cantonese Opera Records at the Canadian Museum of Civilization* https://www.historymuseum.ca/cantoneseopera/opera72-e.shtml

31 D. Moser, *A Billion Voices: China's Search for a Common Language*, Penguin, 2016, pp.30–1.

32 The Editors of Encyclopaedia Britannica, 'Hangul', *Encyclopædia Britannica*, 9 August 2019 https://www.britannica.com/topic/Hangul-Korean-alphabet

33 J. DeFrancis, *Nationalism and Language Reform in China*, Princeton University Press, 1950, p.8.

34 Ibid., p.10.

35 Ibid., p.27.

36 Ibid., p.27.

37 W. Brewster, *The Evolution of New China*, Jennings and Graham, 1907, p.115.

38 Y. Wu and C. Li, 'Reform of the Chinese Written Language', *Foreign Languages Press*, 1965, republished by Pinyin.info http://pinyin.info/readings/zhou_enlai/phonetic_alphabet.html

39 J. DeFrancis, *Nationalism and Language Reform in China*, pp.33–40.

40 P. Chen, *Modern Chinese: History and Sociolinguistics*, pp.12–14.

41 A. Pennycook, 'Language Policy as Cultural Politics: The Double-edged Sword of Language Education in Colonial Malaya and Hong Kong', *Discourse: Studies in the Cultural Politics of Education*, Vol. 17, No. 2, 1996, p.146.

42 R. Levenson, 'Chinese Linguist, Phonologist, Composer and Author, Yuen Ren Chao'.

43 Ibid.

44 Ibid.

45 Y. Chao, *Aspects of Chinese Sociolinguistics*, p.31.

46 'The Boxer Indemnity Scholarship Program', *Shijia Hutong Museum*, 2019 http://www.ebeijing.gov.cn/feature_2/ShijiaHutongMuseum/TheOriginofModernEducationinChina/t1584370.htm

47 R. Levenson, 'Chinese Linguist, Phonologist, Composer and Author, Yuen Ren Chao'.

48 Ibid.

49 J. De Francis, *Nationalism and Language Reform in China*, Princeton University Press, 1950, p.65.

50 D. Moser, *A Billion Voices: China's Search for a Common Language*, p.10.

51 J. De Francis, *Nationalism and Language Reform in China*, p.65.

52 Ibid., p.66.

53 Y. Chao, *Mandarin Primer: An Intensive Course in Spoken Chinese*, Harvard University Press, 1967, p.26.

54 D. Moser, *A Billion Voices: China's Search for a Common Language*, p.18.

55 J. De Francis, *Nationalism and Language Reform in China*, p.68.

56 Ibid., p.68.

57 J. DeFrancis, *Nationalism and Language Reform in China*, p.54.

58 Ibid., p.66.

59 G. Tam, *Dialect and Nationalism in China, 1860–1960*, Cambridge University Press, February 2020, p.178.

60 J. DeFrancis, *Nationalism and Language Reform in China*, p.8.

61 J. DeFrancis, *The Chinese Language: Fact and Fantasy*, p.242.

62 J. DeFrancis, *Nationalism and Language Reform in China*, p.65.

63 Ibid., p.67.

Chapter 11

1 Y. Chao, *Aspects of Chinese Sociolinguistics*, p.27.

2 J. Fenby, *The Penguin History of Modern China*, p.145.

3 Y. Chao, *Aspects of Chinese Sociolinguistics*, p.28.

4 D. Moser, *A Billion Voices: China's Search for a Common Language*, p.24.

5 R. Levenson, *Chinese Linguist, Phonologist, Composer and Author, Yuen Ren Chao*.

6 Ibid., p.1.

7 V. Mair, 'Hu Shih and Chinese Language Reform', *China Heritage*, 2017 https://chinaheritage.net/journal/hu-shih-and-chinese-language-reform/

8 S. Hu, '文學改良芻議', *New Youth* 新青年, Vol. 2, 1 January 1917.

9 V. Mair, 'Hu Shih and Chinese Language Reform'.

10 S. Hu, 'The Chinese Renaissance', University of Chicago, *Haskell Lecture*, 1933 https://web.archive.org/web/20111118100214/ and http://www.csua.berkeley.edu/~mrl/HuShih/

11 R. Levenson, 'Chinese Linguist, Phonologist, Composer and Author, Yuen Ren Chao'.

12 G. Tam, *Dialect and Nationalism in China, 1860–1960*, p.112.

13 R. Levenson, *Chinese Linguist, Phonologist, Composer and Author, Yuen Ren Chao*, pp.2–3.

14 Y. Chao, 'Responses to Objections to Romanisation', *The Chinese Students'* Monthly, 11:7–8, 1916.

15 J. De Francis, *Nationalism and Language Reform in China*, p.85.

16 Y. Chao, *Aspects of Chinese Sociolinguistics*.

17 Y. Chao, *Mandarin Primer: An Intensive Course in Spoken Chinese*, p.23.

18 J. DeFrancis, *Nationalism and Language Reform in China*, pp.82–3.

19 Ibid., p.89.

20 OECD, *Educational Research and Innovation Languages in a Global World Learning for Better Cultural Understanding*, OECD Publishing, 2012, p.136.

21 J. Tetel Andresen and P. Carter, *Languages in the World: How History, Culture, and Politics Shape Language*, 2016, p.111.

22 J. DeFrancis, *Nationalism and Language Reform in China*, pp.93–9.

23 Ibid., p.94.

24 Ibid., p.102.

25 Ibid., p.103.

26 Ibid., p.104.

27 Ibid., p.114.

28 Ibid., p.115.

29 Ibid., pp.111–12.

30 Ibid., pp.119–20.

31 Ibid., p.120.

32 Ibid., p.124.

33 E. Snow, *Red Star over China*, Grove Press, 1968.

34 H. Foster Snow (as Nym Wales), *New China*, Eagle Publishers, 1944, p.144.

35 Ibid., p.139.

36 J. DeFrancis, *Nationalism and Language Reform in China*, p.129.

37 P. Chen, *Modern Chinese: History and Sociolinguistics*, pp.23–4.

38 Y. Chao, *Aspects of Chinese Sociolinguistics*.

39 Y. Chao, *Where I Went Wrong in Matters of Language*, translated by G. Kao, Renditions, Autumn 1973, p.18.

40 R. Levenson, 'Chinese Linguist, Phonologist, Composer and Author, Yuen Ren Chao'.

41 H. Lai and M. Hsu, *Becoming Chinese American: A History of Communities and Institutions*, Rowman Altamira, 2004, pp.6–15.

42 K. Semple, 'In Chinatown, Sound of the Future Is Mandarin', *New York Times*, 21 October 2009 https://www.nytimes.com/2009/10/22/nyregion/22chinese.html

43 H. Yule and A. C. Burnell, *Hobson-Jobson: The Definitive Glossary of British India*, Oxford University Press, p.127.

44 W. Meachem, *The Archaeology of Hong Kong*, Hong Kong University Press, 2009, pp.154–5.

45 J. Wang, 'What Is Mandarin? The Social Project of Language Standardization in Early Republican China', *The Journal of Asian Studies*, Vol. 77, No. 3, August 2018, pp. 611–33.

46 G. Tam, *Dialect and Nationalism in China, 1860–1960*, p.42.

47 H. Dong, *A History of the Chinese Language*, Routledge, 2014, p.146.

48 E. Burney, *Report on Education in Hong Kong*, Government of Hong Kong, 1935, p.25.

49 G. Peterson, *The Power of Words: Literacy and Revolution in South China, 1949–95*, p.110.

50 Ibid., p.110.

51 'Literacy Rate among the Population Aged 15 Years and Older', *China, UNESCO Institute of Statistics*, 2010 http://uis.unesco.org/country/CN

Chapter 12

1 G. Cheung, '50 Years On, Hong Kong Protest Pioneer Has No Regrets (but He's Got No Time for Today's Radicals)', *South China Morning Post*, 3 April 2016 https://www.scmp.com/news/hong-kong/article/1933412/50-years-hong-kong-protest-pioneer-has-no-regrets-hes-got-no-time

2 H. Davis, 'The 120-Year Story of Hong Kong's Iconic Star Ferry', *South China Morning Post*, 16 June 2018 https://multimedia.scmp.com/infographics/article/star-ferry/index.html

3 G. Cheung, *Hong Kong's Watershed: The 1967 Riots*, Hong Kong University Press, 1 October 2009, pp.9–10.

4 Ibid., p.9.

5 R. Kilpatrick, 'Social Activist Elsie Tu', *Hong Kong Free Press*, 31 December 2015 https://hongkongfp.com/2015/12/31/hkfp-person-of-the-month-december-2015-social-activist-elsie-tu/

6   J. Hollingsworth, 'The Hunger Striker Who Sparked April 1966 Star Ferry Riots, and Their Aftermath', *South China Morning Post*, 31 March 2017 https://www.scmp.com/magazines/post-magazine/short-reads/article/2083386/hunger-striker-who-sparked-april-1966-star-ferry

7   G. Cheung, *Hong Kong's Watershed: The 1967 Riots*, p.11.

8   Ibid., p.11.

9   *Commission of Inquiry, Kowloon Disturbances 1966*, edited by J. R. Lee, Acting Government Printer, Hong Kong, 1966, p.148.

10 G. Cheung, *Hong Kong's Watershed: The 1967 Riots*, pp.24–5.

11 Ibid., p.23.

12 S. Tsang, *A Modern History of Hong Kong: 1841–1997*, p.198.

13 I. Scott, *Political Change and the Crisis of Legitimacy in Hong Kong*, University of Hawaii Press, 1989, pp.72–3.

14 G. Cheung, *Hong Kong's Watershed: The 1967 Riots*, p.13.

15 Ibid., p.25.

16 C. Loh, *Underground Front: The Chinese Communist Party in Hong Kong*, Hong Kong University Press, 2010, p.101.

17 Ibid., p.105.

18 Ibid., p.107.

19 G. Cheung, *Hong Kong's Watershed: The 1967 Riots*, p.71.

20 S. Tsang, *A Modern History of Hong Kong: 1841–1997*, pp.196–7.

21 K. Cheng, 'Police Rewrite History of 1967 Red Guard Riots', *Hong Kong Free Press*, 14 September 2015 https://hongkongfp.com/2015/09/14/police-rewrite-history-of-1967-red-guard-riots/

22 C. Loh, *Underground Front: The Chinese Communist Party in Hong Kong*, p.114.

23 Ibid., pp.117–18.

24 A. Pennycook, 'Language Policy as Cultural Politics: The Double-Edged Sword of Language Education in Colonial Malaya and Hong Kong', p.148.

25 M. Chan, 'Hong Kong in Sino-British Conflict: Mass Mobilization and the Crisis of Legitimacy, 1912–26', in M. Chan (ed.), *Precarious Balance: Hong Kong between China and Britain, 1842–1992*, Hong Kong University Press, 1 January 1994, p.36.

26 F. Kan, *Hong Kong's Chinese History Curriculum from 1945: Politics and Identity*, Hong Kong University Press, 2007, p.31.

27 A. Sweeting and E. Vickers, *Language and the History of Colonial Education: The Case of Hong Kong*, Modern Asian Studies, 41, 1, 2007, p.29.

28 'The Session of the Legislative Council of Hong Kong Which Opened 18th October 1972', *Hong Kong Legislative Council*, 18 October 1972, p.40 https://www.legco.gov.hk/yr7273/h721018.pdf

29 J. Griffiths, 'The Secret Negotiations That Sealed Hong Kong's Future', *CNN*, 22 June 2017 https://edition.cnn.com/2017/06/18/asia/hong-kong-handover-china-uk-thatcher/index.html

30 Article 9, The Basic Law of the Hong Kong Special Administrative Region of the People's Republic of China, 4 April 1990.

31 R. Bauer and P. Benedict, *Modern Cantonese Phonology*, Mouton De Gruyter, 1997, p.432.

32 G. Harrison and L. So, 'The Background to Language Change in Hong Kong', *Current Issues in Language and Society*, Vol. 3, No. 2, 1996, p.7.

33 R. Bauer and P. Benedict, *Modern Cantonese Phonology*, p.429.

34 Ibid., p.431.

35 'Shenzhen Basics', *Shenzhen Government Online*, 4 July 2019 http://english.sz.gov.cn/aboutsz/profile/201907/t20190704_18035388.htm

36 R. Bauer and P. Benedict, *Modern Cantonese Phonology*, p.433.

37 Ibid., p.433.

38 S. Tin, '香港地區的語言文字規範問題', *Chinese Language*, Vol. 2, 1992, pp.109–12.

Chapter 13

1 Author interview with Jenny Wu, October 2019.

2 United Nations Population Data, 'Shanghai, China Metro Area Population 1950–2020', *Macro Trends* https://www.macrotrends.net/cities/20656/shanghai/population

3 'Constitution of the People's Republic of China', *National People's Congress*, 2004 http://www.npc.gov.cn/zgrdw/englishnpc/Constitution/2007-11/15/content_1372963.htm

4 B. Qin, 'Shenzhen Becoming Mandarin Outpost in Cantonese Area', *Wen Wei Po*, 6 July 2007 http://paper.wenweipo.com/2006/06/07/zt0606070021.htm

5 H. He, 'Why Has Cantonese Fallen Out of Favour with Guangzhou Youngsters?' *South China Morning Post*, 12 March 2018 https://www.scmp.com/news/china/society/article/2136237/why-has-cantonese-fallen-out-favour-guangzhou-youngsters

6 M. Shek, 'Local Dialect in Danger of Vanishing', *Global Times*, 22 February 2011 https://web.archive.org/web/20111106181706/ and http://shanghai.globaltimes.cn/society/2011-02/625698.html

7 F. Xu, 'Only Shanghainese Can Understand: Popularity of Vernacular Performance and Shanghainese Identity', in L. Bernstein and C. Cheng, *Revealing/Reveiling Shanghai: Cultural Representations from the 20th and 21st Centuries*, State University of New York Press, 2020, p.216.

8 Y. Zhang, 'Shanghainese's Last Gasp', *Global Times*, 3 June 2009 http://www.globaltimes.cn/content/434296.shtml

9 F. Xu, 'Only Shanghainese Can Understand: Popularity of Vernacular Performance and Shanghainese Identity', p.220.

10 H. Pan, 'Proud Shanghainese Asked to Speak Putonghua', *China Daily*, 29 September 2005.

11 F. Jia, 'Stopping the Local Dialect Becoming Derelict', *Shanghai Daily*, 13 May 2011 https://archive.shine.cn/feature/art-and-culture/Stopping-the-local-dialect-becoming-derelict/shdaily.shtml

12 H. Chen, 'Deputy Wants Local Dialect Heard on Metro Trains', *Shanghai Daily*, 17 January 2020 https://www.shine.cn/news/metro/2001170022/

13 P. Chen, *Modern Chinese: History and Sociolinguistics*, p.44.

14 Ibid., p.75.

15 T. Branigan, 'Protesters Gather in Guangzhou to Protect Cantonese Language', *The Guardian*, 25 July 2010 https://www.theguardian.com/world/2010/jul/25/protesters-guangzhou-protect-cantonese

16 '广东颁布规定限制使用方言', *BBC Chinese*, 18 December 2011 https://www.bbc.com/zhongwen/trad/chinese_news/2011/12/111218_guangdong_dialect_putonghua.shtml

17 H. He, 'Why Has Cantonese Fallen Out of Favour with Guangzhou Youngsters?'.

18 S. Cheng and V. Yuen, 'Defending Cantonese', *Varsity Hong Kong*, 20 March 2012 http://varsity.com.cuhk.edu.hk/index.php/2012/03/defending-cantonese/2/?singlepage=1

19 Guangzhou Daily, '粤语易致鼻咽癌？瞎掰!' *iFeng.com*, 19 April 2014 http://news.ifeng.com/gundong/detail_2014_04/19/35888435_0.shtml

20 H. He, 'Why Has Cantonese Fallen Out of Favour with Guangzhou Youngsters?'

21 G. McCulloch, 'Because Internet: Understanding the New Rules of Language', *Penguin*, 23 July 2019, p.2.

22 M. Borak, 'China's Version of TikTok Suspends Users for Speaking Cantonese', *Abacus*, 4 April 2020 https://www.abacusnews.com/culture/chinas-version-tiktok-suspends-users-speaking-cantonese/article/3078138

23 D. Paulk, 'THREAD about How Douyin, the Chinese Version of #TikTok, Is Banning Livestreamers for Speaking Cantonese Instead of Mandarin', *Twitter*, 1 April 2020 https://twitter.com/davidpaulk/status/1245299840944201729

24 Y. Akiyama, '【全程粤語】越來越少的廣東人講粵語，廣州人怎麼看？' *YouTube*, 11 July 2020 https://www.youtube.com/watch?v=RnDDLVtwru8

Chapter 14

1 N. Jenkins, 'Tsang Yok-Sing Wants to Heal the Rift between Hong Kong and China', *Time*, 1 September 2016 https://time.com/4476234/hong-kong-tsang-yok-sing-jasper-china-politics/

2 The Basic Law of the Hong Kong Special Administrative Region of the People's Republic of China, Published by the Constitutional and Mainland Affairs Bureau, July 2020, p.164.

3 J. Wong, *Unfree Speech: The Threat to Global Democracy and Why We Must Act, Now*, Penguin, 2020, p.9.

4 Y. Chan, 'How the Hong Kong Government Tried to Replace Cantonese with Puthonghua as the Medium of Instruction for Chinese Language in Schools', *Medium*, 30 October 2016 https://medium.com/@xinwenxiaojie/how-the-hong-kong-government-tried-to-replace-cantonese-with-puthonghua-as-the-medium-of-a9c7df6e08a7

5 Y. Chu, 'Who Speaks for Lion Rock? Pro-Cantonese Campaign (or Lack Thereof) in Hong Kong', in M. Ng and J. Wong (eds), *Civil Unrest and Governance in Hong Kong*, Routledge, 2017, p.200.

6 'LCQ11: Using Putonghua to Teach the Chinese Language Subject', *GovHK*, 23 January 2008 https://www.info.gov.hk/gia/general/200801/23/P200801230177.htm

7 T. Chen, 'Mandarin Overtakes English as Hong Kong's Second Language', *Wall Street Journal*, 24 February 2012 https://blogs.wsj.com/chinarealtime/2012/02/24/mandarin-overtakes-english-as-hong-kongs-second-language/

8 E. Yau, 'Cantonese or Putonghua in Schools? Hongkongers Fear Culture and Identity "Waning"', *South China Morning Post*, 2 September 2014 https://www.scmp.com/lifestyle/families/article/1583037/cantonese-or-putonghua-schools-hongkongers-fear-culture-and

9 Y. Chu, 'Who Speaks for Lion Rock? Pro-Cantonese Campaign (or Lack Thereof) in Hong Kong', p.197.

10 '驚心動魄(粵普比較之二)', *Hong Kong Education Bureau*, 25 April 2007 https://web.archive.org/web/20140615143649/ and http://resources.hkedcity.net/resource_detail.php?rid=1956736380

11 V. Mair, 'Is Cantonese a Language, or a Personification of the Devil?' *Language Log*, 9 February 2014 https://languagelog.ldc.upenn.edu/nll/?p=10303

12 S. Hui and R. Chan, 'Lam Dismisses Controversies over Education', *The Standard*, 4 May 2018 https://www.thestandard.com.hk/section-news/section/4/195381/Lam-dismisses-controversies-over-education

13 K. Bielicki, 'Hong Kong Identity and the Rise of Mandarin', *The Diplomat*, 14 February 2019 https://thediplomat.com/2019/02/hong-kong-identity-and-the-rise-of-mandarin/

14 '1996 Population By-Census', *Census and Statistics Department Hong Kong*, p.35.

15 '2016 Population By-Census', *Census and Statistics Department Hong Kong Special Administrative Region*, p.45.

16 C. White, 'Cantonese Isn't Dead yet, So Stop Writing Its Eulogy', *Quartz*, 27 June 2017 https://qz.com/1000378/cantonese-isnt-dead-yet-so-stop-writing-its-eulogy/

17 Y. Chan, 'Mother Tongue Squeezed Out of the Chinese Classroom in Cantonese-Speaking Hong Kong', *Hong Kong Free Press*, 22 July 2015 https://hongkongfp.com/2015/07/22/mother-tongue-squeezed-out-of-the-chinese-classroom-in-cantonese-speaking-hong-kong/

18 K. Cheng, 'Baptist University Student Who Protested Mandarin Tests Cuts Mainland Internship Short Following Threats', *Hong Kong Free Press*, 24 January 2018 https://hongkongfp.com/2018/01/24/baptist-university-student-protested-mandarin-tests-cuts-mainland-internship-short-following-threats/

19 E. Ng, 'Baptist University Holds Open Meeting Over Controversial Mandarin Test Following 8-Hour Student Standoff', *Hong Kong Free Press*, 23 January 2018 https://hongkongfp.com/2018/01/23/baptist-university-holds-open-meeting-controversial-mandarin-test-following-8-hour-student-standoff/

20 E. Cheung, 'Hong Kong Baptist University Students Lose Appeal against Punishment for Role in Rowdy Mandarin Protests', *South China Morning Post*, 18 May 2018 https://www.scmp.com/news/hong-kong/education/article/2146834/hong-kong-baptist-university-students-lose-appeal-against

21 Q. Zhang, 'Hong Kong Should Deal Firmly with University Unrest', *Global Times*, 29 January 2018 http://www.globaltimes.cn/content/1087129.shtml

22   C. Zhang, '宣扬"港独"学生陈乐行马上要来内地医院实习？官方：遭投诉，正调查', *Guancha.cn*, 23 January 2018 https://www.guancha.cn/local/2018_01_23_444256_s.shtml

23   K. Cheng, 'Baptist University Student Who Protested Mandarin Tests Cuts Mainland Internship Short Following Threats'.

24   R. Ip, 'Mother-Tongue Language Policy: How Hong Kong Failed Where Singapore Succeeded', *South China Morning Post*, 19 May 2018 https://www.scmp.com/comment/insight-opinion/article/2146704/mother-tongue-language-policy-how-hong-kong-failed-where

25   M. Hui, 'Cantonese Is Hong Kong Protesters' Power Tool of Satire and Identity', *Quartz*, 20 June 2019 https://qz.com/1647631/extradition-law-hong-kong-protests-deploy-cantonese-as-satire-tool/

26   The Stand News, '"Glory to Hong Kong": The Anthem of a Protest Movement', *Global Voices*, 12 September 2019 https://globalvoices.org/2019/09/12/glory-to-hong-kong-the-anthem-of-a-protest-movement/

27   M. Hui, 'How Is Cantonese a Language of Protest?' *Twitter*, 25 July 2019 https://threadreaderapp.com/thread/1154093412330557441.html

28   Tweet from CGTN anchor Liu Xin on 10 August 2019 https://twitter.com/thepointwithlx/status/1160005489213825028

29   Brendan O'Kane https://twitter.com/bokane/status/1160465699682357248

30   R. Cheung, 'Insurgent Tongues: How Loose Cantonese Romanisation Became Hong Kong's Patois of Protest', *Hong Kong Free Press*, 21 September 2019 https://www.hongkongfp.com/2019/09/21/insurgent-tongues-loose-cantonese-Romanisation-became-hong-kongs-patois-protest/

31   @uwu_uwu_mo, 'The Weight of Words – a #HongKong Protest Art Thread', *Twitter*, 13 October 2019 https://mobile.twitter.com/uwu_uwu_mo/status/1183199374056329218

32   Crystal, 'I Went to Eat at Three "Hongkongers Only" Restaurants', *Lausan*, 1 February 2020 https://lausan.hk/2020/i-went-to-eat-at-three-hongkongers-only-restaurants/

33   'In Full: Official English Translation of the Hong Kong National Security Law', *Hong Kong Free Press*, 1 July 2020 https://hongkongfp.com/2020/07/01/in-full-english-translation-of-the-hong-kong-national-security-law/

34   Z. Lin, '香港立法會參選人李梓敬：脫離中間派的「深藍愛國網紅」', *BBC Chinese*, 27 July 2020 https://www.bbc.com/zhongwen/trad/amp/chinese-news-53502659

Chapter 15

1   W. Dong, '西藏，他们的诗和远方', *China Education News*, 7 September 2017 http://www.moe.gov.cn/jyb_xwfb/xw_zt/moe_357/jyzt_2017nztzl/2017_zt06/17zt06_mtbd/201709/t20170911_314110.html

2   M. Yang, 'Moralities and Contradictories in the Educational Aidfor Tibet: Contesting the Multi-layered Saviour Complex', *Journal of Multilingual and Multicultural Development*, May 2019.

3 W. Dong, '西藏，他们的诗和远方'.

4 'Education Investment Increased in China's Tibet and Tibetan-inhabited Areas', *China Tibet Online*, 12 October 2017 http://m.eng.tibet.cn/news/th/1507778632563.shtml

5 M. Yang, *Moralities and Contradictories in the Educational Aidfor Tibet: Contesting the Multi-layered Saviour Complex*.

6 Q. Zhong, '关于"组团式"教育援藏的几点思考', *Tibet Education*, No. 9, 2017, pp.14–16.

7 'China's "Bilingual Education" Policy in Tibet: Tibetan-Medium Schooling under Threat', Human Rights Watch, March 2020, p.58.

8 S. Bu and Z. Geng, 'In Tibet: The Road to Modern Education', *CGTN*, 22 March 2019 https://news.cgtn.com/news/3d3d514d3149544e33457a6333566d54/index.html

9 M. Yang, 'Moralities and Contradictories in the Educational Aidfor Tibet: Contesting the Multi-layered Saviour Complex'.

10 'Gross Entry Ratio to First Tertiary Programmes', *UNESCO Data*, 2017 http://data.uis.unesco.org/

11 'China Statistical Yearbook 2019', *National Bureau of Statistics China*, 2019 http://www.stats.gov.cn/tjsj/ndsj/2019/indexeh.htm

12 G. Postiglione, B. Jiao and S. Gyatso, 'Education in Rural Tibet: Development, Problems and Adaptations', *China: An International Journal*, Vol. 3, No. 1, March 2005, pp.1–23.

13 D. Curtis, 'Learning to Read the Tibetan Script', *Mandala*, June/July 2006, p.52.

14 'Tibetan', *Omniglot* https://omniglot.com/writing/tibetan.htm

15 'China's "Bilingual Education" Policy in Tibet: Tibetan-Medium Schooling under Threat'.

16 Y. Lamucuo, *Becoming Bilingual in School and Home in Tibetan Areas of China: Stories of Struggle*, Springer, 2019.

17 Roundtable, 'Teaching and Learning Tibetan: The Role of the Tibetan Language in Tibet's Future', Congressional-Executive Commission on China, One Hundred Eighth Congress of the United States, 7 April 2003.

18 G. Roche, 'Articulating Language Oppression: Colonialism, Coloniality and the Erasure of Tibet's Minority Languages', *Patterns of Prejudice*, October 2019 https://www.tandfonline.com/doi/full/10.1080/0031322X.2019.1662074

19 Interview with Gerald Roche, expert on Tibetan languages and linguistic diversity at La Trobe University, in August 2020.

20 G. Roche and Y. Tsomu, 'Tibet's Invisible Languages and China's Language Endangerment Crisis: Lessons from the Gochang Language of Western Sichuan', *The China Quarterly*, Vol. 233, March 2018, pp.186–210.

21 B. Demick, *Eat the Buddha*, Random House, 2020, pp.31–3.

22 Ibid., p.44.

23 Y. Lamucuo, *Becoming Bilingual in School and Home in Tibetan Areas of China: Stories of Struggle*, pp.50–5.

24 M. Goldstein et al., *The Struggle for Modern Tibet: The Autobiography of Tashi Tsering*, M.E. Sharpe, 1997, p.186.

25 A. Kolas, 'Teaching Tibetan in Tibet: Bilingual Education Is Survival', *Cultural Survival Quarterly Magazine*, September 2003 https://www.culturalsurvival.org/publications/cultural-survival-quarterly/teaching-tibetan-tibet-bilingual-education-survival

26 'China's "Bilingual Education" Policy in Tibet: Tibetan-Medium Schooling under Threat'.

27 Ibid.

28 S. George, 'Journeys along the Seventh Ring', *That's Beijing*, October 2014 https://www.thatsmags.com/interactive/2014/seventh-ring/

29 E. McKirdy, 'Beijing Set to Take Aim at "Weird Buildings"', *CNN*, 5 December 2014 https://edition.cnn.com/2014/12/05/world/asia/beijing-weird-buildings/index.html

30 Research Report, *'Five Years after the Olympics – Growth in Beijing Has Continued, What to Expect Next?'* Jones Lang LaSalle, August 2013 https://web.archive.org/web/20141113091719/ and http://www.ap.jll.com/asia-pacific/en-gb/Documents/Five_years_after_the_Olympics_EN.pdf

31 S. Jiang, 'China's Ex-security Chief Zhou Yongkang Sentenced to Life for Bribery', *CNN*, 12 June 2015 https://edition.cnn.com/2015/06/11/asia/china-zhou-yongkang-sentence/index.html

32 E. Osnos, 'Born Red', *New Yorker*, 30 March 2015 https://www.newyorker.com/magazine/2015/04/06/born-red

33 J. Leibold, 'Xinjiang Work Forum Marks New Policy of "Ethnic Mingling"', *Jamestown China Brief*, Vol. 14, No. 12 https://jamestown.org/program/xinjiang-work-forum-marks-new-policy-of-ethnic-mingling/

34 Xinhua, 'Xi Stresses Unity for Tibet, Vows Fight against Separatism', *China Daily*, 26 August 2015 https://www.chinadaily.com.cn/business/2015-08/26/content_21709542.htm

35 'China's "Bilingual Education" Policy in Tibet: Tibetan-Medium Schooling under Threat'.

36 'Annual Working Conditions Report', *Foreign Correspondents Club of China*, 2015.

37 Author interview with Jonah Kessel, April 2020.

38 Information Office, 'Regional Autonomy for Ethnic Minorities in China', *State Council of the People's Republic of China*, 28 February 2005 https://www.chinadaily.com.cn/english/doc/2005-02/28/content_420337.htm

39 M. Chan, 'Qinghai Will Not Rush Over Language Reform', *South China Morning Post*, 24 October 2010 https://www.scmp.com/article/728387/qinghai-will-not-rush-over-language-reform

40 E. Wong, 'Tibetans Fight to Salvage Fading Culture in China', *New York Times*, 28 November 2015 https://www.nytimes.com/2015/11/29/world/asia/china-tibet-language-education.html

41 A. Jacobs, 'Tibetan Self-Immolations Rise as China Tightens Grip', *New York Times*, 22 March 2012 https://www.nytimes.com/2012/03/23/world/asia/in-self-immolations-signs-of-new-turmoil-in-tibet.html

42 'Fact Sheet on Tibetan Self-Immolation Protests in Tibet since February 2009', *Central Tibetan Administration*, 28 November 2019 https://tibet.net/important-issues/factsheet-immolation-2011-2012/

43 T. Woeser, 'Tibet on Fire: Self-Immolations against Chinese Rule', *Verso Books*, 2016, p.35.

44 E. Wong, 'Tibetans Fight to Salvage Fading Culture in China'.

45 Author interview with Tashi Wangchuk's lawyer, Liang Xiaojun, in August 2020.

46 B. Demick, *Eat the Buddha*, p.161.

47 Author interview with Tashi Wangchuk's lawyer, Liang Xiaojun, in August 2020.

48 D. Rushe, 'Internet Giant Alibaba Valued at $231bn after Frenzied Debut as Public Company', *The Guardian*, 20 September 2014 https://www.theguardian.com/business/2014/sep/19/alibaba-shares-price-americas-biggest-ipo

49 CGTN, 'Alibaba Released Video for Road Show', *YouTube*, 9 September 2014 https://www.youtube.com/watch?v=uiJJHa6FkYs

50 I told Ilham Tohti's story in my first book, on internet censorship and freedom of speech in China. J. Griffiths, *The Great Firewall of China: How to Build and Control an Alternative Version of the Internet*, Zed Books, 2019, p.131.

51 E. Wong, 'Tibetans Fight to Salvage Fading Culture in China'.

52 J. Kessel, 'Tashi Wangchuk: A Tibetan's Journey for Justice', *New York Times*, 1 December 2015 https://www.youtube.com/watch?v=7HGZXcBq87c

53 R. Rife, 'A Tibetan Language Advocate's Journey to Imprisonment', *Amnesty International*, 7 May 2018 https://www.amnesty.org/en/latest/campaigns/2018/05/tibetan-language-advocate-journey-to-imprisonment/

54 E. Wong, 'Tibetans Fight to Salvage Fading Culture in China'.

55 W. Tashi, 'Here, the Tibetan Language Is Like a Foreign Language', *Weibo*, 29 December 2015 https://www.weibo.com/2029646391/DaGXgE6gk?from=page_1005052029646391_profile&wvr=6&mod=weibotime&type=comment#_rnd1586332639010

56 J. Kessel, 'Tashi Wangchuk: A Tibetan's Journey for Justice'.

57 E. Wong, 'China to Try Tibetan Education Advocate Detained for 2 Years', *New York Times*, 30 December 2017 https://www.nytimes.com/2017/12/30/world/asia/tashi-wangchuck-trial-tibet.html

58 C. Buckley, 'A Tibetan Tried to Save His Language. China Handed Him 5 Years in Prison', *New York Times*, 22 May 2018 https://www.nytimes.com/2018/05/22/world/asia/tibetan-activist-tashi-wangchuk-sentenced.html

59 'Translated Court Documents Expose China's Sham Prosecution of Tibetan Language Rights Advocate Tashi Wangchuk, Raise Fears about Use of Torture', *International Campaign for Tibet*, 29 August 2018 https://savetibet.org/translated-court-documents-expose-chinas-sham-prosecution-of-tibetan-language-rights-advocate-tashi-wangchuk-raise-fears-about-use-of-torture/

60 A. Palmer, '"Flee at Once": China's Besieged Human Rights Lawyers', *New York Times*, 25 July 2017 https://www.nytimes.com/2017/07/25/magazine/the-lonely-crusade-of-chinas-human-rights-lawyers.html

61 '习近平：全面贯彻新时代党的治藏方略 建设团结富裕文明和谐美丽的社会主义现代化新西藏', *Xinhua*, 29 August 2020 http://www.xinhuanet.com/politics/leaders/2020-08/29/c_1126428221.htm

62 I. Yee and J. Griffiths, 'China's President Xi Says Xinjiang Policies "Completely Correct" amid Growing International Criticism', *CNN*, 28 September 2020 https://edition.cnn.com/2020/09/27/asia/china-xi-jinping-xinjiang-intl-hnk/index.html

63 A. Qin, 'Curbs on Mongolian Language Teaching Prompt Large Protests in China', *New York Times*, 31 August 2020 https://www.nytimes.com/2020/08/31/world/asia/china-protest-mongolian-language-schools.html

64 G. Baioud, 'Will Education Reform Wipe Out Mongolian Language and Culture in China?' *The China Story*, 1 October 2020 https://www.thechinastory.org/will-education-reform-wipe-out-mongolian-language-and-culture-in-china/

65 I. Steger, 'China's Insatiable Appetite for Control Is Forcing Even Its "Model Minority" to Rebel', *Quartz*, 4 September 2020 https://qz.com/1899397/inner-mongolians-in-china-rise-up-against-language-suppression/

66 N. Gan, 'How China's New Language Policy Sparked Rare Backlash in Inner Mongolia', *CNN*, 6 September 2020 https://edition.cnn.com/2020/09/05/asia/china-inner-mongolia-intl-hnk-dst/index.html

67 G. Roche and J. Leibold, 'China's Second-generation Ethnic Policies Are Already Here', *Made in China*, 7 September 2020 https://madeinchinajournal.com/2020/09/07/chinas-second-generation-ethnic-policies-are-already-here/

68 C. Humphrey, 'Letter: China's Mongol Region Wants to Stick to the Script', *Financial Times*, 14 September 2020 https://www.ft.com/content/f9378802-90c5-41bb-88c7-90eb9ab62dd5

69 C. Shepherd, 'Authorities Quash Inner Mongolia Protests', *Financial Times*, 10 September 2020 https://www.ft.com/content/c035c3d7-0f96-4e23-b892-2666bc110e20?list=intlhomepage

Epilogue

1 S. Lewis, 'Tynged Yr Iaith', *BBC Radio Cymru*, 13 February 1962 https://web.archive.org/web/20150411225207/ and http://www.llgc.org.uk/ymgyrchu/Iaith/TyngedIaith/tynged.htm

2 L. Hinton, L. Huss and G. Roche (eds), *The Routledge Handbook of Language Revitalization*, Routledge, 2018, pp.495–6.

3 'Cymraeg 2050: A Million Welsh Speakers', Welsh Government, 2017, p.17.

4 L. Hinton, L. Huss and G. Roche (eds), *The Routledge Handbook of Language Revitalization*, p.495.

5 Ibid., p.71.

6 Ibid., p.497.

7 Ibid., p.497.

8 G. Vince, 'The Amazing Benefits of Being Bilingual', *BBC*, 13 August 2016 https://www.bbc.com/future/article/20160811-the-amazing-benefits-of-being-bilingual

9 L. Hinton, L. Huss and G. Roche (eds), *The Routledge Handbook of Language Revitalization*, p.501.

10 I first wrote about Higgs and Duolingo for CNN in 2019. J. Griffiths, 'The Internet Threatened to Speed Up the Death of Endangered Languages. Could It Save Them Instead?' *CNN*, 4 October 2019 https://edition.cnn.com/2019/10/04/tech/duolingo-endangered-languages-intl-hnk/index.html

11 'Language Courses for English Speakers', *Duolingo, Data as of August* 2020 https://www.duolingo.com/courses

12 'Polish', *Ethnologue* https://www.ethnologue.com/language/pol

13 'Greek', *Ethnologue* https://www.ethnologue.com/language/ell

14 A. Kornai, 'Digital Language Death', *Plos One*, 22 October 2013 https://doi.org/10.1371/journal.pone.0077056

15 S. Harrison, '*Welsh Wikipedia Gives Me Hope*', *Slate*, 7 August 2019 https://slate.com/technology/2019/08/welsh-wikipedia-google-translate.html

16 C. Hu, 'Iceland Is Inventing a New Vocabulary for a High-Tech Future', *Quartz*, 2 June 2019 https://qz.com/1632990/iceland-is-inventing-a-new-vocabulary-for-a-high-tech-future/

17 'Projet de loi de finances pour 2020: Action extérieure de l'État: Diplomatie culturelle et d'influence', *Le Sénat*, 6 August 2020 https://www.senat.fr/rap/a19-142-2/a19-142-24.html

18 B. Mussett, 'As Indigenous Language Classes Move Online, Students Discover New Ways to Connect with Elders', *CBC News*, 25 August 2020 https://www.cbc.ca/news/canada/british-columbia/north-island-college-indigenous-language-classes-online-1.5699962

19 E. Ongweso, 'Most of Scottish Wikipedia Written by American in Mangled English', *Vice*, 26 August 2020 https://www.vice.com/en_us/article/wxqy8x/most-of-scottish-wikipedia-written-by-american-in-mangled-english

20 S. Harrison, 'What Happens to Scots Wikipedia Now?' *Slate*, 9 September 2020 https://slate.com/technology/2020/09/scots-wikipedia-language-american-teenager.html

21 J. Griffiths, 'Welsh and Hawaiian Were Saved from Extinction. Other Languages Might Not Be So Lucky', *CNN*, 10 April 2019 https://www.cnn.com/2019/04/09/asia/endangered-languages-welsh-hawaiian-cantonese-intl/index.html

Bibliography

Linguistics and language revitalization

S. Anderson, *Languages: A Very Short Introduction*, Oxford University Press, 2012.

D. Everett, *Don't Sleep, There Are Snakes*, Random House, 2008.

D. Everett, *How Language Began: The Story of Humanity's Greatest Invention*, Liveright Publishing, 2017.

B. Henderson, P. Rohloff and R. Henderson, *More Than Words: Towards a Development-Based Approach to Language Revitalization*, Language Documentation and Conservation, Vol. 8, 2014.

L. Hinton, L. Huss and G. Roche (eds), *The Routledge Handbook of Language Revitalization*, Routledge, 2018.

C. Kenneally, *The First Word: The Search for the Origins of Language*, Penguin Books, 2008.

D. Marmion, K. Obata and J. Troy, *Community, Identity, Wellbeing: The Report of the Second National Indigenous Languages Survey*, AIATSIS, 2014.

G. McCulloch, *Because Internet: Understanding the New Rules of Language*, Penguin, 2019.

J. McWhorter, *The Power of Babel: A Natural History of Language*, Arrow Books, 2003.

M. Tallerman and K. Gibson (eds), *The Oxford Handbook of Language Evolution*, Oxford, 2012.

E. Vajda, *Linguistics 201: The Origin of Language*, Western Washington University, 2001.

M. Walsh, *Indigenous Languages Are Good for Your Health: Health and Wellbeing Implications of Regaining or Retaining Australian Languages*, Northern Institute, Charles Darwin University, 2017.

M. Yoshihara and J. Winters Carpenter, translators, *The Fall of Language in the Age of English*, by M. Mizumura, Columbia University Press, 2015.

Welsh

K. Bohata, *Postcolonialism Revisited: Writing Wales in English*, University of Wales Press, 2004.

N. Brooke, *Terrorism and Nationalism in the United Kingdom*, Palgrave Macmillan, 2018.

S. Brooks, *Why Wales Never Was: The Failure of Welsh Nationalism*, University of Wales Press, 2017.

B. Bryson, *The Mother Tongue: English and How It Got That Way*, HarperCollins, 1990.

J. Davies, *A History of Wales*, Penguin Books, 2007.

J. Davis, *The Welsh Language: A History*, University of Wales Press, 2014.

J. Evas, *The Welsh Language in the Digital Age*, Meta Net White Paper Series, Springer, 2014.

J. Gower, *The Story of Wales*, BBC Digital, 2012.

J. Humphries, *Freedom Fighters: Wales's Forgotten 'War', 1963–1993*, University of Wales Press, 2009.

D. Jenkins, *Nation on Trial: Penyberth 1936*, translated by A. Corkett, Welsh Academic Press 1999.

G. Jenkins, *The Welsh Language and Its Social Domains*, University of Wales Press Cardiff, 2000.

G. Jenkins and M. Williams, *'Let's Do Our Best for the Ancient Tongue': The Welsh Language in the Twentieth Century*, University of Wales Press Cardiff, 2000.

R. Jones, *The Fascist Party in Wales?: Plaid Cymru, Welsh Nationalism and the Accusation of Fascism*, University of Wales Press, 2014.

D. Mac GiollaChríost, *Welsh Writing, Political Action and Incarceration*, Palgrave Macmillan, 2013.

K. Morgan, *Rebirth of a Nation: Wales, 1880–1980*, Oxford University Press, 1981.

J. Morris, *A Writer's House in Wales*, National Geographic Society, 2002.

S. Schama, *A History of Britain – Volume 1: At the Edge of the World? 3000 BC–AD 1603*, Random House, 2011.

N. Thomas, *The Welsh Extremist*, Cymdeithas yr Iaith Gymraeg, 1971.

W. Thomas, *John Jenkins – The Reluctant Revolutionary?* Y Lolfa, 2020.

Hawaiian

T. Coffman, *The Island Edge of America: A Political History of Hawai'i*, University of Hawaii Press, 2003.

T. Coffman, *Nation within: The History of the American Occupation of Hawai'i*, Duke University Press, 2016.

N. Goodyear-Ka'ōpua, I. Hussey and E. Kahunawaika'ala Wright (ed.), *A Nation Rising: Hawaiian Movements for Life, Land, and Sovereignty*, Duke University Press, 2014.

M. J. Harden, *Voices of Wisdom: Hawaiian Elders Speak*, Aka Press, 2014.

D. Immerwahr, *How to Hide an Empire*, Farrar, Straus and Giroux, 2019.

D. Itsuji Saranillio, *Unsustainable Empire: Alternative Histories of Hawai'i Statehood*, Duke University Press, 2018.

S. King and R. Ro, *Broken Trust: Greed, Mismanagement & Political Manipulation at America's Largest Charitable Trust*, University of Hawaii Press, 2006.

J. Rath, *Lost Generations: A Boy, a School, a Princess*, University of Hawaii Press, 2006.

A. Schutz, *The Voices of Eden: A History of Hawaiian Language Studies*, University of Hawaii Press, 1994.

N. Silva, *Aloha Betrayed: Native Hawaiian Resistance to American Colonialism*, Duke University Press, 2004.

H. Trask, *From a Native Daughter*, University of Hawai'i Press, 1999.

S. Vowell, *Unfamiliar Fishes*, Riverhead, 2011.

B. Wist, *A Century of Public Education in Hawaii*, The Hawaii Educational Review, 1940.

Chinese

R. Bauer and P. Benedict, *Modern Cantonese Phonology*, Mouton De Gruyter, 1997.

M. Chan (ed.), *Precarious Balance: Hong Kong between China and Britain, 1842–1992*, Hong Kong University Press, 1994.

P. Chen, *Modern Chinese: History and Sociolinguistics*, Cambridge University Press, 2004.

G. Cheung, *Hong Kong's Watershed: The 1967 Riots*, Hong Kong University Press, 1 October 2009.

R. Chow, *Between Colonizers: Hong Kong's Postcolonial Self-Writing in the 1990s*, Ethics After Idealism, Bloomington, Indiana University Press, 1998.

Y. Chu, *Found in Transition: Hong Kong Studies in the Age of China*, SUNY Press, November 2018.

B. Demick, *Eat the Buddha*, Random House, 2020.

J. DeFrancis, *Nationalism and Language Reform in China*, Princeton University Press, 1950.

J. DeFrancis, *The Chinese Language: Fact and Fantasy*, University of Hawaii Press, 1986.

H. Dong, *A History of the Chinese Language*, Routledge, 2014.

J. Fenby, *The Penguin History of Modern China*, Penguin, 2018.

H. Foster Snow (as Nym Wales), *New China*, Eagle Publishers, 1944.

J. Gibbons, *Code-Mixing and Code Choice: A Hong Kong Case Study*, Multilingual Matters, 1987.

G. Harrison and L. So, 'The Background to Language Change in Hong Kong', *Current Issues in Language and Society*, Vol. 3, No. 2, 1996.

H. Kwok and M. Chan, *Fossils from a Rural Past: A Study of Extant Cantonese Children's Songs*, Hong Kong University Press, 1990.

Llewellyn Commission, *A Perspective on Education in Hong Kong*, Hong Kong Government, 1982.

V. Mair, *The Columbia History of Chinese Literature*, Columbia University Press, 2001.

D. Moser, *A Billion Voices: China's Search for a Common Language*, Penguin, 2016.

T. Mullaney, *The Chinese Typewriter: A History*, MIT Press, 2017.

T. Ngo, *Hong Kong's History: State and Society under Colonial Rule*, Routledge, 1999.

J. Norman, *Chinese*, Cambridge University Press, 1988.

A. Pennycook, 'Language Policy as Cultural Politics: The Double-Edged Sword of Language Education in Colonial Malaya and Hong Kong', *Discourse: Studies in the Cultural Politics of Education*, Vol. 17, No. 2, 1996.

E. Snow, *Red Star over China*, Grove Press, 1968.

A. Sweeting and E. Vickers, 'Language and the History of Colonial Education: The Case of Hong Kong', *Modern Asian Studies*, Vol. 41, No. 1, 2007.

G. Tam, *Dialect and Nationalism in China, 1860–1960*, Cambridge University Press, February 2020.

S. Tsang, *A Modern History of Hong Kong: 1841–1997*, Hong Kong University Press, 2003.

M. Zhou and H. Sun (eds), *Language Policy in the People's Republic of China: Theory and Practice since 1949*, Kluwer/Springer, 2004.

Miscellaneous

A. Brink, *A Fork in the Road*, Random House, 2010.

R. Davies, *Afrikaners in the New South Africa: Identity Politics in a Globalised Economy*, Tauris Academic Studies, 2009.

R. Dunbar-Ortiz, *An Indigenous People's History of the United States*, Beacon Press, 2014.

J. Fellman, *The Revival of a Classical Tongue Eliezer Ben Yehuda and the Modern Hebrew Language*, Mouton, 1973.

E. Freeburg, *The Cost of Revival: The Role of Hebrew in Jewish Language Endangerment*, Yale University, 1 May 2013.

B. Friel, *Translations*, Faber and Faber, 1981.

N. Karlen, *The Story of Yiddish: How a Mish-mosh of Languages Saved the Jews*, HarperCollins, 2008.

A. Korzhenkov, *Zamenhof The Life, Works, and Ideas of the Author of Esperanto*, translated by I. Richmond, Esperantic Studies Foundation, 2009.

A. Krog, *A Change of Tongue*, Random House, 2003.

A. Krog, *Country of My Skull: Guilt, Sorrow, and the Limits of Forgiveness in the New South Africa*, Crown/Archetype, 2007.

H. Giliomee, *The Rise and Possible Demise of Afrikaans as a Public Language*, PRAESA Occasional Papers No. 14, University of Cape Town, 2003.

A. Lang, *The Politics of Hebrew and Yiddish: Zionism and Transnationalism*, The Federalist Debate, Number 2, July 2015.

W. Laqueur, *A History of Zionism*, Tauris Parke, 2003.

R. Malan, *My Traitor's Heart: A South African Exile Returns to Face His Country, His Tribe, and His Conscience*, Grove Atlantic, 2012.

J. Morris, *Heaven's Command: An Imperial Progress*, Faber and Faber, 2010.

S. Ndlovu, 'The Soweto Uprising', in *The Road to Democracy in South Africa, Volume 2*, South African Democracy Education Trust, 2011, pp.331–2.

K. Norman, *Bridge over Blood River: The Rise and Fall of the Afrikaners*, Hurst, 2016.

A. Okrent, *In the Land of Invented Languages*, Spiegel & Grau, 2009.

Y. Rabkin, *Language in Nationalism: Modern Hebrew in the Zionist Project*, Holy Land Studies, November 2010.

A. Sáenz-Badillos, *A History of the Hebrew Language*, translated by J. Elwolde, Cambridge University Press, 1993.

E. Schor, *Bridge of Words: Esperanto and the Dream of a Universal Language*, Henry Holt and Company, 2016.

J. Shanes, 'Yiddish and Jewish Diaspora Nationalism', *Monatshefte*, Vol. 90, No. 2, Summer, 1998, pp.178–88.

B. Spolsky, *The Languages of the Jews*, Cambridge University Press, 2014.

L. Thompson, *A History of South Africa*, Yale University Press, 2014.

D. Tutu et al., *Truth and Reconciliation Commission of South Africa Report*, TRC, 29 October 1998.

Index

Locators followed by "n." indicate endnotes

Abse, Leo 44
Act of Union (1536) 32–3
aerial bombardment (London) 24
African National Congress (ANC) 62,
    64–5
AfriForum 66–70
Afrikaans 58–9, 63–4, 68–9
    critics of 65–6
    and farm murders 66–7
    future of 68–9
    as language of colonialism 60
    as medium of instruction 60–1, 63,
        65, 68
    proliferation 70
    ripple effect 61
Afrikaans Language and Culture
        Association 69
Afrikaners 57. *See also* Afrikaans
    Boer Wars 57–9
    Broederbond 59 (*see also* apartheid
        (apartness))
    bronze statue 62–3
    identity 58, 65
    nationalist hegemony 70
    Peace of Vereeniging 58
    in public sphere 66
aggressive monolingualism 4
AgriSA 67
Akaka, Danny 108
Alders, Ernie 43
Alonsa de Barcena 3
AmaryllisGardener 195–6
Anglicanism 13, 18
anti-investiture bombing campaign 39
apartheid (apartness) 59–60, 63,
        66, 68
    architects of 61, 70

book banned 65
    education 64
Arabic 116, 121, 147
Armstrong-Jones, Anthony 37
Arnold, Matthew 20
Arthur, King 5
Ashkenazi Yiddish 116
Asmal, Kader 65
Atkinson, A.T. 87
Australia, indigenous languages 190
Awodey, Myra 193

Bailey, Alana 68–9
Bantu myth (language) 2
Basque 5, 52
Bauer, Robert 157
Bayonet Constitution 92–3
Beamer, Helen Desha 97–8
Beamer, Peter 98
Beamer, Winona Kapuailohiamanonokalani
        Desha 97, 102
    Hawaiiana 99
    hula and practice 97–9
    missionary stock, descended 100
Beaufront, Louis de 120
Beijing, China 179
    aggressive monolingualism 4
    Cantonese 7, 138
    Commission on the Unification of
        Pronunciation 144
    education 133
    imperial officials writing 138
    Mandarin 138, 140, 145–6, 151
    military intervention 155
    phonological system 150
    trilingualism 169
Ben-Avi, Ittamar 117

Benedict, Paul 157

Ben-Gurion, David 123, 124

Ben-Yehuda, Ben-Zion. *See* Ben-Avi, Ittamar

Ben-Yehuda, Eliezer 113, 115, 123, 126
   Complete Dictionary of Ancient and Modern Hebrew 118
   Hatzvi 118
   Hebrew Language Council 118
   Modern Hebrew 113–14, 117
   in Narodniki 114
   nationalist sentiment 114
   to Palestine 116–17
   A Serious Question 114
   to yeshiva 114

Bēowulf 2

bilingualism 52–3, 161, 173
   education in Tibet 176–7, 180, 183
   fetishization 52
   and multilingualism 192
   in Wales 6, 52

Bingham, Hiram 77, 95

Bishop, Charles Reed 78–80, 93

Bishop, Sereno 96

Bishop Estate 93, 96, 102

Black Lives Matter movement 111, 191

black schools 60–1, 63–4. *See also* Soweto uprising

Blair, Tony 47

Blue Books 17–18, 21, 32–3

bombing and arson campaign 46, 155
   anti-investiture bombing campaign 39
   bombing school attack 26–7, 45
   reservoir work site, attack on 36, 38
   Temple of Peace attack 35–6, 38, 40, 43

bombing school
   attack 26–7, 45
   nationalist opposition to 25
   RAF Penhros 31
   site for new 24–5

Botha, Louis 58

Boxer Indemnity Scholarship 139

Brad y Llyfrau Gleision 17

Brandt, Gladys 99

Breton 55

Brewster, William 137

Brink, Andre 60, 65

Bro Goth agan Tasow (Cornwall) 54

Bro Gozh ma Zadou (Breton) 55

Brooks, Simon 52

Brown, S.R. 133

Brumberg, Abraham 124

Brythonic language 54–5

Caergybi bomb 42

Callaghan, James 42, 44

Cantonese 3–4, 7, 128, 132, 138, 140, 149–50, 152, 159, 168–9, 196
   cause nasal cancer (study report) 162
   as Chinese dialect 170
   distinctive features 128–9
   as dominant language 157
   examples 129
   Heyson (YouTuber) about 163
   marginalization 161–2, 196
   medium of instruction 151
   Official Language Ordinance 156
   Putonghua and 157, 171, 174
   revitalisation 171
   role in protests 171–2
   speakers 128, 151, 156, 170
   vernacular 128, 157, 163
   writing system 128

Cao Xueqin, *Dream of the Red Chamber* 145

Carver, David John 139

Cayo Evans, Julian 37–8

Chan, Andrew 170–1

Chao, Yuen Ren 133, 143
   Boxer Rebellion 139
   early life 135, 138
   Guoyu records 144
   Lion-Eating Poet in the Stone Den 136
   National Phonetic Alphabet 146
   phonographs 146
   polyglottal abilities 144
   Science 144
   study tours 143
   teaching Chinese 150

Charles (prince of Wales), investiture 37–9, 42–3

Chen Duxiu 144
   Chinese Communist Party 144
   New Youth 145

Chen Guofu 146

Chen Zuoru 175–6

Chiang Kai-shek 143, 148, 150

China 148. *See also* Beijing, China; Hong
     Kong, China
  autonomous prefectures 181
  The Boxers 133–4
  Chinese Bibles 136, 145
  civil war 148, 150–1
  Confucian texts 133, 134–5
  extradition bill 166–8
  linguistic change 4, 160, 169 (*see also*
     specific Chinese languages)
  One Country, Two Systems 172
  People's Liberation Army 176
  potential risks 181
  writing system 136
Chinese Alphabet 146
Chung Sze-yuen 156
civil rights movement 46
Cixi (Dowager Empress) 134, 137–9
Clayton, John 85
collision of languages 2
colonialism 150
  and imperialism 5
  language of 60
Coloured Mentality 70
Commission on the Unification of
     Pronunciation 139, 144
Committee for the Preservation of
     Hawaiian Language, Art, and
     Culture 100
Committee for the Promotion of the
     National Language Romanisation
     148
Committee on Unification of the National
     Language 145
Confucius/Confucianism 140, 162
  Analects 135
  Great Learning 135
Cook, James 73–5, 84
Cooke, Amos 77–9, 81
Cooke, Juliette 77–80, 91
Cooper, Henry 86–7
Council for the Preservation of Rural
     Wales 25
Cronjé, Geoff, A Home for Posterity 59
Cruzan, J.A. 91
cultural vandalism 196
Cymdeithas yr Iaith Gymraeg 37, 39, 44,
     46, 53, 192
  civil disobedience campaigns 43
Cymraeg. *See* Welsh

Dakota Access Pipeline protests 111, 192
Daniel, Goronwy 38
Davies, David 19–20
Davies, David William 28
Democratic Alliance for the Betterment
     and Progress of Hong Kong 168
Demosisto 172
Denning, James 16
Derbyshire, Alwen 54
Derde Taalbeweging 68, 70
de Tromelin, Louis 85
Devanagari 177
dialects 49, 76, 87, 128, 135, 137, 145,
     147, 152, 162
  Cantonese as 170
  of Mandarin 138, 145–6, 159
  Shanghai 160
  of Wu 135, 143
'digital language death' 194–5
Dole, Sanford 82, 85–6
Dolman, Eric 37
Donne, M.A. 76
Douyin 163
Dragunov, AA 147
Dubnow, Simon 122
Duolingo 49–50, 193, 195–6, 198
  'incubator' 193
  Irish course 194
  Welsh course 194
du Preez, Max 66
Dutch 58–9, 61
Du Toit, Peter 69–70

Easter Rising 37
educational reforms
  Afrikaans 63
  Inner Mongolia 186
  Thatcher 46
Edward I 37
Edwards, Huw 47
Einion ap Owain 23
Eisteddfod 6, 19–20, 54
'Ekela Kani'aupio-Crozier 101–3, 105,
     110–12, 198
  'Aiea High School 103
  legacy of Hawaiian-language activism
     103
  nascent language movement 104
Elbert, Samuel H. 100
'elder in residence' programme 195

Elementary Education Act (1870) 19
Elipoo 131–2
Emerson, Nathaniel Bright, *The Unwritten Literature of Hawaii* 96
Endangered Language Alliance (ELA) 3, 194
England. *See also* Wales
  bombing school 24
  Declaration of Independence 92
  and Englishness 18, 25
  law of 29
English 3–4, 7, 15, 60, 77–8, 132, 138, 156, 197
  Afrikaans and 59, 61, 68
  Cornwall, adoption 20
  Dutch and 58, 60
  Hawaiian and 86–7, 94, 111–12
  in Hong Kong 133, 138, 169
  imperialism 19
  as instrument of domination 63
  necessity of using 61
  promoting knowledge 17, 191
  trial of Welsh criminal 17, 27–30
  Welsh and 6, 10, 21, 33, 41, 45–6, 51–2
  workhouse schools 13
Esedhvos 54
Esperanto 113, 116, 126
  conferences 119–20
  Dogmas of Hillelism 120
  popularity in France 119
Evans, Gwynfor 45–6
Eyre, Kawika 94

financial crash (2008) 179
First Aliya 117
First Hawaiian Renaissance 95
Fisk, Glen 99–100
Fiske, John, 'manifest destiny' 92
Free Wales Army (FWA) 37–41
The Friend 87, 91, 96
Froneman, Johan 67, 70

Gaselee, Alfred 134
Giliomee, Hermann 66
Gladstone, William 132
Government of Wales Act (1998) 47
Great Leap Forward 178
Great Proletarian Cultural Revolution 154

Great Trek 58–9
Greek myth (language) 2
Grieve, Robert 96
Guangxu Emperor 134, 137
Guanhua 138, 151
Gulick, Charles 84
Guoyu 140–1, 144–5, 150
  phonograph records 144
Gwóngdūng wá. *See* Cantonese
Gwoyeu Romatzyh 146–9

Haddon-Cave, Charles Philip 156
Hakka 149
Hand, David 196
Hawaiian (Hawai'i) 5, 72
  Act 77 86
  annexation by United States 93–4
  anti-Hawaiian campaign (Kaiwi'ula) 94
  The Bird of Paradise 99
  Chiefs' Children's School 77–9, 92
  Christian civilization 95, 97
  colonization 84
  constant/consistent restraint 93–4
  crisis 73–4
  cultural renaissance 109
  distinctive features 72
  examples 72
  extinction 74, 105
  Hawai'i Pono'ī 95
  hula and traditional practices 74, 95–9
  identity, loss 100
  impressions 76
  kahuna 87, 94–7
  kapu 74, 94–5, 97, 99
  lack of consonants 75–6
  language movement 104–5, 109, 111
  as medium of instruction 105
  native sovereignty, loss 85
  Pauahi's 'educational legacy' 102
  politics 82
  Pulolo's case 97
  revitalization 6–7, 110
  rights of Catholics 85
  school system 75, 102
  self-determination 7
  speakers 72
  voting rights/schools, restrictions 86–7, 92
  writing system/language 72, 77

healthy language 189
Hebrew 115–17, 121, 124–6
  Bible 2, 114
  Ulpan method 50
  for Zionist schools 123
Hennessy, John Pope 133
Henry 79
Hermes 2
Hertzl, Theodor 116, 123
Higgins, Michael 193
Higgs, Noah Buffini 193, 195
Hillel the Elder 118
Hilo Boarding School 93
Hinton, L. 192
HMS *Nemesis* 131
HMS *Wellesley* 131
Holy Island 25–6
Holy Tongue 116–17
Homaranismo 120–1
Hong Kong, China 3, 5, 132–3, 174. *See also* Cantonese; Putonghua
  Basic Law (Special Administrative Region) 156–7
  dominance (Cantonese) 157
  education policy/system 151, 155–6, 173
  English in 133, 138, 169
  fascist atrocities 155
  language and self-determination 7, 170
  LegCo, protesters 165–7
  LIHKG 172
  linguistic change 157, 169
  self-censorship 173
  as separate political entity 171
  value system 173
Hoover, Herbert 24
Hopkins, Manley 76
Hua Chunyin 187
Hui, Mary 171–2
Hui Kumulipo (Hawaiian club) 98
Hu Shih 144–5, 149
Huss, L. 192
'hwntw' (dialect) 49

Ige, David 107, 109
The Independent 86
indigenous languages 124, 190–1
Industrial Revolution 19

Inner Mongolia
  educational reforms 186
  linguistic heritage 187
  protests 187–8
Inouye, Daniel K. 105, 109
Insula Sanctorum 23
International Year of Indigenous Languages 5
Iolani Palace 83
Ip, Regina 171
Irish 193–5
'Israel as the Nation State of the Jewish People' 121

Jefferies, Clinton 36–7, 42
Jenkins, Dafydd 202 n.13
Jenkins, John Barnard 38–41
  imprisonment 43–5
  MAC and 38–40
  raid 43
Jephta, Amy 70
Jews/Jewish 113
  embarrassment over Yiddish 122 (*see also* Yiddish)
  Gentiles and 113
  to Palestine 116–17
Jones, Alwyn 42
Jones, Gordon 42–3
Jones, John Albert 38
Jones, Michael D. 19. *See also* linguistic nationalism
Jones, Robert 17
Judaism 113, 115, 118–19, 126
Judd, Gerrit 77, 80, 85
Judd, Laura Fish 76
Junker, Ingrid 63

Kafrissen, Rokhl 125
Ka'ahumanu 73, 75
Kakan 3
Kalākaua, David 77, 82–4, 92, 95–6
Kamakau, Samuel 75
Kamāmalu, Victoria 81
Kamehameha Schools 90–3, 96, 98, 101–2, 105, 110
Kamehameha V. *See* Lot Kapuāiwa (Kamehameha V)
Kamwangamalu, Nkonko 63
Kanaeokana 110

Kānekapōlei 74
Karlen, Neal 122
Kauikeaouli (Kamehameha III) 75, 77, 84–5
Keaoua Kekuaokalani 97
Keʻelikōlani, Ruth 89–90
Kenoi, Billy 107–8
Kerr, Tom 109
Kessel, Jonah 181
    Tashi Wangchuk: A Tibetan's Journey for Justice 184–5
Kīnaʻu 85
Kinnock, Neil 44, 46
Kipling, Rudyard 62
Kolokolov, VS 147
Kong Qingdong 162
Kornai, András 194
Krog, Antjie 64
Kū Kahakalau 105, 110, 198
Kuomintang 143, 148

Labour Party (Welsh) 41, 44
Lam, Carrie 168, 170, 172
Lam Bun 155
Lang, Avi 125
language 1, 197. *See also specific languages*
    collision of 2
    diversity 2, 5, 7, 115, 138, 150–1, 177, 191
    drift 2
    endangerment 4
    evolution 2
    myths 2
    politics 82, 171, 191–2
    resurgence 174
    status and support 195
'language nest' schemes 190
Latin alphabet 128, 136, 141, 146, 197
Latinisation (USSR) 147
Latinised Chinese Reader for Workers 147
Latinised Chinese-Russian Dictionary 147
Latinxua/Sin Wenz 147–8, 152
    Party's literacy programme 149
    restrictions on 149
    'Song of the Graduates' 149
    in USSR 147
Lau Tsz-kei 171
Law, Nathan 172

League of Nations 24, 35, 120
Lee, Dominic 174
Lee, William Little 78–9
Leung, Edward 172
Leung Kai-ping 167–8
Lewis, Saunders 25–7, 43, 46, 191–2, 202 n.13. *See also* Plaid Cymru
    broadcasting, writing and 32
    defence of nationalism 27–8, 38, 43
    first trail, bombing school (Caernarfon) 27–30
    imprisonment 31
    second trail, bombing school (Old Bailey) 30–1
    Tynged yr Iaith 32–4, 189
    Welsh lawmakers, failure of 33
Lewis, Wilfred 27–9
Liang Xiaojun 184–5
Liholiho, Alexander 77, 80, 89, 95
Liholiho, King 73–5
Li Ka-shing 154
Liliʻuokalani 77, 79, 83–5, 92, 95
Lingen, Ralph 13–17
Linguaphone Institute 50
linguistic nationalism 19, 29, 33, 38, 44
Lingvo Internacia 116, 118–19
Lin Yutang 146
Liu Xin 172
Llandovery 13
Llandovery Union Workhouse 13
Lloyd George, David 30
Lloyd George, Megan 31
Llŷn Peninsula 23, 25
    bombing school attack 26–7, 45
    purity of the linguistic tradition 25
    role in Wales's literature 25–6
Llywelyn Ein Llyw Olaf 37
Llywelyn Jones, Emyr 38
Long March (1934) 149
Lot Kapuāiwa (Kamehameha V) 73, 77, 89
    death and failure 80–2
    illness 73
Lugard, Frederick 138
Lu Kan-chang 137
Lunalilo, William Charles 77, 82
Lu Xun 147, 149
Lyman, David Belden 78
Lyman, Henry 78–9

Ma, Jack 182
Major, John 46
Malan, D.F. 59
Malicious Damage Act (1861) 27
Mandarin 4, 128, 132, 135, 138, 140–1,
    143–4, 149, 151
Mandela, Nelson 60, 63, 65
Mangauil, Lanakila 108–9
Mao Zedong 154, 178, 180, 197
Mashinini, Tietsi 61
Mathematics Exercises for Partial Literates
    147
Maui (Hawai'i) 101
Mauna Kea (Hawai'i), movement 107,
    109, 111
Mbeki, Thabo 60
McCulloch, Gretchen 162
Meibion Glyndŵr 45
Mellen, Kathleen 75
Mencius 135
Milner, Alfred, British race 57
minority communities/languages 69,
    178, 194. *See also specific minority*
    languages
    language diversity 191
    promoting 185, 190, 192
    revitalization 190–1
    visibility and legitimacy 191
model ethnic minority (Mongolians) 187
Modern Hebrew 113–14, 117, 125
Modern Standard Chinese (MSC) 163,
    169
Mongolian Language and Literature
    186–7
Monk 223 n.1
Monk, Hugh 131–2, 223 n.1
Morales, Lina, An alternative to
    assimilation and Zionism 125
Mosaic law, principles 118
Moser, David 136
Movement for a Phonetic Alphabet 137
Mudiad Amddiffyn Cymru (MAC,
    Movement for the Defence of
    Wales) 38–40, 43, 46
    battle plan 40
    reservoir work site, attack 36, 38
    Temple of Peace attack 35–8, 40, 43
multilingualism and multiculturalism 197
My Jewish Mother 123

Narodniks 114
National Assembly for Wales 47
Native Hawaiian Education Act (1988)
    105
Nazism 59
Ndolvu, Hastings 60
Netanyahu, Benjamin 121
New Culture Movement 144
New York, ELA map 3
nitroglycerine (explosive) attack 35–6, 38,
    40, 43
Northern Expedition (Chiang Kai-shek)
    143

Ó Doinn, Oisín 194
Official Language Ordinance 156
Okrent, Arika, *In the Land of Invented*
    Languages 115
Old English 2–3. *See also* English
'Ōlelo Hawai'i. *See* Hawaiian (Hawai'i)
Oleson, William Brewster 93–4
'one country, one people, one language,'
    principle 139
one-directional bilingualism 52
online language learning projects 195
Open Stellenbosch Collective (OSC) 65
Opium War 132–3
Orwell, George 115

pagan Saxons 23
Paradise of the Pacific 87
Pauahi Pākī, Princess 74, 77–80, 89, 102
    educational legacy 102
    illness and death 90–1
    Kamehameha Schools 90–3, 96, 98,
        101–2, 105
    marriage and refusal of Lot 80–1
Paulet, George 84–5
Peak Tramway (Amendment) Bill 1972
    156
Pearl, Blaq 70
Pendlebury, Harold 39–41
Pennant, Thomas 23
Perry, Jonathan 194
Philips, Stephen 81
Pierce, Henry 89
Pinyin 152, 162–3
Plaid Cymru 25–7, 31–2, 34, 37, 39,
    40–1, 44–6, 55, 192

Platt, Stephen 132
Poor Laws (1834) 13
Pope, Ida 93
Prah, Kwesi Kwaa 62
Price, Adam 55
Price, Rees 17
Pu'uhuluhulu (Hawai'i) 109–11
Pukui, Mary Kawena 100
Pūnana Leo 105
Putonghua 4, 7, 150, 157, 159–60, 183
    Cantonese and 157, 171, 174
    dictatorship of 152
    employment and Tibetan economy
        178–9
    generation in Guangdong 163, 173
    as medium of instruction 169–70
    as national language (1956) 160
    pro-Cantonese attitude 172
    promoting 157, 160–2, 169–70,
        173–4
    speakers 170
    via Pinyin 162–3

Qing dynasty 133
    Boxers and 134, 137
    Chinese revolution and fall 139
    linguistic uniformity 138
    New Territories 156
Qu Qiubai 147
    Our Views on Promoting the New
        Writing 148
    Putonghua 147

RAF Penhros 31
Rebecca Riots 15, 17
*Reports of the Commissioners of Inquiry into
    the State of Education in Wales* 15–18
reservoir work site, attack on 36, 38
Rhodes, Cecil John 63
Rhodes Must Fall (campaign) 63, 65
Richards, Theodore 94
Ricord, John 79
Roberts, Wyn 46
Roche, G. 192
Romanization of Chinese 141, 145–6
Roodt, Dan 65
Rosetta Stone 3
Rownd a Rownd (S4C) 54
Russell, John 18

San Po Kong strike 154–5
Sanskrit 136
Sau-chung 153
Saunders, Gwenno 194
Schiavone, Toni 52–3
Schleyer, Johann 115. *See also* Volapük
Scots Wikipedia 195–6
Second Hawaiian Renaissance
    100, 104
Sephardic Ladino 116
Shanghainese 140, 159–61
Shifeng, Yang 143
Sianel Pedwar Cymru (S4C) 45–6, 54
Skidmore, Ian 39, 41
Smith, Arthur 137
Smith, John 47
Smith, William 93
Snow, Edgar 149
Snow, Helen Foster 149
Social Darwinism 19
Society for Promoting Christian
    Knowledge 76
Society of Righteous and Harmonious
    Fists 133
So's protest 153
South Africa. *See also* Afrikaners
    despotism 63
    education policy 64
    homicide rates 67
    Union of South Africa 58–9
    white genocide 67
South China Morning Post 153
Soweto uprising 60–2
Stalling, Carl, *Looney Tunes* 95
Star Ferry 153, 155
Strubell, Miquel 190
Sun Yat-sen 141, 151, 197. *See also*
    Kuomintang
Support the New Writing 147
Suzhou Wu 138
Symons, Jelinger 15–17

Tambo, Oliver 60
Tan-y-Llŷn 202 n.13
Tashi Wangchuk 181–2
    imprisonment 184–5
    'inciting separatism,' guilty 184
    lawsuit 184
    political awakening 183

promoting/protecting languages 185
Tibetan education 183
Taylor, George 42
Taylor, Zachary 85
Tel Aviv (First Hebrew City) 121, 123–4
Temperley, A. C. 24
Temple of Peace and Health 35, 37
    aspirations 35
    bombing attack 35–6, 38, 40, 43
Thatcher, Margaret 45–6, 156
Third Language Movement. See Derde
        Taalbeweging
Thirty Metre Telescope (TMT) 107–9, 111
Thomas, Ben Bowen 205 n.40
Thomas, Richard 85
Thompson, Leonard 57, 59
Thompson, Uldrick 93
Three-Character Classic 135
Thurston, Lorrin 85–6, 92
Thurston, Lucy 74
Tianya 171
Tibetan Autonomous Region (TAR)
        176–8
Tibetan languages 184
    Amdo Tibetan 178
    bilingual education 177, 180, 183
    as medium of instruction 177
    promoting and protecting 180, 182–5
    writing systems 177
Tibetan plateau 175
    Buddhism 186
    'educational aid' 175–6
    ethnic and linguistic identity 178
    and Han Chinese 182
    language policy 180
    linguistic diversity 177
    minoritized languages 178
    peaceful liberation 178
    Putonghua and 178–9
Tin Siu-lam 157
Tohti, Ilham (charges of separatism) 183
Tolstoy, The Prisoner of the Caucuses 147
Torah 114, 116
Tories 45, 47
treachery of the Blue Books. See Brad y
        Llyfrau Gleision
treachery of the long knives 17
The Treaty of Versailles 24
Tsang, Jasper 168
Tu, Elsie 153

Umbrella Movement (2014) 166, 169
Uyghurs (Xinjiang) 186

Valentine, Lewis 26–7
    first trail, bombing school (Caernarfon)
        27–30
    imprisonment 31
    second trail, bombing school (Old
        Bailey) 30–1
Vane-Tempest-Stewart, Charles 24
Van Passell, Joseph (parachute jump)
        83–4
van Rheede, Hendrik 59
Vaughan, Ellis 53, 55–6
Vaughan Johnson, Henry 15, 17
vernacular writing 145
Volapük 115–16
von Ahn, Luis 193. See also Duolingo
Vorster, John 61

Wade–Giles system 141
Wales 5, 35, 51. See also Welsh
    bilingualism 6
    during coronavirus pandemic 55
    education in 14–16, 53–4, 196
    England and Englishness 25, 32, 40
    future bombing school 25
    Llŷn role in literature 25–6
    minority-language communities 52, 55
    unemployment 36
Walsh, Conor 194
Wang Pu 144
Wang Zhao 140
Wee, Lian-Hee 171
Weibo 182–3
Weiner, Benjamin 124
Welsh 4–5, 10, 16
    culture 18, 24, 29, 44, 46, 54
    decline of 20–1, 41, 52–3
    development and programmes,
        funding 55
    dialects 49
    distinctive features 10–11
    examples 11, 54–5
    First World War 24
    Hen Wlad Fy Nhadau 54–5
    migrants learning 52
    mockery of English trail 17
    nationalist sentiment 19, 27–8, 30,
        38, 43

priorities 192
revitalization 6, 34, 52, 55, 189, 191
speakers 10, 52, 189, 192
Tan-y-Llŷn 202 n.13
Wikipedia/Wicipedia 194–6
writing system 10
Welsh Courts Act (1942) 32
Welsh Language Act (1967 & 1993) 44, 46
Welsh Language Board 46
Welsh Language Society. *See* Cymdeithas yr Iaith Gymraeg
Welsh National Temple of Peace and Health. *See* Temple of Peace and Health
Welsh stick 17
wenyan (classical Chinese) 135–6, 138–9
Wigley, Dafydd 45
Willemse, Hein 70
Williams, David John 'D.J.' 26–7
    first trail, bombing school (Caernarfon) 27–30
    imprisonment 31
    second trail, bombing school (Old Bailey) 30–1
Williams, Owen 38
Williams, William 14–16, 18–19
Wilson, Harold 36–8, 42
Wiradjuri 190
Wlpan (language programme) 50
Wong, Joshua 169, 172
Woodgate, Ann 43
Woodrum, Marjorie 103–4
The Worker's Way 147
workhouse school 13, 15
Wu 140, 143
Wu, Jenny 159–60, 162–3, 173
Wu Zhihui 140

xenophobia 44
Xi Jinping 175, 179–80, 186–7
Xu, Fang 160

Yang Shifeng (study tours) 143
YesCymru 55
Yiddish 5, 113, 115, 117, 121–2
    Diaspora Jews 124
    Hebrewist opposition to 123
    Holocaust 123, 126
    Jewish embarrassment over 122
    'revival' programmes 125
    Zionists and 123
Yiddish Language and Culture Day 124
Ynys Enlli 23
Ynys Môn 4, 30
Yongzheng Emperor 151
Yuan Shikai 141, 143
Yue 151
Yushu Tibetan Autonomous Prefecture 181
Y Wladfa Gymreig 19

Zamenhof, Ludovik Lazarus 113, 115
    antisemitism 116
    creating own language 115
    death 121
    Esperanto 122 (*see* Esperanto)
    Fundamento de Esperanto 118–19
    Hillelism: A Plan for Solving the Jewish Problem 119
    Homaranismo 120
    'incurable madness' 115
    Judaic mysticism 119
    Judaism, modern form 119
    modernizing Yiddish 126
Zeus 2
Zhang Binglin 141
Zhang Zuolin 141
Zhao Ziyang 156
Zheng Qiao 136–7
Zhitlowsky, Chaim 123–4
Zhong Qiuming 176
Zhou Yongkang 180
Zhuyin 141, 145–8
Zionism 113, 116, 123, 125–6